PORTLAND

The Big City Food Biography Series
as part of the Rowman & Littlefield Studies in Food and Gastronomy

General Editor:
Ken Albala, Professor of History, University of the Pacific (kalbala@pacific.edu)
Rowman & Littlefield Executive Editor:
Suzanne Staszak-Silva (sstaszak-silva@rowman.com)

Food helps define the cultural identity of cities in much the same way as the distinctive architecture and famous personalities. Great cities have one-of-a-kind food cultures, offering the essence of the multitudes who have immigrated there and shaped foodways through time. **The Big City Food Biographies series** focuses on those metropolises celebrated as culinary destinations, with their iconic dishes, ethnic neighborhoods, markets, restaurants, and chefs. Guidebooks to cities abound, but these are real biographies that will satisfy readers' desire to know the full food culture of a city. Each narrative volume, devoted to a different city, explains the history, the natural resources, and the people that make that city's food culture unique. Each biography also looks at the markets, historic restaurants, signature dishes, and great cookbooks that are part of the city's gastronomic make-up.

Titles in the Series

PORTLAND

A Food Biography

Heather Arndt Anderson

ROWMAN & LITTLEFIELD
Lanham • Boulder • New York • London

Published by Rowman & Littlefield
A wholly owned subsidiary of The Rowman & Littlefield Publishing Group, Inc.
4501 Forbes Boulevard, Suite 200, Lanham, Maryland 20706
www.rowman.com

Unit A, Whitacre Mews, 26-34 Stannary Street, London SE11 4AB

British Library Cataloguing in Publication Information Available

Library of Congress Cataloging-in-Publication Data

Arndt Anderson, Heather, 1976– .
Portland : a food biography / Heather Arndt Anderson.
p. cm.
Includes bibliographical references and index.
ISBN 978-1-4422-2738-5 (cloth) — ISBN 978-1-4422-2739-2 (electronic)
1. Cooking, American—Pacific Northwest style. 2. Cooking—Oregon—Portland. I. Title.
TX715.2.P32A824 2015
641.59795'49—dc23
2014024371

♾ ™ The paper used in this publication meets the minimum requirements of
American National Standard for Information Sciences Permanence of Paper for
Printed Library Materials, ANSI/NISO Z39.48-1992.

Printed in the United States of America

To Zephyr, my little fifth-generation Portlander.

CONTENTS

PREFACE

Portland is often seen as a sheltered Waldorf child in a mossy fairy-tale world of chanterelles and huckleberries; a quaint village populated by trust-fund wunderkinds who run food carts, each serving something more precious than the last. But Portland's culinary history actually tells a different story: the tales of the salmon-people, the pioneers and immigrants, each struggling to make this strange but inviting land between the Pacific and the Cascades feel like home.

When my great-grandparents arrived in 1912, ruddy-cheeked and wind-blown from the Russian steppe, they found a city worthy of civilizing them. The Arndts, a German family, had never bothered to learn to speak Russian in the 150 or so years they lived there (such was the impermanence of their stay), but within a few years of living in Portland, they knew they had found their new home. They assimilated immediately. Portland just has that effect on people.

Because John and Elizabeth Arndt chose to settle in North Portland's Albina neighborhood a century ago, I have had the remarkable fortune of having lived a Portland life. My childhood was a tribute to Cascades Indians when I ate sacred salmon and wild trout procured by family menfolk. My girlhood was spent on the Oregon Trail when I ate beans seasoned only with a ham hock, or when my grandmother Laverne baked luscious pies with blackberries picked from Sauvie Island thickets. I was an immigrant child when I ate unripe plums with the wiry Laotian kids down the block—the same kids who dared me into my first taste of hot sauce, and into eating uncooked ramen like popcorn, crunched up in the bag and sprinkled with the salty soup powder.

The 1990s were spent dipping a toe into the twee fairy-world that makes Portland such a destination for food lovers today. During my foray into vegetarianism, there were half a dozen different places to get a Gardenburger in my neighborhood alone, because they were invented here. While rebellious teenagers around the country were lucky to score a Milwaukee's Best or a wine cooler, I cut my drinking-teeth on micro-brews. Before I spent lunch hours pondering the hundreds of food carts inhabiting vast "pods," I spent them pondering Honkin' Huge Burritos' vast salsa collection.

Writing this book has helped me discover all of the Portland-ness of my life. It has given my adoration of this city a depth and breadth that can only be compared to motherhood. This book is a sentimental journey through my hometown.

ACKNOWLEDGMENTS

I have made many new friends and gained several new mentors during this project. For your wisdom, contributions, and camaraderie, I thank my editors Ken Albala and Suzanne Staszak-Silva, The Ben Holladay Society, Doug Kenck-Crispin, Finn J. D. John, Richard Engeman, Tracy J. Prince, Linda Coon, J. D. Chandler, Norm Gholston, Tim Askin, Dan Haneckow, Mike Ryerson, Joe Streckert, Lizzy Caston, Thomas Robinson, Jesse Locker, David Strom, Melissa Lang, Terry Robinett, Ross Pullen, Carter Chase, Steve Humphrey, Dave Conklin, Dana Beck, Michael C. Zusman, Eliza Canty-Jones and the Oregon Historical Society, the City of Portland Archives, the Jack London Bar, the Iwasaki family, Vincenza Scarpaci, Steven Schreiber and the America Historical Society of Germans from Russia (Oregon chapter), Marie Rose Wong, and Darrell Millner.

To my writers' group, Writers Anonymous, for slogging through so many pages of rough drafts, I extend my deepest gratitude. I hope the homemade pickles and cakes made it all worthwhile. For his devoted partnership and for supporting my insatiable vintage cookbook addiction, I thank my wonderful husband, Scott Anderson.

1

THE MATERIAL RESOURCES

Rivers, Valleys, Volcanoes, and Sky

The infant city called The Clearing was a bald patch amid a stuttering wood. The Clearing was no booming metropolis; no destination for gastrotourists; no career-changer for ardent chefs—just awkward, palsied steps toward Victorian gentility. But in the decades before the remaining trees were scraped from the landscape, Portland's wood was still a verdant breadbasket, overflowing with blackberries and hazelnuts, venison leaping on cloven hoof.

"The surroundings of the city were . . . still wild, and the shattered forests seemed excessively rude, having no more the grace and stateliness of nature, and having not yet given away altogether to the reign of art," recalled newspaperman and historian Harvey Whitefield Scott in his 1890 *History of Portland, Oregon, with Illustrations and Biographical Sketches.*[1] Harvey Scott (for whom the dormant Portland volcano Mount Scott was named) did not realize his understatement; Portland has altogether given herself away to the reign of culinary art. In the areas surrounding the city, the breadbasket yet remains.

In the beginning, there was no Clearing. Palustrine meadows typified the pre-European Willamette Valley; today's Greater Portland Metro area was once a vast expanse of ash swales and cattail sloughs that snaked through the thick, black soils of wetland prairies exploding with ultraviolet camas lily, arrowhead-leaved wapato, and tiny, white popcorn flowers.

White oak savannah and its associated thickets of filbert and serviceberry were maintained by fires meticulously controlled by Kalapuya people, and as a result, so were valley quail, elk, and white-tailed deer. Everywhere else was misty rainforest populated by lofty Douglas fir with three-foot boles and long scarves of old man's beard lichen, subtended by dense, multiseral canopies of red elderberry, vine maple, salal, and sword fern.

Before the misty, green beginning, there was fire and brimstone. With Mount Hood to the southeast of town and several extinct cinder cones within the greater metro area, Portland is not just a river city, it is a city of volcanoes. Overlooking Hawthorne Boulevard and a retired sanitarium is Mount Tabor, a volcano located within Portland's city limits.[2] Rocky Butte (formerly known as Wiburg Butte), Kelly Butte, Powell Butte, and Mount Scott are all vents of the Boring Lava Field, an extinct Plio-Pleistocene volcanic field zone with at least thirty-two cinder cones and small shield volcanoes lying within a radius of thirteen miles of Kelly Butte Natural Area. Within twenty miles of Troutdale (just east of Portland) there are ninety volcanic centers.[3] Though Kelly Butte was the site of a Cold War–era civil defense emergency operations center, and there is presently a basketball court in the crater of Mount Tabor, 300,000 years ago these hills raged and sputtered, covering the landscape with lava and ash. The pyroclastic debris weathered into soils ideally suited to growing rhododendrons and huckleberries.

Flowing toward the Sandy River on the western foothills of Mount Hood, the Bull Run River rushes clear and cold atop igneous basalt bedrock, formed when the Missoula Floods scoured away rich soils overlying the lavas that flowed 17 million years ago. This Bull Run water is pure and bright; in 1890, the City of Portland selected Bull Run to supply the city's water and five years later a giant conduit piped the rushing flows, using gravity to move it directly to Portland faucets.

The areas surrounding the watershed to the east of Portland were positively teeming with food. At the turn of the nineteenth century, pre-eminent explorers and travel writers Meriwether Lewis and William Clark called the ten-mile stretch of the Columbia River from The Dalles to Celilo Falls the "Great Mart of all this Country," a sentiment echoed by numerous other chroniclers of early Oregon.[4] Most responsible for this designation were the thousands of pounds of fish hauled out of the river for food and trade.

Figure 1.1.   Mount Hood looms majestically to the east of Portland. Oregon's deep volcanic soils made ancient Portland a superior berry-growing region. The Bull Run watershed produces some of the purest water in the country. Photo ca. 1920. Courtesy of City of Portland Archives, Oregon, 9600-03

WATER

For thousands of years, the Columbia and Willamette Rivers and the babbling tributaries that fed them pulsated with fish. White sturgeon, eel-like Pacific lamprey, and western brook lamprey, signal crayfish, western pearlshell, and western ridged mussels all provided a stable food source for early inhabitants of the area. In the oughts and teens of the twentieth century, North Portland boys fished for channel catfish, brown bullhead, common carp, and crappie in the Columbia Slough using only string, garden worms, and their mothers' hairpins. Of all the fish pulled from Portland's waters, however, salmonids—steelhead, trout, and salmon—were by far the most crucial, sustaining the land and the people.

Salmon and steelhead are anadromous, meaning they are born in fresh water, spend a year or three in rivers and creeks, then as smolts they head out to sea, spending a year or eight in the ocean growing fat and strong. Then, with the scent of their nursery burned into their piscine memory banks, they return to spawn in the very same patch of cold gravels whence they as tiny alevins sprang. They die two weeks later, bruised and beaten, hook-nosed and hump-backed, red as fury.

"The multitudes of this fish are almost inconceivable," marveled Eliot Coues, recalling Lewis and Clark's expedition to the Columbia River in 1805.[5] "The water is so clear that they can readily be seen at the depth of fifteen or twenty feet; but at this season they float in such quantities down the stream, and are drifted ashore, that the Indians have only to collect, split, and dry them on the scaffolds."[6] During the summer months, salmon were so plentiful that they were used as fuel for cooking. To say that salmon was a staple food of indigenous Oregonians would be an understatement of epic proportion; without salmon, Chinookan peoples would very likely not have existed at all.

While archaeologists have dated mass Columbia River salmon harvests back ten thousand years, significant salmon harvest by non-Indians did not arrive until 1866, with the construction of Hapgood, Hume, and Company's cannery. This first cannery was sited sixty-five miles downstream from Portland in Eagle Cliff, Washington, and the vast majority of canneries were stationed at the source in Astoria or The Dalles. However, by the 1890s, one cannery did exist within Portland's city limits—the Burke Fish Company, located at NW Front and Overton, just northwest of today's Broadway Bridge (now a riverfront condo)—and myriad other cannery companies were headquartered in the city.[7][8]

Of the ten species and subspecies of salmon and trout readily available in Portland-area waters, sockeye, or red salmon, fetched the highest price in markets outside Oregon. Salmon species were often given exotic names to appeal to markets outside the Pacific Northwest; sockeye fished out of Alaskan waters might be sold through Portland markets under the brand names "Red Coral" or "Sea Rose."[9] The highest grade of pink salmon, or "humpies," were sold as "Buster," "Peasant," and "Thlinket"; the best-grade chum salmon were sold as "Suwanee" brand.[10]

For those seeking winter runs of steelhead, the northern stretches of the Willamette River have historically provided. "[This fish] is caught in large quantities in the Willamette River, just below the falls at Oregon, which are very difficult to pass," wrote American naturalist and Smithsonian Secretary Spencer Baird in an 1876 report to the US Fisheries Commission.[11] "They arrive at Oregon City as soon as the water rises, about Christmas, at which time they are prime, and are both very fat and of very fine quality." Steelhead do, in fact, make very fine eating, and are worth doing so even when other species of salmon are available.

However, Willamette River fisheries have long paled in comparison to those of the tidally influenced Columbia, even at the productive Willamette Falls located just south of the modern Portland's city limits. "The salmon fishery affords abundant food at a very low price, and of excellent quality: it does not extend above the [Willamette] Falls," reported H. U. Addington, Esq., an underling to British Foreign Secretary George Canning in 1824.[12] "The [lower Columbia River fish] are the richest and most delicious fish I ever recollect to have tasted; if any thing, they were too fat to eat, and one can perceive a difference even in those taken at the Willamette Falls, which, however, are the best kind for salting."[13]

Outside of Portland, salmon connoisseurs were less particular. One nineteenth-century expert on salmon cookery wrote that "as good wine needs no bush, so good salmon should be served sauceless, and only with the water in which it is boiled. The veritable *sauce piquante* is memory and association."[14] The author, Alexander Innes Shand, who wrote on cooking other fish, as well, remarked that complicated medieval recipes "go as far as perverted ingenuity could devise," noting that "the hot spicing and general bedevilling" would have been an insult to even lesser fish.[15] The much-reviled recipe—grilled salmon with a reduction of wine, cinnamon, and onions—may cloy a bit by today's standards, but Shand felt strongly that the only proper way to cook salmon was by simmering in salted spring water.

Anglers' and outdoorsmen's magazines of the late 1800s were giddy with tales of fishing the Columbia River; of reeling in flash after steely flash of fat salmon, constrained only by the speed and strength of a man's hands. A short story titled "Salmon Fishing with the Indians," published in an 1898 issue of *Outing*, rhapsodized angling the Columbia. The narrator Fritz and his friend known only as "the Doctor" are sitting on a high hill above the river watching fish jumping and splashing below. The Doctor thinks he is viewing a pod of whales swimming past, and is incredulous to learn that he is seeing salmon. "I've heard wonderful tales of the fish of Oregon, but I never would have believed that a fellow could sit on a mountain top and see fish jumping a mile away," sputtered the Doctor.[16]

Figure 1.2.   These fisherman in Oswego Creek just outside town had a pretty good day. Salmon fishing in Portland's waterways, even creeks, was a productive endeavor until urban development impacted fish habitat. Photo ca. 1905. Courtesy of Old Oregon Photos

Although these exaggerated fish tales abound in nineteenth-century literature, by the 1870s—only a decade after the first cannery was built—concerns about the decline of salmon had already begun to surface. In 1887, Secretary of the U.S. Senate Anson G. McCook, along with several other officials, reported concerns of over-fishing the Columbia by use of gill nets, traps, and fish wheels.[17] The alarm was not to spare the salmon populations, but over concern that the presence of so much angling was an impediment to the river's navigability. Thirty years after the first Columbia River cannery, the decline of salmon fisheries was officially reported by U.S. Commissioner of Fish and Fisheries, Marshall McDonald. McDonald placed the blame on "the great commercial fisheries prosecuted in the lower river" and prophesied "inevitable disaster."[18]

Salmon runs thrived through more than ten millennia of reverent harvest by Chinookan peoples, so it may come as little surprise that the sharp decline of salmon came on the heels of European settlement of the region.

Overfishing from commercial canneries beginning in the 1860s kicked off the decline most precipitously, but this was followed closely by the habitat impacts that would continue into the present day. To illustrate this point, the lamprey is another historically important fish of native peoples with a life cycle similar to salmon, and although they have never been overfished in the Northwest, their numbers are, too, declining due to the substantial decrease in spawning grounds. Today, Willamette Falls remains the only major site where tribe members can come harvest the serpentine fish.

Once migration and spawning habitat for salmon and trout (and probably lamprey), today Balch Creek in northwest Portland's Macleay Park drains to a culvert that acts as a barrier to fish passage, blocking access for the last run of native cutthroat trout in the city and trapping them in the relatively small tributary to the Willamette River.

Balch Creek is named for Danford Balch, a Portland homesteader most famous for murdering his son-in-law, Mortimer Stump. The Stump family had been engaged in a feud with the Balches, which came to a head a few years after Mortimer and sixteen-year-old Anna Balch eloped to nearby Vancouver, Washington. Danford Balch met Mortimer and other Stump men at the old Stark Street Ferry, and after a heated argument, Balch shot Mortimer with his shotgun. In 1859—the same year Oregon was granted statehood—Balch became the first Oregonian executed by hanging.

Prior to 1903, Balch Creek drained to a wetland called Guild's Lake, which had been leveled and filled with Willamette River dredge spoils in preparation for the Lewis and Clark Centennial Exposition of 1905. Twenty years after the Expo, the Port of Portland began examining the former swamp's potential for siting sawmills, railroads, and other developments, creating the "industrial sanctuary" it remains today.[19] Logging on slopes above streams caused erosion, suffocating redds in the streams before eggs could hatch; sawmill and other industrial pollution had deleterious effects on water quality by raising water temperature (reducing dissolved oxygen for fish to breathe) and introducing harmful chemicals into the water.

In the middle of the twentieth century, one upstream impact had a much larger effect on Portland-area fisheries. After five years of construction, the Dalles Dam was completed. On March 10, 1957, hundreds of onlookers arrived to witness as the water slowly rose, flooding the falls

and village of Celilo—theretofore the oldest continuously inhabited settlement and the most culturally important fishing and trading site on the
North American continent, for at least 11,000 years.[20]

Salmon conservation efforts were often too little, too late, although the
first round of restrictions had been proposed only thirty years after the
first cannery was established on the Columbia. At the first whiff of a
population decline, cannery owners were clamoring for a solution. In
1876, cannery owners petitioned the federal government to open a fish
hatchery on the Columbia; in 1877, when salmon runs plummeted (later
attributed to an El Niño, not overharvest), cannery owners formed a private board to open the first federal hatchery on the Clackamas River,
located a few miles southeast of Portland. Cannery owners continued to
be the most ardent supporters of hatcheries into the early twentieth century; they were also staunch opponents to damming the Columbia and
haphazard fish relocation projects.

Despite the efforts of these unlikely conservationists, salmon fisheries
were in trouble. Lower Columbia canneries accused canneries upstream
of creating an "almost insurmountable barrier to the salmon," while upriver canners claimed that downriver competitors were trying to "Hog-It-
All."[21] Conservation boiled down to not just saving the species, but maintaining one's portion of an ever-shrinking pie. Access to fishing became
so contentious that fistfights or even murders were committed in some
instances. In the 1990s, the National Oceanic and Atmospheric Adminis-
tration (NOAA) Marine Fisheries Service, at last, began its review of
salmonids in the United States under the auspices of the Endangered
Species Act; by the end of the twentieth century, twenty-six evolutionari-
ly significant units (ESUs) of salmon and steelhead received federal protection; five as endangered and twenty-one as threatened.

Though the Pacific lamprey continues its decline, little attention has
been given to the slimy, jawless fish. Fish biologists are not the only ones
to notice the drop in numbers, however. "We have always been harvesting lamprey, taking them back to our longhouses, to our families, to our
feast tables," remarked Columbia River Inter-tribal Fish Commission
spokesperson Sara Thompson, in a 2012 interview with *The Oregonian.*[22]
Thompson continued, pointing out that the species' chances may hinge on
the fact that it will not be winning any beauty contests; "Lamprey are not
the icon of the Pacific Northwest like salmon."[23]

AIR

In early November of 1805, during the expedition down the Columbia, past the area that is now Portland International Airport, William Clark noticed "emence numbers of fowls flying in every direction Such as Swan, geese, Brants, Cranes, Stalks [Storks], white guls, comerants & plevers [plovers] &c."[24] Before the end of the century, Portland already had a reputation for excellent bird hunting.

"A personal experience of ten years added to information gathered from men that have lived here forty years, more or less, convinces me that [western Oregon] has been and is second to none other on earth for waterfowl," wrote American publisher and early game law reformer Charles Hallock in 1891.[25] Hallock wrote effusively of the variety of waterfowl that the Northwest has to offer, of "the exquisite preparation nature has made for their accommodation and the long season for hunting them, with which we sportsmen are blessed," and insisted that the tales of Oregon's duck-hunting affluence bore repeating until they "resolve themselves into blood-curdling, hair raising traditions similar to the Icelandic sagas and the mythical legends of the dark ages."[26] Even today, the Audubon Society has designated twelve Important Bird Areas (IBAs) in the Portland area, each providing waterbirds with crucial overwintering, breeding, or migration support.[27] Before these crucial habitats were fragmented by urban developments, they were separated only by other habitats.

For at least one man, the American dream was in Portland, and that dream was built squarely on duck hunting. Blacksmith David Monastes began earning his keep on the very day he arrived in Portland in 1852. He stopped into a hardware store with nothing but the clothes on his back, and secured enough credit to purchase ammunition for his gun. He set out on foot and returned to town triumphant, having successfully bagged sixteen ducks. He was stopped in the street by an unknown gentleman and solicited to sell the ducks for a dollar a pair. Monastes obliged the stranger and repaid his debt to the hardware store. Monastes continued his bounty hunt, selling what must have been an awful lot of ducks to the same man until he had accumulated more than $1000. In 1866, he used the money to open a smithy on SW First Street, between Yamhill and Morrison; within a few more years, he was a real estate mogul, and by 1883, the Multnomah Rod and Gun Club (later named the Multnomah

Anglers and Hunters Club) was aptly headquartered in the Monastes building.[28]

In the 1850s, Portland was still a largely undeveloped expanse of swampy floodplain, but by the end of the nineteenth century, the city center was fairly well developed and duck hunters had to travel to the north end of town, to Guild's Lake (later drained for the 1905 Lewis and Clark Centennial Expo) or to the Smith and Bybee Lakes. Now known as the Smith and Bybee Wetlands, this 2,000-acre area is the largest protected wetland within an American city. Smith and Bybee Lakes were formerly the city's primary dumping grounds, beginning with the 1940 opening of St. Johns Landfill, and surrounded by port terminals, warehouses, and other commercial developments, it is easy forget that this was once an important waterfowl hunting ground. A few miles downstream, however, hunters can have their duck liver pâté and eat it, too, at the Sauvie Island Wildlife Area.

"If ever nature exerted herself to make a perfect resting and feeding place for wildfowl it was when she got to that part of her labors commonly known as Sauvie's Island," wrote one nineteenth-century hunter in a letter to *Forest and Stream* magazine.[29] Hunters were particularly enamored of Sauvie Island, located at the confluence of the Willamette and Columbia Rivers, and historically inhabited by James Bybee, for whom Bybee Lake was named. Formerly known as Wapato Island after the profusion of water potato growing within the island's wetlands, the island is a main stopping point for migratory birds as they travel along the Pacific Flyway between Alaska and South America. "[W]ho that ever hunted wildfowl in western Oregon has not heard of (Sauvie Island)?" The hunter's love letter continued, gushing that the riverine landmass is "[t]he small boy's ambition and dream and the duck hunter's paradise. The name is as familiar to the hunters of the Northwest coast as that of Chesapeake Bay is to those of the East."

Startlingly, the hunter's letter then takes a dark turn, becoming a bizarre manifesto promising the extermination of swans on the island. "Among the first feathered game to disappear from the face of the earth will be that most notable, majestic and beautiful of them all, the American swan and his cousin, the trumpeter swan. . . . The fact is that the swan, like the bison, is a large bright target, and death loves a shining mark," he wrote ominously.[30] On the precipice of the swan's legal protection in Oregon, the nameless Portland man had a suggestion to other hunters: "let us 'fiddle while Rome burns' and enjoy the fun while it lasts. We may not be able to . . . stuff pillow cases with straw and with these decoys shoot thirty-five swan by moonlight in one night, but we will do our best toward annihilation."[31]

Fortunately for area swans, the ban on hunting did take effect in several states in the late nineteenth century (Oregon included), and the trumpeter swan, once on the brink of extinction, has largely bounced back. The problem, it would seem, was that swans are delicious, a fact firmly established by ancient Romans. Recipes written for swan ranged from a medieval "chawdon of swann," or rich giblet gravy, to a buttery swan-boar potpie best served with a rye pastry crust, according to preeminent seventeenth-century cookbook author Gervase Markham. Like most waterfowl, however, swans were typically preferred roasted.

Although swans were off the table, plenty of other Oregon waterfowl landed in Portland waters and were happily bagged and taken home for supper. Portland is home to twenty-five species of waterfowl, many of whom taste wonderful. "A broiled teal, wood-duck, or butterball [bufflehead], by all means; but a roast canvasback, redhead, or mallard in preference always," declared horticulturist-turned-gastronome George Herman Ellwanger, in his 1902 *The Pleasures of the Table*.[32] Teals, wrote seventeenth-century physician Tobias Venner, "for pleasantnesse and wholesomenesse of meat excelleth all other water-fowle," but as an early modern era doctor, Venner's approval was not necessarily for the bird's flavor; rather, he continued, "for it is easily digested, acceptable to the stomacke, and the nourishment which it giveth, is very commendable and good, lesse excrementall, than of any other water-fowle."[33]

Most Pacific Flyway hunters disagree with Ellwanger's assessment, rating the flavor of wood ducks and teals as most superb, but perhaps they are mistaken. Canvasbacks (*Aythya valisineria*) are named for their favorite food: American eelgrass (*Vallisneria americana*), better known as wild celery; these largest of the local ducks are known to need no sauce. "Immediately they are cut they will fill the dish with the richest gravy that ever was tasted," wrote *New York Sun* editor (and Mark Twain's publisher) W. Mackay Laffan in 1884, declaring that "[t]he triangle of meat an inch thick comprised between the leg and the wing, with its apex at the back and its base at the breast, is considered the most delicious morsel of meat that exists."[34] This morsel, known as the "oyster," remains a favorite nibble of cooks, who are customarily given first dibs; the French call it *sot-l'y-laisse* which translates, roughly, to "the fool leaves it there."

A migratory visitor (and sometimes winter resident) of Sauvie Island, the sandhill crane is Oregon's tallest bird and has one of the longest fossil histories of any bird still found today. Known by hunters of the Central Flyway states as the "ribeye of the sky," the large bird has dark red meat similar to ostrich, and leaner than beef. Natural historian John Shertzer Hittell admitted in 1882 that the sandhill crane was "fit for the table and a good game bird," but the graceful wader was dismissed as merely "eatable" (though "indelicate") by other authors. More derisively, their nickname in nineteenth-century Portland was "Chinese snipe" because it was relished by Chinese immigrants, who no doubt found ways to make the red meat delectable regardless of what white people thought.[35] Hunting for cranes has been banned in Oregon (and elsewhere) since the 1918 Migratory Bird Treaty Act, but the ban was lifted in several Central Flyway states in the 1960s, due to outcry over the birds' abject destruction of cereal crops. Today, Sauvie Island wildlife managers plant millet and corn on public lands to reduce the birds' impact on private lands.

Much as they were with sandhill cranes, Chinese cooks were creative with those birds that dwelled in the hills and fields. Before it was a city of stumps, Portland was the historic home to a variety of upland game birds. Of these, the most plentiful encountered by pioneers were grouse. "'Foolhens,' they called them," wrote zoologist William Thomas Shaw in 1908. Grouse, he marveled, were "birds without apparent fear of man, that stood calmly eyeing him from the path at his feet, or craning their necks from the lower branches of a near-by tree, often to be actually clubbed to death."[36]

Two species of grouse predominated: sooty and ruffed. The ruffed grouse thrived in the brushy willow swamps and creek bottoms of what would become the city center; they frolicked in the young, mixed woods of lower elevations, picking at huckleberries and crabapple. Its percussive mating call rivalled the likes of Art Blakey. This bird, of dappled, dufflike feathers, was nimble, alert, and well-camouflaged. It was no fool.

The sooty, or blue grouse, had an overlapping historic distribution with the ruffed grouse; however, it preferred the edges and openings of the misty old growth western hemlock and Douglas-fir forests of ancient Portland. But unlike the similar ruffed grouse, wrote Shaw, "with the sooty grouse it is different. He is larger and somewhat slow of flight, and in early days at least, before hard experience had taught him the ways of man, was a fool-hen too."[37] Due to the sooty grouse's unfortunate combination of sluggishness and fearlessness, "[t]hey were not meant to withstand civilized progression."[38] Most travelers simply reached out and clubbed the birds for easy meat. The species has since moved out of town; wary of club-wielding travelers, it resides in the safety of the Coast Range and Cascades foothills.

The ruffed grouse may have been wise to the club, but it was no match for skilled marksmen. "The Oregon ruffed grouse . . . was one of our commonest game birds along streams, and in the thick timber of western Oregon," wrote American wildlife photographer and conservationist William L. Finley in an 1896 article for *The Oregon Naturalist*.[39] "It is a very fine game bird and of fine flavor; sportsmen have killed so many about here, that they are becoming scarce," he continued. Echoing this clarion for conservation, another nature writer of the era pled that "[t]he flesh, especially that of the breast, is considered a great delicacy; but the true lover of nature would rather forego the pleasure of feasting on this beautiful bird, and leave him unmolested, to break the deep solitude of the forest with the long roll of his drum."[40]

William Finley perhaps did not know the gustatory joys of roast grouse served strewn with fried bread crumbs and its own rich, brown gravy; he posited that the blame for the red ruffed grouse's fate may have partially fallen on the Mongolian, or ring-necked pheasant, one of many game birds released into the state for hunting. The first successful release of ring-necked pheasants in America took place in Oregon in 1881; eleven years later, Oregon opened a seventy-five-day season and hunters bagged 50,000 pheasants. Cookbooks of the era recommended them stuffed with shallots, wrapped in bacon, and basted with butter.

Pheasant farming was a great way for poultry farmers to earn a bit of extra money."The great Willamette valley is the paradise of the famed Denny or ring-necked pheasant," wrote the Oregon agriculture board in 1898. "A thousand dollars invested in a pheasant-raising plant anywhere in the Willamette valley by an experienced pheasant-raiser will, within a few years, lay the foundation for a snug fortune."[41] Releasing fowl for hunters was then, as it is now, a tidy way to turn a profit, but breeders could also sell their birds to restaurants.

The earliest restaurants in France served pheasant; famed gastronome Brillat-Savarin perfected a technique for cooking them that required them to be hung until "high" or aged and tenderized, then stuffed with chopped woodcock meat, beef marrow, bacon, herbs, and truffles, and then roasting the whole lot atop a bread trencher that has been smeared with a paste of butter, bacon, and the woodcock's entrails. The roast pheasant was then served with the gravy-soaked trencher. Resolutely, Brillat-Savarin insisted that "the peak is reached when the pheasant begins to decompose; then its aroma develops, and mixes with an oil which in order to form must undergo a certain amount of fermentation, just as the oil in coffee can only be drawn out by roasting it."[42] In contrast to the superb roast pheasant à la Brillat-Savarin, French foodie Baron Léon Brisse bemoaned that "[s]imple mortals roast their pheasants in the same manner as partridges, and hang them until they are so high that they are hardly eatable."[43] Even in modern days of household refrigeration, fowl are still often hung, but in sheds or garages, and rarely until they are so high that they are nearly rotten.

Over the decades, numerous other species of upland fowl were released into western Oregon's environs, until there were more aliens than natives: valley quail in the 1870s; Hungarian partridge in 1900; chukar in 1951. By the time Portland native James Beard published his *Fowl and Game Cookery* in 1944, quail were the most widely distributed game bird in Oregon. In *American Cookery* (1972), Beard recommends quail fried in bacon fat for breakfast, served in country gravy, with small new potatoes, hot biscuits, and honey.[44]

LAND

From the West Hills to the Cascades, Portland was once replete with elk and deer. Oregon's mild winters do not necessitate migration, and as such Roosevelt elk are not wont to move around much. They are "staying at-home sort of creatures" that often spend their entire lives in a single drainage basin, and within the city limits, comfortable environs yet thrive.[45] Surrounding the old Balch homestead and interlaced with roads with names like Leif Erikson and Germantown, the 5,000-acre Forest Park—the nation's largest urban greenspace—is still home to deer and elk. The city's proud, cervine ambassador is the leaping deer on the Made in Oregon sign, merrily greeting arriving visitors from the base of the Burnside Bridge.

Deer are far less discriminating than homebody elk, which is a good thing, since they make excellent victuals. In the seventeenth century, English cookbook author and captain Gervase Markham noted that deer and rabbits were the best game for hunting, calling the former "the most princely and royal chase of all chases" and the latter "every honest man's and good man's chase."[46] In Markham's day, venison would have been seasoned with sugar, cinnamon, ginger, and salt, larded with bacon or mutton fat to prevent drying while it roasted, and then served with a sauce of its own drippings combined with vinegar and thickened with bread crumbs.

Larding lean venison with fattier meats or buttered paper was an important technique that carried on to recipes throughout the nineteenth and twentieth centuries. The *Portland Women's Exchange Cookbook* (1913) suggests a roast venison "larded quite thickly with slender strips of pork" and served with *Sauce Robert*, an Espagnole sauce flavored with chopped onions, mustard, and sherry; a century ago, Portland women added currant jelly for flair.[47] The *Chinese-Japanese Cook Book* (1914)—possibly the first American cookbook to include Japanese recipes—features a recipe for pot-roasted *shika shiro* (meaning "white deer"). The recipe calls for pork fat to be diced and rendered in an earthenware *donabe*, and then a venison roast that has been "pickled" in a brine of vinegar, sliced onion, sugar, salt, and "mixed spices" is browned and simmered in soy sauce and miso.[48] These ingredients, possibly including the "mixed spices" that might be the blend known as *shichimi* (made from ground red pepper, orange peel, black and white sesame seeds, hemp seed, ginger, nori seaweed, and sansho, or Japanese pepper) would have been available at grocery stores in Portland's Nihonmachi (Japantown) by the turn of the twentieth century. This recipe resembles those for traditional Japanese venison hot pots that date back several centuries.

Brazen deer continue to inhabit every narrow, green nook of the city, wandering into backyard gardens and grazing along major roads even within the urban centers. In 1978, a security guard on the early morning shift was surprised to see a deer wandering the parking lot of Lloyd Center Mall, located in a bustling Northeast business district. Portland Police were already in hot pursuit; spooked, the deer ran into the mall (then an open-air plaza), darting into Edwin Furnishings, then turned on a dime, ran south toward Manning's Cafeteria, and leapt through a plate-glass window. Hearing what sounded like a loud explosion, Manning's breakfast cook Helen Schneider ran toward the dining room to see the two-year-old buck charging straight toward her. "He sailed over the tables like logs in the forest," remarked a thunderstruck Schneider.[49] The deer was apprehended by Portland Police and, battered and in shock, died en route back to the wilderness of Larch Mountain.

Rabbits have a comparatively easy time maintaining a low profile in the city. Portland's rabbits were plentiful, adorable meat; the two common to the area—eastern cottontail and brush rabbit—are still hunted year-round. Just as Beard's breakfast quails (and much nineteenth-century protein), rabbits were often breaded and fried, served with country gravy or onion sauce. Rabbit was not merely fodder for scraggy pioneers; numerous recipes for rabbit appeared in Fanny Lemira Gillette's 1887 *White House Cookbook*. Like those for stews and soups, recipes for rabbit pie echoed those of other game pies, "excepting that you scatter through it four hard-boiled eggs cut in slices," noted Gillette. Along with recipes for rabbit were several dishes using squirrel, of all things un-presidential. Far be it from Fannie Gillette to judge anyone for eating squirrel, which was certainly on the supper table of more than a few Oregon pioneer households. When cooking squirrel soup, warned Gillette, "[s]train the soup through a coarse colander when the meat has boiled to shreds, so as to get rid of the squirrel's troublesome little bones."

MUSHROOMS

In Portland's warm rain and heavy dew, fungi grow like gangbusters. "Dwellers in the suburbs often have mushrooms growing at their doors," wrote journalist Annie Laura Miller.[50] In her *Sunday Oregonian* article, "Mushrooms are Thick on the Edges of Portland" (1913), Miller noted that in the Irvington neighborhood, then a largely empty land claim with scattered homes, one woman gathered all the shaggy manes she and her husband could eat, while the woman's neighbor picked meadow mushrooms for her household only six blocks away in an empty field.

In the nineteenth century, picking one's own mushrooms was not just a convenience for gourmands, but a necessity for anyone wanting to eat mushrooms. Excepting Italian and French recipes, American cookery did not frequently feature mushrooms until the 1890s, when they were first commercially cultivated in Pittsburgh. As a new item, mushrooms were prohibitively expensive for most people, and many Portlanders had taken to harvesting their own. Responding to a new need, Oregon's first mycological society formed in 1899, as the Mushroom Club of Oregon. Dr. Harry Lane, an outspoken progressive Democrat who would go on to become mayor of Portland (and appoint Portland's first female police officer, Lola Baldwin), was the club's first president. The club was two years in the making, as reported *The Oregonian* in 1897, for the purpose of disseminating information about the cultivation and safety of mushrooms. "Those who do not care to join the club and will insist on eating fungi, can easily learn to distinguish between the wholesome and poisonous species by eating of every species they find, and leaving it to the coroner to do the rest."[51]

Prior to his stint as Mushroom Club president, Harry Lane published several articles in *The Oregonian* with the proper scientific description of various mushrooms and information on habitats within and surrounding Portland, to both encourage mycological appreciation and to deter the consumption of toadstools. A champion of mushrooms as an article of diet, Lane made great efforts to promote them for gustatory pleasure, writing on edible mushrooms that there are a dozen or so that he eats with any regularity, several of which are more delectable than the common meadow mushrooms (closely related to the button mushrooms seen in grocery stores today), but "[m]any more have such unsavory characters of taste and odor when cooked that I have willingly foregone further acquaintance with them."[52] Lane was also keen to dispel myths, noting that the "peppery tang and demoralizing powers" of the mushroom known as "the sickener" could be dissipated by cooking, for instance, or that the fly agaric tastes "sweet and nutty when cooked, giving to the palate no warning of its deadly qualities."[53]

Oddly, Lane did not write about chanterelles, which are plentiful, easily identified, and make superb eating when sautéed in butter and whizzed with cream and fresh thyme into a bisque. And unlike Italians, who hold boletes (better known as porcini) in the highest regard, Lane was unimpressed by boletes. Other mycologists have esteemed the devil's bolete as esculent, for example; Lane wrote, "[b]e that as it may, it was evil to look upon, and had the odor of mold from dead men's graves, and I restrained myself from eating a mess of them."[54] Lane marched to the beat of his own mycological drum, preferring underdog russulas, writing that "[n]o more savory or delicate morsel comes to the pan" than the yellow-gilled russula and purple russula. He had nice things to say about many others, including morels ("one of the best varieties of edible fungi"), of course, and oyster mushrooms ("a fairly good variety"), and called helvellas "the vegetable gnome of the woods."[55] Of beefy porcini, Lane admitted somewhat backhandedly that it could be a desirable addition to the dinner table; "like a singed cat, it is better than it seems."[56]

Though Lane was careful to offer warnings when they were necessary, the ignorant and the cavalier nonetheless took their chances. The real danger in consuming Oregon's most common poisonous mushroom—the destroying angel—is that its effects are delayed. One eating the delectable mushroom feels fine for a day before vomiting, diarrhea, and stomach cramps ensue. The victim then feels a bit better, appearing to have recovered, but the liver has been irreparably damaged. Beginning in the late nineteenth century and every few years after, *The Oregonian* reported deaths due to the unwitting consumption of poisonous mushrooms, or worse: fatalities from picking at the wrong place.

Northern and Eastern Europeans positively adore wild mushrooms. Families of Ukrainians venture out into the woods surrounding fair Portland for a taste of the Old World. The years of lingering toxicity following the 1986 nuclear meltdown in Chernobyl meant that Russian fungi were radioactively contaminated, and by the early 1990s, demand in Eastern Europe drove the prices of wild mushrooms sky-high. Oregon mushroom pickers were happy to oblige the growing need, especially for a few hundred dollars a day. "For greed, all nature is too little," said first-century philosopher Seneca the Younger, and in 1993, twenty-two-year-old picker Phay Eng was murdered and robbed of his mushroom harvest.[57] Eng was one of the hundreds of Cambodians who came to pick Oregon mushrooms with a commercial license. At the time, there had been reports of three other incidents where shots were fired to defend prime picking locations, and other reports of pickers staking out spots and setting up camps armed with assault rifles and pit bulls.

By the early 2000s, matsutake mushrooms were commanding more than $150 per pound on Japanese markets, keeping pistol-packing harvesters in work and in danger. Matsutake have a long history in Imperial Japan, where only royalty were allowed to pick and eat them; because their name refers to a slang description of its phallic shape, women in some courts were not even allowed to talk about the mushroom.[58] Today, the Japanese still covet the matsutake, which are shaved onto soups and rice. A busy picker could earn a thousand dollars within a few hours.

David Arora wrote in his 1979 *Mushrooms Demystified* that the odor of the mushroom is a "provocative compromise between Red Hots and smelly socks," but another Oregon mushroom is even more famous for its tantalizing aroma: the truffle.[59] Like the matsutake, truffles grow beneath the organic duff, but unlike the matsutake, truffles never offer humans a visual clue to their presence. With the help of a hand rake and well-trained dogs (less apt than pigs to eat their score), truffle hunters can unearth truffles of every hue: black, winter white, spring white, and the relatively rare Oregon brown truffle, whose scientific namesake, *Kalapuya*, is the tribe of Native Americans who once inhabited the lands to the immediate southwest of ancient Portland. The first scientific description of Oregon brown truffle was not published until a 2010 *Mycologia* article, but the Douglas-fir symbiont had been collected and described in field guides for many years prior.[60] Coincidentally, there were two main treaty cycles that concerned the Kalapuya Indians in Oregon: those in 1851 and those in 1854–1855. The 1855 treaties were negotiated by Oregon Indian Superintendent Joel Palmer, who founded Dayton, Oregon, twenty-five miles from Portland. Palmer's historic house is the home of the restaurant formerly owned by the man who perfected Oregon truffle oil, Jack Czarnecki. Jack's son Chris is the current chef and owner of the Joel Palmer House.

After sampling them at the 1977 "Mushrooms and Man Symposium" in Albany, Oregon, James Beard declared that Oregon truffles are every bit as good as their Italian cousins; interest in the rare fungi was piqued, and the Oregon-based North American Truffling Society was formed a year later. Naturally distilled American truffle oil was first undertaken by Oregon bacteriologist and enologist, Jack Czarnecki, using Oregon's native truffles. The unmistakable musky, earthy-sweet aroma is most potent in truffle oil, making it ideal for drizzling into a mushroom risotto or onto *oeufs Poche a la Parisienne*—a poached egg dish that, along with numerous other recipes that use truffles, appeared in *La Cuisine Française: French Cooking for Every Home* in 1893. Truffles, perhaps even local ones, were a key ingredient in the goose liver patties presented by Portland's Council of Jewish Women in *The Neighborhood Cook Book* of 1912.

WILD PLANTS

Within the botany chapter of the *History of the Expedition Under Command of Lewis and Clark* (Chapter XXV), more than twenty edible plants are listed.[61] Some of these species were given Latin names that echoed the Chinookan names given by the first peoples to eat them: salal (*Gaultheria shallon*) was "shallun"; camas (*Camassia quamash*) was "quamash." Others are still called by their old names, like the wetland tuber wapato, for which Sauvie Island was originally named.

Early writing on the edibility of plants indigenous to the Portland area reflects the palate of the times. Wild celery (a different species from the one preferred by teals), for example, "is edible and is much relished by the Indians, and is not unacceptable to a hungry White Man," wrote an agrarian for the state agricultural service in 1888, a time when vegetables were not the mainstay that meat and bread were.[62] Some plants were valued not as foodstuffs so much as for the flavor they imparted to meats and fish. Western redcedar, for example, was not eaten, but the bark was indispensible to Chinookan peoples for basket weaving. More recently, planks cleaved from the tree have been used for grilling so that the cooking smoke might season the salmon. Some plants did double-duty: salal branches were used to make rustic grills to flavor fish while it roasted near the flames, and the shrub's blue-black berries were also eaten raw, or dried and mixed with venison and fat to make into the travel rations called pemmican.

Many other plants were staple foods. Camas, like all members of the lily clade, bears a breathtaking inflorescence; the indigo-blue flowers of camas appear in mid-spring in Portland, though the white-flowered large camas is similarly exquisite. The bulb, best roasted in the ground, tastes like a sweet potato; the polysaccharide inulin converts to fructose when heated slowly, and in this way the Chinookan people had sweeteners without the risky trip to a tree full of protective bees. The longer the bulb was roasted (overnight was considered ideal), the more sweet-scented vanillin compounds were created, leading the camas to be known by some as "Indian candy."[63] When dried, the bulb can be pounded into flour to make breads and cakes. Camas was so important to the region's indigenous people that a nearby suburb was named after the plant. Besides salmon, no other food was as widely traded.

By the time the camas bulb is harvested in the late summer, its flowers have withered and faded into dehiscent pods rattling with black seeds. It is worth mention that lovely camas has an equally lovely cousin—death camas—and unfortunately, when camas's bulb is ready to be harvested, death camas becomes her evil twin, indistinguishable from the good lily whose flowers have faded and dropped. The indigenous women had a clever trick, however: in the spring, when camas's blue-violet raceme is unmistakable against the white clusters of death camas's tiny starblooms, the Chinookan gatherer would stroll through the vernal meadows, bending the blue-flowered stems as she went. After the cool September nights sent sugars into the starchy bulb, she only harvested the bulbs attached to the bent stems.

Camas likes a wet meadow, and in ancient Portland wetlands predominated. Before the Guilds and Couch land claims of the mid-nineteenth century, Northwest Portland was a vast wetland cacophonous with whirring dragonfly music and the *conk-la-ree!* trill of the red-winged blackbird. In the low, palustrine marshes and floodplains of what are now the Pearl and Northwest Industrial Districts, cattails—dubbed "supermarket of the swamps" by Euell Gibbons—grew lush, providing stick-to-one's-ribs tubers and sprightly salad shoots. [64]

Another sacred plant, wapato, grew enthusiastically. "This bulb, to which the Indians give the name of wappatoo, is the great article of food, and almost the staple article of commerce on the Columbia," wrote Captain Meriwether Lewis in 1804. [65] A woman would paddle a small canoe out into the water, and upon finding a patch of wapato would hop out of the canoe and pull the tubers out of the thick mud with her toes. The tubers floated to the surface and were tossed into the canoe, which acted as a floating basket. "In this manner," explained Lewis, "these patient females remain in the water for several hours, even in the depth of winter." [66] That there was no off-season for wapato was high on the list of reasons that it was a staple of Oregon's first people.

Another lover of wet meadows is the Indian carrot, or yampah. With its pleasantly crispy texture and nutty, parsnip-like flavor, yampah was so beloved by native peoples that it was harvested nearly to extinction. On the botanical specimens they collected, Lewis and Clark called it a "fennel root eaten by the Indians, of an annis [*sic*] taste." [67] Though he mistook it for dill, Oregon Country explorer John C. Frémont declared yampah "best among the roots used for food," writing somewhat wistfully that "[t]o us it was an interesting plant—a little link between the savage and civilized life."[68] This link was made by the Indians' use of the plant's root as a staple food, whereas the seeds of dill (similar in flavor) are used as a seasoning by those of European descent.

One magical, early September evening in 1843, while camped near Portland in the Lower Columbia, Frémont wrote that "there was a brilliant sunset of golden orange and green, which left the western sky clear and beautifully pure; but clouds in the east made me lose an occultation." (Frémont would be the first of the countless visitors who fell madly in love with Portland under the spell of a warm summer evening.) He continued his account, recalling fondly that "the summer frogs were singing around us, and the evening was very pleasant. . . . For our supper we had yampah, the most agreeably flavored of the roots, seasoned by a small fat duck."[69] It speaks volumes of Frémont's enjoyment of yampah that he considered duck an accompaniment to the root, and not the other way around.

Stinging nettles were gathered as a last resort by local Indians in the early spring, when few other food plants were available, but nettles may have been much relished by European immigrants to the area. The traditional German dish *Brennnesselspinat* (nettle spinach) is a springtime dish of creamed nettles with sautéed onions and butter, served like the *Grüne Soße* from Hessen with boiled potatoes and halved, hard-boiled eggs. Early Italian settlers may have folded nettles into risottos or soft potato dumplings to make the classic *gnocchi di ortiche* in their Brooklyn neighborhood kitchens. Late-nineteenth-century Scandinavians may have been delighted to find the ingredients for an old-fashioned *nässelsoppa* (nettle soup) growing gangbusters in Portland's marshy woodlands.

True to their moniker, nettles *do* pack a potent sting, delivered mercilessly by the fine, silicate trichomes that act as tiny syringes. The sting comes from the venom contained within the trichomes: a combination of histamine, serotonin, and formic acid (similar to the venom injected by stinging and biting *Formica* ants). The pain is a sharp, tingling sting, and on human skin, leaves small white bumps with reddish swelling. Scratching worsens the prickly bite, as it only works the dastardly needles and venom deeper into the dermis. To avoid this, one should always wear gloves when picking, use a salad spinner and tongs to wash, then steam or blanch the greens in salted water to neutralize the venom before eating. Cooked nettles impart no sting whatsoever.

Urban foraging, enjoying something of a renaissance these days, tends to focus largely on weedy, bitter greens growing in sidewalk cracks, or neglected brambles growing on fencerows in alleys. Sour-tasting sorrel, purslane, and miner's lettuce will brighten a salad; experienced foragers know how to find these weeds in vacant lots, while the ignorant and wary spend a pretty penny at the farmer's markets or, increasingly, in restaurants. Sorrel in particular is best reserved for providing a bit of tartness to a dish rather than the base of a meal; the sour taste comes from oxalic acid, which, if one overdoes it, can cause crystals to inconveniently form in the bladder, creating the unfortunate sensation of pissing shards of glass.

Some of the wild plants enjoyed by the region's early explorers and pioneers required no help from wise native women; likewise, some foraging in Portland's wilds requires no handholding from opportunistic "experts." The wild hazelnuts and berries, crabapples, and chokecherries, ripe for the picking and advertising it bawdily, were the precursor to the region's booming agricultural industry. Rose family members like blackberries, saskatoon serviceberries, and woodland strawberries grow well in the fluffy soils that formed in the alluvium and weathered lava flows; these are the rich silts deposited by the Missoula Floods 13,000–15,000 years ago and the volcanic Andisols that blew in when Mount Mazama flipped her lid 6,000 years later. Blueberry cousin salal and its kindred huckleberry and cranberry (both *Vaccinium* species, same as blueberry) beamed in the acidic soil and leafy, fir-needle duff of ancient Portland's moist woods, flourishing in great thickets frequented by cedar waxwings and sun-drowsy black bears.

"[T]here is no country in the known world where wild berries are so common as in Oregon," wrote historian Herbert Lang in 1885.[70] "In the woods and prairies of this part of the State, no less than eighteen varieties of edible berries, some of them equal in flavor to cultivated sorts, exist, abundant, large and delicious." Lang goes on to list a few: "blackberry, strawberry, huckleberry, salmon-berry, sallal, Oregon grape, squawberry and others," remarking on the "enormous quantities of wild blackberries, growing in the woods."[71] Squawberry likely refers to bearberry, an herb much loved by indigenous people.

All of the *Rubus* clan are edible: watery, roe-like salmonberries ("like a raspberry, but more insipid," judged Lang), flat, crunchy, crimson-velvet thimbleberries and finely fuzzy, bruise-purple blackcaps are all a

STRAWBERRIES ARE RIPE
HAZELWOOD STRAWBERRY SHORTCAKE
IS NOW BEING SERVED

Figure 1.3.   Thanks to the region's rich volcanic soils, Oregon strawberries are, according to nineteenth-century historian Herbert Lang, "abundant, large and delicious." Hazelwood Creamery advertisement, ca. 1900s. Courtesy of Norm Gholsto

welcome sight to hikers.[72] Before horticulturists hybridized Oregon blackberries, the native dewberry reigned supreme. Loganberries, marionberries, and boysenberries are all its descendants; the olallieberry is the daughter of loganberry (the son of blackberry and raspberry) and youngberry (the daughter of blackberry and dewberry). "Olallie" is Chinook jargon for "berry"; the fruit was developed in the 1930s in a blackberry breeding program at Oregon State University. The marionberry is dewberry's granddaughter; marionberry's parents are the invasive (but superb) Himalayan blackberry and the Chehalem berry, which is the cross between dewberry and loganberry. The word "Chehalem" is a corruption of the Kalapuyan word ascribed to a band of the Atfalati tribe in 1877; it is also the name of the highest mountains in the Willamette Valley, near Portland at the southern edge of the Tualatin Valley.[73]

Lang noted that blackberries were only approached in bounty by huckleberries, "which have a more contracted habitat, being confined to the mountain regions, where whole townships are covered by their bushes."[74] The Northwest's native huckleberries, also called bilberries and whortleberries by early settlers, were most highly valued by native people, though early settlers were rather fond of them as well. The two most common species, evergreen huckleberry and tart red huckleberry, still grow in Forest Park today, but the bigger, sweeter black huckleberry, once a wildling of the Tualatin Mountains, is now relegated to secret patches in the Mount Hood National Forest forty-five minutes southeast of the city. Black huckleberries were the most highly regarded of the huckleberries in their range, and so important to native people that the month of September was known as "berry month."[75]

Red and evergreen huckleberries were never as sought-after as black huckleberry, nor did any other wild berry experience the same commercial success. By the early 1970s, Oregon's wild huckleberries were already "a dwindling resource" according to forest ecologist Don Minore in a paper for the Forest Service's Pacific Northwest Forest and Range Experiment Station.[76] In the 1980s, when commercial wild huckleberry harvest experienced a resurgence, new management plans were put in place to meet the growing demand.

Just as the areas surrounding Portland are a major berry producer today, Oregon is one of the nation's largest cherry-growing regions. Local Rainier cherries are so highly prized that they may fetch as much as one dollar *per cherry* in Japan. The Bing—the most widely grown sweet cherry in the United States—was invented in 1875, in the Portland suburb of Milwaukie. Sweet Rainiers and Bings are so delicate that the mere spank of a heavy rain can split their skins.

Native bitter cherries and chokecherries were used by early Oregonians, but due to their eponymous bitterness, white settlers with a taste for preserves cooked the cherries into jam, while native people dried the cherries, mixed them with venison jerky and suet, and pressed the fruits into pemmican cakes for storage and travel. Cooking or drying the cherries not only renders them more palatable, but since the bitterness is caused by hydrocyanic acid (better known as hydrogen cyanide), it does the important double-duty of making the fruits a bit less deadly.

In the 1887 *White House Cookbook*, one of the better-read cookbooks in its day, author Fanny Lemira Gillette offers one handy use for wild cherries: cherry bounce.

> To one gallon of wild cherries add enough good whiskey to cover the fruit. Let soak two or three weeks and then drain off the liquor. Mash the cherries without breaking the stones and strain through a jelly-bag; add this liquor to that already drained off. Make a syrup with a gill of water and a pound of white sugar to every two quarts of liquor thus prepared; stir in well and bottle, and tightly cork. A common way of making cherry bounce is to put wild cherries and whiskey together in a jug and use the liquor as wanted. [77]

Since the stones (pits) are the fruit's primary source of cyanide, Ms. Gillette was wise to advise against crushing them. Likewise, the seeds of Pacific or Oregon crabapples are a source of cyanide, just like their stone fruit-bearing cousins. Crabapples are scarcely edible raw; Clark called them "exceedingly ascid," making more notes about the suitability of the plant's wood for axe handles than about the fruit as a food source. [78] The ladies of Portland's Council of Jewish Women included an interesting recipe for sweet pickled crabapples in their 1912 *The Neighborhood Cookbook*. The recipe, included among those for chow-chow and other sweet pickles, chutneys, and condiments, calls to stud the tiny pomes with cloves, simmer in a sweet vinegar syrup spiced with cinnamon sticks until just softened, and then pour into a stone crock.

Settlers and pioneers were fortunate to find indigenous foods reminiscent of those from their homelands, but were even more fortunate for the indigenous people that taught them how to prepare them.

2

THE CHINOOK AND KALAPUYA PEOPLE

Salmon, Camas, and Wapato

Between the aptly named Sandy River and Sauvie's wapato-laden island along the Columbia River, and south along the Willamette to the glissading mouths of the Clackamas and Tualatin Rivers, thousands of people dwelled in the velvet forests and glittering, dewdrop marsh-meadows. Newspaperman Harvey Whitefield Scott noted wistfully in 1890 that "[b]efore the first white settler had sought to secure a habitation in the forest which marked the site of the present city of Portland, the region . . . had passed through the most interesting period of its history."[1] Scott was specifically referring to those years between when Lewis and Clark passed through and the founding of the city half a century later, but the city had been plenty interesting before even the first white men probed the Columbia in the late eighteenth century. The region had been plenty interesting for about fifteen millennia. Some may say that the "most interesting period" had already ended long before Portland became a city.

THE PEOPLE

At the confluence of the Willamette and Columbia Rivers lie an ancient Portland crossroads; not just of two spirited waters, but of two spirited people. The Chinookan tribes of Multnomah and the Cascade peoples converged there, settling the prime real estate on the outskirts of the town site. Not far to the south, the Atfalati (Tualatin) represented the northern-most band of Kalapuya—the skilled hunters of the tip of the Willamette Valley, and these people often came north across the Tualatin Mountains to the rich fishing grounds settled by the Clackamas band of the Chinook. For the half millennium between 1250 and 1750 AD, Sauvie Island, with its bustling villages of Multnomah Indians, was once thought to be the one of the most densely populated sites in North America.[2]

Though there was a high amount of regional similarity among the people of the Northwest, there was also great local variability. Unlike the Upper Chinook (Wasco-Wishram) Indians on the Columbia Plateau, or the Lower Chinook (Clatsop) Indians at the coast, the Chinook living along the middle stretches of the Mighty Columbia—the Cascade tribe—moved seasonally and lived in smaller groups. Because most of them were fluent in the Chinookan dialects called "wawa," trade was easy between the various groups and bands. The people called the Klickitat lived along the Columbia on Portland's eastern edges; the Multnomah tribe lived to the west at Sauvie Island. At the Willamette, the Klickitat overlapped with the Chinook tribe known as the Clackamas, who also lived along the Willamette River east to the eponymous Clackamas River. To the south were the Atfalati band, who traveled on the Logie Trail between Sauvie Island and their West Hills villages on the west side of the Willamette, and overlapping with their traditional rivals the Clacka-mas on the east, competing for prime salmon and lamprey fishing at Willamette Falls.

With their tattoos, wide-gauge ear studs, and septum piercings, many of today's Portlanders pay unwitting homage to those original Chinook and Atfalati, differing only in that today's Portlander has not yet begun the practice of head-flattening. Beginning shortly after birth, Chinook and Atfalati infants were cradled between angled boards by their aristocratic mothers, so that the baby-soft fontanel would harden into the attractive, sloped shape that earned these people the descriptive name "Flatheads" among the first white visitors. Only non-slaves were permitted to bind their babies into cradle boards; high-caste people recognized each other by their slanted crania, and were never taken captive. In Oregon, the practice of flattening the skull was most prominent among the Chinookan peoples; though the practice did spread southward to the Kalapuya, Atfa-lati at the north practiced it most intensely, and the appearance of a flattened head diminished in esteem as one moved south or east from the Lower Columbia.[3]

Besides their penchant for the types of facial adornments and body modifications much loved by the modern counterculture, Chinook and Atfalati bore many other aesthetic similarities. The Chinook and Atfalati were strikingly attractive, with tawny skin and sleek, black hair, its lustre maintained by massaging in fish oils and adorned with shell combs and beads. Although the Chinook were a bit shorter in stature than tribes of eastern states (with men averaging five and a half feet tall), Captain Robert Gray's officer John Boit wrote in 1795, with a certain fondness, that the men were "straight limb'd, fine-looking fellows," and the women "very pretty."[4] As Boit noted, Chinook men preferred to be in a "state of Nature" as weather permitted. The women were only slightly more clothed, typically donning a knee-length skirt of cedar bark strips woven into a fringe of thin cords.[5] During the cold and rainy months, a short robe made of deerskin or goose feather, or a fur cape replaced naturism. Lewis complained that the leather panties of the Multnomah ladies were too tight and skimpy; "this is a much more indecent article than the tissue of bark," he winced, "and bearly [sic] covers the mons venes, to which it is drawn so close that the whole shape is plainly perceived."[6]

A few months earlier, however, on November 4, 1805, Meriwether Lewis, William Clark, and the Corps of Discovery made their first visit to primordial Portland. After having drifted past the Quick Sand River (Sandy River), they eventually settled a bit farther downstream, spending the evening camped on "Diamond Island" (Government Island), in the thickets of hardhack, whiplash willow, and black cottonwood beneath what is now Interstate 205. They hunted swans and geese in Jewit Lake using a canoe borrowed from Indians also camping on the island, sharing some of the meat in return. After the fog burned off, they disembarked at 10:00 a.m., stopping a few miles downstream. In his journal, Clark scribbled a few thoughts in his slippery shorthand: "[w]e landed at a village 200 men of Flatheads of 25 houses 50 canoes built of Straw, we were treated verry kindly by them, they gave us round root near the size of a hens egg roasted which they call Wap-to to eate."[7] The Corps of Discovery had stumbled upon a Chinookan village of Cascade Indians.

John Kaye Gill, publisher and brother of Joseph Kaye Gill (founder of the Portland-based stationer and bookstore J. K. Gill) wrote in his 1909 *Dictionary of Chinook Jargon* that the Chinook "were not as active nor so

Figure 2.1.   Heavily tattooed Chinook woman with her infant in head-binding cradleboard, image ca. 1860. The practice of head flattening by Chinook Indians was noted in the journals of Lewis and Clark. Courtesy of University of Washington Special Collections, NA 4016

robust as the eastern tribes, nor so able to endure hard labor and exposure."[8] Though that may sound a bit insulting, Gill perhaps spoke more to
the ease of living in pre-European Portland than to any lack of hardiness
of the indigenous people. With so much bounty all around them, the
Chinook simply did not need to work so hard at living as did the tribes of
the Great Plains. With their highly productive subsistence economy, the
Chinook were predominantly what are known by many archaeologists as
"affluent foragers." Household-based, complex hunter-gatherer societies
(as they are also known) are more sedentary than typical foragers.[9] However, more recently it has been hypothesized that the Chinook (and possibly the Atfalati) were somewhat agrarian. For example, there is evidence that wapato patches were guarded and intentionally manipulated by
some Chinook women, dismissing the notion that the Chinook were solely hunter-gatherers who lacked any agricultural practices.[10]

The Multnomah—meaning "roses on the water," named for the proliferation of fragrant, wild Nootka roses that bloomed on their namesake
island during the Columbia's summertime high flows—enjoyed a pleasant and relatively easy life. Gill himself noted that

> [t]he Multnomas were specially fortunate in their surroundings, occu-
> pying the lowlands of the Willamette, the greater part of fertile Sauvies
> Island, the lovely slopes and prairies of the Scappoose country, with
> the broad bays and inlets reaching inland from the Columbia and their
> own river, the Multnoma, which was the name of the western branch
> of the Wallamet and also of the main river from its mouth to the falls,
> twenty-five miles.[11]

On the east side of the Willamette, the Clowewallah band of the Clackamas Indians living from Sauvie Island to Willamette Falls enjoyed a
similar luxury, scooping nets full of fat, slippery lampreys and spearing at
the seemingly unending deluge of quicksilver salmon leaping from the
bracing crash of falling water.

Throughout the region, indigenous people enjoyed a similarly high
standard of living. Gill noted that Chinook homes were well-built, cornu-
copian storehouses with wide shelves for holding mats, baskets, and
household items. They put up a wide range of foods: wapato, camas
breads, cakes of dried salal and huckleberries, cattail roots, and bracken
fern fiddleheads; they hung strips of jerked venison and salmon from the

**Figure 2.2.   Chinook lodge interior, engraved by Richard W. Dodson in 1844.
Note salmon hanging from rafters. Courtesy of Library of Congress**

rafters like some kind of meaty tinsel, where they collected flavorful smoke as it passed through the roof vents.

William Clark wrote that the Clackamas people living at Willamette Falls lived on fish and roots, sometimes traveling to Multnomah territory in search of wapato; like their Columbia Riverbank–dwelling neighbors, the Clackamas would

> build their houses in the same form with those of the Columbian vally of wide split boa[r]ds and covered with bark of the white cedar which is the entire length of the one side of the roof and jut over at the eve about 18 inches, at the distance of about 18 inches transvers sp[l]inters of dried pine is inserted through the ceder bark in order to keep it smooth and prevent it's [sic] edge from colapsing by the heat of the sun; in this manner the nativs make a very secure light and lasting roof of this bark. which we have observed in every vilege in this vally as well as those above. [12]

What Lewis and Clark did not know, in their expeditious travels through Portland, was that a great deal of the Clackamas worldview was based on the notion that food was symbiotically linked to people. For Clackamas Indians, all food was anthropomorphized. It was not just the birds and fish that told their stories, but roots and berries had a say in the episodic myths as well. In each episode, a martyr-like food-person announces him- or herself to the deity homologue Salmon or Coyote, saying something along the lines of the following, summarized eloquently by University of Washington anthropologist Melville Jacobs in "World View of the Clackamas Chinook Indians" (1955):

> Dear oh dear. It is during the present season that I appear each year. Were it not for me during this season, the people would be unable to keep their breath. That is, I am of decisive importance to the people right now. It is I who in coming days or weeks make it possible for the people to continue to breathe and therefore to live. Long ago before I came, the people used to die of starvation. Or, they nearly starved. [13]

Salmon or Coyote, listening intently, asks, What is the physical appearance of this claimant? The villagers succinctly explain who the food-person is, using only one or two descriptors: Camas is round-headed. Wild Carrot is long. The handsome one with the sharp mouth is Trout. The final step in each episode is Salmon or Coyote declares the food-person's fate. "We hear, pontifically enunciated, Yes indeed! Poor, poor person! He- or she will be edible," wrote Jacobs. [14] "The people will boil her with hot pebbles, bake her in an underground oven, and cook her on hot rocks. Her name shall be Camas. Or, for Trout: They will boil her to make soup for sick persons. Her name is to be Trout." [15] After their introductions, the importance of each food-person is acknowledged by Coyote with the endowment of a gift: leather armor, furs, dentalia. In some cases, their physical characteristics are part of their gift, as in the case of skunk cabbage's "club" and "shield"—the stubby, studded spadix, subtended by its distinctive yellow spathe.

In a paragraph that must be included in any discussion of first peoples' foodways, Jacobs poetically deduced that

> these Indians regarded their principal foods as persons of a special type. Their view was that these foods wish to attach symbiotically to and be of use and worth to human beings, almost exactly as spirit-powers wish to come to people in order to be accepted, possessed, and used worthily by them. I suggest that the main foods and the spirit-

powers constitute conceptual extremes in a continuum of anthropo-
morphically envisaged spirit entities which need to relate to people and
which are lonesome and unhappy when not related closely to people.
The corollary of this formulation is that foods were not regarded as
pitiable if and when they were cut up, boiled, mashed, roasted, or
smoke-dried, to be used for and by people. All foods were warm,
friendly allies and the major foods were a kind of kin to human beings.
They saved people's lives, just as kin and spirit-powers saved lives.
People, spirit-powers, kin, and many if not all foods were mutually
interdependent and interconnected under certain conditions. These
three categories of beings needed and wanted each other. They were
sad indeed when they were unrelated or unused, that is, when they
were alone. Each food, as the myth says, holds the breath, that is,
maintains the heart and life, of its people. [16]

William Clark was informed by an Indian guide that above Willamette
Falls, the river was turbulent, not unlike the relationship between Clackamas Indians and their nearby rivals, the Kalapuya. Soon, however, neigh-
borly feuds would be the least of their worries. Like all indigenous North
Americans, the Chinook and Kalapuya faced a number of calamities following contact with white explorers. In 1750, smallpox from China
traveled aboard a Russian ship to Nootka Sound, moving south in a wake
of destruction. Thirty years after that, an epidemic of the disease swept
the region. By the time Lewis and Clark breezed into town two decades
later, yet another wave of smallpox had come through the Columbia
River people, introduced by Captain Robert Gray's ship—the first to
enter and navigate the river. In 1805, a Clatsop elder told William Clark
about the bands of people inhabiting ancient Portland, and introduced him
to "a woman who was badly marked with the Small Pox and made Signs
that they all died with the disorder which marked her face."

A series of other indignities arrived with white explorers, stressing an
already greatly reduced native population to its breaking point. In 1830,
the Multnomah were again affected by disease; in the winter of
1829–1830, the Clackamas, too, were exposed to diseases that allowed
the Kalapuya to relocate and occupy Clackamas territory at Willamette
Falls. In 1871, the fifty-five remaining Clackamas Indians dissolved into
the Grand Ronde Reservation. Within a few years, the Kalapuya had also
dispersed.

In 1909, John Gill surmised incorrectly that "the Chinook are probably extinct."[17] Although it is true that there are no longer vast villages of cedar longhouses from The Dalles to the Pacific to sit as reminders of their former power, there were still a thousand or so Chinook living in Portland when pioneers began to arrive (outnumbering whites four to one in 1850), and vestiges of Portland's first people still live on at the periphery.[18] Members of the Oregon's Confederated Tribes of Siletz, the Warm Springs, and the Grand Ronde pulse mightily with Chinook and Kalapuya blood, and Bay Center, Washington, remains a stronghold of the Chinook.

Though smallpox is a ghost of the past for the Chinook, different diseases put the last remaining Indians at risk. Diabetes, heart disease, and cancer have increased in native populations inversely with consumption of the traditional diet, and today, having American Indian or Alaska Native heritage is one of the top-four risk factors for diabetes. The native diet based on huckleberries, salmon, and camas bulbs is, respectively, rich in cancer-fighting antioxidants, heart-protecting omega-3 fatty acids, and inulin—a high-fiber, low glycemic index carbohydrate that lowers blood cholesterol and glucose levels. The taste for processed foods began when the Hudson's Bay Company arrived; wheat flour became a hot commodity, and Cascades people heartily traded for the flour to present as a high-status gift item to chiefs.[19] Eventually, the processed wheat flours grew to replace the inulin-rich camas and wapato flours in the diet. Among modern native people, traditional foods have largely been replaced by convenience foods, but a return to the ancestral diet can prevent and in some cases, even reverse chronic disease.

HUNTING AND FISHING (*MŎW'-ĬCH* AND *PISH*)

One rainy mid-autumn evening near ancient Portland, the Corps of Discovery suffered fitful sleep for the din of southbound fowl all around them. Brants, geese, cranes, and swans, all making their way to sunnier climes, had been up all night honking and chatting in their aerial caravan. "[T]hey were emensely numerous and their noise horrid," Clark grumbled. Though the Corps of Discovery groused plenty about the superfluity of birds (pun intended), the Chinook were not so bothered by the abundance of meat on the wing.

For thousands of years before European contact, native Oregonians craving a duck dinner relied on their archery skills rather than spraying the sky with lead shot and hoping for the best. Their sharp arrowheads were knapped from bits of flint, quartzite, and obsidian traded along a ten-thousand-year-old trade network of Pacific Northwest peoples in Washington and Vancouver Island.[20] The arrow shafts were crafted from strong Saskatoon arrow-wood[21] and fletched with hawk feathers to help them fly true; the bows were hewn from the dense and springy wood of Pacific yew (*Taxus brevifolia*), a close relative of the yews revered by Vikings for carving their own longbows. Thomas Manby, master's mate to George Vancouver aboard HMS *Discovery* in 1792, wrote that the Chinook "never move with out their Quivers, filled with Arrows, all of which are stained with various Colors, and pointed with the flint made exceeding sharp, they seldom miss a mark at twenty yards, and will often kill a bird at forty."[22]

Earlier weapons for hunting were more primitive but no less effective. Bola stones similar to those found at The Dalles were found on Sauvie Island, suggesting that if the technology was not shared, it was at least traded. These small stones were wrapped in leather pouches, linked by rope and thrown at the legs of fleeing prey, knocking the animal off its gait. Snares, pitfall traps, and spears were similarly effective at capturing a wide range of game: small furbears like rabbits and otters, Columbia white-tailed deer and black-tailed deer, mule deer, elk, and black bear were all on the menu.

As they did with all aspects of life, the Chinook infused hunting with their all-encompassing spirituality. According to one myth, the Chinook hunter spirit is a beautiful woman. This supernatural being has brown hair, and her hands and feet are filigreed with tattoos. She gave an orphan boy the power to become the greatest hunter when he released her from his bear trap in which her hand was caught. After their encounter, he needed only carry a painted stick and sing her song; this would drive elk to the water, where one shout would cause them to drown. In this way, the boy killed seventy elk at once, and he excelled all hunters. Chinook boys may have grown up wondering if (or hoping that) they would ever meet a supernatural beauty that could endow them such elk-hunting wizardry, but alas, they would have had to settle for more pragmatic methods.

The Flanagan archeological site located in the Willamette Valley suggests that hunting was of much greater necessity to the Kalapuya than the Chinook and other northwest cultural groups, and that hunting was more important than fishing to the Kalapuya.[23] Though salmon did remarkably leap up the white cascades, Willamette Falls posed a substantial barrier to fish passage upstream. Only about 10 percent of fish who attempt the migration succeed, and as a result, salmon were greatly supplemented with birds and big game for the Kalapuya living south of Oregon City.

The Kalapuya coddled the deer and elk. To simultaneously promote the growth of camas while maintaining a habitat attractive to ungulates, the Atfalati burned the valley floor, a common practice among the Kalapuya, but a method also used by at least some Chinook. Between 1200 and 1400 CE, fires controlled by Clackamas people in modern Lake Oswego (located immediately south of Portland) caused a major vegetation shift and permanently changed the ecology; the once-thick stands of stately Douglas-fir gave way to meadows peppered with ferns, docks, and sorrels attractive to grazing game. One fire history study showed that charcoal evidence decreased to zero by the mid-eighteenth century, almost a century before it ceased in the rest of the Willamette Valley.[24] Evidence suggests that these were anthropogenic fires, not natural, even though they occurred during the period of warmer, drier weather known among archaeologists as the Medieval Climate Anomaly.[25]

Adherence to strict traditions was thought by the Chinook to be crucial to the success of a hunt. If a male elk was killed, for example, twelve men were sent to retrieve the meat; if it was a female elk, eight men fetched it. If many elk were killed, it was dictated by tradition that the meat be dried on-site before returning home. These guidelines read more like helpful suggestions or common sense when one considers the great size of an elk, but reading further into the *Chinook Texts* transcribed by Smithsonian anthropologist Franz Boas in 1894, it is apparent that significant cultural meaning is ascribed to the hunt, during which deeply felt cultural beliefs are upheld. Women were not allowed to eat certain parts of the elk (specifically, the tongue or hooves), nor were they allowed to break the forelegs, which must be carried away by men. Menstruating women in particular were thought to be bad luck, which may be the reason women were required to sit at home during a hunt. "When a hunter is unsuccessful, his child must not go near the water," warned the texts.[26] "When it goes near water, it will fall sick and die at once."[27] Other rules appear more pragmatic than superstitious; women were to stay home with the children to make sure the youngsters did not ruin the hunter's chances. "When he goes hunting, his wife and children sit motionless. When his children make noise, one of them will fall sick if the hunter is unsuccessful."[28]

The introduction of archery to Pacific Northwest peoples occurred during the Middle Pacific period (1800 BCE to 200/500 CE)—the same period that witnessed the advent of fine woodworking. The next step in Pacific Northwest cultural evolution was an explosion of technologies: permanent residence in newly hewn plank longhouses, travel in decorated canoes, and sophisticated fishing equipment each played a part in the significant intensification and expansion of fishing.

Once fishing technology had been developed, it changed little over several millennia. John Gill described Chinook fishing in great detail in 1909, noting that even in the early twentieth century the fisherman used a variety of techniques that deviated little from ancestral methods. Spears and lances with detachable horn points, nets woven from strong, fibrous roots, or simple lines armed with "curious hooks of bone or ivory" were all perfectly effective in the hands of the right user.[29] Some fish were masterfully caught with only bait tied to a line, remarked Gill: "when a fisherman felt a bite he snatched the fish so quickly that he had it in the canoe before it could let go."[30]

To say that salmon was important to the Chinook would be a gross oversimplification. Salmon was alternately a crucial resource provided by the deity Coyote and a sacred spirit on its own. According to one myth, Coyote walked upstream from the mouth of Big River (the Columbia) to Okanagan, Canada, traveling up each of its tributaries and bringing salmon, camas, and berries everywhere he visited, and teaching the people how to catch and prepare salmon.[31] The Chinook Salmon Myth tells of a beautiful chief's daughter who marries the handsome young Iguanat, the salmon-man who sometimes assumed the form of a scabby, sore-covered old man to escape detection. Other salmon myths typically tell of a boy who comes to salmon country and is told to kill some of the children for food. He is cautioned to save all the bones and throw them in the river so that they may be resurrected. When the boy returns home, he brings a bounty of fish to his village.[32]

The Chinook people also had many taboos centered around salmon, which they summarize in their sacred tale of Italapas, another of the many

Coyote myths that was shared among the various bands of Chinook as they traveled to and from the coast. Coyote was fishing in a small creek, and decided that the creek was too small to catch any salmon but silver-side (coho) salmon; "It shall be a bad omen when a fall salmon is killed here; somebody shall die," declared Coyote.[33] The next day, Coyote ran into a bit of trouble: the silver-side salmon had all gone away. Coyote defecated and scried into his excrement, asking the Divine Feces for advice. His excrements spoke to him, replying that the first salmon killed must be cooked right where it was caught. As the days wore on, Coyote faced similarly frustrating challenges, in what amounted to a Simon Says (or rather, Scat Says) of increasingly specific rules for salmon-fishing: Only roast the fish. No steaming the fish unless it was caught upstream. Separate spits for each of the body parts: "one for the head, one for the back, one for the roe, one for the body. The gills must be burnt."[34] All salmon must be roasted the same day as they are caught; if one caught many salmon, one was in for a long day. Cooking fires must then be extinguished with water, not buried in sand.

There were different rules for catching, killing, cooking, preserving, and eating different species of salmon; there were additional rules depending on how far upstream one was fishing, and whether the tide was in ebb or flow stage.[35] When the coprophilic deity finally learned all of the lessons his feces had to tell him, he codified the rules into sacred writ for the Indians. "Even I got tired," said Coyote, after fishing according to the exhaustive fecal law.[36] "The Indians shall always do in the same manner. Murderers, those who prepare corpses, girls who are just mature, menstruating women, widows and widowers shall not eat salmon. Thus shall be the taboos for all generations of people."[37]

To celebrate the first salmon run of the season, a salmonberry was placed in the mouth of the first salmon caught. In some streams, salmon did not run year-round, or were of such poor quality that the people did not use them. The coming of the first salmon marked the end of living on dried meats and roots, and in some cases salvation from imminent starvation. Once the first spring salmon was caught, all fishing was halted until after the ceremony had been performed. Erna Gunther, University of Washington anthropologist and onetime student of linguist Franz Boas, extensively described the ritual in her 1926 *American Anthropologist* article titled "An Analysis of the First Salmon Ceremony," noting that "[t]he fisherman carries the fish to a shaman who cuts the fish lengthwise, taking out the head and backbone in one piece. The fish is baked in a depression in the ground, which is lined with choke-cherry leaves and covered with mats. Everyone is invited and gets some of the fish. They pray at the feast. The bones are not returned to the river." In completing this ceremony, it was thought, the salmon would continue to run, happy to give of itself to feed the people.

Erna Gunther noted that it was due to the general impassibility of Willamette Falls to salmon that the Kalapuya had no such ritual. First Salmon and related ceremonies were based on belief in the immortality of game; that animal spirits do not die when they are eaten by humans. It is symbolic because the Chinook creation myth tells that Salmon was the first animal to offer the gift of his own flesh to the humans. The myths provide insight into the ceremonial practices, because they very frequently dictate the ritual behavior itself.

Though they were not part of the cultural vernacular of the Chinook, some related people had similar ceremonies for the season's first eulachon or Columbia River smelt, a sprightly, anadromous fish that is so rich in oils it could purportedly be burned like a candle if dried and strung on a wick (lending its other name, candlefish). However, the eulachon were also an important fish to Chinook Indians, and Upper Chinooks from east of the Willamette River often traveled downstream a great distance to take advantage of the vast shoals of "ooligan," which could be scooped out of the water with dip nets, or literally raked straight from the water into the canoe with a giant, wooden comb toothed with fishbones. A more passive method of catching the fish used nets woven from the fibers of stinging nettle; these were anchored into the stream bed with poles, allowing the current to drift the fish into the net.

In those bitter days of late winter before the vernal runs of salmon, the eulachon arrived, migrating up the Columbia all the way into the Sandy River to spawn, and were thus thought of as a salvation against hunger after the winter food stores had run dry. Grease could be rendered from the fish to use for cooking, skin and hair care, or for gifting and trading. Today, the distinct population segment of eulachon traditionally fished by the Chinook is listed as Threatened under the federal Endangered Species Act.

Salmon and euchalon are not the only traditional food fish on the decline. Willamette Falls in Oregon City continues to be a sacred fishing ground for descendants of Clackamas and Atfalati Indians, who come to harvest Pacific lamprey. In fact, it is the only lamprey fishing ground used today, because historic Siletz Indian sites no longer support lamprey.[38]

Lamprey somewhat resemble eels, with which they are frequently confused, but lampreys are a far stranger creature. A parasitic, jawless serpent that lacks scales and breathes through a row of holes on the side of its head appears more like a slippery flute than a fish, but as a food, it was as relished by the Chinook as it was by the ancient Romans and medieval royalty. Clackamas people pulled spawning lamprey from the rocks with their bare hands, while standing in the raw chill of the falls.

Today, native people sometimes fish for sacred salmon from power boats, but they still use dip nets and spears. They sometimes wear wet-suits before plunging into the merciless falls, but they still wrench uncannily strong lamprey from the rocks by hand.

GATHERING (HO'-KŬ-MĔL)

Few sacred myths were shared about the process of gathering, and ethnologists have displayed an "astounding lack of interest" in obtaining information about the collection and preparation of food plants, for a number of reasons.[39] First, the work of gathering plant foods was women's work, and most women's work has been either dismissed or overlooked entirely by (primarily male) ethnographers. Also, food plants have typically been deemed less important than the meats and fish procured by intrepid men. Certainly, the shadow cast by salmon was large. Regardless of its significance to ethnographers and historians, a woman's work was never done. Before she got to the task of gathering seeds, berries, and roots, she had other undertakings. She collected rushes from the marshy meadows, bear-grass from the Cascade foothills, and the fine, fibrous roots of western redcedar from the damp woods and riverbanks, and she used these materials to weave her intricate baskets.

Basket weaving techniques spread through Oregon and Washington tribes from the mouth of the Columbia to the interior, but little is known about western Oregon basketry because of the disruption caused by early settlement. Although Chinook baskets served a primarily utilitarian purpose (e.g., collecting and storing food, among a great many other things), the women took the opportunity to inflect the baskets with their aesthetic preference, adding human and animal figures as well as geometric patterns. Several distinctive types of basketry were crafted in the region, and some, like cylindrical baskets and the flat pouches called cornhusk bags, were unique to the women of the Columbia.

At the mouth of the Columbia, finely twined bowls and pouches were made from cattail fibers and decorated in horizontal bands with the black wire stems of maidenhair fern. Upriver, the famous Klickitat baskets of the Gorge were tightly coiled from western red cedar roots with imbricated designs and lightning-bolt zigzags. Klickitat baskets were made not only by the Klickitat women, but along the entire stretch of the Columbia; these baskets, recognizable by their gently flaring cylindrical shape and coiled loops at the rim, are also called berry baskets for their intended purpose: collecting huckleberries.

Another type of basket used for gathering food was the cylinder basket, or "Sally bag." The baskets' nickname comes from the turn of the twentieth century, when unscrupulous traders and collectors, in order to sell their wares at higher prices, deceptively claimed that the basketry was of a rare form on the verge of extinction, being the craft of only one surviving Chinook weaver called "Old Sally." These flexible baskets were tied to a woman's belt and used to carry camas and wild onions. But in order to carry her camas and onions, a woman had to dig them from the rich earth.

Women dug camas bulbs using sticks crafted from cedar or ash—the same wood used for baseball bats today—with the intricate elk- or deer-antler handles for which Chinook craftsmen were well known. The digging sticks caught the attention of William Clark, who sketched them and recorded a detailed description of the device, noting specifically that "[t]he instruments used by the nativs in digging their roots is a Strong Stick of three feet and a half long Sharpened at the lower end and its upper inserted into a part of an Elks or buck's horn which Serves as a handle."[40] American anthropologist and linguist Henry Wetherbee Henshaw made his own observations of the camas digging stick while working for the United States Geological Survey in the western United States in the 1870s. Henshaw elaborated on Clark's description of the stick, adding that "[t]he transverse bar on the end of the handle is an evident improvement on the straight stick, since it can be pressed against the breast and the stick driven into the ground with ease."[41]

Figure 2.3. Klickitat woman Sally Wahkiakus, taken in around 1900 by photographer Lily White. The Klickitat basket she is weaving was of important use to all women of the Columbia River for collecting huckleberries. Courtesy of Oregon Historical Society, Negative 87886

The digging stick was also employed by ancient Portland women to rout out clams (should they visit the coast), as well as to pry loose other roots, corms, bulbs, rhizomes, and tubers. In grassy meadows they found bracken ferns, the crispy-sweet wild carrot called yampah, and cardoon's diminutive cousin, the edible thistle; from the prairies to the Tualatin Mountain woodlands and Coast Range foothills they dug chocolate lily, with its cluster of bulblets that looks like a ball of rice, and the freckled, bright orange tiger lily; from the spongy marshes and mossy stream banks they dug cattails, field horsetail and giant horsetail, cow parsnip, and odoriferous skunk cabbage.

Many of the plants were described in Clackamas Indian oral tradition, transcribed in the 1950s by anthropologist Melville Jacobs. Jacobs had worked closely with the last surviving member of the Clackamas tribe, Victoria Howard, before she died in 1930. Mrs. Howard told Jacobs that in March, the springtime plant folk introduced themselves to Salmon, each beginning her introduction by announcing that if it were not for her, the people would all starve to death. Each plant briefs Salmon on her preparation; the lily Cat Ear[42] says she is eaten raw or baked in the ashes; Wild Carrot (also known as yampah; the only male plant who spoke) professes to be eaten boiled or mashed into cakes. Camas—"the staple type"—would be eaten by everyone, boiled, baked, or cooked on hot rocks.

Spring was not the only season in which a Chinook woman was beholden to plants. The Chinook woman's entire year was structured around the plants she gathered. Autumn was for collecting nuts and seeds; winter meant wapato corms and other fresh roots; the spring was for sweet, green shoots and fiddleheads; early summer was spent following berries and the late summer was for camas. Specifically, the month of August was called *táhápuncœq*, meaning "camas time" in the Atfalati language, and although camas grows in spongy, palustrine meadows, in the late summer the soil was tight and sere, clenching the bulbs selfishly underground.[43] Camas was worth the trouble, though. Derived from the Chinookan word *quawmash*, which means "sweet" or "pleasant tasting," it was a favorite food of the native Oregonians, absolutely relished by the Chinook and white visitors alike.

In one myth, Coyote forbade Clatsop women from digging camas, instructing that they should stick to thistles and lupines. Just to drive his point home, Coyote turned the camas into onions. Typically, however, camas played the role of keeping women busy; it was a prop to provide women with a reason to be in a myth's scene. A woman's relationship with camas was far more significant than the paucity of ethnographers' records would imply, however, and historians benefit greatly from the accounts of botanists. After his visit to Oregon, preeminent British botanist William Jackson Hooker, for whom a Northwest species of willow, lily, wasp, and evening primrose are named (among a great many others), wrote of the camas (then spelled "gamass") in an 1846 issue of the *London Journal of Botany*. He remarked on the plant's ability to determine a woman's suitability for marriage and the great celebratory nature of camas season in the prairies surrounding the Cascades:

> The digging of the Gamass bulb is a feast for old and young amongst the Indians; a sort of picnic which is spoken of throughout the whole year. The different neighbouring tribes meet on the same plain and mostly at the same time, at the same spot where their forefathers met. Here the old men talk over their long tales of olden times, the young relate hunting adventures of the last winter, and pass most of their time in play and gaming; while on the women alone, young and old, rests the whole labour of gathering that indispensable food. They, especially the young women, vie with each other in collecting the greatest possible quantity and best quality of Gamass, because their fame for future good wives will depend much on the activity and industry they show here; the young men will not overlook these merits, and many a marriage is closed after the Gamass are brought home. [44]

According to Hooker, camas's reputation as an esculent preceded it; a colleague of Hooker's, biologist William Stewart, grew it in his Scotland kitchen garden where Hooker saw it growing "in the greatest perfection," and had been told that camas made "a very agreeable and wholesome dish." [45] When the Corps of Discovery first encountered camas, though, the reviews were mixed. "[O]ur men who were half Starved made So free a use of this root that it made them all Sick for Several days after," wrote Lewis. As anyone with a fondness for Jerusalem artichokes can attest, too much of the sweet-tasting oligosaccharide inulin—occurring in high amounts in camas—can cause painful stomach bloating and excessive flatulence.

Throughout camas's range, women were instructed to avoid sexual intercourse before camas season, lest the male essence of her lover taint the harvest. "No man smells on women before digging, or the roots will go away," warned the Chinook's kin to the east, the Nez Perce.[46] Just as women were banned from handling weapons or fishing equipment, men were forbidden from touching root-digging tools, baskets, or root ovens.

Of equal, if not greater, importance was the fingerling potato-like wapato, with its pretty, white flowers and impressive arrowhead-shaped leaves (hence its botanical name, *Sagittaria*, after the mythological archer). Its flavor is somewhat like a russet potato, with an earthy nuttiness and slightly bitter complexity. It does not require peeling, it can be stored wet or dry without rotting, and it has a season 250 days long.

Like camas, wapato is a wetland plant, but unlike camas, wapato is an obligate wetland species, which means it must grow in water rather than being merely tolerant of it. To reach their nutritious carbohydrate bounty, a woman waded knee-deep into the chilly waters between October and March, grubbing out tubers with her nimble toes. Once the corms floated to the surface, she easily plucked them from the water and dropped them into the canoe floating alongside her. John Gill lamented in 1909 that "[t]his root would be a valuable food for whites as well as Indians, and it seems a pity it is not used among our people."[47] Aside from the occasional wild food forager, wapato is still not typically used among Gill's people.

Wapato was a crucial food and trade item for the Multnomah who lived on Sauvie Island, and its value was deemed high. Clark complained that they could not afford the exorbitant fee charged by the Multnomah, noting that "their price's are So high that it would take ten times as much to purchase their roots & Dried fish as we have in our possesion." Clark begrudgingly bought a few single wapato, paying dearly with a fish hook. He stretched his precious score by eating it in elk soup. Wapato cannot tolerate salinity, and the shrewd Multnomah recognized their monopoly, offering no price break to their coast-dwelling kin; Lewis marveled that the "natives of the Sea coast and lower part of the river will dispose of their most valuable articles to obtain this root."

A testament to its productivity, Sauvie Island—the Columbia River's largest island—was named Wappatoo Island by the inhabitants who predated French-Canadian dairyman and Hudson's Bay Company employee Laurent Sauvé.[48] The entire Portland basin contained so much wapato that it was an apt name for the valley before it was changed it to Columbia.[49] Similarly, the 1,500-acre Wapato Lake was a prime harvesting area for Atfalati women to the south of ancient Portland. Wapato Lake was drained by ditches in the 1930s, and converted to farmland for growing onions. The U.S. Department of Fish and Wildlife began acquiring the site in 2007, and is slowly restoring the site's historic migratory bird habitat. Fifteen acres of the historic wapato harvest site have been added as the Wapato Lake Unit to the 4,440-acre Tualatin River National Wildlife Refuge. Another Wapato Lake existed near the present-day Sellwood neighborhood, offering an important source of the food to the Clackamas.[50]

Prime gathering areas were stimulated into growth by the fires started by the Atfalati, and made harvesting small animals, conveniently already cooked, much easier. A particularly relished treat was the nests of yellow jackets that were dug following the fires. The Kalapuya had a saying that testified as much: "*rruoah quatinafoe antealth*," meaning "yellow jacket nests are good eating." The smoke's tranquilizing effect meant the wasps gave up their tasty larvae without a fight. Fires also cleared the path for what ecologists call R-selected, or "pioneer" species—the weeds that thrive on drama. The croziers of bracken ferns shot eagerly from the ashes in the spring following a fire's disturbance, as did the thistles and appropriately named fireweed. These fresh, green shoots were tender and sweet, and added much-needed minerals to a meat- and starch-heavy diet.

Horsetail shoots, cow parsnip, wild celery, and cattail shoots were all eaten raw or steamed with salmon as green vegetables, and some plants were even used as seasonings in much the same way that Europeans were accustomed. "[O]bserved a speceies of small wild onion growing among the moss on the rocks," Clark wrote in March 1806, noting with piqued interest that "they resemble the shives of our gardens and grow remarkably close together forming a perfect turf; they are quite as agreeably flavoured as the shives."[51] Oregon's wild chive is, in fact, the same species as the garden chives cultivated in Europe—the only one native to both the Old World and the New—and was enthusiastically added to the Corps' venison broths and stews. While travelling back up the Columbia a few months later, some of the Corps' men would be given small onions and chives in trade.

Some plants were utilized for their shoots as well as their fruits. The sprightly shoots of salmonberry were peeled and roasted with salmon or eaten with salmon roe, and the warming days of April were known as "salmonberry sprout days." The fruit, a vermilion drupe, was placed in the fish's mouth during the First Salmon ceremony and the "salmonberry days" were celebrated as late spring days lengthened toward the solstice. Interestingly, the Chinook name of the berry is not derived from salmon, but from the Swainson's thrush (known by the Chinook as the Salmonberry Bird), whose ascending-spiral flutesong heralds the ripening of the berry.

Before her death in 1930, Clackamas Indian Victoria Howard shared with Melville Jacobs that her mother's mother had told her many myths about the berry-folk. The berries informed Coyote of their edibility by announcing that they would stab him. "First the wild strawberries [will ripen about the end of May]. Then also those blackberries, raspberries, small grey huckleberries, mountain huckleberries, serviceberries, crabapples, chokecherries. All those things spoke to him like that, 'I am going to stab you, Coyote!'"[52] Coyote would then obligingly pick the fruit and taste it, announcing that it was, indeed, edible. In telling her tale, Mrs. Howard provides a discursive list of the fruits eaten by the Clackamas Indians—the same fruits enjoyed by Chinookan and Kalapuyan people across the region.

Myriad other fruits were harvested by the women of ancient Portland: chewy-dry salal; sour red and tart-sweet blue elderberry; the crunchy cadmium-red thimbleberry; bruise-blue Indian-plum, also called chokecherry if eaten before fully ripe; and the state flower, Oregon-grape, whose roots yielded medicine and yellow dye in addition to the sour, indigo berries. Each of these was eaten raw off the bush, and dried into cakes for storage.

Huckleberries were harvested by Native Americans across the continent; seventeenth-century Algonquins were observed collecting and drying the fruits in the Great Lakes region, as noted in the 1615 journals of explorer Samuel de Champlain. Henry David Thoreau, in addition to being one of the great nineteenth-century nature writers, first compiled the most extensive history on the subject of huckleberries, and chronicled the use of huckleberries in America's infancy. Before Portland was even a wee bairn strapped in its cradle-board, the Chinook were basking in what Thoreau deemed "an unsurpassed luxuriance of fruit."[53]

Of all the berries, huckleberries were of particular cultural significance to the Chinook and Atfalati, who prepared special baskets for the task and made treks to the cool, fir-scented air of the Mount Hood foothills, offering a respite from the late summer swelter. In July and August, the Chinook would amble up the steep, fern-weary slopes not just to collect berries, but also to collect as a people. In addition to providing an important food source for her people, the huckleberry harvest was an opportunity for a woman to make and foster social connections that were maintained across multiple families and generations. Women were in charge in the berry patches; they or their families often laid claim to the best berry grounds, and all the fields were connected by named trails.

Northwest people made special combs of wood or with salmon backbones (similar to those used by the men for scooping eulachon from the river), which neatly liberated the sweet orbs from their twigs, ushered directly into the baskets. It was hard work, but despite the labor involved in collecting all that fruit, the people treated huckleberry season as a sort of pleasant holiday in the mountains before the real work of salmon harvest came in the fall.

As with camas and wapato, the arrival of huckleberry was honored with a First Fruits ceremony, and also as with camas and wapato, huckleberries were appreciated for their ease of storage. Some of the berries were enjoyed fresh, but on the toes of autumn, the people dried a great majority of the fruits as raisins and cakes for leaner times. In 1868, ethnobotanist Robert Brown wrote that great numbers of huckleberry cakes were dried on house roofs and platforms, "superintended by some ancient hag, whose hands and arms are dyed pink with them."[54] In winter, while white settlers of the 1860s were eking out a hardscrabble existence near the fresh townsite, one might imagine that that ancient hag was warm and content, enjoying her sweet huckleberry cakes with smoked salmon, and perhaps a bit of Schadenfreude.

After the berry harvest, women had yet more work to do in the collection of food. In the summer and fall, the seeds of tarweed were harvested by Atfalati in the Willamette Valley, easily accessible to the people after their quick fires burned off the grasses and sizzled the aromatic resins off the plant. The seeds were spanked out of their pods with a wooden paddle and funneled into large, conical baskets. They were ground into a sweet-tasting meal and mixed with camas and hazelnuts. Wealthy Atfalati families laid claim over the rare local tarweed plots and tended them carefully, relishing the large yields. Ten to twenty bushels of the nutritious, oily seeds could be harvested in a single season by just one family's diligent women.

Other seeds, like those from the wild sunflower cousins called balsam-root, were collected and stored whole or ground into meal. Women wandered along dappled forest edges looking for scraggly hazelnut trees. They collected the burnished nuts, which they called *tukwila*, eating some fresh and storing the rest for winter. To the Yakama Indians of the Middle Columbia, hazelnut is a guardian spirit who granted a young boy the power to evade his enemies, which eventually made him a great warrior.

Undulating meadows punctuated with stately Oregon white oaks were maintained using fire. This was not just to promote the proliferation of delectable deer, but of delicious acorns, which were relished by the local people. Acorns could be roasted and ground into meal, or eaten another way. Sometimes, acorns were placed into grass-lined pits outside the door of a family home, covered with another thin layer of grass, then buried in about six inches of soil. Next was added the special ingredient. "Every member of the family henceforth regards this hole as the special place of deposit for his urine," wrote portraitist and traveler Paul Kane in 1859, "which is on no occasion to be diverted from its legitimate receptacle."[55] After marinating for four or five months, the acorns were cooked in another pit, (mercifully) separate from other foods. "Chinook olives," as they were called by white settlers, were "regarded by [the Chinook] as the greatest of all delicacies."[56] One might suppose it was an acquired taste.

COOKING (MĂM'-OOK PĪ-AH)

For millennia, people in the Pacific Northwest all prepared food in more or less the same way: using smoke or open flame, cooking in tight baskets and wrapped in leaves. European cooking vessels were introduced to Pacific Northwest people during the approximately seventy years of contact with Russian and British explorers, French-Canadian fur traders, and Spanish missionaries between the mid-eighteenth century and early nineteenth century. The intended utility of cooking utensils was lost on the people of the Northwest, for whom metals were rare and precious. One eighteenth-century account from fur trader John Meares described the scene as Nootka chief Comekala, having been away with the foreigners on a voyage, returns to present himself to his countrymen. Brandishing a cooking spit that he had purloined from the ship's kitchen, he was dressed in his finest, wearing a copper sheet breastplate and various ornaments in his ears, and hanging from his hair were "so many handles of copper saucepans, that his head was kept back by the weight of them in such a stiff and upright position as very much to heighten the singularity of his appearance."[57] Comekala's proclivity for stealing wares from the galley kept him in a "state of perpetual hostility" with the ship's cook.[58]

In their 1988 Oxford Symposium on Food and Cookery paper titled "Pacific Northwest Indian Cooking Vessels," writers John Doerper and Alf Collins lament that "[t]here wasn't much time to record Indian cooking methods before the arrival of white settlers in the 1850s began changing it."[59] However, most eighteenth-century fur traders in the region did find the cooking methods remarkable enough that they frequently commented on the subject. More specifically, they complained about the reluctance of Pacific Northwest Coast people to try European methods, which made European kettles as a trade item fairly useless. Pewter basins, however, could be filled with hot stones in the traditional style of heating soup, and were highly valuable; women traded sexual favors for these utensils, noted Captain Cook's ship surgeon David Samwell, writing with bemused exasperation that the damsels had "found at last the means to disburthen our young gentry of their kitchen furniture; many of us leaving this harbor not being able to muster a plate to eat our salt beef from."[60] By the time the Corps of Discovery made it to the coast at the turn of the nineteenth century, the Chinook had developed an interest in trading goods (and sometimes services) for copper cookware as well as the usual beads and woolens.

When they were not pilfered or scantily traded, the kitchen utensils of the tribes were few and simple, as described by John Gill in 1891: "bowls and trenchers hollowed neatly from wood, cups of horn, horn spoons, and baskets woven so skillfully as to be water-tight took the place of jugs and buckets."[61] After eating clams procured from the coast, their shells were used as spoons or saucers for broth.

Because of the strict taboos and gender roles assigned to gathering and preparing plant and animal foods, separate methods and vessels were used for cooking camas, say, versus smoking venison. That is not to say that plant and animal foods were not combined in single dishes, but a man was forbidden from using—even touching—an earth oven dedicated to slow-roasting camas. His male essence could taint the oven, and the oven's lady-energy could in turn undermine his hard-won masculinity. Although cooking was primarily a woman's work, there were instances in which a man must cook meat; namely, in adhering to the taboos dictated by Coyote. As previously mentioned, if many fish or elk were killed in one day, all of the meat must be roasted or smoked on-site before the victorious provider could return home. Once he returned with his bounty, the choice to make a salmon-huckleberry stew or cook it *en papillote* with leaves was his wife's.

Once fish were wrested from their watery homes, there were several options for cooking: they could be roasted; wrapped in skunk cabbage leaves and steamed (like the aforementioned French method); they could be pounded to a pulp in a mortar and pestle and dried, to be mixed with huckleberries into pemmican cakes or eaten alone. However, when one thinks of the foods of the Pacific Northwest, it is difficult not to immediately think of smoked salmon. Smoked salmon was by far the most prevalent smoked fish eaten by Chinooks and remains the most common smoked fish eaten in America today. Around the turn of the twentieth century, smoked salmon was brought to the eastern United States by Jewish immigrants from Russia, who may very well have learned it from Pacific Northwest Indians during early eighteenth-century trade.

It was not just salmon that were smoked for later use. Surplus lamprey and sturgeon were split and dried over alder smoke or by the foehn Chinook winds that blew down the Columbia Gorge in the summer. Vast quantities of eulachon, too, were smoked in the roof rafters for later use. Because they are so small, they dried quickly in the heat of the smoke, and it was a good thing that they did. "[T]he Anchovey is so delicate that they soon become tainted unless pickled or smoked," noted Meriwether Lewis while visiting ancient Portland in March 1806. Though he guessed the fish was the wrong species (he described the eulachon at first as "resembling a herring but a size smaller"), Lewis also detailed the process by which they people smoked the little fishes, writing that

> the natives run a small stick through their gills and hang them in the smoke of their lodges, or kindle a small fire under them for the purpose of drying them. they need no previous preperation of guting &c and will cure in 24 hours. the natives do not appear to be very scrupelous about eating them when a little feated [fetid]. [62]

The succulent eulachon were a favorite of the Corps of Discovery's men, and though he raised an eyebrow about the Multnomah's habit of eating the fish a bit on the high side, Lewis was particularly fond of them. "I find

Figure 2.4. Spit-roasting is but one of the myriad ways in which Pacific Northwest Native Americans prepared salmon. Photo by Suzi Trousdale

them best when cooked in Indian stile, which is by roasting a number of them together on a wooden spit without any previous preperation whatever," he wrote wistfully.[63] "[T]hey are so fat they require no additional sauce, and I think them superior to any fish I ever tasted, even more delicate and lussious than the white fish of the lakes which have heretofore formed my standart of excellence among the fishes."[64]

Although the use of cedar or alder planks was widespread among the tribes of the Eastern United States, West Coast tribes skewered fish onto sticks and hung them near the fire to be slow-cooked and kissed with sweet smoke. Nonetheless, the use of planks is synonymous with "traditional Indian cooking," and as such, it continues to erroneously exemplify the Pacific Northwest's foodways. Salmon roasted on sticks were eaten immediately (the heads were particularly savored), but for longer term storage, fish were hung in plank house rafters, allowing heat and curls of smoke to drift up and both cure and flavor the meat.

Pounding salmon created a product that was shelf-stable for years, but was more complicated. As with much of women's work, pounding salmon was arduous, and white explorers were taken aback at the grueling labor the Chinook women performed. Missionary Henry Perkins commented in 1838 that the women of the Columbia "have to labor like slaves. Every day we see them out beside their houses, sitting almost naked on the ground, in the wind and the sun, manufacturing large coarse mats, on which to dry and in which to preserve their salmon. They are untiring at it as the Virginia slaves."[65] However, this inference may not be entirely accurate; anthropologist Lillian Ackerman posits that rather than being a mark of "slavery," the work that women performed in the preparation of fish enhanced their economic autonomy and social position.[66] The end product was owned by the woman, which she could store, sell, or do with whatever she pleased.

The preparation was labor-intensive, but worth the trouble. Freshly caught salmon were cleaned, filleted, and cut into strips, and hung in the hot sun. When the fish was softened a bit, the women shredded the meat and mixed it with salmon roe or berries, then returned it to the parching sunlight to dry. Once the mixture was dry, she pounded it to a fine powder with a maple mortar and stone pestle, then packed it tightly into baskets specifically woven for the product. Because the pounded salmon (called *clatsop* by coastal people) was secreted away in these special baskets, Clark had wrongly assumed that the product was made only for trade (he made the deduction after noting he had never seen it in any lodges). As a highly valuable commodity, plenty of pounded salmon was indeed traded, but the process, which could render 100 salmon down to 100 pounds of shelf-stable protein, created a product that was indispensable to Chinook people for other reasons. To the Chinook, pounded salmon, or *itk'ilak*, hit the sweet spot between practical and delectable.

Once dried, salmon could later be boiled to revive its flavor and texture. In his account of the travels of the Corps of Discovery, Elliott Coues described the process wherein a small wood fire was lit, upon which were laid several round stones. "One of the squaws now brought a bucket of water, in which was a large salmon about half dried; and as the stones became heated, they were put into the bucket till the salmon was sufficiently boiled for use. It was then taken out, put on a platter of rushes neatly made."[67] The resulting salmon dinner was purportedly "of an excellent flavor."[68]

Other wet methods were used in the preparation of food. Steaming, for example, was a preferred way to cook camas bread and sturgeon. Although sturgeon was disdained by mid-Columbia Indians (hence its nickname meaning "the swallowing monster's pet"), the Lower Columbia people relished the fish as a delicacy, as did Lewis and Clark. "[W]e live sumptuously on our wappetoe and Sturgeon," wrote Lewis on March 4, 1806, after noting that nothing else of importance had happened on that late winter day. He then goes on to describe in great detail the process by which the Chinook prepared the sturgeon:

> [A] brisk fire is kindled on which a parcel of stones are la[i]d. when the fire birns down and the stones are sufficiently heated, the stones are so arranged as to form a tolerable level surface, the sturgeon which had been previously cut into large fletches is now laid on the hot stones; a parsel of small boughs of bushes is next laid on and a second course of the sturgeon thus repating alternate layers of sturgeon and boughs untill the whole is put on which they design to cook. it is next covered closely with matts and water is poared in such manner as to run in among the hot stones and the vapor arrising being confined by the mats, cooks the fish. the whole process is performed in an hour, and the sturgeon thus cooked is much better than either boiled or roasted. [69]

Along with steaming, camas and wapato were often baked or roasted underground in an earth oven. Roasting camas bulbs and thistle roots brought out their sweetness, and as such, was a favored cooking technique of the sugar-loving Chinook. Unlike elsewhere along the Columbia, archaeological evidence of Portland-area earth ovens are primarily (though not exclusively) associated with village sites, rather than the areas in which foods are collected. This suggests that Portland-area people returned home from gathering with unprocessed camas and wapato rather than processing the roots into flour at the gathering site. This is probably due to the fact that the Multnomah, Cascades, and Clackamas lived relatively close to their harvest sites, whereas their Columbia Plateau and Pacific Coast kin had to travel great distances and wanted to reduce the weight of their harvest before transport.

During his visit to the region between 1843 and 1844, German botanist Charles A. Geyer observed the Chinook camas ceremony, noting with great interest the process by which the women collected and prepared the bulbs—a process of layering hot rocks with clean grass and then the camas, repeating until the entire four-foot-deep pit is level with the ground. The earth oven was then covered with a fire, which was left to burn for twenty-four hours. This slow roasting allowed the carbohydrates in the bulbs to convert to sugars, which caramelized deliciously. "As soon as the first Gamass are baked, the Indians, young and old, pass from lodge to lodge to eat Gamass: every where is plenty and content," wrote Geyer.[70]

Besides grasses, the Chinook and Kalapuya also used a variety of other leaves to cover camas bulbs during cooking, often layering lady fern or deer fern, which helped retain heat and prevent the food from drying out. Sword fern were particularly effective as nonstick cookware; mashed berry cakes and sticky-sweet camas bulbs could be layered onto its Teflon leaves and easily removed without tearing the confections. It was a good thing, too, because berry cakes were rather labor- and resource-intensive. A single salal cake could weigh as much as ten or fifteen pounds.[71] A woman would be understandably annoyed if she had gone to all the trouble of picking and drying days' worth of berries, mixing them with mashed fresh berries, forming the mix into dense cakes, and baking them for hours, just to have them stick in the oven and fall apart.

As with her other endeavors, a Pacific Northwest native woman left her creative imprint on cooking. An elder woman might have a culinary repertoire of more than 150 recipes, which she guarded closely. Typical of a shrewd trader, a woman was absolutely *quid pro quo* with her recipes; she could be enticed to divulge her secrets only with the offer of another woman's recipe in return.[72] Favorite seasonings included berries and salmon roe (both fresh and dried), along with wild onions, garlic, and chives. In addition to its edible root, the skunk cabbage's leaves were harvested to cover camas and onions while roasting in pits, which imparted "a fine flavor."[73] Chinook women often returned from their subalpine huckleberry jaunts with a basket of juniper berries to add to their culinary arsenal.

FEASTING (HĬ'-YŪ MŬCH'-A-MŬCK)

First Salmon and other first fruits ceremonies all commenced with a feast. Chinookan peoples had established a society that focused heavily on the seasonality of foods and that forged extensive economic ties among other villages and bands through marriage. During their seasonal movements (or when need dictated), Chinookans and Kalapuyans generally went to the localities in which their blood relatives and in-laws lived, rather than blazing trails to new locations. Based on seasonal resource availability, and the rituals and practices that accompanied them (such as Atfalati field burning and the Chinookan First Salmon Ceremony), those cyclical, consonant migrations came to shape relations with white settlers. Ritual feasting is another practice that shaped relations with white settlers, but not in the way of the American Thanksgiving myth.

The "give-away feast," known as "potlatch," was an elaborate gifting ceremony that came with a requisite banquet.[74] Depending on one's social status within the band, gifts could range from a small pot of eulachon oil to, in the case of wealthy eighteenth-century Chinook chief Chinini, gifts of canoes, houses, and women. Chinini's gifts were so outrageously extravagant that some whites (specifically, Captain Charles Bishop of the British ship *Ruby*) misinterpreted them as a sign of a "mental indisposition."[75] Naturally, the traders dropped any side-eyed snickering when the extravagant gifting was directed toward them, and included items such as wild geese, fresh fish, and wapato.

Among the indigenous people of the Pacific Northwest, cooking and gathering to eat as a community has long held high cultural and social significance, and continues to do so today. As with all other rituals, there were rules about the potlatch. When a chief decided to have one (typically for the same reasons people feast today: weddings and funerals), four to six men were sent out to neighboring villages to extend the invitation. Upon hearing the clarion cry, the villagers would titter gleefully, "Oh, we are going to be invited!"[76] The people got themselves all dolled-up, replete with dentalia shells in their noses, red face paint, and goose down strewn about the hair. They wore their good blankets for the occasion, and danced on planks and canoes. The best dancer was selected to be the head dancer, and he or she was required to feign modesty and reluctance before accepting and taking to the go-go stage. Anyone caught dancing out of rhythm was called out and sent to sit down on the sidelines.

If—horrors—the host ran out of food, two youths were asked to go to the next town to retrieve food from a relative's house. (It might have been awkward if the relative had not been invited.) The party continued; people entered the host's house dancing with salmon between their teeth and bags of roots on their backs. The host regaled all of the guests with the most lavish gifts he could afford, such as blankets and long dentalia.

These feasts often lasted for days, strengthening social bonds, economic status, and the sense of community.

Although it is true that the entire point of the potlatch was gifting, the evening feast was, and remains, the most important social and spiritual event of the potlatch, and all attendees were expected to be present.

Based on the assumption that only mental instability could drive such generosity, or because of the anti-capitalist (or anti-Christian) ideals that potlatches perpetuated, in 1884 British Columbian politicians signed into Canadian law a ban on potlatches and prohibited indigenous people from engaging in any "barbarous medicine feasts." The effects on the Chinook's neighbors was minimal; most First Nations people simply moved their potlatches to around Christmastime, to coincide with white celebratory feasting and gift-giving.

No such potlatch bans were ever introduced to the people of the Columbia, but laws banning the sale of alcohol to Native Americans were in effect from 1825 (with the Hudson's Bay Company) to 1953. The need for the law was determined after a century of exposure to European people led to rampant alcoholism and the correspondent boorish behavior, but was viewed by some as the infliction of the dominant white culture's solution to a problem it had, itself, created.[77] Oregon's first temperance law went into effect in 1844—before Oregon was even a state—thanks in no small part to the effects of white man's moonshine on the native population. Devout temperance in early Oregon missionaries was juxtaposed by immoderate drinking and inebriate behavior that was modeled by frontier whites; excessive drinking and violence while under the influence of alcohol are behaviors that were taught to Indians by non-agricultural whites across North America—behaviors encountered with increasing frequency over the nineteenth-century mass exodus to Oregon Territory.

3

THE OLD WORLD MEETS THE WILD WEST, OR: "CONGRATULATIONS! YOU HAVE MADE IT TO OREGON"

Hoisting a five-pound slab of bacon from a barrel of brine, a pioneer shooed away the horseflies and slid the salty pork onto the bench of her family's wagon. She sliced off six rashers—one each for herself, her husband, and her four surviving children, and then returned the slab back to the barrel. She lay the bacon strips into a cast-iron skillet already hot over a fire, and stirred the Dutch oven holding the beans her family had been nursing for two days. She carefully laid a checkered cloth on the dusty ground, smoothing the edges and setting stones on the corners to keep it from flying off in the wind. When the beans were warm and the bacon was sizzled to an aromatic crisp, she swabbed biscuits through the warm grease and spooned her family's supper onto clean tin plates. On this warm August evening there was a special treat: the pioneer had found time at the noontime stop to bake a pie with the wild gooseberries she picked. Life on the Oregon Trail was not all bad, she thought.

Though there were opportunities for grace and gratitude, the overland journey was not for the faint of heart. "Jocular hilarity" characterized the onset of the journey; hope and ambition were perfect exemplifications of the American character, and the promise of free land played no small part in driving hundreds of thousands of pioneers westward.[1] However, as the journey wore on at the excruciating pace of two miles per hour (most wagons achieved around fifteen to twenty miles per day), this glee was eventually eroded by realities of life on the trail. To the chagrin of mothers worried for their daughters' dignity, Victorian propriety was shrugged off as priorities shifted to more pressing matters, such as giving birth in a moving wagon without water, or surviving a pernicious bout of dysentery in the privacy afforded solely by another woman's skirts. Party members dropped like flies from diseases and tragic mishaps, and morale sank to the unsurpassed depths that can only be experienced when burying one's child. For most, the baleful exodus continued for the better part of seven months, concluding mercifully just before the October rains and cold.

There were, by and large, two types of people on the Oregon Trail: coarse frontiersmen and Christian families. The trail had been laid down between 1811 and 1840 by the former—loutish, western-bound bachelors with a penchant for saloons and working girls, and stout mountain men who were perfectly content living in scenic solitude. In the few good years that followed, before the trail became clogged with greedy, gold-drunk emigrants and their hungry livestock, the Great Plains were green and lush, overflowing with abundance. When families joined the wagon trail, the food became "more regular and better cooked," thanks to female hands. A woman's touch—a posy of blue lupine and pink bee flower, a calico cloth spread over the bare dirt—went leagues toward lifting woebegone spirits.[2]

Dairy cows walked alongside the wagon trains, and some pioneers brought chickens along for the ride in the wagons. Hens could be kept in a small, built-in coop, eat kitchen scraps and forbs, and provide a steady supply of fresh eggs and meat. Besides being cheaper, slow-but-steady oxen were preferred over fast, nimble-footed horses for pulling wagons; a bucket of fresh milk hung from the yoke could be churned into butter by the oxen's lumbering gait alone. Fresh butter cooled in a mountain stream could not have tasted sweeter than it did to a dusty, road-weary emigrant.

Based on the strict recommendations outlined in Lansford Hastings's 1845 mover's handbook *The Emigrants Guide to Oregon and California*, items taken by nearly all wagon parties included 200 pounds of flour, 150 pounds of bacon, 20 pounds of sugar, 10 pounds of coffee, and 10 pounds of salt. Though Hastings advised that "the emigrant should not encumber themselves with any other...even by the most devoted epicure," additional foodstuffs might include tea, rice, dried fruit, potatoes, hard tack or crackers, pepper, vinegar, pickles, mustard, tallow, and saleratus to use for baking soda.[3] Some also took whiskey or brandy (strictly for medicinal purposes, they would be quick to assure). Remarkably, Hastings did not include beans in his recommendations, writing that buffalo meat and bacon "can be relied upon, under all circumstances."[4] Regardless, every diary and written account of meals on the Trail mentions eating beans on a nearly daily basis.

As the journey drawled on and draft animals grew tired or wore their feet clean out, many pioneers had to discard frivolous supplies. It was imperative, then, that people packed light. Hastings advised that for the cooking, "[a] baking-kettle (Dutch oven), frying-pan, tea-kettle, tea-pot, and coffee-pot are all the furniture of this kind, that is essential, which, together with tin plates, tin cups, ordinary knives, forks, spoons, and a coffee-mill, should constitute the entirety of the kitchen apparatus."[5] Canteens, buckets, or water bags were brought for liquids, and a rifle, pistols, powder, lead, and shot were brought for hunting game.

Life for the Overlanders somewhat resembled that of other nomadic cultures. Men hunted for supplemental subsistence; buffalo, deer and antelope, sagehens, and jackrabbits all provided protein that did not need to be carried or stored, and fishing offered the promise of a good meal in addition to a much-needed moment of reflection and repose. Women assumed traditional gatherer roles in addition to performing their normal domestic duties. Baking was a daily chore, but doing so in a Dutch oven or baking kettle presented certain challenges, including being frowned upon by early nineteenth-century dietary reformer Sylvester Graham, who wrote that the use of the baking kettle was "decidedly the most objectionable" way to bake.[6] (As a strident vegetarian and general worry-wart, Graham may have not lasted long on the trail.) Regardless of how primitive it may have seemed to genteel women, foraging for fruit offered a change of scenery and something to do; women and children often gathered enough wild berries, plums, or even fern fiddleheads to bake pies. A woman could roll her crust out on the wagon seat and slide the pastry and fruit into her Dutch oven, then affix the lid and bury the pot in the hot coals. Never did ingenuity matter more than on the trail.

Pioneers arrived to Oregon wide-eyed and hungry. Pioneer Catherine Thomas Morris reminisced of her family's arrival to Oregon in 1851. "No longer did we have to eat bacon, beans and camp bread, and not get as much of them as we wanted," she recalled, "for here we could have all the vegetables we wanted, where the hills were full of deer, and the streams full of trout, where when we looked to the westward, instead of seeing nothing but a long winding train of prairie schooners with a cloud of dust hanging over all, we saw waving grass and vividly green fir trees. We looked up at the blue sky with white clouds and to the eastward we could see Mount Hood, clean and clear and beautiful and so wonderful that it almost took your breath."[7]

Originally a trading outpost, Portland—or as it was then known, "The Clearing"—was a stopping place for fur traders decades before the first prairie schooner crested the Cascades. Early trappers lived much as the indigenous peoples: on the land and close to the bone. There were still 1,000 or so Indians living in the Portland area by 1850, and they remained in the city for decades, trading with white settlers well after the city was incorporated.[8]

There had been two separate, vain attempts in the 1830s by Hall Kelley and Nathaniel Wyeth—both from Boston—to attract people from the East Coast to their respective ideas for a town site. Kelley's vision was one of an Oregon Utopia. His was the idea for Americans to travel west in wagons on an (yet-untested) overland trail and claim Oregon from the British, and to establish an orderly, thriving city with the rectangular blocks and straight streets that Portland emulates today. Unfortunately, Kelley had never been west of Washington, D.C., which made his pitch, based solely on the romanticism of the Lewis and Clark journals, a bit less than credible. He did eventually make it to Oregon, traveling via New Orleans, south from Mexico and up through California. He met some traveling companions on the way to Oregon who were headed to Fort Vancouver to sell horses. Kelley's arrival to Fort Vancouver came immediately following news that the Fort should be on the lookout for horse thieves headed north from California. Besides that, the head of Fort Vancouver had read Kelley's subversive writings about to whom Oregon truly belonged (hint: not England). The fort did not let him in.

Nathaniel Wyeth (an acquaintance of Kelley's) had arrived to Fort Vancouver about a month before Kelley, and had begun building log cabins to attempt to set up a trading post. In 1834, he built Fort William at the mouth of the Willamette on Wapato Island, planted wheat, and planned to trade with the Multnomah Indians with the intent to sell dried salmon to Boston. The Hudson's Bay Company had other ideas about who the trading stronghold was, and effectively blocked him. Hudson's Bay Company, the owner of Fort Vancouver, was so pervasive in the Portland area that their well-known initials, "HBC," were said by many to stand for "Here Before Christ."[9] As noted by economic historian Eugene Snyder, if Hall Kelley had been a victim of bad luck, Wyeth was perhaps a victim of bad timing. "If Wyeth had had the resources to engage in the triangular trade—New England, Pacific Coast, Orient—that became so profitable in the 1850s, and if the Willamette-Columbia had developed sufficiently to support such a trade, Wyeth may have succeeded," explained Snyder in *Early Portland: Stump-Town Triumphant* (1970).[10] After Wyeth sailed back to New England with half a shipment of salmon and his tail between his legs, HBC turned Wapato Island over to beef and dairy production, left in the care of their French-Canadian cattleman Laurent Sauvé. The island, now known as Sauvie Island, is still a major provider of Portland-area produce.

The six-foot-four "White-Headed Eagle" John McLoughlin—the man who had built Fort Vancouver and founded Oregon City—was a benevolent host during his governorship of the Fort. Meals in the Fort Vancouver dining hall were legendary, and were shared by Indian chiefs, British dignitaries, and American settlers alike. American author and Oregon Trail emigrant Thomas Jefferson Farnham wrote effusively of his 1839 dinner at the Fort: "Roast beef and pork, boiled mutton, baked salmon, boiled ham; beets, carrots, turnips, cabbage and potatoes, and wheaten bread are tastefully distributed over the table among a dinner-set of elegant queen's ware, burnished with glittering glasses and decanters of various-coloured Italian wines."[11]

Just as the Great Migration was paving the way for other pioneers, a few gentlemen from the East Coast were waffling over whether or not The Clearing had a future. Among them was William Overton, who had arrived from Tennessee in 1841. After a brief sojourn to Honolulu (then the major port for the West Coast), Overton returned to Oregon in 1843 with a mind toward staking a claim. One November day in 1843, Overton and his lawyer friend Asa Lovejoy were making the canoe trip from Fort Vancouver to Oregon City, and he mentioned to Lovejoy his plans for the swampy town site that lay in between. Early settlers had assumed that Senator Lewis Linn's bill would become the law that granted married emigrants to Oregon 640 acres of free land, but before the bill was enacted into law, the Provisional Government at Oregon City required paperwork to be filed along with a small legal fee. The canoe stopped at The Clearing for a mid-trip rest, and Overton talked Lovejoy into filing the paperwork and paying the 25¢ fee; the claim was filed in 1844, with Lovejoy and Overton equal owners.

The cold, wet 1844 spring did not sweeten Overton on the town much (nor did the months spent on the dull task of road-building), and he got the itch to move on. Unfortunately, he was destitute but for his half-interest in the 640-acre claim. He endeavored to sell his half to an Oregon City merchant named F. W. Pettygrove, for $50 worth of supplies and food to help him make his way out of town. Although $50 was a considerable markup from half of 25 cents, Pettygrove was no dummy. Before he accepted the deal, he took a canoe to the town claim site, poked around a bit in the Willamette (taking care to plumb its depths with a surveyor's precision), and realized that the mouth of the Willamette could easily accommodate the type of vessels commonly coming to Oregon for trade. Pettygrove concluded the deal, and Overton went on his merry way to California.

In 1845, The Clearing was now equally owned by Pettygrove and Lovejoy, and haggling over naming the stumpy burg began in earnest. Lovejoy nominated his hometown of Boston as the new town's namesake; Pettygrove, from Maine, famously won the deciding coin toss, two out of three.

By 1850 the population of Portland was about 300, but a year later it tripled.[12] In the early days of the city, Native American encampments lined the hollow near today's Alder Street, and native women sold baskets, kindling, and berries to nearby households.[13] Most pioneers who came to Portland stayed in town only long enough to earn enough money for a final move to Willamette Valley, where good farming could be found and one's full land claim could be staked. Others stayed put. One family took up residence in East Portland, in the heavy timber on the west slopes of Mount Tabor in what is now a water reservoir in the southeast quadrant of the city. The family patriarch, having lopped off all of the toes on one foot while splitting rails, had secured work ferrying people across the Willamette in a dugout canoe. His daughters would lay awake in their beds at night, gripped by the sound of screaming cougars, or wolves howling and circling their home.[14] In 1852, the same year that one diarist arrived to find Portland "a little muddy village of 300," a cholera outbreak on the overland trail slowed the population growth considerably.[15] By 1860, Portland was home to 2,900 souls; less than a decade later, the population swelled to 9,400.

When they traveled west, emigrants brought their foodways with them. Popcorn candy, popular in the mid-nineteenth century at New York's Coney Island Amusement Park, found its way west with the emigrants, as did old English dishes like blancmange (a white, jelled dessert) and Parker House rolls, invented in the Boston restaurant of the same name in the 1870s. Recipes for these foods appear in the Portland-published *Web-Foot Cookbook* (1885), illustrating that food trends from the East Coast traveled to the Northwest with early settlers.

In 1855, Pony Express rider Isaac Van Dorsey Mossman learned to bake bread on a stick while camped in Portland, at what would become the east end of the Morrison Bridge.[16] It is unclear why he chose this bindle-stiff staple; the same year that Dorsey enjoyed his stick-bread, a census of the city was shown to contain one steam flour mill, three bakeries, twelve hotels and boardinghouses, three butchers, six saloons (serving lunch), and a candy store. A few years later, there were counted among other urban comforts twelve restaurants, two additional hotels, and another retail grocery store. There were a staggering fifty-five liquor stores.[17] Stumps peppered the sloggy tracks that interlaced the few false-front buildings. They were painted white so men could avoid tripping over them in the dark.

HUNGRY AS A LUMBERJACK

Portland was growing fast, and above all, it required two things: wood, and the men to pull it out of the forests. Besides felling trees for railroad ties, lumberjacks, sawyers, and millwrights were essential to keep up with the demand for materials necessary for constructing slab roads, sidewalks, and clapboard buildings. In the mid-nineteenth century, timber companies hired twelve-man crews to fell lumber and coax teams of oxen to haul the logs to mills to be sawed into boards for export. These bare-bones crews lacked cooks; in fact, they lacked kitchens altogether. Some men hired a "chore boy" to cook up pork, beans, and bread, but most handled the cooking themselves—typically little more than a pot of beans dangled over a fire—with mixed results. As demand for lumber ramped up, crews with hundreds of loggers, each demanding upward of 9,000 calories a day, became commonplace in the Northwest.[18]

To keep the boots filled, nineteenth-century timbermen often imported "woodhicks" from back east, or hired failed gold miners from California and southern Oregon. Some lured in unhappy sailors commonly found around Portland, with assurances that at least in the forest they would never wake up a slave on a ship bound for China. Loggers insisted on plenty of food as a condition of labor, and all were promised ample meals in addition to regular pay.

Even with the provision of square meals, loggers eked out a fairly tough existence. The term "skid road," or "skid row," now pertaining to an urban area blighted with dilapidated hotels, cheap taverns, and the types of people that frequent such establishments, not only originated in the Pacific Northwest as a logging term (the muddy trails down which logs were dragged, or skidded), but is in many ways emblematic of the infant city. Portland's Old Chinatown was the first urban core and soon became a skid row of saloons in which loggers came to piss away their

Figure 3.1.   Loggers in the Pacific Northwest pause for the camera before sitting down to eat. Photo by Tom Rulson, ca. 1910–1920. Photo © Thomas Robinson

earnings (quite literally, in the case of Erickson's Saloon, which will be discussed in a later chapter).

The quality of camp cuisine was just as important to loggers as the quantity. A man might go work for a competing company if the food offered was appreciably better, and timber bosses knew this. At the turn of the twentieth century, timber company employment pamphlets touted the quality of their logging camp grub as better than the big city hotel's (not that any logger would know how high-class hotel food tasted). Things had begun to improve over plain, old pork and beans by the late nineteenth century. "In the matter of food, for instance, the logger of the present is much better off than his predecessor of the period of the once puissant axe," wrote one journalist in an 1898 article for *Lippincott's Magazine.*[19] Once roads wended their way out to the trees, the ease with which supplies could arrive to camps increased manifold. Beans with the requisite cube of salt pork now came with beef and sauerkraut, served in generous portions; there were potatoes with gravy, and hot, buttered bread. Piping hot tea and coffee sweetened with sugar and condensed milk washed down plates of cookies, doughnuts, cakes, and pie. Pacific Northwest loggers had it significantly better than their New England and Midwestern counterparts.

During World War I, however, despite the knowledge that hardworking men needed good food to power them, many timber companies tried to cut corners by offering smaller portions and lower quality of product. Numerous articles published in trade magazines offered tips to timber barons on how to save on food costs; one promoted improving the appearance of dining halls to encourage slower eating to reduce the amount of food consumed, while others recommended putting the onus on logging camp cooks to maintain scrupulous food cost records and personally account for product loss. Meanwhile, there was an exponential increase in demand for light, strong, and flexible Pacific Northwest spruce for building war planes. During the war, life for lumberjacks and logging camp kitchen staff was demoralizing; living and dining conditions were squalid and the labor was bone-crushingly arduous. Something had to change. With help from the radical labor group the Industrial Workers of the World (IWW, or the "Wobblies"), they went on strike in the summer of 1917.

Although there was plenty to complain about, even the most ardent critics of the timber bosses found the quantity of food in the camps adequate. James Rowan, the militant leader of the Wobbly lumberjacks, admitted begrudgingly that the food was "fairly substantial and plentiful as necessary to enable the men to endure the long hours and hard work."[20] However, among their demands was "wholesome food in porcelain dishes, no overcrowding; sufficient help to keep kitchen clean and sanitary."[21] Their strike began with a walkout over bad food.

With the strike's marked decrease in wood production, the government predictably stepped in. The Loyal Legion of Loggers and Lumbermen, or Four L, was a militarized labor union created by the U.S. War Department to counter the widespread lumber strike brought about by the Wobblies. War Colonel Brice Disque was dispatched to call a meeting of timber industry leaders in downtown Portland to come to a solution; timber baron Simon Benson graciously hosted the event at his hotel. Patriotic civilian and soldier volunteers, totaling 45,000 men, pledged loyalty to the American war effort and took up residence in barracks just across the Columbia from Portland.[22] Those who did not take the oath were suspected of being saboteurs, anarchists, or traitors.

Following the formation of the Four L, things improved markedly. Fresh fruits, vegetables, eggs, dairy, and meats were added to the loggers' diet, in abundance and as a matter of course. A wider variety of foods was served, rather than beans and salt pork every day. Clean cookhouses for dining and food preparation became common place, and men were given the dignity of plates and silverware. And for the first time, women started working in Pacific Northwest logging camp kitchens, finding employment as cooks, bakers, dishwashers, and waitresses. Affectionately known as "flunkies," camp waitresses had to work fast, and soon picked up the skill of carrying six plates at a time on one arm, plus a seventh in her other hand.[23] Colorful cookhouse jargon enlivened the cookee's work; hollered requests for spuds (potatoes), java (coffee), a nosebag (lunch bucket), cow (canned milk), smear (butter), fish eyes in matter (tapioca), sinkers (doughnuts), and hen fruit (eggs) added to the merry din of a busy kitchen.[24]

In the morning, the cook's shanty churned out sizzling, broiled bacon, hash brown potatoes, medium-boiled eggs (hitting that custardy sweet spot between pale, dry yolks and runny, golden gravy), rolled oat porridge, and hot, buttered toast. The cook kept a pie tin filled with melted lard next to his or her stove, periodically dipping a clean, rolled-up burlap sack to swab the griddle between flapjacks. The chore boys and flunkies would load the tables with pitchers of milk and plates of cake and dough-nuts. Breakfast would be eaten quickly; boiled eggs were crumbled be-tween hot cakes and covered in butter and syrup to more fleetly usher the meal into one's gob before setting off to work. A few slugs of scalding hot coffee would flush it all back before the men abandoned their rough-hewn tables and headed off to labor.

In the 1870s, just as the demand for lumber and lumberjacks was mounting, San Franciscans were pouring into the burgeoning Portland. Railroad travel was affordable and brought the promise of new places to live and do business in an unsaturated town that was growing fast. William Whitlock, an Oregon City courthouse recorder, wrote in a letter to his friends, the Treadgolds, who had left Oregon City to return to the UK, that "Portland is quite a large place at this time and improving fast, fine large brick and stone buildings, you would hardly know the place. Emigration is coming in very fast, fare from California is low. . . . [I]t brings some very bad stock from Frisco."[25] Whether Whitlock was inti-mating about miners or the Chinese is a mystery, but many of the "low stock" would find residence in buildings owned by Portland's prominent families—landlords to the gambling dens and after-hours saloons. More typically, railway traffic between Portland and San Francisco went the other way, and instead of carrying people, it brought wheat and flour, apples, and berries.

AGRICULTURE

At the end of the nineteenth century, the call for agrarianism was loud and clear. "Every effort must be put forth to bring wild lands in cultiva-tion," implored Harvey Whitefield Scott, "to increase the area of orchards and the number of flocks and herds, and, if possible, to render substantial assistance to settlers who find the difficulties of pioneer life too great to be overcome."[26] The problem with agriculture in the West, as Scott iden-tified it, was that aggressive ranching and farming driven by off-site capitalists led to exhausted lands, and ultimately resulted in the type of land barony and feudalism seen in England and Ireland. "Portland wants nothing of this," he wrote.[27] Scott's vision for Portland was an artisanal paradise of apple-cheeked families, sun-ripened vegetables on micro-farms, and velvet-nosed, doe-eyed milch cows. "For this reason [Portland] will principally encourage such industries as fruit raising, dairying, sheep and stock raising by small farmers on small farms; the raising of poultry and the labor of small manufactories, and of persons in rural communities."[28]

Portland had been doing a commendable job of adhering to Harvey Whitefield Scott's utopian vision from the covered wagon days of the 1850s until the postwar Baby Boom of the 1950s, when most of Portland's small neighborhood farms were razed for ranch-style housing. And yet today, with the rise of heirloom-bred backyard chickens, home lacto-fermenting, and beer brewing, Scott's American dream is thriving in the Portland of today.

From the beginning, clearing the land had been an urgent task. In the 1820s, before the piney weald was flecked with tiny, glowing cabins, a fire had swept through the east side of Portland, clearing large swaths of the girthsome Douglas-fir, western hemlock, and bigleaf maple forests, burying the earth in rich, organic carbon and opening the door to agriculture.[29] Volcanic buttes covered in fluffy, acidic soils meant that sweet berries—already happily living in ancient Portland—were a natural fit.

The first fruits intentionally planted were not all berries, however. In the 1840s, a Quaker abolitionist named Henderson Luelling had, like many others, been stricken with Oregon fever. He had already pulled up stakes in Indiana and gone to Iowa in 1837, but ten years later he found himself with a twinkle in his eye for greener pastures. To the incredulity of his friends, he decided to bring his beloved nursery business with him. He filled one wagon with humus and charcoal, laying his strongest little whips and toddler saplings into the growing medium. He hitched three oxen to the heavy wagon and set off.

Luelling's Traveling Orchard, as it came to be known, rode in the 100-wagon train captained by Lot Whitcomb, a wealthy entrepreneur who went on to build the Willamette's first steamship. Of the 700 grafted saplings Luelling selected, there were eighteen apple varieties, eight types of pear, six different cherries, and three peaches; there were quince, plums, black walnut, and a shell-bark hickory. He doted on the little trees, cooing at them as his own children and giving them water even when there was none to spare. "[E]very day, no matter how scarce the water, nor how far the distance between watered camps, each and every one of those little 700 trees were carefully sprinkled with water," recalled one pioneer.[30] "Each little tree was a saga in itself."[31] Some fledged leaves and bloomed during the nearly eight-month trip. Some of the gooseberry and currant bushes bore fruit. Confounding doubters' belief, half of them made it all the way to Oregon.

What the naysayers did not realize was that the Great Spirit was dwelling within Luelling's trees. At any rate, that is what the Native Americans thought, a fact that stayed the hands of those bands otherwise unfriendly toward pioneers. Luelling later learned that the divine protection enjoyed by the tiny trees growing out of his wagon may have extended to the entire party. Not only did Luelling's party have no "Indian trouble," but when his pregnant wife, Elizabeth, went into labor en route, the awe-struck Columbia River people merrily canoed her to The Dalles for medical attention, excited to have a hand in divinity.[32] Before they made it, Elizabeth gave birth to the ninth Luelling child, a son that they dutifully named Oregon Columbia Luelling.[33]

After giving birth on the riverbank, the Luellings still had to finish the trip down the treacherous Columbia Cascades. The Native Americans helped again, guided by their reverence for Luelling's collection of sacred trees. When, finally, they arrived to the outer Southeast Portland enclave of Milwaukie, the trees stretched out their roots and thrived. The orchard was the first known orchard where grafting occurred. Some have said that Luelling's trees were the mothers of all of the fruit trees in Oregon. Recalling his detractors, Luelling later said that the return on his effort was "a dollar a drop for the sweat I lost in getting the necessary water to keep them alive while we crossed the desert; and their luscious fruit repaid me many times over the jeers, ridicule, and contentions of my comrades."[34]

Bringing scions and grafted saplings, though cumbersome, was a necessary labor. The apple *does*, in a good many cases, fall far from the tree. Apples do not "come true" from seed; that is to say, planting apple seed is a crap-shoot. The genetic material captured in each seed is diverse, even from one individual apple—each seed from that single apple grows into a tree bearing vastly different fruit. One tree may produce sweet, red fruits that are perfect for eating out of hand, though most will grow into scraggly wildlings with inedible fruit that, according to Henry David Thoreau, is "sour enough to set a squirrel's teeth on edge and make a jay scream."[35] These hard, scrabbly apples are fit only for pressing into cider, and hard cider was the fate of many apples before Prohibition.

The first apple trees planted at Fort Vancouver in the spring of 1827 were from seeds that came out of an apple eaten for dessert at a London dinner party. One of those trees, called the "Old Apple Tree," still grows just across the river near the Fort Vancouver National Historic Site, about a half mile southwest of the original orchard. These first apple trees in the Greater Portland Metro Area did not produce the succulent fruit of Luelling's babied trees. In 1841, one officer with the U.S. Naval Wilkes Expedition wrote of his visit to McLoughlin's seed-borne apple orchard at the Fort, remarking about the fruits that "to my taste the majority were better adapted for baking than for a dessert," but admitted that in a new country they were better than nothing.[36] Another early pioneer said in 1906 that she had been eating the fruit for fifty-five years, and that it was "of fair quality."[37] These and the other fruits and vegetables grown at the Fort were never destined for export; they merely kept the officers in fresh produce while staying at the barracks.

When apple trees do make the cut, it is for good reason. Among the 350 trees to survive Luelling's continental journey were sublime eating apples with names like old-fashioned poetry: White Winter Pearmain, Red Astrachan, Winesap, Baldwin, Gloria Mundi, Red-Cheeked Pippin, and a few other varieties now considered heirlooms. There were Fall Butter, Winter Nellis, and Seckle pears, cherries, grapes, and plums.

Henderson's brother Seth Lewelling (who spelled his name differently) had arrived to Oregon in 1850, and after working at Henderson's old nursery, he took over the horticulture even though he had very little nursery experience. Business had been slow at the Luelling and Meek nursery, as Lewelling recalled in 1892:

> The great difficulty was to get stocks on which to graft. They tried the wild crabapple and thorn brush [hawthorn] for seed fruits and the wild cherry for stone fruits, but with poor success. In the fall of 1849 a Mr. Pugh brought from the States some seed of various kinds which Meek and Luelling bought and planted, and from which in the fall of 1850 they had splendid stocks from two to four feet high. They grafted 18,000 which in the fall of 1851 averaged about four feet. . . . The apple trees sold readily for $1 apiece, and plum, cherry and peach for $1.50 each.[38]

It was not just trees that the brothers were selling. The little teenaged trees had started producing fruit that fetched a handsome price in San

Francisco, where the gold money was flowing. Garnering a price as high as $2 per pound (roughly $57 per pound in 2013), a few boxes were shipped down, secured with iron straps to protect them against fruit thieves. By 1856, the orchard and its offspring had grown enough that Oregon orchards shipped 20,000 boxes of apples. At the California selling price of $20–30 per bushel, that single year's shipment of apples would be worth between $11M and $17M in today's market.[39] In 1858, the Luelling orchard alone produced 2,800 bushels of apples.

By 1854, Henderson Luelling saw fit to take advantage of California's weather, wide-open space, and ostentatious fruit prices. He sold out his holdings to his brother Seth and his son-in-law William Meek, and he and his son Alfred went on to start apricot and cherry orchards in their very own town of Fruitvale, now a predominantly Latino enclave of Oakland. In 1860 Luelling started a group called the Free Lovers, sold his Fruitvale property, left his wife, and sailed to Honduras. He lost most of his money, then returned to San Jose to live with friends. In 1878, Luelling died of a heart attack while clearing land for another orchard.

William Meek had brought apple and cherry seeds and a few of his own scions along for the ride on the Oregon Trail, but the Oregon life turned out to not be quite what Meek had in mind, so in 1859 he, too, sold out his share of the business and moved to California. Unlike Luelling, Meek wisely quit while he was ahead; after ten years of running a thriving stone fruit enterprise, he built a 7,900-square-foot mansion on his 3,000-acre orchard.

Seth Lewelling stayed put. He planted five acres of Italian prunes—the first such orchard west of the Rockies. Although he had only a few years' experience as a nurseryman, he was a natural; he began to tinker with the *Prunus* genome by hybridizing cherry varieties. Before long, he had propagated a new cherry, which he named the Black Republican. The Black Republican, a dark-skinned, firm-fleshed fruit that withstands long-distance shipping and has an intense black cherry flavor with hints of rose, almond, and herbs, was a favorite among western fruit growers. As wildly successful as it was, it turned out to have been created accidentally. It had volunteered from seed in Lewelling's garden, and he had no idea who its parents were.

Like all Quakers, Lewelling was a strident abolitionist. As a thumb to the nose, he named the cherry after a nickname that he had been maliciously given by his pro-slavery colleagues back east. "I will make it a term of honor," he promised, "and I'll make you relish Black Republicans."[40] The Oregon Horticultural Society later renamed the cherry "the Lewelling" in honor of Seth, but the new name never caught on anywhere but the South, where, in the 1860s, the name "Black Republican" had been something of a sales deterrent. Lewelling had succeeded in making anti-abolitionists literally eat their words, a fact of which he was very proud.

For all his accidental success, there were at least a few intentional wins. Perhaps the best known of these is the Bing cherry, which, despite having been boldly named after his Chinese orchard foreman Ah Bing, sold fine in the South. It did fine in Portland, too, even at a time when anti-Chinese sentiment ran high. The cherry, an offspring of a cross between the Black Republican and the native, wild sweet cherry (*Prunus avium*), was growing in an orchard row managed by the six-foot-tall Manchurian. In 1889, at the end of his thirty-five-year-long contract with Lewelling, Bing returned to China to visit his family, and was not granted permission to return to the United States. The cherry that bears his name is still the most widely produced cherry in the country.

Oregon was built on apples and cherries, but it is berries and hazelnuts (also known as filberts) that characterize the regional cuisine today. Oregonians blend hazelnuts into pesto instead of pine nuts, and Oregon boasts hazelnut-fed pork that rivals (some even say exceeds) the Spanish acorn-fed ham (*jamón ibérico*) that fetches around $90 per pound. It is difficult to avoid hazelnuts in grocery stores, on menus, and in farmers markets in Portland. As late as the 1930s, SE 104th and Stark Street, now the site of an Adventist hospital, was still populated by hazelnut orchards, and today, 99 percent of American hazelnuts are produced in Oregon, and a great many of which being grown in Yamhill County, only twenty-five miles south of Portland.

But the story of hazelnut growing in the region is rather disappointingly prosaic; the industry as it is known today only dates back to the turn of the twentieth century, and seems to have been a knee-jerk reaction to the booming success of orchards in general rather than to a deep cultural need to grow a local food. The Oregon Agricultural Experiment Station (part of the Oregon Agricultural College, now Oregon State University) pragmatically published its guidance on the cultivation of hazelnuts in 1898, after a decade of growing a dozen English hazelnut trees given to the college by a Salem nursery owner. These had possibly been derived from those planted by Sam Strictland, a retired Hudson's Company officer who started a small grove of hazelnut trees in Scottsburg (near Roseburg, about 150 miles south of Portland) in 1858. The trees did just fine in the Valley's climate and soils, they reported, and would make a fine orchard specimen.

Twenty years earlier, that conclusion had already been drawn by Felix Gillet, a French-born nurseryman living in California. Gillet believed his "Barcelona" variety of hazelnuts would fare far better in the Mediterranean climate of the Willamette Valley than the drier, hotter climate of California, where it had been failing. Five years later, another Frenchman, David Gernot, planted fifty trees along a fence row in the Willamette Valley, and hazelnut growing began to ramp up. In 1886, Portland postmaster (and later Oregon Senator) George A. Steel bought 165 second-generation seedlings from Gillet, and planted them in the hobby farm he kept at his pastoral estate a few miles south of Portland. Twenty years later, the very first commercial hazelnut orchard had been started by George and Lulu Dorris in Springfield in 1905 on a site presently used as a living history orchard. At around the same time, a handful of farmers from Clackamas and Yamhill Counties purchased nursery stock from Gillet and started the hazelnut orchards just outside Portland, in the rows now seen growing along Wilsonville Road between Wilsonville and Newberg. Others followed suit, and soon small groves of filberts grew throughout Portland's east side.

Dorris's nephew Ben later wrote that "in no other case will Nature aid you in the Willamette Valley as she will with the filbert, the first cousin of the wild hazel which is the only nut indigenous to Oregon."[41] Though there are technically other edible, native nuts (recall the "Chinook olive"), Ben Dorris had a salient point about the hazelnut's hardiness in the region. Everywhere else in the country, the plant was susceptible to the fungal disease Eastern Filbert Blight, which devastated orchards in the early 1900s. That Oregon already had a native hazelnut is perhaps a good reason for its horticultural success. Its commercial success was largely because of demand for alternative protein during the war.

Wartime cookery books instructed in the clever use of hazelnuts for creating meatless "meat loaf," rissoles, and other savory main courses, though home cooks might also have turned to so-called hygienic or scientific cookbooks for advice on preparing filbert "sausages" and the like. Nuts were an important mainstay during World Wars I and II, but once meat rationing was over following the wars, nut consumption dropped off precipitously. Filberts were relatively unappreciated following World War II, and for decades recipes for the sweet nuts appeared almost exclusively in German dessert recipes. Hazelnuts did not reach their apex of popularity in Oregon until the late 1980s, when the Hazelnut Marketing Board began its first successful promotion program and landed the filbert as the official State Nut of Oregon. It would seem that the hazelnut is beloved in Oregon only because Oregonians were told to love the hazelnut.

In addition to filberts, Felix Gillet had dabbled in growing berries commercially. "[T]he Pacific Northwest takes the lead as the berry section of the Union," proclaimed an 1899 article in *Oregon Native Son* magazine, and this was a sentiment already understood before Oregon's statehood.[42] Even before berry bushes came along for the ride on Luelling's wagon train, blackberry plants from the Sandwich Islands (Hawaii), brought by the Hudson's Bay Company, thrived on the other side of the Columbia. Heady-sweet strawberries grew wild in the mountains, valley, and on the coast, making them a natural crop for farms and homestead gardens. Blackcap raspberries and scrubby huckleberries had not only been relished by innumerable generations of Native Americans, but also provided genetic material for early horticultural experiments.

Although the rolling suburbs beyond the West Hills were an expanse of wheat and other verdure, throughout Portland's east side, families found extra income growing and harvesting berries on parcels of rural land checkering the suburban neighborhoods. Most lands to the east of 82nd Avenue were still fairly wide-open spaces in the early 1900s, and after 1915, green grocer Nick Sunseri's wholesale produce stand on the east bank of the Willamette meant there was a single market to sell the fruits and vegetables rather than having to peddle them door to door.

In 1904, Japanese families began pouring into the Montavilla neighborhood on the east side of Mount Tabor, and by the close of the decade there were hundreds of Japanese residents growing and harvesting raspberries and loganberries on a thousand or so acres. By 1914, Montavilla was considered one of the most prosperous suburbs on the east side, thanks in large part to urban gardening and produce markets. The Lynch area (now known as the Centennial neighborhood) in outer Southeast was another nexus of urban berry production, and as late as the 1950s the David Douglas neighborhood consisted of nothing but berry fields, a

"Piggly Wiggly store and a service station."[43] East Portland's berry-growing prowess could not be denied, and the farther east one traveled, the longer the berry fields remained. Gresham (adjacent to Portland to the east) was once known as the "Raspberry Capital of the World"; vines of the sweet ruby-drupes continue to line SE Stark from Park Rose to Gresham today.

In the years leading into (and during) the Great Depression, berry picking offered a way for women and children to contribute to household financial survival. In July 1922, a labor newspaper bulletin announced that in Portland "[b]erry picking is in full swing. A good family man with 13 children helping can earn as high as $2.75 a day if he exercises strict economy and they all pick from sunrise to sunset."[44] Unfortunately, this was a reality for many Portland kids, as child labor laws and the eight-hour workday were still more than a decade away from federal enactment.

Figure 3.2.   Berry picking was a way for Portland women and schoolchildren to earn extra money or to contribute to their family income. Photo ca. 1900. Courtesy of Old Oregon Photos

After the Depression, Portland children were still expected to pitch in during berry season. In 1945, berry pickers were even recruited by Portland Public Schools, who organized school picking groups to get students to and from work. During peak production, upward of forty-five school groups toiled away to keep the fields picked, and thousands more acres still needed picking. Postwar, the USDA continued its recommendation that children were the perfect choice for light agricultural work, depicting in one pamphlet a Portland boy working "6 hours a day during raspberry-picking season. Youth provide ideal labor for this work."[45] During the sunny mid-century summers and for decades beyond, berry-picking offered Portland's Baby Boomer children a way to stay out of trouble and earn a little spending cash for popcorn and chocolate malteds.

All the fruit coming out of fields and orchards meant that not only were agricultural workers staying plenty busy, but Portland was home to a thriving fruit canning industry, as well. Whereas salmon canneries dominated in Astoria and The Dalles, Portland was a center for fruit packing. In 1914, when Gresham was kicking off its first commercial raspberry enterprise, Portland had already been home to several fruit canneries and packing plants for about thirty years.

Numerous Portland businesses cropped up to produce jams, conserves, jellies, and vinegars. The Kerr Glass Manufacturing Corporation—makers of jars for home canning—opened its offices in Portland in 1903 as the Hermetic Fruit Jar Company (Ball Corporation bought Kerr Glass in the 1990s). The Kerr brothers also sold jarred fruit products and condiments with their partner, William Wadhams, from their building on NW 13th and Davis. Before the century was up, numerous others opened to take advantage of Portland's ideal location at the nexus of fruit production and shipping ports. Roseland Preserving Company sat at the corner of SE 50th and Powell Boulevard, on what is now a Taco Bell parking lot. Mutual Fruit had a plant on SE 3rd and Morrison, where the streets are still half-cobblestone and old rail lines lurch out of the pavement. California Packing Corporation had its Kenton Station on N. Columbia Boulevard, on what later became a sawmill site and stove factory, and is now a cleanup area managed by the Oregon Department of Environmental Quality.

At the end of the nineteenth century, fruit and vegetable canneries were the primary employers of women in the Pacific Northwest. The development of more efficient transport systems meant that the superfluity of fruits from the Willamette Valley could be processed in Portland and shipped to San Francisco or the new markets on the East Coast. Between 1900 and 1910, fruit production in Oregon nearly quadrupled, while the value increased by 268 percent. Canning was a way for Oregon agriculturalists to take advantage of both the boom in fruit production and the growing markets. Sorting, cleaning, and packing the fruit were considered to be light, unskilled labor; for these reasons, and because of the seasonal, temporary nature of the work, employers preferred women and children who would presumably not be looking for full-time jobs and could be let go at the end of the season.

The canning room at Oregon Packing Company employed approximately 200 women and teens under the supervision of a forewoman. Although the work itself was dismissed as facile, it was nonetheless understood that if the crops were to be saved, it was imperative that women and teens do their part; the financial health of Oregon rested on them. Admittedly, the work was not all that physically taxing. Pears, for example, would be washed, then peeled, then halved and cored before being packed in cans and sent down a conveyor to be sealed and steamed. Other workers would label and box the cans for shipment. The work itself, however, was not the problem. The problem, as identified by Progressives, was that work took women away from home.

Unlike other professional fields undertaken by women (of which there were very few), many women maintained their employment in canneries even after marriage. This led early activists to call for regulation of women's labor—not because women deserved better work/life balance, but because it threatened women's roles as wives, mothers, and homemakers. In 1908, the ten-hour workday for women had been successfully defended before the U.S. Supreme Court when attorney Louis Brandeis declared that women were simply too weak to work longer days and that the long hours interfered with her ability to complete her domestic duties at home.[46] Each of the labor issues identified by Progressives pointed to one belief: that a woman's place was truly at home.

The women working in the fruit canneries had different ideas about what they needed, and this started with fair pay and sanitary working conditions. Reports of the working conditions alleged that there were no clean toilet facilities, no changing rooms for getting out of filthy work clothes at the end of the day, and that the cannery lacked proper first aid for skin rashes caused by prolonged exposure to fruit acids. The strikers' press committee claimed the level of sanitation at the plant as unsafe not just for the workers, but for the company's customers, as well:

> The company handled fruit so rotten and filthy that it was nothing but a slime and mush and the girls had to dig their arms into the mess as they worked. The girls testify also that the fruit juice that falls to the floor to a depth of a half or one inch, is mopped up, wrung out into a bucket and used for JAM. A woman of 61 said the report was true and that she had refused to use this refuse for preserves. [47]

These claims of feculence were serious and egregious, but worker pay was the real problem that the employers were not inclined to address. Workers in the canneries were paid a "piece-rate" by the amount of fruit they processed, typically measured by the weight of the boxes filled. In the beginning of the season, women could earn about a dollar a day hulling strawberries, but when the plant switched over to cherries later in the season, the fragile fruit's quality was often so poor that it was impossible for workers to earn a livable wage. A worker could spend three hours trimming away rotten bits and end up with only a dime's worth of usable fruit. At its lowest point, pay was around 40 cents a day, which was about one-third of a livable wage in Portland at the time—a rate low enough to drive some women into less wholesome professions to make ends meet. Elsewhere in the Pacific Northwest, high attrition rates were the cannery workers' only response to low pay, but in Portland the women took matters into their own hands and went on strike. On Friday, June 27, 1913, fifty women walked off the job at Oregon Packing Company. The following Monday morning, 200 of them didn't come to work.

"GIRLS MAKE GOOD FIGHT," announced the *Portland News* headline at the dawn of the strike. [48] As momentum gathered, more than a thousand protestors, agitators, and police officers joined in the fray. Strikers and sympathizers were beaten with clubs and suffered injury by Portland's mounted police when horses were driven onto the women. A few people were hospitalized, and dozens were arrested (one man was charged with "sitting on the curb . . . and singing ribald songs" and fined $20). [49] Intimidation flew in both directions; protestors threatened arson of the plant, and police promised to clear the streets, even if it meant the use of force. *The Oregonian* portrayed the police as not only justified in committing violent acts against strikers and agitators, but insisted that their actions were endorsed by the public. The police actions were not supported by the public, however, and many came out in support of the women workers, by providing donations and free lunches of sandwiches, coffee, candy, and ice cream to the strikers.

Marie Equi, a well-known medical doctor and suffragist, came to the strike in support of the cherry sorters and provided medical attention to those injured during the protests. When IWW organizer Tom Burns was jailed during the strike, Equi visited the jailhouse and cussed out the officers, punching one in the face. She had to be physically thrown from the building. After battling police over free speech a few days later, Equi was arrested herself. She retaliated by stabbing an officer with her hat pin and declaring to the crowd that although she had begun the fight a Socialist, she was thenceforth an anarchist.

The Portland strike had been an anomaly among cannery workers in the Pacific Northwest, and it was apparently effective. Oregon Packing Company finally agreed to raise pay and provide better facilities to the workers. Two years later, Oregon Packing Company moved its operations across the river to Vancouver, Washington.

FLOUR AND CEREAL MILLS

Just as the Portland area had served as a cradle to the ever-bearing fruit bowl of the West, the Willamette Valley had been similarly gaining a reputation as the future breadbasket of America. Wheat had been brought to Fort Vancouver in the 1820s; a decade later it was being grown in French Prairie and the Tualatin Plains, where the Atfalati Indians had spent millennia fortifying the soils and clearing trees with fire. Retired trappers set up wheat fields in the 1840s, and most emigrants planted cash crops of wheat within weeks of landing on Oregon soils. The first plank road in Portland—Canyon Road—was built in the 1850s to transport wheat from the Tualatin Plains (in what is now Beaverton) to Portland's markets and shipping docks. By the turn of the twentieth century, Portland shipped more wheat than all other Pacific Coast ports combined.[50] Wheat put Portland on the map.

Just as Portland became a major grain port, it was also becoming a major center for milling it. Entrepreneurs lined both banks of the Willamette with an array of docks, meat packing plants, and flour mills, including William Ladd's Portland Flouring Company in the 1880s. Though the mill was successful, Ladd's attentions were divided among his myriad other economic interests, not the least of which was opening Oregon's first bank. What Portland's flouring industry needed was "one large man" to take on all of the Orient.[51] That man, recruited by Ladd himself, was Theodore B. Wilcox.

When William Ladd died in 1893, Wilcox took over Portland Flour's presidency and began executing his plan for regional domination in earnest. The flour magnate established silos and warehouses all over Portland, and then throughout Oregon and Washington. He engaged in obdurate price warfare with the explicit goal of crushing his competitors—primarily small mills across the Pacific Northwest. His callousness toward fellow millers prompted one distraught competitor to write of the "wicked Mr. Wilcox," that he was "grinding the millers between their own millstones" and that

> [w]hen the milling magnate of Oregon and Washington, who handles a dead banker's millions, passes to his final accounting, it is very doubtful if any truthful writer will indite any . . . kind words of him. This magnate openly says he proposes to have the flour trade of the Orient, and with favors from railroads and steamship companies he is sacrificing the smaller mills to his greed.[52]

These kinds of complaints were music to Wilcox's ears, and only served to steel his resolve to forge an empire out of their failed endeavors. By the turn of the century, with his regional competitors completely under water, he made good on his threats to begin exporting his surpluses to China. The prospect of gaining 400 million new customers meant that Wilcox could continue expanding indefinitely.

Unfortunately, the Hong Kong flour brokers, merchants, and noodlemakers were loyal to their San Francisco–based Sperry brand and were unwilling to shift their money, even for a superior product at a lower price. Wilcox's lasers had a new target. He hired Canadian diplomat Albert Rennie—a man with no flour experience but plenty of people skills—and in one year Portland Flour sales in China nearly doubled, going from 116,935 barrels in 1894 to 235,523 barrels the following year. In 1898, meager harvests throughout most wheat-growing regions of the world, particularly California, seriously impacted global supplies. Fortuitously, 1898 was a bumper year for the Pacific Northwest, and that year

Oregon exported almost 2 million barrels of flour, of which nearly 325,000 barrels went directly to China.[53]

With his foothold firmly established, Wilcox made a concerted effort to edge out California and Washington competition in China and corner the Asian market. He understood the power that the Hong Kong flour brokers had to influence sales, and proceeded to form a syndicate with Hong Kong's wealthiest and most influential brokers. He promised substantially lower prices (even if it meant taking a significant loss in profits), in exchange for the rejection of flour from competing companies.

As Wilcox envisioned, the syndicate crippled the competition, and amid the vociferous complaints emerged one formidable opponent: Washington State's Centennial Mills president and former Dutch sea captain Moritz Thomsen. Though Thomsen was unable to gain control of the transpacific market, he did succeed in getting one of the syndicate's brokers to jump ship and buy Centennial Mills flour, eventually leading to the syndicate's dissolution. Unfortunately, the Chinese merchants and noodlemen were already loyal to Wilcox's brands. Wilcox was the irrefutable king of the multimillion-dollar Asian flour trade.

In 1907, Wilcox's diplomat Rennie took a gamble on his relationships with Hong Kong brokers and set up his own flour mill in China with the express purpose of competing with Portland Flour. His endeavors were an epic failure, and bankrupt, he committed suicide a year later. By then, Chinese entrepreneurs had begun importing the most advanced milling technologies from America and Europe and set up their own mills in China. Eventually Chinese wheat replaced Portland Flour as the dominant flour producer in Asia, and after Wilcox's death in 1918, Portland Flour was purchased by Sperry before being absorbed by General Mills. Although he had been a cutthroat businessman, Theodore Wilcox had opened the door to Asian commerce and greatly enhanced the prosperity of the entire Pacific Northwest.

Such ready access to wheat and flour meant that large-scale baked goods companies were right at home in Portland, and by the turn of the last century a great many of them had set up steam-powered factories in Portland's industrial districts on both sides of the river. The first crackers and matzos in Portland were made in 1880 by Oregon Steam Bakery; these were mostly plate-sized pilot bread (hardtack) sold to the government for soldiers or sent to trade with Indians at Astoria. For a few years,

Oregon Steam Bakery was the only cracker game in town, with a fruitful monopoly enjoyed by just two men.

In 1883, at the age of twenty-two, a Kansas-born son of Oregon Trail pioneers named Herman Wittenberg bought a half-interest in the German Bakery and Coffee House, located on 3rd and West Burnside. In addition to selling pastries, cookies, and coffee by the cup, they retailed baked goods including crackers made by Oregon Steam Bakery, co-owned by Thomas Liebe. In 1886, Liebe and Wittenberg had a difference of opinion over the cracker retailing, and severed ties. To supply the German Bakery, Wittenberg started his own Portland Cracker Company on NW 11th and Davis, with financial backing from the Nicolai brothers (for whom the NW Portland street was named). A year later, Wittenberg sold his interest of the German Bakery to focus on building his cracker empire.

An 1887 sales book from Portland Cracker Company listed the popular cookies and confections of the era: lemon snaps, Jenny Linds (a caraway-spiced sugar cookie named after the nineteenth-century opera soprano called the "Swedish nightingale"), picnics (a snickerdoodle-style cookie with a raisin dotting the center), ginger snaps, fruit biscuits (crispy sugar cookies with candied orange peel), vanilla bars, coconut taffy, and nicknacks (a sugar cookie flavored with sour milk and lemon oil). If one trudged upstairs to the second floor of the factory, broken cookies could be purchased at a discount—sold in the amount of "two bits" worth. This was customary until around the middle of the twentieth century, when broken bits were ground into crumbs and reincorporated into the cookies.

Wittenberg was somewhat old-fashioned when it came to flavoring his cookies. Rather than rely on chemical flavoring, Wittenberg made his own vanilla extracts by steeping a puree of aromatic vanilla beans in grain alcohol. The company stored barrels of alcohol for this purpose, and one day an employee, looking for a wee tipple, went snooping around the top floor of the factory. He struck a match, peeked into a nearly empty barrel, and "went boom."[54]

The burgeoning Portland Cracker Company was doing brisk business, and it certainly did not escape notice. In the same ruthless practice used by flour baron Theodore Wilcox, Oregon Steam Bakery cut prices down to bedrock in order to freeze out their new competition. The plan backfired, and Portland Cracker Company summarily absorbed Oregon Steam Bakery, only two and half years after it rolled out its first sheets of crackers. Soon, Wittenberg's co-owner, Louis Nicolai, wished to dissolve the partnership and Wittenberg partnered up with none other than Moritz Thomsen—the very same Dutch sea captain and head of Centennial Flour Mills who had been hell-bent on taking down Wilcox.

In 1891, after moving into the spanking-new brick building on 11th and Davis (now a Pearl District parking garage), Wittenberg began swallowing up smaller cracker and cookie companies across the region, including several in Washington State. He ran Washington Cracker as a separate company, and took over Oregon Cracker Company (on NW 6th and Glisan), eventually turning it into a macaroni factory. These takeovers began a sort of snack war, and soon confectioners in San Francisco were helping Wittenberg's competitors try to take him down. He had no other choice but to diversify, and as a result, he barged into the candy-making business. He purchased the Seattle Steam Candy Company in Seattle and the Bernheim-Alisky Candy Company in Portland, the two largest confectioners in the Northwest.

Although his expansion tactics may seem aggressive, some maintained that it was the quality of Wittenberg's product that allowed him to succeed so profoundly. One writer gushed that "[w]herever one may go in the northwest, the name of the Portland Cracker Company may be seen, and its brand on a box is a guarantee that the contents are equal to the best made anywhere in the world."[55] By the turn of the twentieth century, their business manufactured two-thirds of all of the crackers and candy consumed west of the Rockies.[56]

In September 1899, Wittenberg sold the Portland Cracker Company (which included Washington Cracker), to the Pacific Coast Biscuit Company, becoming vice president and manager in the process. Wittenberg's stately brick building in Portland's gleaming industrial district would become emblazoned with Pacific Coast Biscuit Company's memorable logo: the swastika.

The bright white swastika would not become a symbol of unfathomable hatred for another twenty-five years. For centuries, the broken-armed cross had been a Buddhist emblem of good luck, and it was for these reasons that the logo had been chosen in the first place; "[t]hese biscuits are sold under the 'Good Luck' seal!"[57] squealed an advertisement in 1916. "Aren't the Grahams of this brand wonderfully good for children?"[58] That the symbol is shocking today is undeniable, and it is for this reason that the swastika was removed from the building. What is most shocking, however, is that it remained in plain sight until 1998.

In only thirteen years, Wittenberg had made millions of dollars, employed thousands of people, and established Portland as the cracker capital of the West. By the time he sold out to Pacific Biscuit, his company had eight factories and had eaten up fourteen other biscuit and candy companies from Seattle to Los Angeles. Wittenberg died at the age of fifty-two, well before the first Swastika Biscuit ever appeared in *The Morning Oregonian*, but Pacific Coast Biscuit continued, eventually becoming part of the National Biscuit Company (NABISCO) brand.

Grandma's Cookies (which also made cakes) had been in Portland since its inception in 1914, and Wittenberg's son Ralph bought Grandma's in 1945. He ran the factory at the corner of N. Williams and Broadway, churning out ginger snaps, vanilla sandwich cookies, and chewy molasses, oatmeal-raisin, and chocolate chip cookies for nearly three decades. A four-alarm fire claimed the building in 1970, and the company relocated to Beaverton. In 1980, under the updated name Grandma's Foods, the company was purchased by Frito-Lay Company, making the cookie matriarch a household name outside the Great Northwest.

Other bakeries paved the path followed by the early cracker companies. In 1897, fifteen-year-old Engelbert Franz asked his uncle, who had opened United States Bakery on Front Street in 1880, to secure his passage from Rothsaifen, Austria, to America. Franz worked at the bakery for eight years, and after he repaid his debt to his uncle, eventually sent for his brother Joseph. The two of them bought their own bakery in 1906, and then opened Franz Bakery at NE 11th and Flanders in 1912, creating an instant Portland landmark with the later addition of the giant, rotating loaf of bread to the building's roof. In the late 1920s Engelbert invented the industry standard five-inch hamburger bun for the burger restaurant Yaw's Top Notch. Prior to that, hamburgers had been served on toast or Kaiser rolls; today Franz supplies nearly every Northwest fast food restaurant with hamburger buns.

Davidson's Bakery was another Portland institution, started by Eugene Davidson in 1918 with his first location on NE 24nd and Broadway. Davidson had come from a long line of bakers; he was a descendent of the baker who invented angel food cake, and Davidson's bakery followed suit with its line of sweets; butterhorns, coffee cakes, cinnamon rolls, and doughnuts were all top sellers along with his "butter-made" Sunbeam Bread. During World War I, the company sold Liberty Bread made with rye, rice, and cornmeal to conserve wheat. Davidson ran the company for fifty years before selling to Hansen's Northwest Bakers, Inc.

Portland is still a hotbed of whole grain and artisanal bakeries, with numerous vegan and gluten-free offerings. One organic, vegan bakery has come into the spotlight over the past decade, not just because of the quality of its product, but because of its unlikely hero. Dave Dahl had grown up in his family bakery; his father had been raised Seventh Day Adventist, and whole grains were a way of life that culminated in opening Nature Bake bakery on SE Division Street in the 1950s, experimenting with sprouted wheat breads that would have made nineteenth-century health reformers like Graham, Jackson, and Kellogg proud. Dahl struggled with depression as a teen, and began using methamphetamines in the 1980s. After spending fifteen years in and out of prison for burglary, armed robbery, assault, and distribution of controlled substances, Dahl found the bakery an ideal place to get back on his feet. He took a job at his father's bakery in 2005, working for his older brother, Glenn. Dahl started baking the bread he had craved while he was in the clink, and the loaves from that first batch were "killer." Dahl began selling the loaves under the name Dave's Killer Bread at the Portland Farmers Market later that year, and as of 2012 had expanded to sixteen varieties with distribution in eleven states.

VEGETARIANISM

Portland's history of whole grain breads and Adventist health regimens long predated Dahl's organic, vegan loaves, and less-processed versions of indispensable products came a century before Portland's Pacific Foods and Salem's Kettle Chips. By the late nineteenth century, Portland's reputation for high-quality baked goods and grain products was well known. In the 1860s, Seventh Day Adventists had already begun to move to Oregon, and like their kin back in Battle Creek, Michigan, these people adhered to strict tenets regarding health and diet. In 1893, right at the time that Portland was hitting its stride with wheat and flour exports and cracker production, a student of John Harvey Kellogg's named Dr. Lewis Belknap came to town. Having been scurrilously robbed of all his possessions while waiting at a San Francisco dock, Belknap arrived to Portland with nothing but the clothes on his back and a dream of spreading the hygienic gospel.

He borrowed enough money to pay the rent on an eight-bedroom house, where he set up a six-patient sanitarium. After a few years he needed to expand, so he began renting a mansion from Simeon Reed, for whom Reed College was named. A year later, Belknap moved on to California, but his sanitarium remained in Portland. The Seventh Day Adventist Church took over his sanitarium, and by 1897 they had added a health food company.

The Portland Sanitarium Food Company, located at SE 60th and Belmont (now the site of an elderly care and assisted living facility), was a branch of Battle Creek Sanitarium Health Food Company, producing vegetarian products and prepared foods such as protose, a canned meat substitute that looks not unlike dog food. The company ran a restaurant at the same location, touted by John Harvey Kellogg himself as being among those "[e]ating-houses where food prepared in accordance with the principles of rational dietetics and scientific cookery may be obtained," where one could find a bloodless meal for a few pennies. [59] In 1900, the company published *The Sanitarium Eclectic Cook Book* featuring the recipes from the sanitarium's dining room.

At around the same time, several other vegetarian restaurants and boardinghouses, unaffiliated with the Sanitarium or Adventism, began popping up around downtown Portland. In January 1898, *The Oregonian* offices were visited by "a pallid, wild-eyed young man with a starved look," rambling enthusiastically about his plan to open a vegetarian café. He launched into a description of the process by which he created "vegetable turkey" using peanuts, turkey eggs, butter, and bread crumbs (seasoned with sage, salt, and pepper). [60] He was informed by amused *Oregonian* staff that although it sounded "very excellent," his prospects of a profitable business would be "mighty slim," and that he should perhaps wait until Thanksgiving to mention it again. [61]

Later that year, the young man's vegetarian restaurant was opened on 4th Street between Yamhill and Taylor, in the house built in 1847 from a do-it-yourself kit by Captain Nathaniel Crosby (this same building, known as "the old Crosby house," was the home of Rose City Waffle House in 1905, and the restaurant was converted to a shaving parlor a few years later). Before the century was up, the Portland Medical Mission, an Adventist-affiliated facility promoted by John Kellogg, had opened their

Figure 3.3. Portland's first vegetarian restaurant was opened in the former home of Captain Nathaniel Crosby on SW 4th, ca. 1898. Courtesy of Oregon Historical Society, negative Orhi3594

Good Health Restaurant. Another vegetarian café, located at today's 6th and Stark, had been financially successful, but according to an article in *The Oregonian*, the prices were so low that "the better class of people avoid his place, thinking it had been established for the benefit of those who are hard up."[62]

That Portland already had four vegetarian eating establishments by the start of the twentieth century reveals much about the city's long history of supporting alternative lifestyles and esoterica, as do the actions of one proponent of the diet, Lora Little. The libertarian health reformer was an indefatigable writer and speaker on a variety of subjects including, but not limited to, why the smallpox vaccine should be abolished. Little insisted that all of life's ills, no matter how virulent, were natural, and therefore beneficial. In 1916 she crusaded for—and, terrifyingly, nearly won—a complete ban on vaccinations for Portland schoolchildren. Her proposed alternative was food, specifically a Grahamist diet of brown rice and whole grains, and although she did not completely eschew meat, she advocated eating very little of it. "Eat right, live right, and all your injuries, of whatever kind, quickly disappear," she insisted. [63]

The Oregon Vegetarian Society began meeting in the "Advance Thought" parlor at the Hotel Mallory (now Hotel DeLuxe) on SW 15th and Yamhill in the early 1900s. One member, Charles Piggott, is fondly remembered as one of Portland's earliest eccentrics; in 1892 he built an ostentatious castle called Mount Gleall on the top of the West Hills, but lost it a year later during the Panic of 1893, earning it the nickname "Piggott's Folly." The parlor that hosted the meetings was owned by Lucy A. Rose Mallory, the daughter of the founder of Roseburg, Oregon (her mother, Minerva Kellogg, had died during childbirth), and the wife of Oregon Congressman Rufus Mallory (for whom Mallory Avenue in Portland's Albina District was named). Mrs. Mallory, a native of Michigan, was a proponent of "mental healing" as outlined in her monthly publication and 1915 book *The World's Advance Thought* (of which Leo Tolstoy was a fan), and she hosted the Vegetarian Society meetings in her home. Portland's followers of the New Thought movement of the turn of the twentieth century met in the same parlor to study the Hindu epic *Bhagavad Gita* and the works of poets Walt Whitman and Ralph Waldo Emerson, both noted vegetarians.

Although Lucy Rose Mallory had been born near Battle Creek to a Kellogg mother, in Portland, not all nineteenth-century vegetarians were affiliated with the Seventh Day Adventist Church. The president of the Oregon Vegetarian Society, William H. Galvani, was a Russian Jew and later a Buddhist; he was the author of a book on Theosophy ("divine wisdom") and a 32nd-degree Mason of the Scottish Rite, or a "Sublime Prince of the Royal Secret." [64] In 1896, his letter to *The Oregonian* on "Bills of Fare for That Plantigrade Frugivorous Mammal Known as Man" was mocked by the newspaper's editor as having been written by "a crank," but may have been to some great use to vegetarians in need of tasty Christmas menu options. [65]

An astonishing array of dishes graced Galvani's suggested bill of fare: a grapefruit half to start, followed by a tomato soup with cheese straws, and Turkish rolls with Béchamel sauce. The main courses would be scalloped lima beans in a creamy Hollandaise sauce spiced with mace, riced "potato snow" with beets and a vinaigrette, and broiled mushrooms on toast with extra wheat bread and rolls for passing around the table. A pineapple sorbet to cleanse the palate, and then a celery salad with coconut cream (celery was very fashionable in those days, and was featured on all menus in better homes). A relish course of sweet pickles, salted almonds, and olives finished the meal. The desserts would consist of a fruit platter, apple-sago pie (sago is a palm whose starch is similar to tapioca), mince pie, and plum pudding ("the mince pie without meat, the plum pudding without suet"), and further entremets accompanied the tea: cake, blancmange pudding, roasted chestnuts in cream, and a nut tray.

Vegetarianism remained at the fringe of society for decades, relegated to sectarian Christians, zealous health nuts, and esoteric philosophers until the upwelling of the counterculture of the late 1960s. Hippie philosophies bore an uncanny similarity to the type of dietary hygiene and "mind over matter" spiritualism of the New Thought and Christian Science movements. Portland was no different; by the early 1970s there was a vegetarian hot dog stand on NE Sandy, and the anti-war and pro-recycling radical collective called Terrasquirma had set up an urban commune on SE 40th and Main Street. They hosted potlucks to fuel their social justice study groups; two of the group's founding members baked bread twice a week, and one made yogurt. One of the members ran food buying clubs out of the basement, and another became the produce buyer for Wapatu Produce Co-op, which supplied various food co-ops in town. The Terrasquirma house was notably vegetarian, for reasons of "economy and ecology," a theme outlined by Oregon native Francis Moore Lappé in her 1971 book *Diet for a Small Planet.*[66]

In the 1980s, vegetarians would finally get a break from alfalfa sprouts and canned protose nuggets in soy gravy, with the merciful launch of Gardenburger by Portland-based chef Paul Wenner. In 1981, Wenner invented the meatless burger in the kitchen of his Gresham eatery, Garden House Restaurant. One day he was experimenting with ways to use up the restaurant's leftover vegetables and rice pilaf, added some egg, oats, and seasonings, and formed the mix into a loaf. He served slices of the veggie loaf on what he called a "Garden Loaf Sandwich." Next he tried serving the creation on a hamburger bun, which he coined the Gardenburger.

To his delight, his dish was a huge hit among the restaurant's patrons, and soon made up half of all of Garden House Restaurant orders. Wenner soon realized he might have a market outside the restaurant, and when the Garden House Restaurant closed during Oregon's recession in 1984, he got his chance. He started the company Wholesome and Hearty Foods, Inc. (later changed to Gardenburger, Inc.) and began aggressively promoting his product at restaurants around the country. His big break came in 1986, at the Natural Food Expo in Los Angeles, where he arranged to have his nutritious patties served in the cafeteria during the event.

For America's convenience-starved vegetarians, Gardenburgers were a revelation. Unlike other meat analogs, Gardenburgers were based on whole grains and vegetables instead of soy. Within months of the launch, Northwest-based fast food chain Burgerville, USA, included the Gardenburger on its menu, and national burger chains followed suit. Gardenburger's rise was dazzling; Wenner's energetic visage graced the pages of *Forbes* and *Fortune*. Even confirmed meat lovers were on board; "the brown, chunky patty tastes like something that's worth ordering again," conceded *Oregonian* staff writer Mike Francis.[67] The Massachusetts Institute of Technology (MIT) hailed Paul Wenner as "Inventor of the Week." Wenner went from being nearly penniless to owning an art deco mini-mansion in the Hawthorne District.

Although the Gardenburger production plant relocated to Utah in 1999, its headquarters and research facility are still based in Portland (Wenner is currently working on several savory flavors of a meal-replacement bar called Gardenbar). And however many ups and downs Gardenburger stock takes—the company filed for bankruptcy in 2005, and was bought by the Kellogg Company in 2007—Portland reigns as the capital of American vegetarianism.[68]

DAIRIES AND BUTCHERS

On a crispy, late-summer day in 1860, little Mary Emma Marquam (daughter of Philip Marquam, for whom the bridge was named, among other Portland landmarks), was out for a stroll with her brother Will. The fragrant Rambo apples were in their prime, and the two Marquam children stopped by the old Kelly farm just in time to see that Reverend Albert Kelly had just slaughtered a beef cow. The sight of the cow's head was distressing to Will, and he kicked the reverend in the shin for killing the cow. Poor little Will was thunderstruck when he was informed where steaks came from.

The next morning, Will and Mary and another boy were walking to Portland's Central School, on what is now SW 6th and Morrison. Mary was carrying their lunches in a basket, and the boys rode stick horses.

Along the trail the children were approached by a very large brown dog, who sniffed the lunch. The little boy Gus whacked the dog with his stick, yelling, "Get away from us, you big, ugly dog!" Mary felt sorry for the poor thing, so she walked up to it and stroked its fuzzy head. "As I patted it," Mary later recalled, "it made bread with its paws, like a cat does, and purred as loud as a coffee mill."[69] The "big, ugly dog" turned out to be a cougar that had filled its belly on a quarter of Reverend Kelly's fresh, hanging beef, and was too sated and happy to eat the children.

Fresh beef was aplenty in early Portland, but getting cattle to Oregon had taken some doing. In the 1830s, pioneer Ewing Young arrived to Oregon, responding to Hall Kelley's "note of alarm" to Americanize the Wild West. He had his sights set on establishing a new trading post in the region. However, the Hudson's Bay Company (HBC) had a stake in preventing Americans from settling and attempting to conduct business in then-British Oregon. Worse, Young was wrapped up in that unfortunate "horse thief" debacle with Kelley (they had been traveling with criminals unawares or were possibly wrongly accused). Not only was Young completely blacklisted from Fort Vancouver, but his attempts to trade with even Canadians were met with a hostile boycott, as well, thanks to the control Dr. McLoughlin had in the region.

Consequently, Young elected to purchase a cauldron from the dismantled Fort William on Sauvie Island, and built a distillery to get even with McLoughlin. If he would not be allowed to conduct his business at the Fort, he would make a product that everyone wanted and that the HBC did not sell. Furthermore, he knew that the HBC *would* not sell liquor to the Indians because they feared it riled them up. Young thought he would stir the Fort's pot, so to speak, and "offer a commodity for which white man and Indian would risk the danger of the displeasure of the Hudson's Bay Company and their own destruction as well."[70]

Lieutenant William Slacum, agent to President Jackson, was sent to Oregon to evaluate the region and its inhabitants, and after a little chat with McLoughlin he set out to dissuade Young from raining calamity on the Fort with his white lightning. Young reluctantly dismantled his still, and Slacum was celebrated by Dr. McLoughlin as a hero. Perhaps sensing Young's verve, Slacum appointed Young the leader of the Willamette Cattle Company. The HBC would not sell any cattle to settlers, opting instead to rent cows and maintain their tidy livestock monopoly. If the Willamette Cattle Company was going to get off the ground, they had little choice but to return to California (then still a part of Mexico), and bring the cattle north, a task that called for "diplomacy as well as daring and sagacity."[71]

The daring and sagacity were needed to ford the droves of cattle across the San Joaquin River; the diplomacy was required to achieve the task without becoming victims (or perpetrators) of violence with the bands of Umpqua people they encountered along the way. Of the more than 800 head of longhorn cattle that left California in 1837, 630 arrived to the greener pastures of the Willamette Valley (some were killed by Indians, some were eaten by the party, and some just wandered off).

The successful journey of the Willamette Cattle Company had ended settlers' dependence on HBC. Young was so wealthy after the venture that when he died four years later, Oregon's first provisional government had to be established to divide his heirless estate.

Naturally, the longhorns increased in numbers and began to escape, running in terrifying, semi-feral herds of fifteen to twenty. "[O]f course they were a real menace, especially to anyone afoot," recalled one old-timer.[72] The problematic bovines had to be eliminated, and were eventually replaced by the gentler, short-horned Durham cattle that came west with pioneers on the Oregon Trail. By the latter half of the nineteenth century, it had nevertheless been deemed necessary for Portland to create a city ordinance prohibiting the running of cattle through certain streets in the city center. Specifically, north of SW Hall and south of NW Flanders, and east of 9th to the river were off-limits; Front Ave (now partially Naito Parkway) and SW Jefferson were approved beef thoroughfares. Milch cows were granted clemency and were allowed to traipse escorted through town, unimpeded.

Meatpacking developed on a massive scale in 1880s Portland, and cattle ranching largely moved to eastern Oregon. SP Market, opened on SE 21st and Powell in 1880, served the carnivorous needs of Southern Pacific Railroad laborers working in the Brooklyn rail yard a few blocks away. (Now called SP Provisions, the same family-owned meat market has relocated to the NW quadrant of town.) During the Gilded Age, beef was seven cents a pound and a "Good Meal" set one back $1.50, or half the day's wages for the average laborer. In the 1880s, several independently operating local butchers—Thomas Papworth, Morton M. Spaulding, and William Spaulding—formed the Portland Butchering Company. The company made regular appearances in *The Oregonian*, with advertorials outlining the best way to ensure success in making first-class meals (hint: use meats from Portland Butchering Company). "Whether the meal be a breakfast, with its accompaniment of a delicious chop or a succulent steak, or whether it be a dinner, which includes a fine roast done to a turn," it was imperative that a housewife use Portland Butchering Company's meats if she cared about the health and happiness of her family.[73]

Papworth and Morton Spaulding split off from Portland Butchering Company, joining downtown butchers Adolph Burckhardt and the O'Shea brothers to form the American Dressed Meat Company. In 1892, American Dressed Meat Company, with slaughterhouses in Troutdale and offices in Portland, consolidated with Portland Butchering Company to form the Union Meat Company. At incorporation, Union Meat Company ran meat markets around town and maintained processing operations at the Fourth Street Market on NW Glisan, while slaughtering continued to take place out at the Troutdale plant. As a result of Union Meat Company's formation, beef and pork prices in Portland dropped by nearly 40 percent.

The Oregonian was initially high in its praises of Union Meat Company, but within a year, the bloom was off the rose. Independent packing companies attempted to share the market, but Union Meat Company maintained a sizable dominance. Although the company had essentially been a cooperative of nearly a dozen independent butchers, there were intimations that the company was a monopoly. "The people of Portland have been dependent for a number of months past upon the pleasure of one concern for their supply of meat," read an ad in *The Oregonian* on October 22, 1893.[74] It was "deplorable," surmised *The Oregonian*, and perhaps even a crime, that there was only one purveyor in town for "toothsome, tender, palatable and healthy" meats.[75]

In the late nineteenth century, Chicago-based meat companies had already begun sending agents out west to canvas the city for potential new abattoir and packing sites; the big eastern companies wanted to expand, and Portland was primed. Portland was near rail lines and fresh water, and was still sparse enough that stockyards and factories could be sited far away from the urban core. In 1906, Swift Meat Packing Company arrived with its refrigerated railroad car technology, which meant that live cattle no longer needed to be shipped to the meat-eating markets. Swift purchased Union Meat Company along with 3,400 acres near the

Northern Pacific Railroad in North Portland, set up its Portland Union Stockyards, and began setting sights on bigger plans for the city.

Before the 1900s, the Kenton neighborhood was just a farming community similar to other townships in the area such as University Park and St. Johns, but in 1908, Swift bought up 300 acres south of Columbia Boulevard to build a complete city for its employees. Rather than build company housing, however, Swift sold its employees inexpensive lots upon which they could build, and many did build small "kit" bungalows. Promoters of the model community proudly claimed that Kenton had been situated such that "prevailing winds tend to blow down the river away from the home section, thus dispelling and dissipating disagreeable odors attendant with its operation."[76]

Derby Street (now Denver Street), the town's main thoroughfare, was equipped with an electric streetcar line that connected to the main city line and ran all day. There was a cattlemen's bank; the illustrious Chaldean Theater (later the Kenton Theater), second only to the downtown Egyptian in beauty; and the first-class Kenton, MacArthur, and Rowley Hotels for cattlemen visiting the livestock exchange. By 1919, Kenton was annexed into Portland and Swift employed 800 workers, jumping to 1,800 in the 1920s and '30s. Swift offered lengthy paid vacations and pension plans to loyal employees, male or female. The spanking-new town of Kenton butchered more beef than any other city in the Northwest.

The development of new highways in the 1960s was the first nail in the little beef town's coffin; traffic no longer flowed through the commercial district, and businesses began relocating closer to the freeway exchanges. The closure of the Swift plant in 1966 was Kenton's death knell, and ten other slaughterhouses closed one by one over the following years. The Pacific Livestock Expo held its last show in the 1980s, and the Union Stockyards closed during the same era.

Although beef, lamb, and pork are no longer raised and slaughtered inside the city limits, buying meat *en carcasse* is still possible through the many meat shares and community-supported agriculture (CSA) that Portland has to offer. Local meat enthusiasts and culinary renegades can hone their charcuterie craft or learn to break down a whole hog through the Portland Meat Collective, started in 2009 by food writer-turned-butcher Camas Davis to teach "Ladies' Home Pig Butchery," among myriad other indispensable skills. Davis's education program allows Portland's meat eaters to connect with a heritage from which they have been separated for a century, while imploring one to make "informed decisions about where they want to sit on the spectrum of eating factory-farmed meat and veganism."[77]

Not all cows that made it to Portland were destined for the steak knife. When the first Overlanders arrived to settle the wilds of Oregon, most brought along a dairy cow as a ready source of milk and butter. These were not anything like Ewing Young's frightful longhorns; they were sweet Jerseys with lanuginous noses and soft, chestnut eyes. They were strawberry-blond Guernseys and auburn Herefords and classic, black-and-white Holsteins. Holsteins made the most milk by far, but fawn-brown Jerseys were unrivaled for the quality of their cream, and their milk yielded the most butter.

Just next door to the urban center, clover-scented Hillsdale provided exquisite grazing for gentle dairy cows and was producing the state's finest cream in the 1890s. With Swiss immigrants (and generations of Swiss dairy experience) at the helm, Portland's milk displayed "an astonishing degree of purity."[78] Among the first of these was the Raz Brothers Dairy, run by the ten siblings on a ninety-three-acre tract in southwest Portland. One of the Raz grandchildren (John, born in 1906) built his own farm on Dosch Road, down the hill from the old amusement park at Council Crest. According to John Raz, who died in 2005, his was the "last working dairy farm within the Portland city limits" before the site was purchased by a church in the late 1980s.

There was dairy land all over the city. Portland International Airport and the golf course next door were once pasture, and the northern parts of the city, now St. Johns, Kenton, Beaumont-Wilshire, Concordia, and Cully neighborhoods, also sprawled with dairy farms. East of 82nd Avenue, any land that was not growing fruit thrummed with the bellows of milch cows. There were dairies in Lents, Mount Tabor, and Mount Scott in old East Portland; pastures in Hayhurst, Multnomah Village, and Portland Heights sprawled out along the West Hills. Automobiles brought an easier mode of delivery for dairies, and shiny, white milk wagons were a familiar sight. Prior to that, horse-drawn carriages conveyed crates of gently clinking bottles to neighborhood homes. Starting in 1900, Hazelwood Creamery used such horse-power to deliver its fine creams, butter, ice cream, and milk-fed poultry from a storefront downtown (later opening a confectionery and restaurant, as well).

Alpenrose Dairy, still in operation, was started unofficially in 1891, when Swiss immigrant Florian Cadonau began delivering three-gallon cans of milk from his farm near today's SW 35th and Vermont Street to restaurants downtown. His son Henry married Rosina Streiff, a nice local girl whose father happened to be the consul of Switzerland. For their dairy, located next door to the Cadonau seniors, Rosina chose the name Alpenrose because it reminded her of the delicate blooms of her father's homeland.

The dairy's milk was known for its high quality, but a labeling mishap in 1929 resulted in a citation with the health department. Cadonau's employees evidently had run out of "pasteurized" bottle caps and simply began using the "raw" labels instead. Health officials demanded that he lose his license, but he was acquitted of wrongdoing. Regardless, health inspectors thenceforth began inspecting dairies on a surprise, drop-in basis instead of notifying dairy owners ahead of time. Dairymen were advised to "watch their step," by City Commissioner John Mann.[79] It was no wonder that the health inspectors had scrutinized milk so closely. Twenty years before Portland's milk earned the reputation for being

Figure 3.4.   Hazelwood Creamery delivery driver watering his horse at Skidmore Fountain, ca. 1900. Courtesy of Norm Gholston

among the purest in the world, Portland led the nation in a more sinister contest: baby deaths related to bad milk.

Prior to the work of city health commissioner Dr. Esther Pohl (who later became Esther Pohl Lovejoy), inspection of dairy products for public consumption could, and often did, consist of little more than a food commissioner tasting the milk and shaking hands with the dairy farmer. In 1907, after finding conditions at Portland's dairy suppliers to be "vile and foul," Pohl proposed an ordinance that required dairies be visited by a health inspector, rather than a food commissioner.[80] Because impure milk had disproportionately impacted the health of children (including Pohl's son Freddie, who died in 1908 from milk poisoning at the age of six), it fell to women to take up the fight. Pohl called upon the Portland Women's Club, the Oregon branch of the National Consumers' League, the Visiting Nurse Association, and the Multnomah County Women's Christian Temperance Union. An ordinance was passed in March of 1909, but any celebrations would have been premature. It would appear that the Oregon dairy and food commissioner, J. W. Bailey, had not been enforcing it.

Six months after Pohl's successful ordinance campaign, a farmer noticed that his barn cats kept dying, and before long he figured out that it was his own cows' milk that killed them. The farmer called on Commissioner Bailey for advice. Bailey listened to the dairy man's description and made his diagnosis: bovine tuberculosis. "Tuberculosis milk may kill cats," he reportedly reassured the farmer, "but it will fatten babies."[81] The incredulous farmer (who had been continuing to ship his milk to Portland all the while) could not believe the commissioner's nonchalance, particularly when so many infant deaths had been reported recently. The dairyman decided to make one more stop in Portland on his way back to the farm, and paid a visit to the offices of the *Oregon Journal*.

Oregon Journal reporters Marshall Dana and John Wilson were on the beat, and went to Bailey's office to learn the facts. Wilson began the interview by calling Bailey a "baby killer."[82] Predictably, this set things off on the wrong foot; Bailey denied the accusations, and demanded to know what business it was of the paper's, anyway. Wilson called Bailey a liar, and "thereupon, they tangled," recalled Dana.[83] Bailey, according to his retelling of the incident to *The Oregonian*, "retaliated by seizing the newspaper man by the throat and throwing him across the lounge" before giving the featherweight Wilson "a severe tongue-lashing."[84] Dana, who was new on the job, had to break it up before someone was seriously injured. The next day, Wilson left his post at the *Oregon Journal* for undisclosed reasons, possibly related to getting into a fistfight with a public official.

The paper's editor put Mr. Dana on the story. When the reporter visited Portland's dairy farms, what he saw was appalling. "Out on the Columbia Slough road there was a dairy operated by a dairyman named Mike," Dana recalled forty years later in his 1951 book *Newspaper Story*.[85] "The door of the dairy barn stood open. When (we) got a little closer the disturbed flies flew up in a cloud. In front of the barn lay a dead calf. Evidently it had been there quite a while."[86] Taking a look around the farm, it had been easy for Dana to see why the calf had died: the conditions were filthy, with cows covered in dirt and wading through their own manure. Some of the cows' udders were covered in weeping sores that leaked pus into the milk. Farmer Mike admitted that although he had gained a bad reputation with the state dairy inspectors, it had not been for his egregious shortcomings in sanitation. It had been for watering down the milk.

Dana found another farmer on the southwest side of town that had been transporting milk into the city in metal pails that he also used for hauling garbage back to his pigs, giving the pails a quick rinse before filling them with milk again. The farmer had a customer whose child died in convulsions after drinking his dairy's milk. As Dana discovered further horrors, he surmised that it might be no coincidence that Portland had the nation's highest incidence of infant mortality related to gastrointestinal illness. Dana returned to his desk and got to work. "BAD MILK KILLS PORTLAND BABIES," read the shrill, red letters on the cover of the *Oregon Journal*.[87]

By late August 1909, at least 300 Portland babies had already died, and Dr. Pohl and her sister, too, found themselves hospitalized with the same milk poisoning symptoms that had taken the life of little Freddie Pohl the previous year. She joined Dana in his exposé against impure milk, sharing her story with the press. "As a mother, I am vitally interested in this compelling of the dairy commissioner to do his paid duty," Pohl lobbied.[88] "I have paid for this laxness by the life of my son. ... I say and I know that the milk supply of Portland is rotten, literally rotten. Commissioner Bailey doesn't pretend to do what he is paid to do. The consequence is, I've lost my boy."[89] As a doctor, Pohl's story gave merit to Dana's claims, and as a grieving mother, she put a human face on the story.

After Pohl bravely spoke about her personal tragedy, the state veterinarian and the Portland Chamber of Commerce joined the battle; after all, bovine tuberculosis was an animal welfare concern, and high infant mortality was not good for Portland's reputation as a desirable place to relocate and start a business. Angry letters poured in criticizing the dairies and demanding Bailey's resignation. Dairy farmers, resistant at first to government involvement and the imposition of regulation (and very likely feeling a bit attacked), eventually got on board when they realized the city regulations would essentially be protecting them from having to compete with unscrupulous dairymen who undercut good farmers by taking shortcuts that gambled with people's lives. Finally, in October of 1909, irrefutable data linked the city's milk supply to the child deaths, proving correct everything that Bailey had been stubbornly denying for months.

In late November of 1909, a grand jury investigation of Bailey resulted in a "severe reprimand," and a new milk ordinance was unanimously passed by the city council and the mayor. With this, the food and dairy commission's control over the process ended, and the safety of the city's milk became the responsibility of the health department. Within a few years, Portland's milk supply had made a full recovery and earned its national reputation for purity.

Twenty years after the milk's overhaul, the Dairy Cooperative Association was formed, and 1,300 dairymen signed on. Farmers from around Multnomah County could sell their milk to the dairy co-op for pasteurization, bottling, and processing. By the 1930s there were more than seventy-five independent dairy processors in Portland, including Mayflower (later bought by Darigold), Alpenrose, and Sunshine, which are still in operation today. The Dairy Cooperative Association building can still be seen on the east side of the Ross Island bridge, with its yellow and white hand-painted letters still peeking through nearly a century of rain and sun. A great complex of abandoned feed silos and grain elevators, and modern Darigold facilities, are still visible between SE 6th and 8th, between Woodward and Division.

In 1905, Portland hosted the worldwide Lewis and Clark Centennial American Pacific Exposition and Oriental Fair, better known as the Lewis and Clark Expo, to celebrate the 100-year anniversary of the Lewis and Clark Expedition. The area known as Guild's Lake (now the NW Portland industrial district), once a swampy expanse of wapato and waterfowl, was drained and built into a vast arcade, complete with an esplanade and full-size buildings. Between June 1 and October 14, Portland hosted 2.5 million visitors from around the world. The theme, decided by the Oregon Historical Society, was "Westward the Course of Empire Takes Its Way"; this was a way to focus the festivities and to boost Oregon's regional pride.

Portland's regional identity, though young, came through in the foods offered by the dozens of restaurants and concessionaires that catered the event. Hazelwood Cream Company offered waffle cones of its gold medal–winning ice cream. Oregon fruit growers, who were declared the stars of the Expo (by *The Oregonian*), displayed their wares for the tasting, "for the fame of the state's fruit is becoming worldwide."[90] Portland's famous cookie and biscuit companies offered samples and sold popcorn, peanuts, candy, and chewing gum for festival-goers to enjoy; mom and pop soda fountains sold their homemade sodas. Hotelier Theodore Kruse and restaurateur Frank Huber built restaurants for the occasion.

The American Inn had also been created specifically for the Expo. The restaurant featured popular dishes of the era, such as relishes of then-trendy celery and a range of seasonal cold dishes, but also highlighted a few local fruits sold separately. Oysters from Tokeland and Shoalwater Bay in southwestern Washington (places once occupied by Chinookan-speaking people) and crabs from the coast were top-selling items. After the Expo, the grounds were the site of the Emancipation Celebration.

Much as they are in the city today, African Americans were rare in nineteenth-century Portland. Despite the laws that made them unwelcome in the state, there were four free blacks counted in Portland in 1850. Two of them were Abner and Lynda Francis, who opened the first African American–owned mercantile at the corner of Front and Stark in 1856.[91] This was no small feat; provisional and territorial governments in the 1840s and the 1850s Oregon banned slavery while also excluding free blacks from residing legally in Oregon (the punishment for being more than one-quarter Negro in Oregon was either corporal punishment or forced labor). Despite their risk, the store stayed in operation for more than a century, finally closing in 1960. Prior to completion of the Northern Pacific Railway in 1883, two-thirds of Portland's black people worked as either cooks or domestics, and following its completion many more worked as waiters aboard the train's dining cars. When the luxurious Hotel Portland opened in 1890, seventy-five black men from Georgia and South Carolina were recruited to work as waiters and barbers, bringing their families and Southern foodways with them.

Despite Portland's growing African American middle class, coming north had not guaranteed freedoms that many blacks expected. Most black families lived in neighborhoods near Union Station, west of the Japanese neighborhoods near the North Park Blocks. Segregation laws left it up to black-owned businesses to serve the community, and many opened restaurants on the main drag, NW Flanders: Mack Oliver's grocery store and Hedspeth's Restaurant on 10th (and Hedspeth's private club for black porters, waiters, and cooks), Chandler & Ballard's Club Café (including a barber shop and soda fountain) on 9th, and Mrs. Emma Moore's Restaurant on 7th. In 1906, entrepreneur W.D. Allen launched the Golden West Hotel on NW Broadway and Everett, which became the social hub of Portland's African American community. In the ground floor of the building, Richardson's café both employed and served blacks, and neighborhood children could stop by A. G. Green's confectionery and ice cream shop for a sweet treat.

For decades, Portland's African Americans quietly lived their lives, started families, and built businesses. With the shipbuilding boom of 1941, however, American industrialist Henry J. Kaiser transformed Portland into the country's leading producer of military cargo ships, swelling the city's population by a third, or roughly 160,000 people. Approximately 40,000 of the new residents were black, mainly recruited from New York City. To house the new city of people, Kaiser built Vanport City (a portmanteau of Vancouver and Portland) in the floodplain between the Columbia Slough and the Columbia River, where Portland International Raceway sits today. In 1943, 10,000 worker homes were hastily constructed to keep up with the influx of people. Vanport became the second-largest city in Oregon, and the nation's largest wartime public housing project.

Vanport was the only place in Oregon where people of different ethnic and racial backgrounds lived together in relative harmony, presumably because they were all on equal socioeconomic footing and had predominantly all come from bigger cities that had larger ethnic populations and more racial diversity to begin with. Vanport had all the comforts of home where its residents gathered: church potlucks, a grocery store with a bakery and butcher's counter, a store where men could get tobacco and the newspaper, and "a cafe that had great food."[92] One resident recalled that when his mother ran out of wartime meat ration coupons she would sometimes drive to a butcher shop in St. Johns to buy horse meat. "When Mom put the platter with a horsemeat pot roast on the table," he reminisced, "Dad would sometimes joke, 'Now nobody say Whoa!' . . . I never thought I could eat horsemeat, no matter what, but once I got the thought of what I was eating out of my head it wasn't bad-tasting."[93]

When the war ended, most laid-off white workers left for other cities or other parts of Portland, but many black families remained, limited by ongoing discrimination in both hiring practices and real estate sales. Some of those that left were replaced by returning veterans, so by 1948, the population of Vanport was approximately 18,500 people. Vanport remained nearly half black (and the other half low-income whites), all living together in housing designed to be temporary.

Then, in late May 1948, the Columbia River was turgid and roiling with vernal rains. On the morning of Memorial Day, amid concern over water levels, the Housing Authority of Portland issued the following statement:

REMEMBER: DIKES ARE SAFE AT PRESENT. YOU WILL BE WARNED IF NECESSARY. YOU WILL HAVE TIME TO LEAVE. DON'T GET EXCITED.[94]

At 4:17 p.m. on Memorial Day of 1948, the waters broke through the railroad dike. Within minutes, ten feet of water swept over the city. Vanport was washed away.

Because many people had left home for the holiday weekend, there were only fifteen fatalities from the flood; however, the official warning of the flood had been issued only two hours before the levee was breached. When the waters subsided, people returned to what was left of their homes and salvaged what they could before moving on to surrounding neighborhoods. Whites made a fairly seamless transition into new homes, but black people faced the indignity of having to move away from wreckage into areas that actively did not want them.

Portland already had a shaky race-relations record, but the flood forced racial integration in predominantly white North and Northeast Portland—particularly in Albina, which was largely inhabited by German families who had immigrated to Portland thirty years prior. Four years after the flood, the National Urban League director Lester Granger posited that the flood had perhaps done Portland's African Americans some good, calling Vanport a "nasty, segregated ghetto" where "[N]egroes lived in the same patterns as they did in the South."[95] The flood had allowed blacks to further integrate into Portland's society, the benefit of which was not fully appreciated by Portland's white population. African Americans still faced discrimination in nearly all aspects of life.

Although many of Portland's first African Americans were from New York, Portland's black culinary identity is heavily influenced by the South. Charmaine Coleman, a black community leader and educator living in Eugene, Oregon, recalled foods from her Southern childhood that traveled with her to the Northwest: beans and ham hocks, corn bread, chicken feet gumbo, which "used to be common fare. Now it is reserved for very special occasions," and sweet potato pudding casserole:

> Sweet potatoes, cooked and mashed, are mixed with cream, eggs, cinnamon and nutmeg—as you would mix filling for a pumpkin pie. This mixture is baked as a custard. Poured into a crust, it becomes sweet potato pie. There is a saying among Afro-American people: "We don't eat pumpkin pie; we eat sweet potato pie."[96]

The South's first blacks brought their African foodways, which became enmeshed with the Southern culinary identity; today, black-owned restaurants in Portland are as likely to be owned by immigrants from Africa as they are by African Americans. In Portland's traditionally black neighborhoods, the deeply rooted, black-owned soul food restaurants and corner stores are variegated with Ethiopian cafés and halal food markets. Some of these straddle both worlds through food, offering greens cooked in the traditional Eritrean manner alongside American sweet potato pie. Portland's culinary landscape has always been—and continues to be—injected with freshets of inspiration from other cultures.

4

IMMIGRANTS

Their Neighborhoods and Contributions

Early Portland was often characterized as a Wild West version of a New England commercial town, and if one focused only on its founders and architecture, this may be a fairly accurate assessment. However, founders and architecture alone do not a city make; a city is also its people, and for a good, long while, a great many of those people were foreign-born.

In 1860, a quarter of all Portlanders were born outside the United States; as early as 1870, roughly half of Portlanders were ethnic, foreign-born, or had at least one immigrant parent, and twenty years later the percentage jumped to nearly 60 percent. More than a sixth of all Portlanders could not speak English in the 1890s, and among the eight major cities of the Far West, Portland was second only to San Francisco in its proportion of immigrants per capita.[1] Jews and Italians settled in South Portland and opened delis and vegetable stands; Germans moved to Goose Hollow and started bakeries and breweries; the Chinese, Slavs, and Scandinavians in Northwest Portland opened up fish markets and sold produce by the cartful; and German-Russians (also known as Volga Germans), Central Europeans, and Scandinavians in the Albina District in North Portland started dairies and meat markets.

When the growth rates of immigration slowed, it was not because fewer immigrants were arriving, but because the emigration of native-born Americans into Portland kept a greater pace. For decades, Canadians and the British remained in the top-five immigrant groups adding ingredients to the melting pot. Although they contributed little to Portland's ethnic diversity, British and Canadian foodways were the most similar to those of nineteenth-century Americans heading west, largely because early American and Canadian cuisine had been introduced by the first colonists and their cookbook authors.

Irish families settled along Canyon Road and kept flocks of geese that had a propensity for getting loose and wreaking havoc on neighborhood gardens, where they, according to *The Oregonian*, "demolish every vestige of the vegetables."[2] In August 1875, police officer Charles Lawrence was called in to drive the geese away.[3] The women attacked with sticks and stones to protect their geese, and instead, Lawrence was the one driven away (one woman, Mrs. Tierney, pressed charges against Officer Lawrence, and he was charged with assault and battery). After much ado, the judge on the case threatened to jail "the first woman to start another ruckus over geese."[4] The image of a bunch of women squabbling about geese running amok in a gulch could not leave the minds of Portlanders, however, and the name Goose Hollow stuck.

Some of Portland's early immigrant groups were never very populous, such as the Hungarians and the French, who were represented by only around 500 people each. Nonetheless, these groups left their culinary mark; a Hungarian restaurant was opened at the Lewis and Clark Expo by a Portland restaurateur, and by 1920 Portland had its own French *patisserie*. Other immigrants appear to have always maintained a low profile; a few bands of Roma Gypsies were seen in Portland as early as the 1870s, camping near Guilds Lake until the area was turned into an industrial park ten years after the Lewis and Clark Expo. They found ingredients in the surrounding hills to prepare traditional foods like snail soup fortified with wild mushrooms and foraged greens.

Greeks, too, settled in Portland in 1910, though only about 700 of them made it that far west, during that colossal Greek immigration to the United States. They had primarily been peasants in Greece, but these early immigrants were not interested in agricultural endeavors in the New World. They did not squander their American opportunities; rather than taking jobs in manual labor, they focused mainly on opening businesses—primarily restaurants, candy stores, and fruit and vegetable stands. In the 1920s, Portland's first coffeehouses were opened by Greeks; the *kafeneio* were like small community centers where Greek men met after work to socialize. In 1936, a Greek started Sunshine Dairy, still open today. An annual Greek festival has been held to celebrate Portland's Greek community for more than sixty years.

In the twentieth century, immigrant population growth was slow and steady until the 1970s, when Portland's immigrant population began to include a great number of refugees fleeing their war-torn homelands. This brought people from Laos (and small populations of ethnic Hmong and Yao people fleeing Laos), Cambodia, and Vietnam to the Brooklyn neighborhood in inner SE Portland. Just as Southeast Asian immigrants were becoming established enough to start opening restaurants serving *pad thai* and salad rolls, Ukrainians and Russians fleeing the Soviet Union had put down roots in the Foster-Powell area of SE Portland, eventually opening cozy corner stores selling pickling cucumbers and smoked mackerel along busy thoroughfares. Today, Ukrainians, Russians, and Romanians are clustered together in outer SE Portland and in Clackamas County suburbs to the southeast of Portland, and the best places to find fresh cheese and traditional black bread are between Foster and Powell. East Africans have mostly settled in the traditionally black neighborhoods of NE Portland, opening cafés and halal markets next door to generations-old barbecue restaurants and barber shops.

A new wave of Asian immigrants continues to arrive seeking jobs, much as they did more than a century ago, but these are young, educated people headed for professional fields in the top-rated medical school on Pill Hill, and the high-tech sector nestled in the Silicon Forest. With these new people, more of the culinary world comes to Portland's suburbs: South Indian delights such as the lentil-based breakfast cake *idli* and savory chickpea doughnut *vada*; Pakistani *korma* spiked with ginger and placated with cashews and cream; Hong Kong–style noodle joints that sell roasted pork and crispy duck by the pound to eat alongside shrimp wonton soup; Korean *dol-sot bibimbap*—grilled beef and tidy little heaps of vegetables, served atop rice sizzling in a hot stone bowl and topped with an over-easy egg.

In the 1930s, Portland's District of Parents and Teachers (the precursor to the Parent Teacher Association, or PTA) had its own Americanization Department, which compiled a thirty-nine-page booklet, *Cook Book of Many Lands; Foreign Recipes*. In it, the author, Leora Sidwell, included a thoughtful foreword about getting to know one's foreign neighbors. [5]

GERMANS—BREWERS AND BUTCHERS

At first, Germans were the largest non-English speaking group in Portland, but in the 1880s, Chinese immigrants almost doubled other immigrant populations. At around the same time, Portland Flouring Mills and Pacific Coast Elevator had new rail access for shipping their grain products. Scandinavian, Irish, Polish, and German immigrants were drawn to these new job markets; they began filling up the Goose Hollow neighborhood in southwest Portland and later, the Albina neighborhood on the east side of the Willamette. Germans caught up in numbers with the Chinese by 1900, and a decade later, they made up the majority of immigrants.

Many Germans left the Fatherland at a time when Germany was evolving toward industrialization. The American Midwest and West, with their vast and vernal landscapes, offered agricultural opportunities for those families that were not interested in moving to German cities for factory jobs. Unlike Portland's Irish, who favored shepherding and textile-based work (and predominantly relocated east of The Dalles to Morrow County, Oregon, to engage in these endeavors), many of Portland's German farmers were also interested in culinary enterprises. They brought with them traditional recipes and techniques for baking and confections, for processing meats, and for brewing beer, along with their particular styles of serving it, like the Fountain Saloon's "Celebrated Hot German Beer."[6]

Charles Alisky was one of Portland's earliest and best-known restaurateurs. He grew up in Frankfurt, the son of an accomplished musician in a prominent family. After his father died, Alisky began apprenticing in his uncle's confectionery across the river in Mainz. He came to the United States as a nineteen-year-old, working as a confectioner in a first-rate hotel in Georgia for awhile before relocating to the West Coast. In the 1860s, Alisky opened a restaurant and treat shop on SW First, between Morrison and Alder; though he served oysters "in every style," he was best known for his sweets.[7] "He was the first to put this business on a high plane," recalled Harvey Whitefield Scott in 1890, "and during all the years he was connected with it, it was the leading establishment of this kind in the city."[8] Alisky partnered with his brother-in-law Charles Hegele and treated Gilded Age Portlanders to German tarts and other pastries, but it was the "delicious ice cream" and "STRAWBERRIES & CREAM!!" that drove the customers wild.[9]

During World War I, attitudes toward Germans shifted in Portland from jovial kinship to fear and disdain. The German-named streets Bismarck, Frankfurt, and Frederick in the Brooklyn neighborhood were changed to the more patriotic Bush, Lafayette, and Pershing, named after an Oregon pioneer and two war heroes, respectively. By World War II, anti-German sentiment seemed to have faded somewhat, likely due in part to the leader of the free world having the name Eisenhower. As noted by Portland historian Eugene Snyder, trustworthy German-Americans were aplenty by the 1940s, both as civilians and in the military. "Especially were they dominant in that vital defense industry with this Pantheon of Teutonic names: Blitz, Blatz, Schlitz, Pabst, Budweiser, Busch, Heidelberg, Hamm, *und so weiter*."[10]

More than one member of the "vital defense industry" hailed from Germany and had been long established in Portland. Henry Weinhard immigrated to Portland from Württemberg in 1856, a bright-eyed chap twenty-six years of age. He worked for and with a variety of other German *braumeister*s before realizing that the thirsts of Portland's lumberjacks, fishermen, and sailors had been woefully unslaked. By the time he arrived in Portland, there were two other Germans making beer. He partnered with one—the aptly named George Bottler—before opening his own brewery, and buying out the first brewer, Henry Saxer. He eventually became the kaiser of a vast beer empire, whose brewing complex swallowed four city blocks of Northwest Portland real estate and produced beer for a century (discussed further in Chapter 7). After marrying Louisa Wagenblast (a nice Württemberg girl he met in Oregon), he helped found the Portland German Aid Society, which helped innumerable German immigrants get on their Portland feet. The Society's first president was yet another German brewer, Henry Saxer. When the German Aid Society opened its elderly home, Altenheim, on SE 79th and Division, it was reported that "the cooking is excellent and the meals vie with those served at first-class hotels."[11]

Weinhard sold his lagers to most local drinking establishments; he not only advertised his beer for "steamboats, steamships, hotels, restaurants, saloons," but also offered daily delivery service to the homes of "private families."[12] Beer was not just vital to the happiness of Portland's roughnecks and laborers; importantly, it had a place in the German home as a matter of course. As an upstanding member of Portland high society (among myriad other prominent Germans, such as merchant/banker

Frank Dekum), Weinhard did much to elevate attitudes toward beer when the temperance movement was in full, ax-wielding swing.

Also serving the needs of Portland's German families was Otto's Sausage Kitchen, started by immigrants Otto and Selma Eichentopf. They had initially settled in Aberdeen, Washington, in 1911, where Otto started his first sausage market. In 1921, the family relocated to Portland following the accidental death of their four-year-old daughter. They opened a meat market on Woodstock Street, and their son Edwin went to Woodstock elementary school just up the street. (His mother was a notable asset to the PTA board, which was likely among the better-fed of all Portland Public Schools PTAs, since Selma was always tasked with providing refreshments.)

Edwin grew up to run the family business after he returned from World War II, and his son Jerry took over the business in 1983. Jerry and his wife, Gretchen, still run the little sausage shop and deli today with their children—the fourth generation of Portland Eichentopfs. The smokehouse built by Otto still billows with fragrant tendrils of alder smoke, kissing the bockwurst and wieners that have been prepared from Otto's original family recipes for nearly a century. Today, Otto's deli menu reflects the changing face of their customers; one can still order liverwurst on dark rye just as one has for the past century, as well as a meat loaf sandwich that harkens back to the 1950s, and one specialty sandwich filled with sausage and Granny Smith apples speaks to the modern Portland palate with a nod to the traditional.

Another meat market still in operation, Zenner's, came next. George Zenner opened his shop on NE 53rd and Glisan in 1927 and began churning out smoked meats and sausages that are sold in grocery stores throughout the Northwest. Products like Louisiana Red Hots, linguiça, and andouille appeal to the tastes of a broader market, but like Otto's, their use of local alder for smoking leaves an indelible mark of the Northwest. Gartner's Meats was started later, after World War II. Jack Gartner, a Portland native, had learned sausage making from his father, Hans, who brought the family recipes and master techniques from Germany. Gartner's is famous among well-heeled Portlanders for their colossal rib eye steaks and the meltingly tender, marinated *flanken* short ribs that caramelize like beef candy.

Cooking in German households sometimes required adaptation to local ingredients. Chanterelles were savored by Germans as *pfifferlinge*, and would have brought joy to the hearts of cooks missing traditional chanterelles in cream with spaetzle. Trout and salmon would have been a welcome sight to homesick Germans, who would cook the trout by pickling in vinegar before simmering in water, serving the fish with melted butter and horseradish, or perhaps mixed with other fish (salmon and eel were common) to make a salad. Salmon, cheap and ubiquitous, could be baked in a pie or mixed with mashed potatoes and fried in little cakes.

JEWS—DRY GOODS AND DELICATESSENS

A small but significant portion of ethnic Portland during the boom years included the foreign-born Jews who began immigrating to the young town in the early and mid-1850s. The Jews who immigrated to Portland in the nineteenth century overwhelmingly brought with them their mercantile trades, acting as Portland's early shopkeepers and innkeepers. A third of all German immigrants were Jewish; in fact, Jews were the first German immigrants to arrive in Portland, when Jacob Goldsmith and Lewis May opened a general store in 1849. In the late 1850s, there was an influx of Jews from gold boom towns to the south, including Aaron Meier, who opened a department store with his business partner, Emil Frank, in 1870 after spending a decade owning various dry goods stores downtown.

Most Jewish families settled into communities alongside the Germans of Goose Hollow, taking up residence in South Portland, between the Willamette and the West Hills, from the Marquam Bridge to the Sellwood Bridge. In the 1860s, it was not just South Portland that bustled with Jewish-owned businesses; the center of downtown was astir with German- and Jewish-owned eateries and groceries. Alisky's famous strawberries and cream were being sold right next door to an established saloon and ice cream parlor owned by a Mr. Bergmann (who was also in the wholesale candy trade), whose brother ran a butcher shop down the street.

On First and Taylor, Henry Engel ran a grocery store that sold fresh produce, eggs, and lager; on Front and Stark the same was offered by Blumauer & Rosenblatt. Mrs. Rosenblatt's recipe for German-style braised cabbage with fried onion gravy appeared in Portland's *Web-Foot Cook Book* in 1885. The same book featured a few recipes for German cakes and pastries, translated into English by Mary Bodman Strowbridge, a German-American and wife of Portland judge Joseph Strowbridge, as well as one for German wine soup by Fannie Meier, the heiress to the Meier & Frank department store empire.

Many of the other Jews in Portland were immigrants who had lived for some time in New York before relocating west. The Industrial Removal Office (IRO) helped place Jews from all over the country into housing and work in their new cities. Sometimes the Portland IRO would make requests to New York's IRO for men and women of specific professions in order to meet the needs of Portland's Jewish community. In August of 1908, for example, Zion Meat Market (formerly located at today's SW 1st and Lincoln) sent a letter to the New York IRO in search of a *shochet* who could slaughter meat animals according to Jewish religious ritual.

First Street, in the early days of South Portland, was likened to a smaller version of Delancy Street on New York's Lower East Side. Kor-

Figure 4.1. Baker Harry Mosler lost his bakery during urban renewal projects that razed vast portions of Old South Portland in the 1960s. Courtesy of the Jewish Heritage Society OrHi 89445

sun's kosher deli, Maccaby's grocery store, Zion Meat Market, and Mosler's Bagel Shop were among the dozen or so grocery stores, bakeries, and butcher shops along the street. Nina Weinstein, a Portlander who grew up in South Portland during the 1920s, recalled that "there were other grocery stores where I lived, but [my mother] insisted on going to Mrs. Macoby because she was a widow and she was Jewish."[13] Mrs. Weinstein remembered her mother buying live chickens on Front Street and then walking them to the shochet on First to be butchered, and plucked by "a poor, little old lady named Shifra."[14]

Mrs. Weinstein—in her late nineties when her oral history was recorded for *Stories from Jewish Portland*—attributed her longevity to her mother's cooking, which deviated from the rich roasts and buttery noodles of most Jewish mothers and centered around seasonal fruits and vegetables procured from an Italian gardener who parked his truck in the neighborhood every other day.

Jewish families in Portland adapted their traditional foods to local ingredients. The Ashkenazi who poached fish dumplings known as gefilte fish even got a Portland makeover. Co-author of *Artisan Jewish Deli at Home* and great-grandson of a South Portland butcher, Michael Zusman recalled his grandmother Edith's "pink gefilte fish," which used a combination of salmon and halibut instead of traditional pollock or whitefish; her use of shredded carrot and onion is a common way to stretch the fish, and the savory flavor profile points to her family's Eastern European origins. The pink gefilte fish made by Edith Zusman was also featured in *The Neighborhood Cook Book* published by the Council of Jewish Women in 1912, produced as a fund-raiser for the Neighborhood House.

The Neighborhood Cook Book also showcases an interesting take on classic sweet and sour fish (*suz und sauer fish*), a dish that exemplifies the Ashkenazi fondness for pairing vinegar with honey. It seems that in Portland, the classic dinner staple not only uses salmon instead of white-fleshed carp or shad, but replaces the traditional rye bread and molasses with crumbled ginger snap cookies to thicken the sauce—a preference of German Jews. This ginger snap version is also seen in Mrs. Meier's recipe, which was published in the *Web-Foot Cook Book* in 1885:

Sweet and Sour Fish. Jewish Dish.
Four pounds of fish—salmon, trout or porgies if salmon, cut in slices;
one cup water, one cup vinegar, one large onion sliced, a little salt, a
few whole cloves, half cup seedless raisins, one cup brown sugar; cook

about one hour and then take out the fish carefully and keep warm. Thicken gravy with powdered ginger-snaps, boil it a few minutes and serve with fish. —Mrs. A. Meier

The Neighborhood House, founded by established German Jews, was an important Jewish social center and offered the second wave of Jewish immigrants—predominantly from Russia—access to resources for building lives in America. One such resource was a cooking class, which, despite the quality of recipes offered in the charity cookbook, was reportedly not well-attended.

Jews from Russia had often grown up with food insecurity before coming to America, and Portland's bounty was alluring. In *Stories from Jewish Portland*, one elder reminisced about growing up in South Portland in the 1920s. Her father grew tomatoes in the family garden, he shopped at the fruit and vegetable stands at the Fifth Street Market (not far from today's Portland Farmers Market), and he purchased chickens from the neighborhood kosher butcher Harry Schnitzer, Edith Zusman's father.

VOLGA GERMANS—BAKERS AND HOP-PICKERS

Excepting their religious beliefs, the Russian Jews shared many similarities to the wheat-growing Volga Germans. The Germans who followed Catherine the Great's manifesto to "civilize" the Russian steppe farmed the Volga River Valley in the 1760s and came to Portland between the 1880s and World War I. Both the Russian Jews and the Volga Germans came from and settled in tightly knit, somewhat isolated communities, and both spoke their own version of German: Russian Jews spoke Yiddish (a High German language), whereas Volga Germans primarily spoke a Low German dialect whose vernacular had remained relatively unchanged for hundreds of years. The *Wolgadeutsche* all relocated to the same insular enclave of Albina between NE 10th and 15th, from Fremont to Prescott. Albina was not unlike the Norka village back in the port town Saratov, from whence most of Portland's Volga Germans came. Then known as "Little Russia," some people remarked that it was as almost as if Norka had picked itself up and moved halfway around the world.[15]

Volga Germans were accustomed to living as outsiders; they had done so for more than a century in Russia, maintaining their German ethnicity and language during the entirety of their settlement in the Volga River Valley. Volga Germans maintained their foodways, as well, with few influences from their Russian neighbors. There are exceptions, however; the Volga German word for pancake, *belina*, comes from the Russian *blini*. The traditional Volga German dish *bierock*, a bread stuffed with cabbage, onions, and ground beef, resembles *pierog* in etymology and is typical of the Russian meat pie *pirozhki*. Dishes like *Fleischkeukle*, a fried meat pie originating in Turkey, appear to be influenced by the Tatars that also lived along the Volga.

Culturally secluded Volga Germans did not eat tomatoes until they arrived in the United States, because these crops had not yet been integrated into German cuisine before they departed for Russia (like many northern Europeans, Germans were wary of the nightshade and stuck to keeping tomatoes solely as decorations until the late eighteenth century). Consequently, Volga German versions of some Russian dishes reflect this distinction. Volga German cabbage rolls called *halupsi*, for example, are based on Russian *goluptsy*, but whereas the Russian version is often served with tomato sauce, traditional Volga German recipes never called for tomatoes until they were Americanized.

Volga German immigrants largely took work as laborers in Portland, but several well-established businesses, like Herman Wittenberg's German Bakery, Portland Cracker Company, and Thomas Liebe's Oregon Steam Bakery, hired *Wolgadeutsche*. "It was the custom to hire teenage boys in those days, and the factory was full of mostly lads from Russian and German families living in Albina," recalled Wittenberg's niece Lucille Saunders McDonald in 1960.[16] "In fact, the Germans and Russians seemed a part of the secret success of the early-day bakeries. They literally carried their recipes in their heads."[17]

In the 1920s and 1930s, many Volga German women and children took seasonal jobs picking berries, but more frequently they worked picking hops. Several families would travel together, thirty miles south, to the German-owned hop fields in St. Paul on what they thought of as sort of summer retreats. They packed tents and two weeks' supplies with them: homemade *roggebrod* (rye bread), cured bacon and other meats, baking supplies, and staples like potatoes and onions that traveled well.

Figure 4.2. In the 1890s, the "Russian" bakery workers at the Portland Cracker Company were actually Volga Germans. Courtesy of Oregon Historical Society, negative Orhi5764

The hop pickers' camps were tended by two or three women who were in charge of cooking and taking care of little ones, in addition to working a full day stripping fragrant hop flowers from their vines. Mollie Schneider Willman, an Albina woman, reminisced about the summers she and her mother spent picking hops in the 1930s:

> The women cooked meals outside where wood-stoked cook stoves were situated, sometimes under an open-air shelter filled with picnic-style tables and benches. With no ice boxes available for cold storage, we would fill heavy bottles and containers with perishables (milk, for example) then seal them tightly and sink them in the creek. A truck from the local grocery came by every afternoon when the field work was finished, providing us with a veritable market on wheels. The driver sold fresh meat, eggs, and other groceries.[18]

Picking hops was backbreaking work, often in blistering summer heat, and the vines tore up one's hands unless they were protected by thick leather gloves. However, once the day's quota was met, the workday was done, even if it was only the middle of the afternoon. This was when children went splashing in nearby swimming holes and women picked fruit. Some hop field owners grew berries, grapes, and fruit trees along the edges of their fields or in adjacent orchards, and some allowed their hop pickers to take fruit home at the end of the trip. Some started batches of blackberry wine; others canned peaches with the canning supplies and jars they brought along. Women also filled a spare pillowcase with hops to take home for brewing the family beer. At the end of each day, pickers turned in their haul and were given a ticket to tally the weight of hops they had picked, and before heading home at the end of the trip, workers turned in their tally tickets for cash. Because of the late-summer season for hops, children often started school late, but Portland teachers were kind and lenient, understanding the importance of picking hops not only to the livelihood of Volga German families but to their culture, as well.

Over only one generation, Portland's *Wolgadeutsche* became American—much faster than the Volga Germans elsewhere in the United States, and despite the fact that they had remained ethnically German for nearly 150 years while in Russia. The first-generation immigrants to Portland made efforts to shed their ethnicity. They insisted their children speak English even at home; they preferred packaged, white Franz bread to the working-class brown rye of their homeland. Their sons married nice, local girls and moved out of the neighborhood (some of these local girls nonetheless learned the ethnic recipes of their mothers-in-law). After World War II came the Vanport floods; as water rushed into that doomed lowland, African Americans rushed into Albina to live alongside the remaining Germans of Little Russia.

CHINESE—VEGETABLE GARDENERS AND CHEFS

What began as a trickle of immigration in the 1850s, soon became a deluge of skilled laborers and opportunists in the 1880s. Portland's Chinatown is the second-oldest Chinatown in the United States, and between 1890 and 1910, it was also the second largest.

Due to its geographical location in southeastern China, Guandong had had the most contact with the West, and because the region was in the midst of civil war, the 1850s was a fine time to head across the Pacific in search of better opportunities. Guandong Province had had plenty of con-

Figure 4.3. Volga German women and children spent the last few weeks of summer picking hops on German-owned fields outside of town. Women often brought home a pillowcase or two of hops for brewing the family beer. Photo © Thomas Robinson

tact with Portland specifically, taking imports of wheat and timber and shipping in exchange for imports of tea, opium (still legal in the nineteenth century), and laborers. Some Chinese men had already made the journey to the West Coast a decade earlier in search of gold, but by the 1850s, the gold had dried up, and hundreds of Chinese men came north in search of railroad jobs. Hundreds more continued northwest to take work in the salmon canneries in Astoria.

Although the Burlingame Treaty of 1868 initially opened the doors of Chinese immigration, discrimination and later anti-Chinese laws deprived Chinese men of a family life. Because laws made it exceedingly difficult for Chinese women to immigrate to the United States, as late as 1910, there were still only forty-eight Chinese-born women counted on the census to more than 4,700 Chinese-born men. Because miscegenation laws prevented Chinese men from marrying white women, Chinatown was populated almost solely by men, and the merchants of men's needs.

At best, the Chinese were treated as an exotic novelty, but usually they were treated much worse. Of the 1,700 or so Chinese that were in Portland by 1880, a few escaped derision; notably, the cherry's namesake Ah Bing, who was well respected by his employer, Seth Lewelling (but was nonetheless denied access back to the United States after he returned to China for a family visit). Like some black domestic workers in the South, some Chinese domestics were doubtless treated warmly in sympathetic households. James Beard adored the Chinese amah who raised him and wrote fondly of his family's cook, Jue Let, who "became a part of the family. He was the one person that Mother never could dominate."[19] As a people, the Chinese tended to carry a reputation of being hard workers (which is likely behind the fear that they would steal jobs from white men). This "respect" for the industriousness of the Chinese was immortalized in 1905 with the first mechanized salmon butchering machine, ignobly dubbed the "Iron Chink."

In all, Portland has had three distinct Chinatowns. Between 1850 and 1943, Chinatown was located in the heart of today's downtown, between SW 2nd and 4th Avenues, running only six blocks between Taylor and Yamhill. When Japanese families were interned during World War II, Chinatown's residents moved into Nihonmachi (Japantown) to take up the empty spaces left behind, and the places the Chinese left behind were razed to make way for the downtown business district.

Today, vestiges of Chinatown are seen between NW 3rd and 5th, from Burnside to Glisan, in an area now called Old Town Chinatown. At first, this was called "New Chinatown," but today there are less than a dozen Chinese businesses in this neighborhood. Instead, the area is dominated by homeless shelters and social services offices, echoing the long history of the city wishing to hide all of its unwanted people (and their vices) in red-lined ghettos on the edge of town.

The "New Chinatown" moniker would be more accurately applied to the thriving district five miles east. New Chinatown, for all intents and purposes, very clearly lives along SE 82nd Avenue, between Powell and Burnside, where its people dwell. The truly New Chinatown is an area conspicuously lacking grand lion-statue gates, pagoda rooflines, and walled gardens; it is a staccato of car lots and Vietnamese bakeries and hooker-hotels and grocery stores that sell the freshest *taku choy*. It is where one sees roasted ducks hanging in gilded windows and where one buys red-stamped mooncakes and paper-wrapped balls of smoky gunpowder tea.

OLD CHINATOWN (1850–1943)

"The territory of Portland's Old Chinatown was better defined by the relationships of residents and their commercial activities than by the locations of structures and their uses," explained Asian American Studies professor Marie Rose Wong.[20] Wong carefully notes that unlike San Francisco's Chinatown, which was an urban enclave that grew from legislative restrictions, Portland's Chinatown was built by social organizations, and as such, there was no spatial containment of Chinese people. Instead, as Wong explains, Portland's Chinatown epitomized a "nonclave" immigrant community, giving Chinatown the freedom to relocate itself as needed.[21]

For a long time, Chinese people lived in encampments near the sources of their livelihoods, and in Portland, that was mainly railroad companies and private homes (a great many other Chinese immigrants lived in Astoria, where they worked in salmon canneries). To serve the needs of these workers, a number of merchants set up businesses, and soon laundries, opium dens, and places of worship called Joss Houses followed suit. In Portland's early days, men far outnumbered women of any race, and wherever women were in shortage, the Chinese population was the largest. Chinese men filled the roles typically occupied by women: cooking, washing, and domestic work.[22]

For about thirty years, there were two distinct Chinese communities in Portland. The urban Chinese settled in downtown tenements and either acted as merchants or took on the aforementioned "women's work," and their country cousins settled the raw hillsides and marshes, in areas west of downtown. These areas were dubbed the Chinese Vegetable Gardens by Portlanders, and in the latter half of the nineteenth century, market-oriented vegetable gardening had become another moneymaking venture for Chinese people. As it was unlikely to compete with white jobs, gardening was an "acceptable" Chinese occupation (from the white perspective, anyway), and as Italian immigrants on the east side of the river would come to find, growing and selling vegetables was an important element of Portland's economy. The eastern foothills of the Tualatin Mountains (today known as the West Hills) were well irrigated with natural seeps and springs, and south- and east-facing slopes captured plenty of light even in overcast weather.

Before flood control measures were in place, Tanner Creek Gulch in the Goose Hollow neighborhood was undesirable for real estate development, and the Chinese Vegetable Gardens were first documented there in 1879. Other vegetable gardens sprawled across Johnson Creek Gulch in NW Portland's old Slabtown, along the Balch Creek watershed and Guild's Lake.[23] A writer for *The West Shore* magazine marveled in 1889 that "[i]ncongruous as it may seem to find turnips, beets and cabbages growing in such luxuriance and profusion . . . such a sight can be witnessed in Portland every day in the 365 that make up the yearly round. . . . By utilizing every available inch, by cropping the same ground several times a year, and by constant use of irrigating ditch and watering can, [the Chinese gardener] secures a marvelous quantity of vegetables from a very small patch of ground."[24] The article also commented on the contrast between the "palatial residences of [Portland's] wealthiest citizens" in the hills, with the "shanties of these industrious Orientals."[25]

One of Portland's Chinese merchants, Ah-ning, wrote home to China in 1861 lamenting the lack of proper things for Chinese people to eat and the high price of chicken, and criticizing American farming techniques, specifically, the lack of composting. "They grow food, but not like in China. They don't feed the land with land food; they waste land food and

Figure 4.4. Chinese vegetable gardens in Tanner Gulch. The wealthy residents living at the top of the slope did little to interfere with the gardens, but eventually city ordinances made it illegal for Chinese gardeners to sell their wares. Courtesy of City of Portland Archives, Oregon, A2004-002.2544

there are weeds all over. Land food is all saved in China, and the land is made very good, with great crops. That is not so here."[26] It is perhaps for these reasons, then, that the gardeners grew Chinese vegetables that they had no intention to sell to white Portlanders, like bok choy for stir-fries and *tung qua* (winter melon) for making soup. However, western crops like carrots, corn, onions, and radishes, along with blackberries and strawberries, were enjoyed by Chinese cooks and relished by Portland housewives looking for a bargain on seasonal produce.

Because of this disconnect in the availability of ingredients, most Portlanders dipped only a wary toe into Chinese cooking at home. An Americanized recipe for the stir-fried meat and vegetable mélange called chop suey appeared in *The Oregonian* in 1915 at the request of a curious reader living in Tillamook.[27] The letter's respondent, cooking advice columnist Lilian Tingle, suggested that the home cook may have to make a few substitutions, or omit some ingredients (like canned bamboo shoots) entirely. To make the "Spanish" version, one simply added chili powder.

Chop Suey, Americanized. 3/4 pound lean pork or chicken, 2 ounces lean ham, 1 onion, 3 stalks celery, 1/2 cup mushrooms, 3 tablespoons tried out (rendered) pork fat, 1 tablespoons flour, 1 teaspoon salt, pepper to taste, 1 level tablespoon sugar, 1 teaspoon lemon juice, 2 tablespoons soy, ½ cup bamboo sprouts, ¾ cup chicken stock. Cut the meat and the vegetables into very narrow strips about 2 inches long, and brown them lightly in the fat, doing a few at a time to prevent drawing out the juice too much, and reserving the strips as cooked. Sprinkle in the flour, and cook it in the fat. Add the stock and let boil up. Add the prepared meat and vegetables with all the seasonings, except the soy. Flavor to taste with Chinese spice if available, and liked. Cover, and simmer very slowly until the meat is quite tender, then add the soy and serve with plain boiled rice, boiled so that the grains are dry and separate. Pass soy for those who like more. [28]

Although chop suey is widely regarded as an American invention, anthropologist E. N. Anderson wrote in the *Encyclopedia of Food and Culture* that it is possibly based on *tsap suei* ("miscellaneous leftovers" or "odds and ends"), commonly prepared by vegetable growers in the Guandong Province—the same area from which Portland's Chinese immigrants had originated. Others claim that chop suey was invented by Chinese railroad workers on the West Coast. Nonetheless, once restaurants and high-profile hostesses began serving it, the dish was all the rage in Portland at the turn of the twentieth century.

Gardeners lived in a shanty town of ramshackle lean-tos next to their plots. Disparately, the tops of the canyons above the garden-villages were where the view-hungry upper classes lived. The view of gardens and easy access to affordable produce may have offset the visual blight of the gardeners' hillside hovels, because there are no records of the upper classes making any attempts to remove the gardens.

Vegetables grown in the Chinese gardens were sold by street vendors carrying baskets yoked to long poles that they draped across their shoulders. Both Chinese and Italian vegetable peddlers would set up their farmers markets on SW 3rd Street, between Salmon and Madison. Every morning in the summer, starting at 5:00 a.m., these pop-up markets jockeyed for the best sales and would be finished by 7:00 a.m. After buying out stock in the morning, Italian green grocers (operating their markets on the east side) typically resold the wholesale produce at a retail markup. Haggling sometimes got a bit out of hand, and minor skirmishes occasionally erupted between the rival vegetable dealers. One came when an Italian vegetable retailer was arrested for badly beating a Chinese vendor who refused to sell him a bag of corn for $1. Another time, market owner Frank Amato got into a legal scuffle with Lin Foon and a few other Chinese vegetable growers over assault and battery charges filed against each other. *The Oregonian*'s coverage of the court hearings was a painful attempt to re-create pleadings from two immigrant groups as they grappled with the English language, but the evidence presented at the time spoke for itself. "Amato was without a scar, yet poor Lin Foon had almost been beaten to a jelly," summarized the sympathetic deputy district attorney.[29] Amato was fined $15.

Eventually, other Portland vegetable markets started to complain that their profit margins were suffering from the competition of Chinese street vendors who had virtually no overhead costs. Vendor ordinances went into effect in 1910 that barred the vegetable growers from peddling their wares in certain downtown districts, one of which was Chinatown. And although there had not been complaints about the gardens or shanties, the plots nonetheless slowly made way for other developments as property owners found more lucrative ways to use the land, namely, mansions and the Multnomah Athletic Club. The changing land use and produce ordinances were a one-two punch against the vegetable growers, and Chinese vegetable gardens disappeared from Goose Hollow and Slabtown in the early twentieth century.[30]

By the late nineteenth century, not only did the Chinese have a reputation for being hard workers, but their culinary prowess was becoming well known. Even during the height of anti-Chinese sentiment, when some restaurants bragged that they had "no Chinese in kitchen," most restaurateurs knew the value in having Chinese kitchen staff. In 1873, Abigail Scott Duniway wrote on the front page of her newspaper, *The New Northwest*, that when it came to cooking, Americans and the English had a thing or two to learn from the Chinese. "Our 'civilization' in this is over a hundred years behind the age; and in this respect the Chinese are far our superior."

Portland's oldest restaurant, Huber's, was headed by—and is still operated by the descendants of—Chinese immigrant and cook Jim Louie. Frank Huber hired twenty-one-year-old Jim Louie in 1891, and three years later, Louie became a local legend by serving turkey sandwiches and clams on the half shell during the midst of a 100-year flood, purportedly selling them from a rowboat floating in the middle of the saloon.

Other savvy restaurateurs and hoteliers knew that Chinese chefs were a secret to success, as well. In the 1890s, a young widow named Elizabeth Brennan (who would later marry John Beard and give birth to a cherubic James) ran a twelve-room boardinghouse in a four-story Victorian downtown, which she dubbed the Gladstone Hotel. Disenchanted with fickle French and Italian chefs (who tended to wander off to San Francisco once they had saved enough money for the ticket), Brennan decided to hire and train three Chinese chefs instead—Jue Let, his sous chef, Gin, and his pastry chef, Poy. [31]

Let was a phenomenon in the kitchen. His beef stew, which was an effective way to use tougher cuts of meat, had an Oriental flair that made it a hit with the Gladstone's paying guests. The beef was browned a long time in fat before the vegetables were added, and the juices from the vegetables would mix with the fond and pan drippings to make a sauce. The sauce was thickened with grated potatoes and flavored with what James Beard vaguely (or coyly) described as "a variety of seasonings, including a good dose of soy sauce." [32]

Elizabeth Beard did not know where Let lived, a fact that drew no end of frustration for her. Let was loyal and promptly arrived when she called—unless he did not want to. If they had gotten into one of their friendly spats (one time Let came after Beard with a kitchen knife, and she parried with a log of firewood), he could disappear for days and there was little Beard could do but send hopeful messages and wait until he cooled off.

At the turn of the century, Let announced to Elizabeth Beard that he was tired of working in hotels but wanted to continue working for her. She admitted that she was selling the hotel anyway and that she wanted to take a break and have a baby with her new husband, John Beard, an assessor of imported goods who was well known among Portland's Chinese merchants. Let became the Beards' personal chef at the house on SE 23rd and Salmon, where the family lived and took in boarders. Although Let never moved into their home, he became a great inspiration to young James. Growing up with a Chinese home cook as well as a Chinese godfather (a friend of John Beard's whom James described as an aristocrat and a tyrant) gave James Beard a familiarity with ingredients like dried shark fins and dried turtles for making curative soups. He had a comfort with Chinese cooking that lasted throughout his life.

Other prominent Portland households employed Chinese private chefs, as well. Lee Sing was the chef at the opulent mansion of Portland socialite Charlotte "Sudie" Green, grandmother of Communist journalist Jack Reed. During his freshman year at Harvard, Reed wrote that Lee Sing was an "honest, reserved [and] thrifty" man and "a real artist" in the kitchen. Like many Chinese immigrants in Portland, Sing had converted to Christianity but continued practicing some traditional Chinese rituals, such as burning joss sticks and eating shark fin seasoned with chicken gizzard. Like many chefs, Sing did not abide the presence of others in his kitchen and was a rumored alcoholic.

With so many members of the upper crust employing Chinese cooks and exotic dishes like chop suey coming into fashion, Oriental influences began to surface in the homes of Portland Progressives. Elizabeth Beard decorated with accents of Chinese art, rugs, and vases, and Chinoiserie was making appearances in Portland's social elite. *The Oregonian*'s Society page detailed one party thrown in 1903 by Mrs. Cornelia Rockwell, a friend of Abigail Scott Duniway's and a board member of the Young Women's Christian Association (YWCA).[33] The house had been decorated with softly glowing Chinese lanterns and the table festooned with Japanese embroideries. There were little ginger jars filled with burning incense, and each place setting was marked by a placard with the guest's name written in Chinese characters set atop a pair of ivory chopsticks.

The chopsticks provided no end of entertainment for the women, as no one knew how to use them properly and the ladies all tittered as they fumbled with the fifteen courses, the first of which was the on-trend chop suey. "[N]ot a thing on the menu was American," relayed the dazzled correspondent. The meal ended with "sweet pickled rinds of no one knows what; candies, peach pits in place of almonds, and the most curious biscuits in the world, each one adorned with a little red painted flower." The curious little biscuits would have been moon cakes; they could have been filled with any of the traditional fillings, such as sweet adzuki bean paste, lotus seed paste, or a mixture of nuts and the sweet pastes. Moon cakes are often served sliced in wedges, and are typically eaten with tea. At this party, the "tea was poured from queer little Chinese bowls, set in brass trays, and"—most shockingly—"served without sugar, lemon or cream."[34]

By the time Portland society became enrapt with Oriental exoticism, the first Chinese restaurant had already been in place for more than half a century. In December 1851, after the same year Portland became incorporated as a city, *The Oregonian* ran an ad for Tong Sung Restaurant and Boardinghouse, located on SW Second Street. It is unknown whether or not Mr. Sung prepared Chinese or American foods, but he promised that he employed the very best Chinese chefs and his aim was to please.[35] Numerous others came and went, and in 1928 restaurateur Wong On opened Hung Far Low (meaning "almond blossom fragrance") at the corner of NW 4th and Couch, in New Chinatown. A decade earlier, a different restaurant by the same, snicker-inducing name was located at the edge of Old Chinatown. As this earlier Hung Far Low ran continuous "waitress wanted" ads in *The Oregonian* during the summer of 1917, the restaurant may have had some trouble staying open at that location.

NEW CHINATOWN (1920S–1990S)

When the second Hung Far Low opened its doors on NW 4th and Couch, Portland's Chinatown had begun its relocation from the heart of downtown to the area that came to be known as New Chinatown. Between 1900 and 1915, Portland was undergoing a building boom in response to the City Beautiful movement that was sweeping the nation's major cities. Old Chinatown had been in the center of a disastrous fire in 1906, and property values were climbing. There had already been plans (mostly by white property owners) to relocate Chinatown to the north, and although some Chinese merchants resisted the change, Chinatown gradually lost its core in the center of downtown and moved north ten blocks, overlapping with the black neighborhood between Everett and Flanders. By 1926, the backbone of New Chinatown was along NW 4th. As a final act of acceptance, the Chinese Consolidated Benevolent Association (CCBA) celebrated the opening of its new social hall in 1931, twenty years after first opening the CCBA building.

The next big change to New Chinatown (today referred to as Old Town Chinatown) occurred with the bombing of Pearl Harbor. Japan had invaded China in the 1930s, and with the onset of World War II, the United States and China suddenly had a common enemy. The Chinese were unexpected beneficiaries of the new anti-Japanese sentiment. When

Japanese-Americans were rounded up and shipped off to internment camps in 1942, many of the vacancies left in their homes and businesses—conveniently located right in the center of New Chinatown—were snatched up by Chinese Portlanders. With the repeal of Chinese exclusion laws in 1943, Chinese people had finally regained the right to own property and become naturalized citizens.

When communities who have a long history of industriousness and thrift suddenly gain the right to own property, they tend to quickly, and rightfully, prosper. For better or worse, the economic boom enjoyed by the rest of Americans postwar enabled Chinese citizens to move out of Chinatowns and into the suburbs. With the decline of the nation's Chinatowns in the late 1940s, Chinese food was pulled out of ethnic enclaves. In 1949, sociologist Rose Hum Lee worried that "American-owned enterprises serving Chinese dishes bring an end to the tourist-attracting features of Chinatowns" and that, in turn, more Chinese would shift focus to providing the home cook with packaged food products and spices to accommodate the desire for Chinese food. Lee observed that World War II was an accelerant in this trend, and that this shift in the American economy was occurring outside Chinatowns.

Although Chinese cooking had been gaining popularity in mainstream Portland as early as the 1920s and 1930s (even the *Joy of Cooking*'s 1931 issue included a recipe for chop suey), the love affair that America had with Chinese food seems to have exploded postwar. This was especially evident with the introduction of Hawaiian and Polynesian culinary influences along the West Coast, and the cocktail culture of Don the Beachcomber and Trader Vic's integrated Cantonese cooking into Tiki culture with dishes like the pupu platter and sweet and sour meatballs. Cloying, lurid red sauces changed the face of Chinese food across the country. In Portland, that change occurred at the Alibi in 1947; soon, Portland had a Kon Tiki at the Sheraton and its own Trader Vic's at the Hotel Benson. Canton Grill, which opened in 1944, served the Honolulu cocktail (a blend of gin and fruit juices) with its fried shrimp and full Chinese menu.

In her 1949 article, Rose Hum Lee predicted that no new Chinatowns would be created. While it is true that there are no new giant red gates to inform visitors that they have arrived, Portland does, in fact, have a *new* New Chinatown.

NEW NEW CHINATOWN: THE JADE DISTRICT (1990S–TODAY)

Although the cultural centers of historic Chinatown like the Lan Su Chinese Gardens and the Chinese Consolidated Benevolent Association headquarters remain in Old Town, the culinary center of Chinatown now largely resides along SE 82nd Avenue, spilling east and west for a mile or two down the arterial main streets. The transfer of sovereignty of Hong Kong to the People's Republic of China in 1997 sparked a significant movement of Chinese to North America at the turn of the twenty-first century. Unlike Portland's first Chinese immigrants of the mid-nineteenth century, these people from Hong Kong were wealthier and more educated. They had business savvy. As Marie Rose Wong puts it, the economic standings of these two groups of immigrants are polar opposites. [36]

Canton Grill and New Cathay were anchors to the relocated Chinatown on 82nd even in the 1940s; later, Legin added grandeur to the area with its three-story pagoda and lavish banquet hall. Immigrants from Hong Kong and Southeast Asia found the new neighborhood's affordable housing and commercial space attractive, but resentments over the Portland Development Commission's habit of siting homeless services in the heart of Chinatown has played no small part in the exodus to the east side. Nonetheless, new residents have had opportunities to build restaurants and markets right in the neighborhood where they live. Over the past ten years, 82nd Avenue has become the location of three new Chinese megagrocery stores and dozens of strip malls and shopping centers serving Chinese barbecue and steamed pork buns, but it has also become the new home of Portland's oldest Chinese restaurant, Hung Far Low, which relocated to the Avenue of the Roses in 2005.

Whereas the original Chinatown housed Chinese cooks and gardeners in nineteenth-century Portland, and the second Chinatown catered to the city's developing palate for sticky-sweet General Tso's chicken and other Chinese-American delights, the Jade District appears to be a perfectly self-contained, thriving community that primarily serves food for the immigrants who live there. There is an aura of culinary authenticity that was hidden in earlier iterations of Chinatown. Perhaps all that has changed is that concurrent explosions in globalization and culinary fanaticism have brought Portland a new community of eaters more open to experience the real flavors of Chinatown, like garlicky pea shoots and the distinct alkaline *kee* aroma of yellow lye noodles swimming in clear broth. Maybe the "secret" Chinese menus are just no longer secret.

JAPANESE—STRAWBERRY FIELDS AND TOFU-TEN

Like the early Chinese immigrants, Japanese immigrants, or Nikkei, were predominantly unmarried men who were drawn to Oregon by railroad jobs. When Chinese exclusion laws created labor shortages in the 1880s, Japanese workers filled the roles. These railroad laborers typically survived on threadbare conditions, eating a flour dumpling soup called *dango-jiru*, fortified with salt pork and vegetables, and occasionally padded out with bread. Some labor contractors used food as a weapon for Americanizing their workers, insisting that Japanese laborers eat western foods. In some camps, miso, *shoyu* (soy sauce), and rice were banned.[37]

Many left Portland for salmon cannery jobs on the coast, but by the 1890s, Portland had several Japanese-owned hotels and restaurants catering to the first-generation immigrants—the *Issei*—serving indigent laborers a decent meal for 10 or 15 cents. Because cards and prostitutes were such common wage sinks in this town of bachelors, some waiters had to carry sticks during shifts to thrash deadbeats attempting a dine-and-dash.

Predominantly arriving from Okayama, Yamaguchi, Hiroshima, and Fukuoka Prefectures, Portland's Japanese population grew from just twenty men in 1890 to nearly 1,500 residents in 1910.[38] Between 1910 and 1920, Japanese women began to move to Portland, tipping the gender balance closer to equal. Nihonmachi, or Japantown, developed in a few blocks right in the center of Chinatown, between Ankeny and Glisan, from Front to Fifth Avenue. When people married and started families, Nihonmachi went from a seedy district of drifting laborers to a blossoming community. Restaurants, grocery stores, and a fish market opened; Portland's School of Domestic Science started holding "Japanese classes" for home cooks on Saturday evenings in 1906.

In 1905, Anzen opened its doors in the heart of Nihonmachi; it moved to its current location in a diminutive building on Martin Luther King Jr. Boulevard in 1968, and is still Portland's best-kept secret for those seeking centrally located, sushi-grade tuna. A *shoyu* company came next; the first in the state to import soybeans. In 1911, Saizō Ota came from Okayama and started Ohta Tofu-ten (Ota Tofu Company) and soon began making a variety of soybean products such as *aburage* (fried tofu pouches) for filling with sushi rice or slicing into miso soup. It also made gelatinous, bruise-colored blocks of voodoo-lily paste called *konnyaku* to add to bubbling pots of hearty *oden*—a warming comfort on a squalling Portland evening.[39] Ota Tofu relocated to the east side of the river in 1981 and is still in operation, making it the oldest tofu company in the United States.[40]

Although Portland's white residents did not necessarily appreciate the wares of master tofu makers in the 1910s, the specific regions from which Japanese people immigrated influenced the way Portlanders ate. In Japan, the greatest culinary deference is given to what is known as *meibutsu*, literally, "famous things," or the food for which a given region is known—the specialty that the region does better than anywhere else. One of the *meibutsu* of Hiroshima (and to only a slightly lesser extent, Okayama) is oysters.[41] Portland's once-flourishing oyster saloon scene was bolstered by the Nikkei; being inland, Portland was never a producer of oysters, but the city's residents were enthusiastic consumers of the bivalve. The Pacific Northwest's commercial oyster industry was started in the mid-1880s and exploded with the introduction of Japan's Pacific cupped oyster, brought to the West Coast in the 1920s.[42]

Many Issei had avoided the trouble and vice of Nihonmachi in its early days, opting instead to settle areas outside the urban center. The Montavilla neighborhood on the northeastern foothills of Mount Tabor was the first, and one of the two largest, Japanese farming settlements in the Portland area; the other came later, as farmers expanded a few miles even farther east to Gresham. By 1908, according to historian Eiichiro Azuma, Montavilla was home to thirty-six Japanese farmers who rented 655 acres of farmland; three years later, more than 200 Japanese people lived in the "Japanese farm village" of Montavilla, with an additional hundred or so field hands to pick up the slack during the harvest season.[43]

The rural outskirts of town offered more opportunities for farmers. The Iwasaki family began growing row crops of strawberries and vegetables in the suburb of Hillsboro in 1916. According to Jim Iwasaki, the sansei grandson of Iwasaki Brothers' founder Billy, growing strawberries was a skill that Japanese farmers learned in Oregon.[44] Whereas many people took their money back to Japan to retire comfortably, some families, like the Iwasakis, put down roots. By dint of their ingenuity and earnest, by 1920, Japanese farmers produced 90 percent of all strawber-

ries grown in Gresham; within twenty years, 90 percent of all broccoli
and cauliflower, 75 percent of celery, 70 percent of peas, and 45 percent
of the asparagus grown for the entire state was done so by Japanese
farmers.[45]

For those who stayed in the city, however, the 1920s and 1930s were
Nihonmachi's golden years. The children of the first and second generation of immigrants—the *Nisei* and *Sansei*—played in the streets and attended neighborhood schools and churches. Families got together in shady, early-summer meadows for *undokai*—the weekend "sports days" accompanied by vast picnics. They spread out blankets in the soft bluegrass
and languished over big basketsful of the earthy, stewed root vegetable
nishime; hand-patted triangles of *onigiri* (rice balls) with a filling of tuna
salad or the salty, red *umeboshi*; chicken, either fried or smeared in teriyaki sauce; and an endless variety of sushi rolls and pickles.

In the 1920s, Portland's Japanese restaurants often served non-Japa-
nese cuisine, as advertised in the Japanese-language newspaper, *Oregon
News*. Japanese-owned Mary's Café served roast beef and mashed potatoes, pancakes, and other American foods, and Ichikiri Restaurant served
both Chinese and Japanese food. *Shina soba* ("China noodles," better
known as ramen) were commonly advertised by Japanese restaurants,
observed Dave Conklin, a scholar of the history of Portland's Japanese
food.[46]

Shina udon was not the only foreign food interpreted by Japanese
Portlanders. A recipe printed in the 1932 *Cook Book of Many Lands . . .
Foreign Recipes*, published by the Portland Parent-Teacher Association's
Americanization Department includes one "Japanese" recipe. The recipe
is an example of *yoshoku*, or "western food," the Japanese versions of
European foods popular in Japan after the Meiji restoration period of the
1850s.[47] In this case, a gratin:

Crab—Japanese Style

    1 can crab meat
    Juice ½ lemon
    1 teaspoon Worcestershire
    Few grains cayenne
    1 tablespoon butter or oil
    1 tablespoon flour
    1 cup milk

1 small can mushrooms
1 teaspoon grated onion
1/8 teaspoon paprika
2½ teaspoons salt
3 hard-cooked eggs

Combine crab meat, mushrooms and lemon juice, onion, Worcestershire sauce and seasonings. Make a white sauce from the fat, flour and
milk and add to the crab mixture and the eggs, which have been finely
chopped. Heat all thoroughly and serve on toast. Or, fill greased rame-
kins and sprinkle with grated cheese and cracker crumbles, and bake
12 minutes in a very hot oven. Serves 6.[48]

In the 1930s, trouble began to brew on the other side of the Pacific. Japan
invaded Manchuria, and the ripple effect was a rift between the Japanese
and Chinese in Portland. Chinese restaurants discouraged Japanese clientele, so Japanese restaurants started serving the Chinese food that they
enjoyed eating, rather than risk being turned away at Chinese-owned
establishments. By the end of the decade, Chinese foods were no longer
advertised by Japanese restaurants.[49]

By the 1940s, Portland had the seventh-largest community of Japanese
in the United States. In the spring of 1942, Nihonmachi was shuttered as
Japanese Portlanders were forced to liquidate their property under Executive Order 9066. By May, 3,500 people were rounded up and assembled
at the Expo Center (still the Pacific Livestock Expo at the time) for five
months before being evacuated to the Minidoka concentration camp near
Twin Falls, Idaho. Life in the Expo Center was demoralizing; people
were fed army rations (supplemented with some Japanese foods) in com-
munal mess halls. There was a dysentery outbreak. A cook was shot in
broad daylight by a military police guard when he tried to obtain ingredients from the assembly center kitchen. During a heat wave, the fire
department sprayed hoses on the floors of the center to cool it off. The
water seeped into the plank floors, turning the dry dirt and manure beneath them to fecal mud, and the resulting stench and hordes of flies were
unbearable. One sixty-year-old man attempted suicide by slashing his
own throat with a razor.

During the war, many farmers who were deemed loyal (non-enemy)
were relocated to sugar beet farms to earn a pittance while they waited it
out. On Portland's waterfront, a granite boulder reads, "Black smoke rolls

/ Across the blue sky. / Winter chills our bones. / This is Minidoka."[50] Japanese-American and fifth poet laureate of Oregon, Lawson Inada still remembers his interred childhood.

After the war, the American-born Nisei and their children made pensive steps toward reintegrating into society, but Nihonmachi never returned. Some Japanese business owners had friends in the white community, who either rented out their spaces or otherwise kept them safe while they were away. The Ota family was one such lucky case; a sympathetic landlord held their space and tofu-making equipment during the internment, and they were able to pick up where they left off after the war. Postwar Portland directories listed Ota as a wholesale bakery, perhaps a move by Ota to downplay the Japanese identity of their product, or due to a lack of American understanding about what a soybean cake actually was. Although the American perspective on Japanese culture had been forever altered, the survival of food-based businesses like Iwasaki Brothers, Anzen and Ota Tofu show that four generations after first arriving, Portland's Japanese community has persevered.

ITALIANS—FIG TREES AND FARMERS MARKETS'

In 1872, *The Oregonian* reported among its "Local Brevities" that "Portland boasts of a fig tree which bears fruit." Although Portland did not yet boast a large population of Italians during that newsworthy event, those first to arrive brought more cuttings to start fig trees of their own. By the turn of the century, Italian grandmothers walked all over South Portland, gathering figs in their aprons to distribute among the neighbor ladies.[51]

In the 1860s and 1870s, there was a baker's dozen or so of Italians in Portland, who set up groceries, fish markets, and fruit stands, and then left town for other opportunities.[52] The earliest Italian families, like many immigrants, were attracted to Oregon by railroad jobs, but it was the bounty and verdure that hooked them. The first to stay put were from northern Italy and lived alongside Eastern European Jews near what is now Duniway Park in South Portland. They set up gardens that grew vegetables both for family consumption and for sale to other households; market gardens that grew produce for local delivery were known as truck gardens. SW Patton Road, a winding street that connects downtown to

Hillsboro, was once a main thoroughfare for Italian truck gardeners to get their wares across the West Hills.

One northern Italian truck gardener, Delfino Antrosio, happened to grow and deliver produce and teach recipes to James Beard's mother. Elizabeth Beard ardently embraced Italian food, paying little regard to the "significance of garlic as a social influence in Portland"; namely, that the smell of the stinking rose on one's breath might out a person as ethnic. [53] Antrosio would stop and chat with Mrs. Beard, and one day made her polenta—a dish unknown outside Italian homes and the first James Beard ever tasted. Although Antrosio was from Piedmont (a region famous for its dairy products, love of crudités, and the heavy use of garlic), his pesto recipe was a keeper, and one Mrs. Beard eagerly added to her repertoire. Zucchini was another favorite crop of hers, introduced to Oregon by Italian gardeners, and grown along with favas and artichokes by her friend Joe Galluzzo. [54]

Most of the early Italians were working-class, as were those who settled and built gardens in Parkrose and Milwaukie. However, one of Portland's early restaurants (and later, one of the earliest fine hotels) was opened by Milanese seaman and polyglot Samuel Arrigoni. The next sizeable group mostly came from southern Italy and settled homes and vegetable gardens in Ladd's Addition (then still known as "Ladd's field") and surrounding neighborhoods, just a mile east of the rows of retail produce stalls. Like Arrigoni, the southern Italians arrived to start businesses of their own, as well as to provide better education to their children.

In the early 1890s, there were already several Italian hotels, including Campi's Hotel at SW 1st and Oak. Campi's featured a saloon and a restaurant, and although they served such tempting items as "Macaroni, Raviolli, Tagliarini, Lasagne, Spaghetti, and Risotto served in [the] Italian Style," most of Portland society had not yet caught on to the Italian love of garlic. [55] Nonetheless, other Italians who arrived to Portland sight unseen to unfamiliar faces would have been heartened to have a place to stay where the food and language spoken were their own.

After the unification of Italy (and the subsequent end of feudal systems) in 1861, Italians suddenly had access to medical resources and a steady food supply. The resulting demographic boom led to overpopulation in southern Italy, one of the driving forces in Italian diaspora reaching an all-time high at the turn of the century. The years between 1900 and 1910 saw a fivefold boom in the Italian population in Portland alone. Some of them came from Liguria, land of the pesto, but the majority of Portland's Italian immigrants came from Calabria, a region in southern Italy whose cuisine includes a focus on preserved foods like oil-packed vegetables and meats, as well as dry sausages. The Calabrian influence was still evident by the time *Cook Book of Many Lands* was published in the 1930s; nearly half of the Italian recipes are for vegetable dishes, especially Calabria's beloved eggplant.

Italians never made up a great proportion of Portland's immigrant population, but those who did live in Stumptown stayed busy and were visible community members. Most Italians in Portland had agricultural experience, and the vast majority of them went into the business after immigrating. The Italians did not want to live in rural areas, however, and instead focused on growing, transporting, and selling vegetables from plots of land around town to produce stalls and markets near the urban center. They also kept kitchen gardens for home use, which is why one sees so much marjoram, lemon balm, rosemary, and fig trees growing wild in southeast Portland's back alleys and along property edges. Lemon balm, which proliferates in Portland's Mediterranean climate (much to the frustration of modern gardeners), was soaked in white wine to make a digestif for curing stomach cramps and headaches.

By the time Portland's first farmers markets were built, the vast majority of the city's produce vendors in Portland were Italian. The Italian Gardeners' and Ranchers' Association formed at the turn of the twentieth century, and a large marketplace soon followed. The market was located just south of the west end of the Hawthorne Bridge (built in 1910), offering a central location for the Italians both living near Hawthorne and in South Portland.

With the centralized market, the farmers and peddlers had a core location to enable them to standardize their prices and ensure quality control. The Italian Gardeners' and Ranchers' Association building also provided a place for farmers and grocers to meet and socialize, as well as housing Italian restaurants from the storefronts that faced onto busy Martin Luther King Jr. Boulevard (then called Union Avenue).

A portion of what is now called the Central Eastside Industrial District was referred to as "Italian Row" by the 1893 *Portland Register*.[56] After a number of other produce wholesalers and grocers built stores near the Italian Gardeners' and Ranchers' Association building, many Portlanders

Figure 4.5. Independent Produce Company, ca. 1932. Italian vegetable vendors like this one were common in the area of Southeast Portland known as Produce Row. Courtesy of City of Portland Archives, Oregon, A2008-001.86

began to refer to the area as "Produce Row," a name that has been acknowledged by the café of the same name, which opened in the neighborhood in 1974.[57] The colloquial neighborhood name was confirmed again in 1989, when members of the Hawthorne Boulevard Business Association applied to add the Italian Gardeners' and Ranchers' Association building (constructed in 1922) to the National Register of Historic Places.[58] In 1929, the Association moved into a larger building a half mile east to SE 10th and Belmont, where Gatto & Sons Fruit is still located.

In the 1970s, historian Charles Gould demarcated the boundary of Italian influence as including everything from Powell to Hawthorne, from the river to 50th, or approximately two and a half square miles of southeast Portland real estate. Corno's Market, which opened in the 1950s, graced Produce Row with its cheery, yellow façade and its Carmen Miranda-esque hat of giant fruit for about forty years before it was demolished, but this is still where Portland's Italian gardening heritage is most evident. Although they sold out to Del Monte in 1998, Grazianos sold produce from the neighborhood for more than seventy years. Agostino Graziano's son and grandson grew the business into the Northwest's largest purveyor of precut produce. Anyone who ate at Taco Bell or Pizza Hut in the 1990s ate onions, tomatoes, and lettuce grown and chopped by the Grazianos. Names like Gatto and Rinella still appear on fruit and vegetable trucks in Produce Row, revealing glimmering traces of the neighborhood's past.

Not all of Portland's Italians were in the fruit and vegetable trade. Joe Chiotti came to Portland with a background in baking, a business into which his wife, Marcella, had been born. One might say that bread was in Marcella Chiotti's DNA; she was the great-great-granddaughter of baker Michelangelo Dompè, whose family bakery has been continually operating in Piedmont, Italy, since 1687.[59] When Marcella married Joe in 1903, she was unable take over her family's business, because women were not allowed to inherit property. Instead, the newlyweds came to Portland, where Joe's brother Alessio was the president of a baking company. Joe went to work for Alessio, and in 1915 the Chiotti brothers opened the New French Bakery at SE Hawthorne St and Grand Ave. Joe and Marcella's sons opened Pierre's French Bakery in 1932. (Because of ongoing anti-Italian racism, many bakeries at the time added "French" to their names to illustrate the European nature of their product, but most "French" bakeries were actually filled with Italian bakers.) Joe and Marcello's grandson, Dean Chiotti, took over Pierre's in the 1970s before opening his own bakery, Alessio's, named after his uncle. Marcella's great-great-granddaughter, Sarah Willett, works at this bakery, where bread is still made from the 1687 Dompè family recipe.

Santo "Sam" Porco was another well-known baker in Portland. He grew up in South Portland, the child of Calabrian immigrants, and after wooing a dark-eyed girl into marriage with the power of his cakes, he opened a bakery next door to the SP Meat Market on SE 21st and Powell. From the little storefront where a bike shop and kung-fu studio sit today, SP Bakery produced bread, cakes, cookies, and pastries. Because of its location a few blocks from the Brooklyn rail yard, the bakery and meat market had been given the name "SP" by its previous owner to cater to the needs of Southern Pacific railroad employees who lived in the neighborhood. It was a happy coincidence for Sam Porco that those were also his initials.

Sam Porco was the toast of the town, and baked for the highest-profile clientele, including the mayor. Porco was beloved by neighborhood children for his habit of passing out free samples. He gave the little girls gentle pinches on the cheeks and dazzled them with promises to bake their wedding cakes one day. His kindness paid off when those girls returned at the bakery doorstep as young women with new sparkle on their fingers, asking Porco to make good on his word.[60] "There are quite a few families in Portland where I've made wedding cakes for three generations of brides," he recalled in 1978.[61] It was not just wedding cakes that Porco excelled at; he also baked birthday cakes for the children of Portland's upper crust, including the governor of Oregon. He transitioned away from baking and into food inspection in the late 1950s, but even after he retired he had a miniature replica of his bakery built in the basement of his SE Portland home. In 1978, at the age of seventy-one, he came out of retirement to help restaurant Yaw's Top Notch improve their baked goods.

Although most of the Italian restaurants in Portland were opened in the 1970s (during a period of growing national appreciation for Italian-American cuisine), a few earlier restaurants managed to appeal to a broad enough audience to survive to this day. In 1949, Joe Fracasso and his partner, Ken Baker, opened Portland's first pizza joint, Caro Amico, in a three-story Victorian on Barbur Boulevard at the edge of old South Portland. It was originally intended to be a speakeasy, but new mayor Dorothy McCullough Lee (Portland's first female mayor) had won the election on promises to "clean up" the city, and she put the kibosh on speakeasies and gambling houses because these establishments had a tendency toward debauching women. Fracasso and Baker had no choice but to create a restaurant instead. Baker's sons joined the business in the 1950s, but Jack Baker left in 1959 to open "The Pizza House" Amalfi's in NE Portland. In 1963, when the neighborhood was in the midst of the urban renewal project that demolished fifty-four blocks of South Portland to make room for Keller Auditorium and I-405 (displacing hundreds of Jewish and Italian families and businesses), Caro Amico's three-story house burned down. The new building, constructed fifty years ago, is a wonderful testament to mid-century architecture a-go-go and still serves pizza and other Italian-American specialties.

MEXICANS—SUGAR BEETS AND TACO TRUCKS

Unlike other immigrant groups, there was never one big deluge of His-
panics to the city of Portland. Because of the shared border with Mexico,
migration north had rather been a steady stream of people coming and
going as needed to seek work and other opportunities. There were already
Mexican cowboys (*vaqueros*) in Oregon when Ewing Young brought
cattle to the state in the 1830s. As Oregon was still on the Mexican border
at the time, it was from Mexico that the cattle came in the first place.

By the late nineteenth century, Portland was actively engaged in trade
with San Francisco, and food trends traveled both ways. To the delight of
Portland's thrill-seeking gastronomes, tamales made their way north by
the mid-1890s. Tamale parlors—a trend with which Mexicans had little
to do—originated in San Francisco in the 1880s, and the eateries were
warmly embraced in Portland. The first *tamaleros* in San Francisco were
typically Mexican street vendors and sold steaming-hot tamales from tin
kettles on the street, but Portland did not have roaming Mexicans selling
freshly made tamales until a century later. The tamales hawked in Portland parlors were a purely gringo affair, having been diluted through San
Francisco parlors for ten years before heading north. According to advertisements in the local papers, most tamale parlors at the turn of the century were in the oyster business, as well; tamales seemed to be a hot item
that oyster saloons were happy to tack on to their menus. The Mobile was
an oyster and tamale parlor on SW 3rd and Yamhill that not only served
tamales and oysters with crawfish "cooked in the best of wines," but also
included private dining rooms for ladies. [62]

In 1905, the interest in Mexican cuisine had expanded beyond tidy,
husk-wrapped packages. The Portland Tamale Parlor, located on SW
Park between Alder and Morrison, was "the only place in town where
enchiladas [and] chile con carne with frijoles, Mexican style ... are
made." [63] It was also the location where "the celebrated Fritz's tamales"
were made, so it is uncertain whether the tamales were made by a German
cook or if Mexican cooks took German nicknames. Pleas for "a good
Mexican cook" certainly did appear in Portland newspaper want ads at
the time. [64]

By the 1910s, while revolutionaries were leading an uprising in Mexico, Portland housewives were clamoring for "hot Mexican tamale" and
"real chile con carne" recipes. [65] In 1912, a woman from Lents (still its

own town at the time) wrote to Lilian Tingle of *The Oregonian* wanting one, but with the added request that it be the real deal. "I would like the genuine Mexican article, if possible, but do the best you can, please."[66] The three different recipes provided, which Miss Tingle obtained from a "genuine Mexican," were somewhat more complicated than an earlier one published by the cooking expert, adding chopped peppers, onions, boiled eggs, and olives to the sauce and chicken mix. Adding to their air of ethnic authenticity, they also featured considerably more garlic and tabasco sauce.

Recipes for tamales and chile con carne were also featured in *The All-Western Conservation Cook Book* (1917).[67] Early recipes called for regular cornmeal instead of the *masa harina*, which has been slaked with lime to break down the corn's cell walls. Slaking the corn also allows the masa to bind to itself nicely to make dough, and improves the corn's nutritional value, preventing diseases like pellagra. Using regular cornmeal would have yielded a disappointingly crumbly exterior, but otherwise, the Americanized recipe was somewhat traditional, calling for a filling of chopped, poached chicken in a chile-spiked tomato sauce, and tying the husk at both ends as seen in the tamales of San Francisco.

The Mexican Revolution (1910–1917), which ultimately resulted in the Mexican Constitution, also created widespread poverty for its citizens, which increased immigration to Oregon as people sought work.[68] Thus began what would become a long pattern of the United States treating Mexicans as a temporary labor pool; immigration increased during World War I when the United States needed men to fill the empty spaces left by soldiers. In 1924 this freedom of migration ended when the US Border Patrol was created, and without work available, the Great Depression further reduced immigration. Immigration picked up again during the Second World War, but this time policies were put in place to remind Mexicans that their stay was temporary. Nonetheless, with the creation of the Bracero Program during World War II, American employers—largely sugar beet farmers—were allowed to hire Mexicans during emergency labor shortages. Mexicans quickly became Oregon's primary agricultural workforce (which was convenient, since Japanese farmers had all been rounded up and shipped off to Idaho).

The Bracero Program essentially allowed American land owners to import Mexican laborers and then unceremoniously dismiss them back to Mexico when they were no longer needed. The program was renewed in

1951, and since most Japanese Portlanders did not return to farm work after the war, Mexican immigrants and Mexican Americans maintained their roles as the leading agricultural workforce. However, the rhythms of daily life were interrupted as Latino communities searched for a sense of place. "During the 1950s and '60s, Oregon's Latino communities were small and isolated and had difficulties maintaining traditional life," explain folklorists Nancy Nusz and Gabriella Ricciardi.[69] Women had real difficulty preparing traditional foods, because key ingredients simply were not available so far from home. At a time when Van Camps canned tamales or Rosarita complete four-can Mexican dinners were the only option, many Mexican women had little choice but to make their own tortillas.

Cooking advice columns aimed at "business girls, working women and busy mothers" continued to rally for Mexican dishes both as time savers and affordable family-pleasers.[70] However, the "cornmeal pancakes called tortillas" were still elusive and required explanation.[71] By 1952, a few Mexican food companies that sold canned tortillas began to gain placement in Portland grocery stores, and bagged tortillas like those seen in modern grocery stores appeared a few years later. Home cooks would still have to import *masa harina* from California for another twenty years, when grocery stores began selling it.

Postwar tourism to Mexico had increased the American palate for authentic Mexican foods, and by the 1950s, Portlanders were ready to move beyond packaged supermarket dinners. *The Oregonian* ran Associated Press stories from Mexico City, including one on how to use "The Gourmet Touch," using fascinating new foods like tortillas.[72] "The tortilla, a thin, round toasted sheet of unleavened corn flour, is standard," explained the report. Newly educated gourmands would have been shocked to continue reading; they would have learned about such traditional dishes as *gusanos*, the fat grubs that feed on the Maguey cactus.

Mexican restaurants began popping up all over the city in the 1950s. Among the first authentic eateries was the Del-Mar Club on SW Barbur Boulevard. The chef was half-Mexican and half-Scottish, going by the name "Don Miguel," and he went to great pains to avoid Americanizing his food. He could not abide chili con carne made with hamburger instead of "good, honest beef"; he ground his own corn on a *metate* stone and made the tortillas in-house.[73] The tongue-searing hot sauce "was purely extracurricular," but would have been a far cry from the tabasco-laden ketchup seen in most Mexican-American food at the time.[74] Don Miguel made his own salsa using chiles he imported from Los Angeles. His ultimate goal, he relayed to the papers, was to see his customers "swathed in red and white checked bibs, using their fists to shove in tacos and tostadas."[75]

Soon, Portland had restaurants peppered throughout town, like Estrellita on SE 25th and Clinton. Although the restaurant has been the location of hipster dive paradise Dot's Café since the early-1990s' grunge era, the velvet damask walls reveal the original establishment's Spanish flair. Estrellita (meaning "little star") had been named after the wildly popular singer and flamenco dancer Estrellita Castro, whose popularity reached its heights in the 1930s and 1940s. The menu featured not only the familiar tacos and tamales, but the relatively exotic quesadillas and chiles rellenos.

The Immigration Act of 1990 sought to tighten the limits on legal immigration to the United States, but resulted in an increase in the number of visas granted, mainly for employment and to reunite families.[76] Portland's historically low Mexican immigrant population experienced a surge during the 1990s.[77] Today, Latinos make up Oregon's largest minority group. Besides the Hispanic-owned taco trucks, *supermercados* (supermarkets), *panaderias* (bakeries), *carnicerias* (meat markets), and neighborhood bodegas serving the residents of Hillsboro and the Lents and other outer East Portland neighborhoods, national-chain supermarkets in the inner city reflect the growing presence and culinary traditions of Hispanic families. Mainstream supermarkets often have an entire row dedicated to Hispanic foods and sell a dozen different varieties of dried and fresh chiles, crinkly bags of fragrant spices, canned salsas, and *dulce de leche*. Some even sell hard-to-find items like fresh chickpeas still in the pod.

Other fresh produce is available directly from local farmers. Lents International Farmers Market, which began in 1999, is Portland's only farmers market with a focus on international foods, primarily uncommon Hispanic herbs, as well as Southeast Asian and Russian heirloom vegetables.

Over the past decade, Portlanders have come to enjoy the rise of food cart cuisine, the earliest of which came from the *taqueria* trucks scattered throughout the city's industrial areas. For a buck or so apiece, taco trucks catered to hungry workers on their lunch breaks by serving legitimate tacos—not the U-shaped Frito filled with hamburger and iceberg lettuce, but warm corn tortillas topped with highly seasoned, flattop-grilled meats, minced onions, and a few sprigs of cilantro served with a wedge of lime and a little plastic tub of homemade hot sauce. While taco trucks certainly did not originate in Portland (nor were tacos the first food to be sold from carts), their ubiquity launched an entire style of cooking and eating for which Portland has become nationally renowned.

SOUTHEAST ASIAN—PAD THAI AND PHO

Escaping political upheaval (and in many cases, atrocious human rights violations) in 1975, refugees from Laos (including Hmong and Mien or Yao people), Cambodia, and Vietnam began to arrive in the United States, many of them settling in Portland. After the initial first wave of immigrants (primarily well-educated Vietnamese and to a lesser extent, Laotian and Cambodian refugees), the second and third wave arrived in the early 1980s, largely settling in the Rose City Park and Roseway neighborhoods along Sandy Boulevard, as well as the Montavilla and Hosford-Abernethy neighborhoods.[78] Today, Vietnamese Americans represent the city's largest group of Asians; in fact, Portland has one of the largest populations of Vietnamese in the United States.

It did not take long for Vietnamese immigrants to put down roots in their new home, and for many, restaurants were the first step in attaining the American dream. With over three hundred Vietnamese and Thai restaurants in the city, Southeast Asian immigrants have had the most visible impact on the way Portlanders eat, at least in the past few decades.

By 1978, after a very short settling-in period, Portland already had at least one Vietnamese restaurant and market; Mai Restaurant on NE 58th and Glisan attracted diners with a menu of Vietnamese and French dishes, a blend of cultures that arose from the long history of French colonization in the tropical country. For those who preferred cooking at home, Viet-Nam Market on NE 40th and Tillamook offered refugees a chance to prepare the foods of their war-torn homeland. Thanh Truc Restaurant opened a year later on SE 12th and Powell, near a small community of Brooklyn neighborhood Laotian refugees.

By the early 1980s, there were a handful more markets and restaurants opened by Vietnamese, Cambodian, and Laotian immigrants. Thanh The on NE 68th and Sandy served traditional Vietnamese fare without the French influence. The most popular dish, according to owner, Van Ly, was the *my tho*—a hearty soup with rice noodles, shrimp, and Chinese-style barbecued pork, topped with bean sprouts and peanuts for crunch.[79] In 1984, the restaurant was sold and reopened as Yến Hà Restaurant and Lounge, which still serves an eight-page menu of traditional Vietnamese offerings.

Southeast Asians adapted well to Portland's temperate climate and its botanical offerings. Refugee children in the early 1980s played Chinese jump rope with their American neighbors; they climbed the same neighborhood fruit trees searching for free snacks. The Lao saying, *"van pen lom; khom pen yan,"* means "sweet makes you dizzy; bitter makes you healthy," and was further translated into Portlandese by the use of foraged, unripe plums to make a modified *tam maak hoong*—the spicy, shredded salad traditionally made with green papaya.

In the mid-1980s, just as the *New York Times* declared Thai food to be the Next Big Thing, Thai restaurants joined the scene. Although Thais immigrated in much smaller numbers than other SE Asians, Khmer and Lao cuisine bears many similarities to Thai food, and many of Portland's Thai restaurants were likely run by Cambodians and Laotians.

Whereas Northeast Portland was where Vietnamese refugees settled, Beaverton's tech jobs drew a larger Thai population. The first Thai market, Lamthong, opened in 1980 at the location now anonymously named "Asia Supermarket," across the street from a bakery that has been in operation since 1925. Twenty years before Pok Pok drew crowds with its sticky-garlicky hot wings and drinking vinegars, Portlanders lined up for lemongrass-slathered pork satay, basil-laced coconut curries, and silken pad thai noodles at Tara Thai on NW 23rd. The restaurant has continued to serve the same Thai and Lao menu for three decades, whereas most other Southeast Asian restaurants have been much more ephemeral, either shifting location or closing entirely.

By the 1990s, there was an explosion of Vietnamese restaurants in Portland. Signs depicting beautiful maidens wearing mandarin-collared tunics and conical straw hats became ubiquitous, and if the sign included an illustration of a cow, diners knew the house specialty: phở. The rich oxtail broth scented with star anise and charred shallot beckoned, and for only a few dollars, diners could eat their fill of chewy rice noodles and thinly sliced beef that cooked in the heat of the fragrant broth. In most places, the phở menu is split; shaved brisket and rib eye for the average American diner, and tendon and tripe for those craving the real deal. The giant bowls arrive with a plate of cooling bean sprouts, wedges of lime, and sliced jalapeños, plus a pile of fresh herbs like Thai basil and culantro—a flat, jagged-edged herb related to cilantro, but with more peppery bite. Portland was smitten.

Like the Chinese who came a century earlier, the Hmong in Portland often engage in urban vegetable gardening, growing a range of Asian produce. Although they are not a very populous people, their small enclaves are apparent at a glance. One garden in SE Portland appears to have been built upon an apartment complex parking lot; the asphalt has been chipped out and tilled with rich soil, its perimeters dug and churned to produce rows of birds'-eye chiles. The center of the garden plot features a tall, ramshackle trellis draped in luffa gourds, scarlet runner beans, and chayote squash, and borders of potted taro are interspersed with cannas, daisies and dahlias bearing flowers as big as one's head.

By not placing the same value on traditional cooking (or intentionally abandoning foods from their homeland to blend in), some Portland immigrants have assimilated more quickly. While that certainly yielded some benefit, the loss of one's cuisine is the loss of cultural continuity. By being in the business of preparing traditional foods, either for profit or personal use, some immigrants have been better equipped to maintain ties to their heritage in ways that others perhaps cannot.

5

TO MARKET, TO MARKET

Going Grocery Shopping

In the 1850s, Portland was, in the words of Belgian gold-seeker Jean-Nicolas Perlot, "nothing but a warehouse."[1] Perlot's assessment was fairly accurate; in Portland's toddler years, merchants and stumps were aplenty, but refinement was yet burgeoning. Before the Transcontinental Railroad made it to the West Coast, it took nearly five months for goods to make it to Oregon, sailing from New York Harbor, around Cape Horn in South America, and up to San Francisco, so food products were never very fresh unless they were produced locally. Because of this fact, most merchants dealt in dry goods and liquor wholesaling in town, or got rich selling timber and wheat to San Francisco. This was fine for the bachelors who dominated the town; they could always just eat out. But if Portland was ever going to become the gleaming metropolis of the Pacific Northwest, it needed merchants to set up shop and put down roots.

In 1857, the Belgian Perlot had given up gold prospecting for the gardening life in Portland. Fortunately for Perlot, he arrived just before the Italian immigrants, and was Portland's first landscape gardener, establishing flower and vegetable gardens for the city's wealthy black-thumbs. He also grew astounding amounts of produce, which he sold directly to Alexander Ankeny, who, in addition to being a steamship builder and sea captain, was one of Portland's first grocers.

MERCHANT PRINCES TAKE REIGN

Technically speaking, Francis Pettygrove—the man who famously won the coin flip to name Portland instead of Boston—owned the first store in town. It was a log cabin in the forest, located on the waterfront near today's SW Naito Parkway and Washington. Pettygrove did a brisk business from 1845, after he finally convinced a carpenter to tolerate the mosquitos and fleas long enough to construct the log building, to around 1847, when the Gold Rush changed everything. For a few years, all the able-bodied men left town to get rich in the Sierra Nevada (some accounts say only three men remained), but Pettygrove stayed put and developed a tidy monopoly on the town's business. By 1848, after more than one shady business deal that left him on the outs with his former friend Benjamin Stark, he was one of the wealthiest men in the territory.

Pettygrove's heart was not really in groceries, though. He sought greener pastures, and after burning a few bridges, he resettled in Washington with the intention of creating a new mega-city that would dwarf Portland. Port Townsend, where he eventually died in 1887, never even came close.

Lucius Allen came to Portland in 1850, on behalf of New York wholesale merchant John DeWitt. He opened a store next door to Couch & Co., visible in the very first photograph taken in the Pacific Northwest. Allen, DeWitt, & Company closed after only one dolorous month of business. DeWitt cut Allen, replacing him with Cicero Lewis, a childhood friend of Allen's who had come to Portland at the same time. By 1853, DeWitt was out of the picture and the two chums had their own store on Front and Burnside. They had built their business by nurturing loyalty, keeping firm on fair prices, and offering goods of interest to Native Americans. Within thirty years, Allen & Lewis became one of the largest grocery wholesalers in the Pacific Northwest, although neither man has a street named after him to prove it.

Henry Corbett also arrived in 1851, opening a white clapboard storefront on Front and Oak. Thomas Pritchard, whose store is also seen in early Portland photographs, sold coffee, candy, spices, and dried apples, along with baskets likely provided by the Chinook women camped in the Douglas-fir thickets still surrounding the one-street town. Next door, a man named Baker stayed true to his name and ran a bakery with his partner, Clark. There was a butcher shop that also sold hides to the tannery, and a few dry goods stores.

William Ladd had opened a liquor store in the spring of 1851, but sales were so sluggish during those first, muddy months that he could not even afford to pay his $6 property tax. He had to earn the money by digging stumps out of the street. After he paid his tax bill by completing a public works project, business picked up and he soon added groceries to his store. Selling chicken, eggs, and produce from the farms in the Tualatin Valley helped him gain a foothold, and then a stroke of great luck occurred when his father's friend W.D. Gookin arrived with a ship full of goods to sell on consignment. Now Ladd was a one-stop shop, selling his own fresh foods and liquor alongside tobacco, shaving soap, and paper, plus blasting powder and farm tools to help other newcomers clear more of the town. In only five months, his revenues exceeded $1,000—equivalent to around $30,000 in 2014.[2] In a year, he tripled that.

Unlike Portland's so-called merchant princes (those men for whom several of today's streets are named), John Wilson, a former clerk for Lewis and Allen, had achieved some success without financial backing from his friends and family.[3] He bought a business from Corbett's former partners in 1856, and began selling dry goods and groceries like so many merchants before him. However, he took a different tack; instead of relying solely on Tualatin Plains goods, he began trade routes to the Willamette Valley, as far south as the Umpqua River. Wagons full of fresh eggs and butter, slabs of bacon and ripe fruits and vegetables ambled up Scholls Ferry Road to bring the wholesome goodness of the Willamette Valley to the mean city streets. Historian E. Kimbark MacColl reported that Wilson slept on the second floor of the store with an "old iron club" in case thieves tried to break in.[4]

The grocery store was successful enough that Wilson was able to move into a new building on First a year later—the first commercial building west of the waterfront. By 1870, he moved into an even grander brick building on Third, going into partnership with William Parker Olds. Realizing that further business expansion was somewhat hampered by the limitations of domestic and foreign trade in Portland, Wilson eventually sold his business to Olds, who would slowly grow the company into a five-story department store. The Olds, Wortman, & King building still stands on SW 9th and Morrison, and is the home to Le Cordon Bleu College of Culinary Arts.

ANKENY'S MARBLE PALACE

Portland's first merchants had begun with good enough intentions; they wanted to get the city up and running, and provide the goods to the people who would build. The 1853 plat map by Captain T. O. Travailliot, created two years after the city's incorporation, designated an entire two blocks to a public market.[5] One of these blocks, Market Block (Block 132), would eventually become the site of two marketplaces, but it took two decades, even though the people of Portland were clamoring for a place that would allow them to engage in business directly with producers. They wanted to avoid the trouble of having to spend all day shopping at several different stores, all while getting gouged by retail middlemen who were wont to change their prices on a whim.[6]

Captain Alexander Ankeny was a natural pick to start the city's first public market. He had arrived to Portland in 1850, just ahead of Ladd and Corbett. After dabbling in various enterprises for a few years, he opened a meat market in 1856, and then began selling produce once Perlot started growing it. As a successful businessman, he understood what it took to build a marketplace, and he also had the capital to back up his ideas. In 1868, he began drafting plans to build the Ankeny Block on land he owned near the river, on today's First and Ankeny, and in early October of 1872, when Portland was at its loveliest, the New Market and Theater was complete. It was a thing of beauty; it was hailed as "an architectural ornament to the city."[7]

The high-ceilinged and gas-lit New Market and Theater, better known as the Central Market, included twenty-eight stalls for a variety of food retailers. Marble arches, grand columns, octagonal mirrors, and potted palms interspersed the rows of berry baskets and paper-wrapped pork chops. One market stall sold cordials and liquors, another butter and lard, and yet another pastries, bread, and crackers; indulgent luxuries and pragmatic household staples were presented unblinkingly side by side. Against a frescoed wall, other vendors sold fresh salmon, cleaning the fish right behind a neat partition to hide unsightly mess and odor, presenting the coral-pink fillets on cool marble counters. One purveyor even sold fresh venison and live game birds. It was an epicurean wonderland.

Its glittering success was short-lived, however; by the mid-1880s, Portland's residential areas began to expand outside the urban core to the new "suburbs" west of Nineteenth Street. Businesses had to follow them or fail, but a large, centralized market could not easily pick up and resettle in the suburbs, so Central Market opened its doors to other ventures. By the end of the decade, the ornate brick palace was a sales floor for farm tools.[8]

After a few years without a public market, Frank Dekum—an unlikely combination of confectioner and banker—opened a new public bazaar in the Market Block, occupying an abandoned pavilion. Unfortunately, this pavilion was abandoned once more by 1895, and in 1911 the building was razed to build the Civic Auditorium.

"A HOPELESSLY INSANITARY STATE"

With a central market no longer in operation, Portland shoppers were once again left to shop at smaller neighborhood markets. This would have been a grand idea, if not for the fact that many of the markets were in dilapidated buildings and left plenty to be desired. Food purity ordinances, on the books since 1851, were rarely enforced. In 1905, when everyone else was getting the city dolled up for the Lewis and Clark Centennial Expo, a few plucky householders decided it was time to take action regarding the insalubrious condition of Portland's markets. The appearance of modern markets across America, with their brightly lit aisles, sparkling glass cases, and fresh foods, is in no small part thanks to the efforts of Portland women more than a century ago.

After journalist Upton Sinclair's exposé on the meatpacking industry of Chicago, meat sanitation was at the front of everyone's minds (leading many to become vegetarian). His articles, which appeared in serial form in 1905 in the socialist magazine *Appeal to Reason*, culminated in the 1906 book *The Jungle* and eventually to the federal Meat Inspection Act of 1906. His intention had been to expose the working conditions of America's factory workers, but the public, including Portlanders, fixated on the issues of food safety presented in the work.

While Sinclair was conducting his undercover research in Chicago's slaughterhouses, Portland was undergoing its own battle with bad meat. In 1902, local reports began to surface of butchers slaughtering hogs that were already half-dead from cholera and selling this meat to the public; arrests were made, and it was discovered that the offender simply made it a practice to kill sick hogs and send them off to Portland. He had never taken precautions to prevent disease in the first place, stating that "the sick ones were as good to kill as any."[9]

Over a three-year period, updated meat and milk inspection ordinances had been introduced by City Council, violently opposed by various meat and dairy retail associations, failed, redrafted, "indefinitely postponed," and eventually passed in 1905.[10] The big slaughterhouses were in favor of regulations that forced the smaller meat retailers to adhere to the same rules that they were forced to follow. This support merely inflamed the resistance. Retail butchers accused the commissioner's office of intentionally bolstering the beef trust. The retail butchers perhaps had a point; the big slaughterhouses, operating in Portland's Kenton neighborhood, were Chicago-based Swift (under the local business name Union Meat Company) and Armour—two of Chicago's three largest meat companies who worked cooperatively to form a monopoly. (Little did anyone in Portland know, but Swift and Armour were soon going under the federal microscope in antitrust proceedings back east.) Whether or not the David-versus-Goliath battleground should be the bowels of Portland's citizens, however, was the issue taken with Commissioner F. W. Mulkey. Inspections needed to happen.

Between 1902 and 1903, more stories emerged. Once the screws were turned on them, some butchers reluctantly admitted that putrid meat was regularly embalmed with borax, salicylic acid, or even, reportedly, formaldehyde to slow decay. Bologna was frequently painted red to make it look fresher, and sausage meat was mixed with iron and other additives to mask putrid odors. It is uncertain if that is a worse practice than selling carcasses with the hides still attached, in order to mask that the animal had already "decomposed an inch deep under the hide," as was the case encountered by one seller.[11] "Of course, I refused to handle them," he offered, "but they were sold and eaten in Portland. I don't wonder that epidemics result from such food."[12]

City ordinances were finally passed in 1905 (still a year ahead of the federal law), but it was not just the meat shops and slaughterhouses that were to blame for Portland's ills. As domestic science expert Lilian Tingle wrote in *Good Housekeeping* in 1907, Portland's neighborhood markets were "often in a hopelessly insanitary state."[13] As might be expected, back alleys and cellars of these business were typically operated without regard to hygiene, but more shockingly, as Tingle reported,

Figure 5.1. Publications like *Puck Magazine* illustrated that bad meat was a national problem in the early 1900s. Courtesy of Library of Congress

Many were open to the street, so that flies, dust, and dogs did damage unchecked; and the late passer-by at night might catch glimpses of rats holding high carnival in the midst of unprotected food material of all kinds. Joints of meat, whole carcasses of sheep and hogs, hanging outside unscreened doors and windows, convened many a fastidious newcomer to vegetarianism. Piles of fruit and vegetables on the pavement made vegetarianism as uninviting; conscientious housekeepers made protest from time to time; but nothing came of it. [14]

Many did, in fact, take up the cause of vegetarianism in response to the tainted meat epidemic, an item that did not escape notice from the papers. A surge in membership in the Oregon Vegetarian Society in 1905 was in direct response to the repulsive state of meat shops. "The plant-eating brethren say kind words for the women crusaders who swooped down on the filthy flesh markets," reported *The Oregonian* in 1905. [15] Vegetable stands were no picnic, either, but at least people would not die from food poisoning after eating lettuce that had half-turned to compost. Portland's vegetarians were smug about the turn of events. "Filth," they said, "is inseparable from flesh." [16] (Blissfully for period vegetarians, the discovery of the pathogenic qualities of spinach-loving *E. coli* was still twenty years away.)

Lilian Tingle did not care much if the meat eaters had it worse than the vegetarians; her unending mission was to clean up fruit stands, bakeries, and butcher shops alike. As the newly appointed chief inspector, she assembled a posse of women from the school of domestic science, accompanied by the secretary of the State Board of Health. The Board's authority granted them access to back rooms and storage areas where customers were typically not admitted. In many places, they found conditions even worse than they had suspected.

Although there was a fair amount of grumbling, some market owners expressed relief that a new standard would be enforced. Whitewashed walls, fly screens, and display cases became the new norm, keeping pastries, cheeses, pickles, and deli foods safe from flies and dust. Refrigerated cases for meat markets became commonplace, whereas not a single one had existed prior. The market inspection committee began circulating flyers to householders to report their findings while out shopping. If a market had sufficiently complied with the new standards, they earned a gold star and a spot on the "clean list." The papers began a regular habit of listing those markets that had received the clean bill of sanitation so women would know where to shop; soon, the theory went, "competitors, for self-protection, will 'breaks their necks,' so to speak, to follow the lead." [17]

Within months, things had improved markedly, and the volunteer inspector was so overwhelmed with work that she had to resign from her post. A full-time inspector, prominent Portland club lady Sarah A. Evans, took her place. (Sarah A. Evans was a member of so many Portland ladies' clubs that she was eventually elected the president of the Oregon Federation of Women's Clubs.) Householders and newspapers were her greatest ally, but without ordinances in place, Evans had no jurisdiction to punish offenders. Some shoppers were still ignorantly shopping from dirty markets, providing little incentive to market owners to make costly improvements. As to the blithe ignorance of these shoppers, Tingle lamented that "women as a rule seem far more careful about the protection and handling of their millinery than of their food material."[18] The problem required a two-pronged attack: an educational campaign in concert with pure foods ordinances.

Lilian Tingle described in *Good Housekeeping* how she urged the women of Portland to take a stand against filthy markets. In doing so, she inspired the entire nation. Tingle's call to arms caused an uproar, and after receiving many letters and inquiries, *Good Housekeeping* declared November 13, 1907, to be National Visiting Day, imploring housewives "throughout the length and breadth of the land" to take to the streets, give their neighborhood markets the old once-over, and to act as the agents of their own cities' market reform.[19] Tingle's words of advice to women seeking change were to make investigations, educate their neighbors, and "keep everlastingly at it."

Some of the suggestions for improving produce markets went a bit far. When interviewed by *The Oregonian*, man-about-town (and future Rosarian) G. M. Hyland demanded that all fruits and vegetables be kept behind glass for the sake of "attractiveness and certainty of hygienic purity. Everybody knows that things in glass look more pleasing to the eye than when scattered pell-mell."[20] Hyland had other humorously grand ideas about how to display vegetables, too, casually suggesting that the best way to present vegetables was in an iron fountain that sprays a fine mist over the produce to keep it clean and fresh. In Hyland's eyes, there could be no happy middle ground for vegetables; they were either in the squalor or on a pedestal. Although his let-them-eat-cake problem-solving approach is charmingly laughable, grocery stores did eventually employ fine misters to keep produce refreshed.

PUBLIC MARKETPLACES

During the city's sweeping market reforms, socialite Rose Hoyt (wife of County Commissioner Ralph Warren Hoyt, for whom the Washington Park arboretum is named) had gone on the record as being in favor of cleaning up markets, but had expressed doubts about the practicality of opening a public market. "I am very certain that an open market place, which has been suggested, would never succeed in Portland," she nay-said. Her reasoning was that "we all have telephones and do nearly all our marketing by telephone." In 1903, only around 10 percent of American households had a telephone; to suggest that everyone simply phoned in orders for grocery delivery was perhaps a bit delusional.

In 1908, when the nation was still up in arms about the "beef trust" among Chicago meat companies, *The Oregonian* published an editorial titled "A Move Toward Monopoly," imploring the city to open a public market on the grounds that Portlanders have the right to buy "clean, cheap, fresh and abundant" produce without resorting to buying from truck gardeners.[21] Italian truck gardeners were already organized and unified in the Italian Ranchers' and Gardeners' Association (IRGA), one of the duties of which was to regulate produce prices.

The best solution against a trust forming among the farmers, who were accused of "demoralizing" prices with their lack of overhead costs (and thereby undercutting retailers), was to open a public market with stalls rented to farmers and other producers at a fair enough rate as to eliminate the need for street vending. Roving vegetable peddlers, begged the editorial, "should not be permitted to obstruct the streets or to annoy house-holders by importunity."[22] Grocery retailers heartily endorsed any measures that would prevent competing vendors from selling produce at a lower rate (and presumably of fresher quality) in the streets directly outside the stores.

Catering to the demands of grocery retailers was certainly a factor, but the bottom line was pleasing those who held the purse strings: housewives. "The home is quite as important as the retail grocery stores," the editorial concluded matter-of-factly.[23] "While we value both, if one must be sacrificed it should not be the home. We should never forget that all these efforts to place the public at the mercy of monopolies are direct blows at the welfare of home and family."[24] Whether Rose Hoyt liked it or not, Portland was once again ready for a centralized public market.

Portland's Italian truck gardeners had already become well established in East Portland by the early 1880s, setting up a string of businesses in Produce Row. They soon founded the IRGA, and after a decade or so on the west side, they moved from a river-addled waterfront building back to the east side to be nearer the growers. By 1908 they had a fully dedicated building, acting as the social and commercial hub for growers and buyers alike. The IRGA's move back to the east side just made Portland's lack of a central marketplace more painfully obvious.

John F. Carroll had come to Portland in August 1903, after having been ousted from a newspaper job in Wyoming. Cattle barons protested his alliance with small cattle ranchers in what was known as the "Rustlers' War." Nonetheless, his background in journalism made it easy to find a job elsewhere, and after a stint in Denver, he soon found himself editing and publishing the Portland paper *The Evening Telegram*. He used the publication as a platform for his ideas for a range of civic projects, eventually culminating in Portland's Rose Festival. As another public service, he openly declared the need for a public market in a 1913 editorial. "We believe no investment could be made that would be of greater general benefit to the whole community than this," Carroll wrote.[25] He gathered up some of his business-minded colleagues, formed the Producers' and Consumers' Public Market Association (PCPMA), and got to work.

"What is wanted is a market without partnership run in the interests of the producer and the consumer," pled one member of the building committee.[26] Another insisted that fairness was key; that there needed to be a standard of honesty in weights and measures. Perhaps most importantly, Portland's housewives—the ones doing the shopping—had been vociferously demanding a clean marketplace that offered fresh, wholesome foods in excellent condition. Food purity and sanitation were still at the front of everyone's minds a decade after the first reports of dirty markets.

After a few years of tireless advocacy, the PCPMA opened its first market in North Portland on Knott Street, between Williams and Albina.[27] Albina Market had its grand opening at the end of April 1914. (One can imagine what a remarkable sight it must have been for the Volga Germans, fresh off the boat from the Old Country, to arrive to their new American home to see a bustling marketplace swollen with bounty— complete with parades—right in their neighborhood.)

The market was the first to serve Portland's east-side shoppers with wares from across town, and was greeted with much fanfare. One woman sold homemade marmalade, and growers from Mount Tabor sold lettuce, potatoes, and spinach. Another vendor sold live chickens, and as an extra-special treat, one farmer promised to bring a fat hog to slaughter and sell right from his wagon.[28] Housewives were urged to ready their shopping baskets; in anticipation, area department stores held a sale on baskets.

Happily, Albina Market had gone gangbusters, and after much celebration, another market was opened a month later on NE Alberta, for children to sell food from school gardens. May of 1914 was a busy month for Portland's public markets; only two weeks after Albina Market's grand opening, *another* one, called the Carroll Public Market, was opened on SW 4th and Yamhill. Yet another parade rang in the market's opening day, and the 35,000 or so shoppers reported to have visited descended on the site like joyful locusts, snapping up nearly every single fruit and vegetable by midafternoon.

The Carroll Public Market (often called Yamhill Market by the papers) had something for every palate; Mayor Albee bought six boxes of strawberries, noted the papers, and other farm-made victuals were equally as tempting: jams and jellies, honey, pastries, buttermilk and cream, fresh and cured meats, in addition to an array of berries and salad fixings. *The Oregonian*'s ceaseless boosterism ultimately led to traffic jams and clamor, but for the time being, Portland could not have been more thrilled. The open-air market had the rustic charisma of European agoras, while offering products of a quality rivaling any of the high-end shops of London or Paris. The prices were affordable for shoppers and the dime-a-day vendor rents were far lower than the overhead on any storefront.

The Carroll Public Market was a stupefying success; so much so that plans immediately began to turn the one-block curbside pop-up into a permanent fixture. Within six weeks, the city commissioner's office was petitioned by the Public Market Board to take the helm.[29] A brick-and-mortar market was surely needed, but in the meantime, new market ordinances, a market master to enforce them, and some shade canopies were direly needed to oversee the 400 or so vendors operating daily. Within only a few months, the market had engulfed several more blocks of downtown real estate, and new sites were explored to find a permanent home large enough to accommodate the market's rapid growth.

Naturally, Carroll Market had its detractors. Retail grocers were irate about losing so much business to the bewitching lure of the festival-like public market. Libertarian market vendors were less than enthusiastic about having to follow new ordinances. And as always, there was the issue of cleanliness. Most complaints were chalked up to garden-variety squabbles between neighbors, but it was simply impossible for the market master and his single assistant to keep up with enforcing all regulations.

Dr. Esther Pohl Lovejoy, the ardent supporter of food sanitation reform who had successfully lobbied to enforce visitation on dairies by health inspectors (rather than just winking food commissioners), was on the job at Alberta Market to assist farmers and sellers, and to ensure food safety. But by 1919, problems with Portland's markets once again surfaced, and ever-vigilant, women once again rallied for reform. This time, the suggestion was to hire a new market master and two women to replace the market master's assistant.

After about fifteen years in operation, agitation arose to relocate the busy market. Congestion along Yamhill was unbearable. By the 1920s, there was new urgency to move the Carroll Public Market when plans for the Morrison Bridge construction were revealed to include an access point on Yamhill Street. The city had five years to find a new home for the market, and after weighing the various options, the riverfront was finally selected. The privately held Public Market Company of Portland stepped up to the plate with offers of substantial capital for building a new facility, much to the chagrin of the Yamhill Market Producers' Association, who had concerns that the privatization of the city-run Market would eat into individual producers' profits. The whole affair, which dragged on for years, was heavily politicized. Threats flew; name-calling ensued. Portland sat divided.

PORTLAND PUBLIC MARKET

Regardless of the built-up animosities, finally, on December 15, 1933, "Portland's Marvelous New Million-Dollar Market" was opened on "Portland's new $2,000,000 seawall" on the waterfront, spanning 620 feet between the Hawthorne and Morrison Bridges.[30] *The Oregonian* ran a four-page center spread that could scarcely convey the city's jubilance. Exclamation points abounded. The opening reception featured "plenty of music and fun!" (thanks in no small part to Slim Taft's twenty-one-piece swing band), "galaxies of lights!" and "entertainment every breathless, surprising hour!"[31]

Portland Public Market, also known as the Sea Wall Market, was touted as America's largest and "History's Greatest Food Market" by Max Zimmerman in his 1937 book, *Super Market: Spectacular Exponent of Mass Distribution*.[32] Adding to the original Yamhill Market's European appeal, the shopping aisles in the new Portland Public Market were given names taken directly from the famous markets of Europe: Rue St.

Figure 5.2.   Opened in 1933, "Portland's Marvelous Million Dollar Market" (aka Portland Public Market) was eventually torn down to create Tom McCall Waterfront Park. Courtesy of Library of Congress

Germain, Covent Gardens Road, and Belfre Lane hearkened back to Paris, London, and Bruges.[33]

There were beauty parlors and flower shops in addition to "the nation's longest counter of fine foods."[34] The refrigeration and storage cellars, the ad gleefully noted, were completely insect- and vermin-proof. Most sensationally, Portland Market had its "own unique *sugar mill*—a miracle of modern science—where automatic scales controlled by photo-electric eyes weigh sugar to within 1-1000th of a pound accurately!"[35]

The Market was an astonishing city of food. It boasted twelve bakeries, ten creameries, seven meat markets, six delis, eight seafood stalls, another dozen produce stalls, four pickle shops, and seven stalls for treats like candy, popcorn, and nuts; stalls from the best stores around town could now all be visited in one convenient location. Within those market walls, Zimmerman effused, one could "discover every conceivable food product. It was theirs to satisfy and enjoy every wish, every caprice and every appetite in food. . . . The good things to eat are spread out in a delightful panoply."[36] Zimmerman's praise did not stop there. He continued in almost frothing adulation:

> Even Epicurus who wrote with gusto of the delights of the palate as a satisfaction for the soul, never walked into a garden so heavily laden with delicious delicacies as was the great Public Market. Perhaps he dreams of a land like Oregon with this myriad of tasty viands which has found their way to the counters of this modern food edifice. [37]

The Market was not just a food emporium; it was an entire shopping mall inside a four-story, 220,000-square-foot glittering palace of a building, and a complete game-changer for Portland's housewives. It featured an auditorium with a fully equipped modern kitchen for cooking demos; there was a Home Economics Department to help uninspired shoppers with menu planning, "Handy Ann" shopping carts with quiet, rubber tires to convey one's purchases about the market, and uniformed assistants to help carry purchases to one's car when the shopping day was done. A day at the market was no longer the housewife's doldrums. Market day was now, as Zimmerman put it, "a social holiday."

Although it had been the toast of the town from the get-go, the Portland Market seems to have been something of a flash in the pan. It never really took hold as anything but a novelty, and only a few short years later, the Market was already struggling to secure vendors and attract shoppers. By the time Portland began rounding up Japanese internees and setting up shipbuilding yards at Swan Island, Portland Public Market was shuttered, eventually ceasing operations only a decade after it had opened. One great mistake identified by early critics was that it had launched during the Depression. Another is that it had opened on the west bank of the river when Portland was largely developing residentially on the east side and its commercial growth was expanding westward instead of along the waterfront. The grand building was rented out to the United States Navy before becoming the new headquarters of the *Oregon Journal* in 1948. In 1969, following Governor Tom McCall's lead to convert Portland's waterfront into a public park, the building was demolished.

During the years of squabbling before Portland Public Market had been built, Hollywood Arcade Public Market had quietly opened in December 1931, one building west of the Hollywood Theater on NE 41st and Sandy Boulevard. The Hollywood Arcade Market was the first in Portland to offer the open-air feel of the previous markets with the luxury of curbside service for the time-strapped and around-the-clock hours of operation in some of the Arcade's stores. Although the Hollywood Arcade had opened to "throngs of housewives" still desperate for a new shopping experience, the thrill was short-lived. Once Portland Public Market was up and running, even curb service and twenty-four-hour operation were no match for the new belle of the ball. By the 1940s, when Portland was closing its grandest public market, the Hollywood Arcade was largely used for office space until it closed for good at the end of the century.

SUPERMARKETS AND CHAIN STORES

Neighborhood markets never lost their popularity the way a centralized mega-mart like Portland Public Market had. After the war, with suburbs bubbling out from the simmering urban core, the neighborhood supermarket reclaimed its place in the hearts of Portland's housewives.

In the early days of Portland's neighborhood groceries, merchants typically operated on credit and provided delivery service. Shoppers indicated what items they wanted, and these items were collected by a clerk or an assistant working behind the counter, who would then wrap them up. Tidy, brown paper packages tied up with jute twine were the cherry on top of what was, for some women, a pleasant social excursion out of the house.

All that fuss and attention, though a treat, was expensive and time-consuming. One had little choice but to stand there and wait patiently for her groceries to be wrapped, or pay even more to have them delivered if she could not be bothered to stand there tapping her fingernails. The traditional mode of payment was to put everything on store credit and then settle up at the end of the month. Be they spendthrifty or just down on their luck, many families accrued more debt than they could afford to pay when the grocery bill arrived.

The 1910s saw the birth of chain grocery stores nationwide; because they operated on a cash-only basis (and thanks to the spread of the automobile, which eliminated the need for delivery), they enjoyed an explosion in the 1920s. By the 1930s, the chain store had hit its zenith, with nearly half of all American groceries being sold from chain stores.[38] Whereas independent stores were owned by Portland shoppers' friends and neighbors, many chain stores were owned by outside interests. For

Figure 5.3. Typical of neighborhood markets in 1910, August Storz Grocery on N Williams and NE Thompson sold groceries on credit and delivered to neighborhood households. Courtesy of City of Portland Archives, Oregon, A2004-002.791

better or worse, independent stores granted credit; chain stores were strictly "cash and carry."

In 1915, independent grocery retailers in Portland, Oregon, formed the wholesale grocers' cooperative United Grocers, a few years ahead of the arrival Portland's first chain store. With the unification came the benefits typically enjoyed by only chains: combined buying power and economies of scale. Later, when the country was gripped by the Great Depression, Pacific Mercantile Cooperative formed to develop affordable store brands that would allow United Grocers' independent retailers to compete with national chain brands. The brand Western Family Foods (based in the Portland suburb of Tigard) was established by Pacific Mercantile Cooperative thirty years later, and is still the major store brand offered by Portland's independent grocers like Zupan's and New Seasons.

In 1920, Portland got its first taste of chain store shopping when Canadian merchant Ross McIntyre moved to Portland to open his Twentieth Century grocery stores, triggering an inundation of chain stores in the city. A year later, Marion Skagg relocated from American Falls, Idaho, to a pretty Alameda neighborhood bungalow, and opened four new Skaggs United stores all at once, resulting in the takeover of the independent store Freeman grocery and a well-established coffee company.[39] Portland, said Skagg, was "a city with a future and second to none in the country," in the process casting an invitation to widespread commercial encroachment. Piggly Wiggly opened two stores in Portland a few months later, introducing the concept of self-service shopping to the city. The deviation from full-service groceries was at first a welcome change. Piggly Wiggly was the first store to feature checkout lines, price-mark each item in the store, and as a result of the decreased service, charge lower prices.

The Skaggs United stores also differed from the independent stores of Portland in that they did not operate on credit, which had a reputation of driving families deep into debt and increased the costs of basic goods for everyone. MacMarr stores further improved the shopping experience by offering clear glass refrigerator cases to allow shoppers to "look within the refrigerator space and see all the perishable foods on display" before making a selection, and by offering drive-in service in addition to the still-new self-service (though presumably, not at the same time).

By 1926, while still living in Portland, Skagg merged his stores with Los Angeles–based Sam Seelig stores, which had been freshly renamed

"Safe-Way." This decisive move, while bold, was completely dwarfed by that of Ross McIntyre's. In 1929, *The Oregonian* announced a major change to Portland's retail landscape. "Huge Chain Store System Born Here," read the headlines, to reveal the merger of McIntyre's ninety-eight Twentieth Century stores with the hundred or so stores owned by Charles Marr, as well as dozens of other stores each owned by various grocery men throughout the West.[40] MacMarr Stores, Inc., was a multimillion-dollar, 396-store grocery super-group. In 1931, MacMarr merged with Safeway. By the time McIntyre died in 1947, not only had he started an entirely new chain of stores (Columbia Food Stores), but his MacMarr chain operated 3,000 stores in the western United States.

As the nation was slipping into the Depression, the temptation to buy from chains that offered better prices was too great for many Portlanders, and chain stores rapidly took over smaller neighborhood stores. This emerging trend did not escape the notice of independent retailers. The 1926 merger between Skaggs United and California-based Sam Seelig Company as well as the one in 1929 between MacMarr and Piggly Wiggly had both been brokered by Charles Merrill (of Merrill Lynch), which raised some hackles. Profits generated by these stores were bleeding out of the local community and into the pockets of Wall Street fat cats, the critics noted, and although there would be local jobs provided in the stores, the work was typically unskilled labor that contributed little to the long-term vitality of neighborhoods. The affronts to economic equity and social justice were too much for Portlanders to swallow. Soon, the chain stores' critics got organized.

"The anti-chain-store movement made strong inroads in the state of Oregon, where traditions of independent business and hostility to outside control had long existed," wrote historian David A. Horowitz.[41] An anti-chain crusade began in 1931 when the Independent Business Men and the Western Merchants and Manufacturers' Association sponsored a bill to begin taxing chain stores a certain dollar amount for each store they held in the city. Pacific Northwest radio stations ran broadcasts backing the fight, given by popular anti-chain store propagandist Montaville Flowers.

Flowers was invited to speak at a Portland rally given by the Western Merchants' and Manufacturers' Association and wrote an inflammatory book on the subject of how chains were destroying the country. *America Chained; A Discussion of "What's Wrong With the Chain Store"* (1931), which included an entire chapter on the "Portland Fights," called chain stores both a voracious predator, "insatiable like a great tiger," and a marauding "parasite" that fed upon the community's very social foundations (including churches and schools).[42] The chain store, in Flowers's eyes, was a Leviathan hell-bent on global domination. "Its god is money, its process is annihilation, its purpose is to master the world. That's what's wrong with the chain system and that's enough."[43]

Although Flowers was a Republican, chain stores had their detractors on both sides. Democrat Robert G. "Fightin' Bob" Duncan (who called himself "The Oregon Wildcat") was a Ku Klux Klan–backed, anti-Catholic diatribe-machine of a man. He got on the anti-chain soapbox at around the same time as Flowers, targeting his ire at the MacMarr grocery chain that had been opening stores across Portland. Duncan criticized chains' habit of commercial homogenization, and said that they were "ruled by a contemptible oligarchy of Wall Street magnates."[44] He compared the stores to pillaging Vikings. He slung a stunning array of colorful epithets at his critics on the radio, too, calling out by name numerous upstanding members of Portland society and landing himself in hot water with the Better Business Bureau. Although the charges of slander did not stick, the Wildcat spent six months in the county jail for using profane language on the radio, making him history's first radio jock to get busted for cussing on the air. After his time in jail, with his word devalued, he slipped out of the anti-chain spotlight.

In the early 1930s, the Independent Merchants' Association petitioned the Portland Chamber of Commerce for federal regulation of pricing by grocery chains. The proposed tax bill would require chain stores to pay a fee for each of its stores; the more stores a chain had, the higher the tax. Portland's influential City Club published a thoughtful piece opposing the tax (largely because its membership was composed of a number of wealthy merchants). In 1933, *Oregon Merchants Magazine* editor G. J. McPherson openly blamed the Depression on the growing power of chains. The tax bill passed in 1932, making Portland the first city in the country to pass anti-chain store legislation.

Piggly Wiggly refused to pay the full tax once implemented. The City Council retaliated by refusing to grant Piggly Wiggly a license to sell beer, and then ordered the arrest of the store's executives for selling beer without a license. The store paid up, but a few days later, the city became embroiled in a legal battle with Safeway that lasted for years. Safeway eventually paid up, as well, plus interest and court costs. Within a few years Safeway had swallowed up MacMarr and, by extension, the Oregon Piggly Wiggly stores.

The chain tax was on the books for a full decade, but it did not staunch the growth of chain stores like Safeway, nor could it halt the demise of many mom-and-pop grocery stores. In 1938, McPherson acknowledged that the efforts may have been fruitless, when he wrote that the "[c]hain store tax has not reduced chain store competition and only in rare instances reduced competitive conditions or reduced the number of stores."[45] Price wars gouged independent businesses again in the 1960s, resulting in another antitrust food price law in 1963. Piggly Wiggly changed its Portland stores to 3 Boys' Markets in 1966; there is still one faded 3 Boys' Market ghost ad on the building that sits on the corner of NE Dekum and Martin Luther King Jr. Boulevard.

Other chains came and went, with scattered stores remaining in or near Portland. Anderson's, Albertson's, Red Apple, and IGA all had their day in the fleeting Portland sun; Kienow's closed in 2000, after ninety years of business in Portland; Thriftway still operates within the Unified Grocers cooperative. One Portland-based grocery chain, Fred Meyer, even survived the 1932 tax and went on to become the nation's fifth largest grocery chain before its 1999 merger with Kroger, making it America's largest grocery chain.

"WHAT'S ON YOUR LIST TODAY?"

In 1908, after a few years on an educational westward journey, Frederick Grubmeyer, the twenty-two-year-old son of a Brooklyn grocer, moved to Portland. The city's outlying areas were still largely rural, so Grubmeyer changed his name to Fred G. Meyer and began selling coffee to workers at the farms and lumber camps on Portland's outskirts. His business did well, but he wanted to branch out from the coffee-delivery service. After a brief and fruitless sojourn in Alaska, Meyer stopped off in Seattle for a while, where he became interested in Rosicrucianism—an esoteric, altruistic, mind-over-matter philosophy that informed his business sense. He also met a slippery shyster who convinced Meyer that his future was in retailing and to purchase, sight unseen, a fantastic new store conveniently located near the hub of Portland's railroad and commercial district. It was the business opportunity of a lifetime, too good to pass up.

When Meyer arrived with the keys to his new store, he saw that, as promised, it was right near the train station. However, it was a complete hovel, and about mile north of the new shopping district. Nonetheless, he made the most of it, and used the store to restart his wagon delivery business. In about 1915, he bought a stall at Pioneer Market on Front Street and began his new Java Coffee Company, selling coffee, tea, and spices. A couple of years later, he moved Java Coffee Company into its own building on Yamhill, between 4th and 5th.

By the early 1920s, Meyer had his hands in a lot of different pies; he was the president of Pioneer Market Company; he was liquidating market stalls and selling off the market's restaurants.[46] Java Coffee Company was being rebranded as Mission Tea Company. In 1921, Meyer sold Java Coffee Company to M. B. Skagg, who used it to open one of the four stores in Skaggs United chain. A few months later, Meyer bought a seventeen-year lease on the quarter-block on 5th and Yamhill, which at the time held a small market and the home of Edward Failing (younger brother of early Portland resident and three-time mayor Henry).[47] Meyer tore down the buildings, and within a year, he and his brother opened a new two-story building that would become the Fred Meyer flagship store, named Mybros (short for "Meyer brothers") Public Market.[48]

This first store was right in the thick of Carroll Market and next door to the Sanitary Butter Store. Taking a cue from the successful public markets like Yamhill and Hollywood Arcade, Fred Meyer was the first to the offer "one-stop shopping" in a single, neighborhood market, as well as offering the self-service shopping experience previously offered only by chain stores. Rather than having to stop by several different stores to complete her shopping, now a housewife simply visited one store's different departments to tick off the items on her list: meat, delicatessen, lunch, grocery, homemade mayonnaise, coffee, and even tobacco.

In 1923, Fred Meyer opened another store with the addition of a dairy department and Fred Meyer, Inc., was incorporated in the state of Oregon. More stores opened, adding more departments. Excited by the idea of new-fangled chain stores, he and Harry also began operating a few Piggly Wiggly stores. Meyer had a change of heart a little while later, wanting to keep his name on the stores and maintain creative control over the way things were done. Harry disagreed, and the ensuing fraternal rift was irreparable.[49]

Fred Meyer soldiered on. In 1928, Fred Meyer became the first store in the world to offer a self-service pharmacy. At around this time, Meyer noticed that the business at his downtown store was beginning to slump. Upon closer investigation, he came to realize that the police had been issuing tickets for illegal parking. Ever the champion of the customer, Meyer collected the parking tickets from the cars and payed them at the police station. But then he took it a step further: he got the names and addresses of the cars' owners, which he plotted on a map back in his office. He started to notice a trend; shoppers were driving in from another part of town to shop at his store—the fast-growing "suburb" of Hollywood. He took this insider market data and got started on his masterpiece.

On June 26, 1931, Meyer confided in his wife, Eve, that he was worried. Building the new store had drained them financially, and if this new store was not a success, they would be ruined. The next day, the brand-new, full-square-block shopping center opened to much fanfare. In addition to the full supermarket, the new store featured men's and women's apparel departments. It also did not hurt that the store was located along Sandy Boulevard, which the papers at the time noted "accommodates more automobile traffic than any other arterial avenue in the city."[50] This was the world's first "hypermarket"—a supermarket combined with a department store under one roof.

Meyer's stores were successful because he was willing to take a loss to keep his customers happy. One of his philosophies (of which there were myriad, known affectionately as "Fred-Speak") was to "think like today's customer," and during the Depression, his customers wanted to save money.[51] He was the first in Portland to offer coupons and discounts, sometimes selling items at below cost to get the crowds in. He would site the sale items at the back of the store, and customers just found themselves leaving with more items than they intended. Besides the leading brands and generic brands, Meyer offered a third level of products with his mid-priced store brand My-Te-Fine. The My-Te-Fine products were still made by major manufacturers; so as long as customers could get over the difference of label, they could buy their favorite higher-end brands for a lower price.

Over the decades, Fred Meyer stores branched out farther into the suburbs, eventually entering markets in other states. By the mid-1950s, the stores began including Eve's Buffet restaurants, named after his wife. Fred G. Meyer had no hobbies besides walking and the opera, and after

his wife died in 1960, his interests were singularly fixed on his business.[52] He died in 1978, at the age of ninety-two, after spending fifty-six
years turning his company into a billion-dollar empire.

HEALTH FOOD STORES

A few years before his death, Fred G. Meyer saw another new opportunity for innovation: the health foods market. A few health food and vita-
min stores had begun opening around town, and by 1973 Fred Meyer
stores included their own Nutrition Centers, where health-conscious
shoppers could find alfalfa sprouts and Bragg's liquid amino acids.

In the late nineteenth century, when health fads were sweeping the
nation, Portland had several grocery stores that offered a variety of glu-
ten-based health foods for diabetics, "carbon wafers" and Graham crackers. At around the same time, the Seventh Day Adventist Church added a
vegetarian health food company to their Sanitarium and began distribut-
ing their "nut preparations" to the F. Dresser & Co. grocery store. One
such product was an instant nut milk called Bromose, tantalizingly described by John Harvey Kellogg himself as "an exceedingly palatable
food preparation, [that] consists of cereals and nuts, in which the starch is
completely digested, the nuts perfectly cooked, and their fat emul-
sified."[53]

By the 1920s, plenty of brands were calling their products "health
foods"; Borden's canned chocolate malted milk was advertised as such. A
few Adventist-owned stores such as Brammert's Radiant Health Food
Store (which stayed open into the 1950s) and the Bio-Chemic Health
Food Shop opened downtown to sell products like Burbank Concentrated
Vegetable Tablets. By 1930, the city had at least one secular health food
store, with the opening of Urling's Natural Foods Store, "dedicated to the
promotion of Real Health by Natural Methods."[54] The official "Oregon
State Branch" of the store was cordially opened by Sergeant Texas Urling, a mysterious man who had just the previous year published a book
titled *Astrological Bio-Science of Food Chemistry for Self Analysis*. Urling's products helped people easily move from the "cellar of existence to
the living room of life," which, he screamed from the advertisement, "is
RADIANT HEALTH AND HAPPINESS."[55] Within a few weeks, he was

hosting lectures and demonstrations, but then appears to have abruptly vanished that same year.

For a few decades, the Seventh Day Adventists ran the health food game in Portland, but when the new hippie health craze burst onto the West Coast in the late 1960s, local health nuts and secular vegetarians could shop at Rose City Nutrition Center on SW 3rd and Alder, which opened in one of the old Ann Palmer Bakeries. Rose City Nutrition Center advertised papaya enzymes, yogurt, vitamins, and juicers in addition to "fresh fruit and organic veg. juices."

In 1970, *The Oregonian* ran a spread on the new Sunshine Natural Food Company that opened up on SW 7th and Madison. "Organic Food Store Taps New Market," the headline announced from the business page. The window of the store featured a sign that defined for Portland's groovier residents what the word "ecology" meant. The editorial provides a description of the scene inside the store:

> [A] young man taps his fingers on the lunch counter to the tempo of the East Indian music and a loose fitting young lady in a mother hubbard skirt makes sprouts and avocado sandwiches; and a redhead, who looks out of place in a tailored skirt, puts up an order at the herb counter. [56]

One of the owners, twenty-six-year-old former department store buyer Michael Bidwell, offered adroit journalist Gerry Pratt a shot of unfiltered apple juice and chatted him up. "The idea is to teach people to eat local products, as much as possible," one of the proprietors explained, somehow not realizing that Oregon does not grow avocadoes. [57] Pratt appears to be having a transcendental experience with the "Harmony Grits" and organic yeast. The redhead at the herb counter began talking about the teas, to be used internally and externally. "You want to ask about that 'external tea,'" notes Pratt, "but you just cannot. After all, these people have been so good and now you do not even notice your socks down around your ankles as you follow her out the door, through the sunshine in the glass and carrying your own apple juice, too." [58] The good vibes did not last long; the store was put up for sale the next year.

Other stores followed, and the resurgence in granola-appreciation gave post-Kellogg Adventists the invitation to go mainstream with health foods. The vegetarian grocery store called Daily Grind Natural Foods and its Urban Onion deli, run by Adventists, opened on SE 40th and Hawthorne in 1973, selling the same Kellogg-approved canned meat analogs as the Sanitarium, as well as the best vegan brownies Portland had theretofore tasted. The store closed in 2007, the result of slumping business, the owners reported. One longtime employee gave anonymous testimony stating that the owners had not been paying their vendors, and another implied that the owners had been engaging in crooked business; for the health food store to have failed on one of Portland's early counterculture main streets was, according to the employee, "most likely a real crime."[59]

A few years after the closure of Daily Grind, the site was purchased by another grocery store, the Portland-based chain New Seasons. New Seasons was born in 1999 of a sort of health food love-in; one founder, Brian Rohter, was the general manager at now-defunct Nature's Fresh Northwest (Nature's was purchased by GNC in 1997, who in turn sold it to Utah-based Wild Oats in 1999, which was eventually purchased in 2007 by Whole Foods). Another of New Seasons's founders was Chuck Eggert, founder and CEO of Pacific Natural Foods, a Tigard-based brand of boxed broths and soups that is one of the nation's largest organic foods producers. Nature's president, Stan Amy, the third founder, provided capital for New Seasons's startup. Once up and running, New Seasons opened branches in old grocery stores throughout Portland: its Sellwood branch was formerly a Piggly Wiggly, the Seven Corners store was once a Red Apple, and the flagship store, at Raleigh Hills, opened in an old Kienow's.

New Seasons had a lot to learn from Nature's, and its success is largely thanks to the pioneering Nature's had done in the natural foods industry; namely, the idea of offering conventional brands alongside organic brands. Just like in a New Seasons today, in a Nature's one could buy, say, imported tagliatelle, Tom's of Maine toothpaste, and a Diet Pepsi, all in one place. Stan Amy got started with the Nature's Food and Tool, the health food store that opened in 1969 and was renamed Nature's Fresh Northwest in the mid-1980s. Amy was early to recognize that eating served a purpose beside the biological. "It can be a multi-faceted experience," he told *The Oregonian* in 1982, "refueling plus entertainment."[60]

Amy aimed to make his stores crisp and clean while being simultaneously warm and friendly; he wore a beard, but kept it neat. (Similarly, New Seasons has adopted the motto, "the friendliest store in the neighborhood.") Shedding the hippie image went far in promoting Nature's brand—the same types of products typically used by long-hairs with trust funds were happily snatched up by professors and yuppies when sold by cleaner-cut staff. Not only did this ideal become integral to Portland's cultural identity—that of the slightly crunchy intellectual—but more importantly, in 1969, Portland midwifed the birth of the upscale supermarket chain, several years before the first Whole Foods.

Zupan's first store opened a few years later, securing Portland's place as the nursery for high-end grocery chains. Founder John Zupan had spent his teen years working for Sheridan's Fruit Company and a decade as Fred Meyer's regional produce manager. The store is still family owned nearly forty years later.

CO-OPS

Although health food stores were old business, and grocery cooperatives were certainly nothing new, in the early 1970s, cooperative health food stores were the apex of far-out counterculture; they were *synergy*, man. First formed as a nonprofit food-buying club, People's Food Store (now People's Food Cooperative) opened its doors on SE 21st in 1970, just a block down the street from Sam Porco's old Powell bakery, in a building that had been one neighborhood grocery store or another for sixty years. People's is one of only two grocery co-ops that remain from the old "food conspiracy" days—the period starting in around 1970 when activists on college campuses began to shift their focus from fighting The Man to building grassroots alternatives in their neighborhoods.[61] It was time to get back to the land, co-op founders were saying, to think about ecology, and to buy organic.

In 1969, when the "SE Food Conspiracy" announced its plans to open a storefront, they needed help getting their idea off the ground. They put out ads in the local alternative papers asking for donations. When they incorporated a year later as People's Food Store, their goal was altruistic: offer affordable, healthy food to all the people. Whereas most other co-ops were hotbeds of radical politics, People's wanted to be welcoming to the little old ladies and other regular folks in the neighborhood.

Unfortunately, only a few of these "regular" neighborhood folks shopped at the store, which was only open three days a week. The housewives and blue-collar neighborhood people would come in for "cigarettes, ice cream or meat," reported an article in the now-defunct under-ground newspaper *Portland Scribe*, "and then just turn around and walk out when they find they can't get them."[62] The store, when it was actually open, mainly attracted Reed College students and members of the health-conscious bourgeoisie. Eventually, on the verge of shutting down, they decided to hire a manager. In 1972, People's opted to buy the building that still houses the store, using rent generated by the upstairs apartment to help with maintenance costs.

Over the years, People's went through many changes: they cycled through different managers, they came close to closing more than once, refocused their vision, and remodeled their building. People's somehow survived while making a conscious decision not to compete with high-end "natural" foods stores, choosing instead to remain funky, homey, and owned by the people. Although they adapted to the changing needs of the neighborhood and allowed their vision to evolve over time, their core principles remained. The other of Portland's original vegetarian grocery co-ops, Food Front, not only changed with the times, but expanded, as well.

Before NW Portland was filled with restored Victorian mansions and high-end restaurants, it was filled with dilapidated old flophouses occupied by transients and industrial steel workers. In the early 1970s, when the neighborhood was still spacious and the rents low, a few people got together to start organic gardening and recycling programs. When Food Front opened its doors on NW 26th and Thurman as the Real Good Food store in 1972, the neighborhood was filled with the lingering smell of hashish and what one founding member called "free-spirited people who live loose, casual, spontaneous lives."[63] The store sold organically grown produce at 25 percent above wholesale to the general public, and only 5 percent above cost for active co-op members. The store thrived, and within a few years, it upgraded to a sunny new building up the street.

In the mid-1970s, the flourishing vegetarian and organic foods scene paved the way for businesses like King Harvest, who started selling hummus and carrot juice from their own natural foods store on SE 24th and Ankeny in 1976. True to the late 1970s/early 1980s macrobiotic *modus operandi*, they also sold house-made wheatgrass juice and pita pockets filled with curried tofu "egg" salad, shredded carrots, and just for kicks, a black olive on top. Eventually, they relocated to SE 15th and Morrison;

they dropped the storefront, juice bar, and deli and switched to a whole-sale hummus operation.

"Evolve or Die," reads the bumper sticker. Businesses like King Harvest survive by adapting, and by focusing on what they do best. Food Front added a second store in a growing part of Southwest Portland to ride the changing tide. And in 1994, People's bounced back from the brink of ruin by adding its Wednesday afternoon organic farmers market. Two years earlier, Portland Farmers Market opened to showcase a collection of the region's finest products in one centrally located bazaar. Like many of Portland's great market ideas, it was conceived of a group of produce-minded friends with money burning holes in their respective pockets and idealism burning holes in their respective hearts, and like fire, it spread. It has thrived because whether it realized it or not, in its hearkening back to the old Portland Public Market days and yon, it respected Portland's past.

6

PERUSING THE MENU

Eating Out in Stumptown's Oldest Restaurants

Portlanders have always loved eating out. "Well appointed restaurants where choice viands are served, play an important part in metropolitan existence," urged Edward Gardner Jones in his 1894 *Oregonian's Guidebook to the Pacific Northwest.*[1] Creating a cosmopolitan existence was important to early Portlanders, tired of living in San Francisco's shadow and desperate to make over the Wild West with some *My Fair Lady* magic.

A century before Portland's restaurants and chefs were put it in the spotlight—before Andy Ricker and Gabe Rucker were the toast of the *New York Times* and before Jenn Louis and Naomi Pomeroy were gracing the Food Network—Portland was just a small town, happily feasting. A hundred years before Portlanders lined up for Salt & Straw's pear-blue cheese ice cream, the Hazelwood Creamery's ice cream parlor and restaurant drew the crowds. Once upon a time, food carts were strictly for working-class lunches—not for thrill-chasing gastronomers following the advice of the latest food blog.

The city's first eateries were boardinghouses and saloons catering to the broad-shouldered brutes slogging into town looking for work loading merchant ships and felling colossal trees. The saloons were a good place to get a square meal and a stiff drink, and according to popular lore, a fabulous place to get shanghaied. Between the 1870s and Prohibition (1916, in Oregon), saloons typically offered free lunches to keep patrons drinking. These ranged from a bowl of peanuts to Erickson's Saloon's famous "dainty lunch." With the purchase of a nickel beer or one of Erickson's surprisingly prim cocktails (evidently a big hit with the rough-necks in from the forests and the sea), one could eat his fill of the stagger-ing array of foods laid out. According to a 1954 *Esquire* piece written by Oregon journalist Stewart Holbrook, the "dainty lunch" was anything but:

> Erickson's free lunch centered around the roast quarter of a shorthorn steer, done to the right pink turn that permitted the juices to flow as it was sliced. Bread for sandwiches was cut precisely one-and-one-half inches thick. The Swedish hardtack bread, round and almost as large and hard as grindstones, stood in towering stacks. The mustard pots each held one quart. The mustard was homemade on the spot; it would remove the fur from any tongue. Round logs of sliced sausages filled platters. So did immense hunks of Scandinavian cheeses, including *getost* (of goat's milk) and *gammelost* (meaning "old"), the latter of *monstrous* strength. Pickled herring swam in big buckets of brine. At Christmas, large kettles of *lutfisk* were added to the dainty lunch.[2]

While New Englanders were building Portland's mercantile empire, most of Portland's early restaurants were opened by Germans straight from the fatherland. Sometimes, the twain met; C. S. "Boss" Schenck, a duck-hunting buddy of Alex Ankeny's, had a triangular watering hole on NW Front and Flanders. Boss' Saloon (renamed Boss Lunch in the 1890s) served blue-collar men lunches from the 1870s until 1950, when it was torn down during the alignment of the Steel Bridge with Highway 99W. Being right on the waterfront, Boss' Saloon was a central hub for mer-chants and mariners looking for shipping information. The bartender grew so tired of answering questions about this ship or that, that he put up a chalkboard above the bar highlighting the details of the arrivals, where-abouts, and loading information for ships visiting the local port. Those who came to eat lunch and check the board eventually incorporated into the Portland Merchants' Exchange Association in 1879.

Being on the waterfront, Boss' Saloon was also rumored to be a noto-rious hangout for crimps like Jim Turk and "Mysterious" Billy Smith to shanghai sailors into slavery for grain ships. The two-story saloon had a sailor hiring hall in the upstairs office, so sailors frequently came in between jobs to find a new gig. According to local legend, crimps would greet a sailor with a smile and a friendly clap on the back, buy him a meal and a few rounds, and then slug him in the back of the head and drag the hapless kid off to a ship whose captain paid a tidy fee for the new crew member. Once the poor sap came to, he was already halfway to Astoria. Turk and Smith were so ruthless, it was claimed by some old-timers, that their own sons were among those who mysteriously disappeared from Boss' Saloon.[3]

EARLIEST RESTAURANTS

Most of Portland society stayed away from these gritty saloons, opting instead for a restaurant meal. One of Portland's first restaurateurs, Charles Alisky, was "a man of unusual energy," possessing "ability and originality . . . gifted with genius and persistence in a greater degree than any of his fellows."[4] He was born in Germany, coming from a long line of skilled confectioners. Before Alisky's became a full-service restaurant, he and his partner, Charles Hegele, ran an ice cream saloon and candy shop on First and Alder specializing in "caramels and cream bonbons." Being the 1880s, they also obligatorily served oysters, both imported from the East Coast and "of local growth," prepared "in first class style."[5] Based on cookbooks from the era, "first class style" could have meant anything from escalloped oysters in dainty patties to oyster pie in a rich pastry crust.

Though the restaurant is all but forgotten today, Alisky's was once Portland's gleaming, culinary pearl. "As Delmonico's is to New York so is Alisky's to Portland," fawned an op-ed piece in *The Oregonian*.[6] "Good livers invariably seek the place they can be assured of the best. The fame of Alisky's has gone abroad, and travelers of the section know it so well that it has become to them a matter of course to go to Alisky's. . . . Alisky's is one of the institutions Portland should be proud of."[7] According to Harvey Whitefield Scott, Alisky's was the "first to put [the restaurant] business on a high plane, and during all the years he was connected with it, it was the leading establishment of this kind in the city."[8]

The Louvre was another early high-class restaurant in Portland that set the stage for Portland's emergence from the gley muck of incivility. It had a separate gents-only dining room, festooned in palms, white linens, and mirrored walls, which made it much nicer than the plainer family side of the establishment. Connected to the Belvedere Hotel on 4th and Alder, the restaurant was first owned by Charles Barenstecher and Fritz Strobel. After running the esteemed restaurant for sixteen years, Barenstecher went on to buy a tavern on 6th and Alder and reopened it in 1908 as The Hof Brau Grille and Café, which he tended like his own baby. Built in replica of the Hofbrau in Munich, the restaurant was the toast of the town. "Within [the interior] all is beautiful," cooed the papers.[9] Chef Albert Haller, who had worked at the Louvre, presided over the kitchen, fresh from a trip to Europe and armed with the finest ingredients to "make the fare of the new grille a keen gastronomic delight."[10]

The Louvre was bought by Theodore Kruse, a wealthy German hotelier who had dabbled in restaurants and catering for a while after moving to Portland. Kruse had a flair for the dramatic; one day in August 1911 he simply disappeared, worrying his wife enough that she finally placed an ad in the paper inquiring on his whereabouts. He was spotted the next day in Seattle, in the company of two men, and returned to Portland the following spring, saying he had needed "to merely get away."[11] He and his wife divorced shortly after.

The Louvre had a wild reputation; shortly before Kruse's abrupt disappearance, the Louvre had been on Judge William Gatens's short list for its "immoral atmosphere." It was one of the "gay refectories" where the "gay laugh" could be heard, and a regular venue of the Hungarian violin virtuoso Jack "Gypsy" Rigo.[12] In November 1912, however, a "Bestial Story from Portland" erupted in the papers; soon, the Louvre became embroiled in scandal when it was revealed that it had been a prominent meeting place of Portland's homosexual underground.[13] Gypsy Rigo was arrested, along with about thirty other Portland men in what was dubbed the Vice Clique Scandal.

In 1913, shortly after the Vice Clique Scandal, Kruse wanted to maintain a low profile so he closed the Louvre and opened the Rainbow Grill in the Morgan building on SW 7th and Washington. A grand party celebrated the opening night on October 2, 1913. The papers were all atwitter over the décor: "Rainbow Grill Outdoes Nature in Its Decorative Beauties," sang the headlines.[14] "The familiar rainbow in the sky looks like a poor job when contrasted with the delicate shades and colors of the rainbow glow coming from concealed lights in the Rainbow Grill."[15] The op-ed piece went on for days about the glory of the interior, going so far as to say that the grill was the handsomest and most unique in the entire coun-

Figure 6.1. The Louvre interior in 1913, with proprietor Theodore Kruse on the right. Photo © Thomas Robinson

try. It comes almost as an afterthought that "[t]he Rainbow Grill is a good place in which to eat. That is its real purpose," but the only thing the piece says about the menu is that the food was clean, kept at the proper temperatures, and cooked with modern appliances. An additional report of the opening night found the food "appetizing, tempting and satisfying."[16]

Advertisements peppering the full-page spread do suggest that the Rainbow fed its patrons well. They served "fat, juicy, delicious" Blue Point oysters, champagne, and steaks. Having evidently learned nothing from the ongoing gay sex scandal, the Rainbow featured a "Special Men's Grill," where a gentleman could select his own cut of meat (a juicy sausage, perhaps), have it cooked to order, and eat it in the company of other gentlemen. Due to lagging profits—very likely due to a now more deeply closeted gay population—the Rainbow closed in June of 1915, less than two years after first opening its fabulous doors. A year later it reopened as a new restaurant and candy store. "Grill Site to Grow Gay," the papers announced, but it was doubtful to ever become more gay.[17]

Before Portland's restaurants had issues with gay sex, they were having issues with the fairer sex. Just when Portland's fine new restaurants were starting to get a foothold, problems had already begun to simmer. Laws in the late nineteenth century already banned women from singing, dancing, or waitressing in saloons, and in 1908, an ordinance was drafted by suitably named Councilman George Cellars, allowing women to drink liquor only in restaurants. To skirt the law (no pun intended), saloons simply began billing themselves as "eating houses."[18] This was not much of a stretch, since nearly all the saloons in Portland offered a free lunch, but the contingency for distinguishing between a restaurant and a saloon with sandwiches was, according to Cellars's ordinance, that the establishment had to be greater than 400 square feet to qualify for a liquor license. This distinction led Councilman Allen Rushlight to draft a counter-amendment to level the playing field.

Rushlight rationally pointed out that "there is no sane reason why a man's wife should be compelled to consume a full meal at an aristocratic restaurant in order that she may be served with a glass of beer." Although married women on fancy dinner dates with their husbands were very likely the furthest from Cellars's concern, Rushlight made a salient point, and his use of married aristocratic women as an example of whom the law was hurting was strategic. Food was still required by Rushlight's amendment, but if a woman wanted a beer with her light lunch in a little café (or a free lunch in a saloon, say) instead of a ponderous meal in a grand hotel restaurant, that was her business.

The size restriction was what really stuck in people's craws. Cellars's ordinance gave an unfair advantage to big restaurants like the Louvre and the Portland Hotel (which some assumed might have been Cellars's intention all along), whereas a small restaurant like Palmen Garden, a well-established bierstube that served cheese herrings and imported frankfurters—German specialties not offered at big restaurants—would be at risk of being shut down after nearly twenty years in business. Rushlight's amendment to Cellars's ordinance reduced that to 300 square feet; Cellars had also proposed removing the phrase "eating houses" from the bill and changing wording from "restaurants serving liquor with meals" to "licensed restaurants." Popular beer garden restaurants, like the Hof Brau, and fashionable restaurants with a reputation to maintain, like the Louvre and the Portland Hotel, quickly applied for licenses to maintain their right to offer adult beverages in their dining rooms.

A third opinion emerged that stated perhaps women should not be allowed to drink, period. Councilman Henry Belding warned that the size of an establishment mattered little; restaurants, he felt, were actually much worse. "You can't get a girl to go into the so-called low saloon, but it is comparatively easy to persuade any unsophisticated girl to enter a hotel or café, under the pretense of a meal; then purchase a little liquor, dull her senses and she is unable to protect herself."[19] (Portland's date rapists, interest piqued, began taking notes.) Worse still, he ranted, were Chinese noodle houses, which he called "the most vicious resorts in Portland."[20] At a time when Chinese food was exotic and trendy, he said it was easy to lure a girl in on the novelty alone, "but the results are so baneful that, in my opinion, the Council ought to revoke every one of their liquor licenses at once."[21] Belding continued on his hyperbolic soapbox, stating that women should be only be allowed to drink at home (if at all), "for [liquor] is so ruinous it is appalling."[22]

Rushlight's amendment was vetoed by Progressive Democrat Mayor Harry Lane, and the law returned to the version written by Cellars: for their own good, women were only allowed to drink in large restaurants, and only so long as they had food and there were no screens or partitions dividing up the restaurant and hiding their actions from plain view. Restaurateurs won the battle for a lady's business. Soon, it would not matter; Oregon enacted a ban on alcohol in January 1915, five years ahead of national Prohibition.

Fancy hotels and private clubs had always been places for the upper crust to find a proper meal. The grand opening of the opulent Hotel Portland in 1890 brought wealthy visitors and dignitaries from around the country, in addition to bringing a new labor force of black service industry workers. After 1913, the Benson Hotel became the new pinnacle of urban elegance, and by 1951, Hotel Portland was demolished, but for those sixty years, the Portland was the bees' knees.

The Portland was where Mark Twain stayed overnight during his only visit to the City of Roses (he called Portland "a pretty nice town," but said the city needed more macadamized roads to make it more bike-friendly). During Vice President Theodore Roosevelt's stay in July of 1893, the hotel served a private party dinner featuring a French menu of clams, a

Figure 6.2.   A profusion of bars was a common sight in downtown Portland. By
the 1910s, the Hong Kong Café and chop suey houses were just as popular as the
cafeterias and lunch buffets. Courtesy of City of Portland Archives, Oregon,
A2004-002.1162

truffled cream of chicken soup, and caviar canapes for the hors d'oeuvres.
Next came a fish course of Chinook salmon with duchess potatoes (pu-
reed potatoes piped through a fluted tip and baked until golden), followed
by a larded filet of beef with *Sauce Richelieu* (a rich reduction of Madeira
and beef stock with tomatoes). The entrée was *vol-au-vent à la Toulouse*
(puff pastry garnished with sweetbreads, foie gras, and truffles), served
with white beans; fried chicken with white sauce and baby peas; and a
Benedictine sorbet to cleanse the palate. The roast course was pigeon
with potato puree, and the salad was shrimp with mayonnaise. Charlottes,
watermelon, petits fours, ice cream, and pudding were served for dessert.

Although the hotel pulled out all the stops for the vice president, the
Portland's normal menu was nothing to sneeze at, either. In 1921, no
fewer than 247 items appeared on the dinner menu—seventeen of which
were different styles of potato. Most were classic, European-style dishes
such as lamb with mint sauce or reindeer steak with orange sauce, but a
few Oregon specialties got the gourmet touch. The steelhead meunière
would have been a delightful marriage of local ingredients with French

technique; a steelhead fillet, lightly dredged in flour and sautéed in butter and sauced in brown butter with lemon juice, capers, and parsley. Hazelnut ice cream would have been the highlight of the late June menu, as would the loganberry cream pie, prepared with fresh berries at the peak of the season.

The Arlington Club, that private social club of Portland's royal families, has long held dinners of the highest esteem, and was where Mark Twain dined on his brief sojourn to Stumptown. In 1896, the Arlington held a dinner for English Shakespearean actor Frederick Warde. The menu, printed on parchment and inspired by the works of the Bard himself, was a work of art all its own, each course accompanying an apt verse from Warde's play. For example, the Terrapin a la Maryland (a creamy turtle stew popular in the nineteenth century) came inscribed "You shall be ruled and led by some discretion," a verse from the second act that makes a coy nod to the proclivity of a turtle to duck into its shell.[23] The meal so impressed the stage actor Frederick Warde that he recalled it fondly in his 1920 memoir. The 1855 Schloss Johannisberger Riesling probably helped make it memorable.

Most Portlanders would go their whole lives without tasting a forty-year-old vintage in the city's most exclusive club or eating Shoalwater bay oysters on the half shell in a five-star hotel. Luckily, there were plenty of other options, especially for lunch. Before shopping mall food courts, department stores typically featured in-house cafés or restaurants to offer hungry shoppers a little pick-me-up and keep them in the store. For the first half of the twentieth century, these were often some of the nicest places to dine. Olds, Wortman & King had its Paris Tea Room, Newberry's had a lunch counter serving superlative grilled cheese sandwiches, and later, Fred Meyer stores had Eve's Restaurants. When Meier and Frank opened its new building on SW 5th and Morrison in 1915, it was the largest department store west of the Mississippi and its tenth-floor restaurant, the Georgian Room, was a destination unto itself.[24]

The tea room at Meier & Frank's, noted historian Jan Whitaker, "was said to be one of the top dining spots in that city, if not the entire Pacific Coast."[25] Although it is unknown just when Meier & Frank opened its Georgian Room (the earliest mentions in the newspapers are from the 1920s), the store may have had a café right from the moment it first opened in 1857; a restaurant and tea room on the seventh floor were advertised by the store in 1910. The earliest American department stores often featured cafés, and later in the nineteenth century, tea rooms. Department store restaurants were one of the services among the "strategies of enticement" offered to pamper customers, according to historian William Leach.[26] Department stores primarily catered to women, and the Georgian Room reflected this: opulently decorated with paneled wainscoting, soaring ceilings, and pictorial wallpaper, the room created an ambience of wealth, and dainty menu items such as chicken salad and curry crab reinforced that this was a place for ladies to lunch.[27] It did not hurt that a young Clark Gable also worked there (after a stint as a logger in Seaside), selling neck ties, right around the time the restaurant first opened.

Although it was mainly a meeting place for Portland ladies, the Georgian Room was also a favorite of James Beard, who gushed about the restaurant in his autobiography. Chef Don Daniels, Beard wrote, was one of the best he had ever known.

> [H]e produced food of rare quality—veal birds with a rich, creamy sauce, flavored with dill or tarragon; a beautiful salmi of duckling; and a remarkably good salmon soufflé with a Hollandaise sauce. And he did superb clams, shipped from Seaside and Gearhart as fast as possible, which were sautéed *meunière* or with parsley butter and served with an excellent tartar sauce.[28]

Chef Daniels also made a variety of ice cream for the restaurant called Frankco. It was made with "the heaviest cream possible," which was whipped and then frozen quickly at a very low temperature to produce large crystalline shards, Beard recalled.[29] The four seasonal flavors in Beard's day were maple for autumn, cognac for winter, lemon for spring, and strawberry for summer.

Meier & Frank's was not just for elegant ladies' lunches; the Pine Room Men's Grill, also on the tenth floor, offered businessmen a place to meet for midday steaks and cigars. For working-class ladies who shopped on their lunch breaks, the two basement floors of the store featured a coffee shop and a dairy lunch counter for a quick meal. The basement floors also featured a delicatessen and grocery shops to buy meats, cheeses, candy, pastries, and wine.

Meier & Frank closed its illustrious Georgian Room in 2005. In 1960, with the completion of the Lloyd Center shopping mall, Meier & Frank had another restaurant, the Aladdin, which closed in 1990 during mall renovations and is now the location of the mall food court. Today, the Georgian Room has been restored into a private dining room at the upscale steakhouse Urban Farmer, and the Meier & Frank Building is home to The Nines Hotel and Macy's. The store's Cobb salads, a Georgian Room top seller, are still offered by a different descendant of the restaurant. Gerry Frank, the great-grandson of store founder Aaron Meier, still serves the "Famous Meier & Frank Cobb Salad" at his Salem café Gerry Frank's Konditorei. The salad is a full meal: crispy romaine lettuce topped with shredded chicken breast, a fan of sliced avocado and hard-boiled egg, and neat little piles of cherry tomatoes, black olives, crumbled bleu cheese, and bacon.

Department store restaurants were a nice alternative to fine dining for lunch, but many regular folks preferred the speed and affordability of cafeterias. In 1907, Portland got its first taste of the new dining craze that had been sweeping Seattle and Los Angeles when The Cafeteria opened on SW 6th and Stark. The timing for cafeterias was great; visibility of the kitchen assured customers that sanitary conditions were being maintained—a high priority during the widespread hygiene crises in the first two decades of the century. Another benefit was that the prices were "less than one-half the cost of other first class Portland restaurants" and one could "avoid tip nuisance."[30] Most persuasive was the time savings. "For the busy man there is no delay," the papers said; "[t]he novelty of going directly himself and getting what he wants—not having to put in an order and lose half his noon hour waiting for it—appeals to everyone."[31]

The food was typical working-stiff's fare: roasted chicken with stuffing or turkey with cranberry relish; a choice of local salmon, halibut, or fried smelts; beef ribs or pork chops with applesauce; and a variety of vegetable sides and desserts. A diner could come away with a proper three-course meal for just a few nickels. Within a few years, other eateries followed suit: Rosarian Cafeteria and the C & C Cafeteria—each one tried to one-up the last by offering higher-class and a more modern setting, or breakfasts, respectively.

By the 1920s, cafeterias were highly popular nationwide and later, during the Depression, they offered an affordable respite from the tedium of poverty. By 1921, however, Portland was evidently bored with them and ready for "a radical change from the standard methods of cafeterias!"[32] In the case of C & C Cafeteria, the "radical change" was to go back to a partial restaurant service; those wanting breakfast had to place a slip on their tray and wait for their food to be brought out.

With three Portland locations by 1920, Seattle-based Manning's Coffee Café (also called Manning's Cafeteria) was long-lasting and very popular. When the price of coffee was at a new high in 1950, Manning's began filling the blue coffee cans in their displays with rock salt because people kept stealing them. Twice, people had the gall to return the salt-filled cans, demanding either money or coffee in return.

CELEBRITY CHEFS

Chefs have always been valued in Portland. In 1851, Andrew Skidmore's chef, the New York–trained Peter Loudine, earned a respectable $150 per month (more than $4,000 in 2013 dollars) cooking at Skidmore's hotel.[33] And before there was Wolfgang Puck, there was Horst Mager. In 1959, at the age of twenty-eight, the moon-faced German took a job at the newly opened Lloyd Center Sheraton Hotel. He had only been in the United States for two years, having grown up in his father's restaurant in Hesse, Germany, but after visiting his sister in St. Louis, he decided to try his hand at the American dream.

Mager worked at the St. Louis Sheraton for a year or so, and when the Lloyd Center shopping mall was being built in the late 1950s, he was recruited to open the new Portland hotel restaurant. He bought a Plymouth Fury and drove it to Portland. After sufficiently proving his mettle as a sous chef in a first-class hotel kitchen, Mager bought into widow Maria Kald's restaurant, Maria's Swedish Dinners, in 1963 and took over as head chef. At Maria's, Mager was able to relax a bit from stuffy hotel fare and cook the food of the Fatherland. German and Swedish specialties came naturally to the seventh-generation chef.

His ascent was celestial; in 1964, he was selected for a Chef's Choice award by the Chefs du Cuisine Society of Oregon. The menu he prepared for the selection committee was a lentil soup with sliced frankfurters, then Swedish herring salad, followed by a salad of butter lettuce and hard-boiled eggs. His entrée was a classic Rhenish sauerbraten: pork roast marinated in wine vinegar and seasoned with juniper and allspice berries, draped in a rich, raisin-sweetened gravy. This was complemented by similarly sweet-and-sour red cabbage and crispy-savory potato pancakes.

The following year Mager changed the name of the restaurant to the one it bears today: Der Rheinländer. And then, the television offers began to roll in. In 1965, Mager began to appear on a show called *Chef's Gourmet*, a feature broadcast by the local CBS affiliate, KOIN. Throughout the late 1960s and early '70s he was a regular guest on the cooking program KOIN Kitchen, before becoming the show's host in 1973. He played up the jolly Bavarian persona slightly more than the real-life version of himself (who, it has been rumored by numerous local industry professionals, was something of a bear to work for). Julia Child appeared on the show in 1975. It was not until 1977 that Der Rheinländer got its first proper restaurant review, but by then it mattered little; Horst Mager was a force of nature.

In the 1970s, he expanded his culinary territory by opening a series of other (sometimes ill-fated) restaurants as part of his Specialty Restaurants, Inc., empire: the Irish-inspired Blarney's Castle; Chateau La France; the upscale (no pun intended) Couch Street Fish House, and a half dozen or so others. His L'Omelette was evidently much loved by Julia Child and James Beard, but succumbed. Although none of those restaurants survived the 1980s, his bierstube Gustav's—with four locations in addition to the one attached to Der Rheinländer—has endured, proving that Mager does German best. It is still the only place in town where one may eat while someone strolls around in *bundhosen* and a Tyrolean hat, playing an accordion and yodeling.

Mager did not stop at restaurants and television spots; he even opened his own culinary school. The Horst Mager Culinary Institute opened in the Olds, Wortman, and King building in 1983, later to be renamed Western Culinary Institute (now Le Cordon Bleu College of Culinary Arts). He also had a series of food product endorsement deals; Reser's Fine Foods gave him his own line of Bavarian potato salads; with a dressing of bacon, red wine vinegar, herbs, and "just the right touch of sugar," the salad, claims Reser's, is "a more sophisticated, less sweet version of German Potato Salad."[34] Throughout his career, Horst Mager has emphasized that cooking is an art as much as a business, and that a creative mind is what is needed to succeed.

During Portland Community College's Oregon Chefs Week in March of 1983, Mager presented classes on how to prepare chicken in a variety of inventive ways. Another Portland chef was featured in the series, a former employee of Mager's named Ross Pullen. Decked out in his chef's whites and toque, and of a mountainous stature (6 feet, 2 inches and 300 pounds), Pullen looked like a caricature of a big, bad French chef, but had the approachable nature of a regular working stiff (he still does, although his physical stature has become somewhat less foreboding with age). Pullen and Mager went way back; after moving to Portland in the late 1970s, Pullen worked a stint for Mager before opening his Sellwood restaurant, Belinda's.

By the time Belinda's opened, the rising trend of *nouvelle cuisine* of the late 1960s had a full decade to become assimilated into the American middle class, and French restaurants were big in Portland. Belinda's was Portland's first real taste of the kind of restaurant to which New York and Los Angeles was becoming accustomed. The restaurant featured Oregon's longest wine list, and introduced French Provincial cooking technique and rustic proteins like rabbit and mussels to local palates. The formidable Pullen was one of the first chefs in Portland to contract directly with local farmers to grow shallots and basil for his restaurant, at a time when heavy sauces and dried herbs were the culinary norm. His restaurant topped the city's Best Of lists, but then the pinch of the space—a tiny, fifty-four-seater next door to a laundromat—began to show its limitations.

Pullen had been thinking of relocating downtown to the historic Glisan's Building (before Kell's Irish Pub moved in), and even after a long talk with Horst Mager about the crushingly high downtown rents, he decided to do it anyway. A year later, in 1983, he split from his Belinda's partner over differences of opinion and left the restaurant. He took a turn at a restaurant in Tualatin, then another as the executive chef at Father's American Broiler and Nightclub, and yet another at Jack's on Alder in the old L'Omelette location. Unfortunately, Jack's on Alder had never actually been financed, and it closed five weeks later. He had arrived to Portland "bursting onto a much more primitive local restaurant scene in a shower of chanterelles and chardonnay," wrote *Oregonian* journalist David Sarasohn, and after his series of restaurant hopping, he became Portland's gastronomic "prince in exile."[35]

When asked why things had gone in such an unexpected direction for him, Pullen had a logical theory: the 0.08 blood alcohol limit and the invention of the VCR. In the mid-1980s, people began to stay home rather than risk a drunk driving ticket from a night on the town. In his trademark off-the-cuff way, he summed things up neatly: "People don't go out," he said. "They pick up a movie for a couple bucks, the old lady gets a Lean Cuisine for $3.98, some burgers for the kids and some beer for the old man, and it's not a problem that she can't get him to wear anything but shorts and a T-shirt because he's been wearing a business suit all day."[36] After bouncing around from restaurant to restaurant into the 1990s, trying to recapture that magical spark, Pullen quietly receded into the backdrop. He now writes and mentors budding restaurateurs.

Pullen was not the only chef to find fame in Portland just to have it unceremoniously wrested away. Caprial Pence's series of cookbooks and nationally broadcast television shows, *Cooking with Caprial!* and *Caprial & John's Kitchen: Cooking for Family and Friends*, could not save her Westmoreland Kitchen from bankruptcy and, after seventeen years, closure. Adding to that sting must be the fact that in recent years, the city has gained national acclaim for its hundreds of food carts, often owned and staffed by chefs who enjoyed illustrious careers at noted restaurants before relocating to Portland. Success, it would seem, comes to those who pay their dues somewhere else.

LIVING LEGENDS

For children growing up between 1963 and 2001, Farrell's Ice Cream Parlor was *the* place to celebrate one's birthday (or to lie and say it was one's birthday, should one particularly crave the searing spotlight that comes with an entire crew of ice cream parlor employees, singing, banging drums, and blaring a manic, hand-cranked siren while fully bedecked in 1890s garb). The Organ Grinder was the only other acceptable place for parents to take birthday children if maximum happiness was to be ensured, but the animatronic monkey enthusiastically crashing cymbals atop a spectacular four-story Wurlitzer organ was no match for that rat Chuck E. Cheese. The Organ Grinder closed in 1996 after twenty-two years, even though its pizza was vastly superior to the rat's.

Before there was a Hooter's to bid farewell to those leaving Portland across the Mighty Columbia, the bright red sign with the giant clock commanded that one *EAT NOW AT WADDLE'S*. Lost restaurants like these will live on in the gustatory memories of Portlanders of a certain vintage, even as chain restaurants try their damndest to erase them. Fortunately, there are still a number of restaurants that have hung on, not just

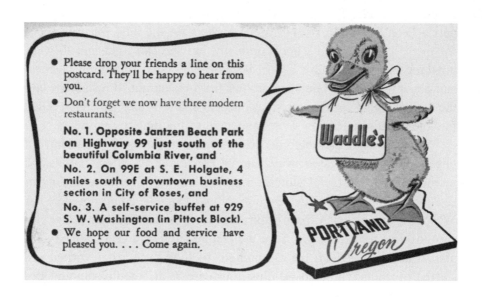

- Please drop your friends a line on this postcard. They'll be happy to hear from you.
- Don't forget we now have three modern restaurants.

  No. 1. Opposite Jantzen Beach Park on Highway 99 just south of the beautiful Columbia River, and

  No. 2. On 99E at S. E. Holgate, 4 miles south of downtown business section in City of Roses, and

  No. 3. A self-service buffet at 929 S. W. Washington (in Pittock Block).

- We hope our food and service have pleased you. . . . Come again.

Figure 6.3.   Before Hooter's moved to Portland, there was family-friendly Waddle's beckoning drivers in for a burger and milkshake at the bank of the Columbia River. Courtesy of Norm Gholston

for a decade or two, but for a century or more—the restaurant equivalent of geologic time. These are Portland's living legends.

HUBER'S, 1879

Portland's oldest restaurant was founded as the Bureau Saloon in 1879. At the time, it had been touted as the finest in town. When Frank Huber bought the White House Saloon down the street in 1893, the papers noted that "now he owns the two finest saloons in town." The Bureau Saloon was originally on SW 1st and Alder, then upgraded to the Railway Exchange Building (also known as the Oregon Pioneer Building) on SW 3rd between Stark and Washington in 1910. The new building paid breathtaking homage to the Arts and Crafts movement: a vaulted ceiling with Povey Brothers art glass skylights, terrazzo flooring, marble wainscoting, and solid Philippine mahogany columns and fixtures.

As with so many saloons of the time, Huber's offered patrons a free lunch with the purchase of a drink to keep the men drinking. But unlike other saloons, the food was what kept drawing people back. In 1891,

Huber had hired a twenty-one-year-old chef named Jim Louie, who had been working at the Peerless Saloon since nearly the moment he arrived from China nine years prior. However, it was his roasted turkey that was truly peerless.

"A young fellow, he cook 10,000 turkey, he know a little bit," Louie once said.[37] "Cook 50,000 turkey, he know something about it."[38] Truly, Jim Louie knew something about turkey. His moist turkey sandwiches and creamy coleslaw soon gained a reputation. Louie once told Portland's consummate storyteller Stewart Holbrook about the time "when he sat in a rowboat [in] back of the lunch counter in the Bureau and served steamed clams and turkey sandwiches to a party who entered the place in what was then known as naptha launch."[39] (In 1894, Portland was in the middle of its most famous 100-year flood; its citizens happily posed for photos with ducks swimming in the foreground and conveyed themselves from points A to B by all manner of watercraft, small motor boat included.)

Frank Huber died suddenly only a year after moving into the Railroad Building, leaving the management of his beautiful new restaurant to Louie.[40] Louie was beloved by Portlanders, even while wearing a peculiar jade bracelet and a queue during the height of anti-Chinese sentiment. He cut off his queue in 1912, a little after the death of Frank Huber and the fall of the Qing Dynasty ("Four hundred million Chinamen can't be wrong," he told Holbrook), but continued wearing his lucky bracelet.[41] One day in 1946, seventy-six-year-old Louie felt a bit off after finishing his shift. His cooks helped him into a booth to rest. After lying down for a few moments, he died. Six years later, his nephew Andrew bought the restaurant from Frank Huber's son. The restaurant is still managed and is now fully owned by Louie's descendants.

During Prohibition, Huber's fell back on its sage-flecked turkey dinners to keep in business, but bird was not the only thing on the menu, if one knew how to ask. Huber's speakeasy did not require a secret knock for entry, but a request of "special tea" resulted in a Manhattan served in a coffee mug.[42] By the 1970s, Prohibition long over, Spanish coffees became the restaurant's second trademark, when Jim Louie (grand-nephew of the original) introduced the cocktail to the menu.

The cocktail is a dance, theatrically prepared tableside by a handsome, smartly dressed man. He pours long trails of bracing liquors into swirling glasses: 151 and triple sec. With the click of a brass lighter, the vapors are ignited into blue wraiths, safely contained in their sugar-rimmed cages. With twirling wrist movements, the handsome man keeps the wraiths gyrating until the sugar on the rims begins to caramelize. Another swan dive of liquor: kahlúa. The blue wraiths continue their samba until they are drowned by a pour of coffee and a cap of nutmeg-kissed whipped cream. The cocktail—a tribute to the fire god—is complete.

JAKE'S FAMOUS CRAWFISH, 1892

Crawfish are beloved by Northern Europeans, and the many German names in Jake's history is a testament to that fact. Jake's originated from two separate crawfish houses: Mueller & Meier and the Quelle.[43] Mueller & Meier was a saloon on SW 18th and Washington, which opened in 1892. In 1911, Mueller & Meier moved six blocks away to the Whitney and Gray building on SW 12th and Stark (the one that still houses Jake's today). They added a soda fountain during Prohibition, and then sold the business in 1920.

The Quelle (German for "source," pertaining to a spring or a stream's headwaters) opened in 1880, advertised as a crawfish house and "first class beer hall."[44] John Schlenk, a baron from Germany, blew through his fortune relatively quickly after arriving in Portland, so in 1892 he opened a crawfish house to generate income. Schlenk and his partner, Fred Sechtem, took over the Quelle in 1902 and moved to a new location on SW 6th and Stark, catering to the after-theater crowd. "This grille, which is intended only for families, theater parties and women with escorts, will be served the far-famed crawfish that has given the Quelle a reputation throughout the length and breadth of this land," wrote *The Oregonian*.[45] "Those who have once eaten the Quelle crawfish want no other."[46]

The Quelle put Portland on the map as a crawfish-eating people, and journalist Samuel Blythe wrote an article for the *Saturday Evening Post* saying as much.[47] The Quelle's secret was that the crawfish were cooked in wine. After the lease ran out on the Quelle (following Baron Schlenk's death), John Sechtem closed the restaurant and bought the Hof Brau from Charles Barenstecher (who had owned the Louvre before Theo Kruse). He ran the Hof Brau as Hof Brau-Quelle for a few years, bringing the best of both establishments together: the Quelle's crawfish and the European entertainments (like the Austro-Hungarian royal orchestra) of the Hof

Brau. Without wine for cooking (or drinking), the restaurant withered during Prohibition, and not its tapestries nor its red velvet-cloaked gypsy orchestra could save it.

In 1920, former Quelle waiter and Portland native Jacob Louis Freiman merged his crawfish expertise and loyal customer base with the business savvy of local saloon owner John Rometsch—the man who had purchased Mueller & Meier. (The restaurant was renamed to Jake's shortly after Rometsch sold out his half of the business.) Jake Freiman was passionate and charismatic, and he had a devoted following of regular customers from the upper echelons of society, despite the fact that he had a reputation for being something of a loose cannon.[48] One painting hanging in Jake's, a portrait of a woman, is rumored to have been of Freiman's lover—the wife of one of his customers. He had purportedly commissioned the painting to hang up behind the bar in order to taunt the cuckold, but when Freiman saw that the portrait was a nude, he flew into a jealous rage, drew a gun, and shot at the artist.[49] The bullet hole is still in the painting that hangs above the bar. This story, while entertaining, is at least a little apocryphal. After the Louvre closed in 1913, and Prohibition closed the Rainbow Restaurant, the Louvre's famous nude, *Venus at the Bath*, was lost until it was sought out and purchased for the restaurant by Walter Holman (Jake's owner in the 1940s and 1950s). Rumors that the nude is the portrait of Freiman's mistress are simply that, despite the "bullet hole" in the painting.[50]

Regardless of his volatile reputation, Freiman knew the Quelle's secret to succulent crawfish. Jake's served the same plump, juicy crawfish fresh from the Yamhill River as the Quelle (before the Yamhill became polluted by agriculture).[51] The real magic touch was to cook the crustaceans in a flavorful court bouillon fortified with white wine, but most Germans, Scandinavians, and Russians use beer in their broth, adding flowering heads of dill, caraway seeds, peppercorns, shallots, garlic, and a pinch of nutmeg for seasoning. The Pacific Northwest's *Pacifastacus* crawfish is larger, milder, and sweeter than the mudbugs of the Southeastern United States. Local crawfish hail from crisp streams and placid lakes instead of muddy swamps and backwater sloughs, and their subtle flavor does not require a bludgeoning of Old Bay seasoning to become palatable. The crawfish used by Jake's today strictly come from Oregon waters, Central Oregon's Lake Billy Chinook, to be specific.

Jake's crawfish was so well known that through the middle of the twentieth century, the Jake's menu declared that their "delicious and different" crawfish could be shipped anywhere in the United States, sending them nationwide in chilled, five-gallon tins. Today, it is one of only a handful of surviving restaurants of its kind, serving seafood prepared simply, in an environment that has changed very little in more than a century.

BESAW'S CAFÉ, 1903

After retiring from logging, French-Canadian lumberjack George Besaw Jr. ran a gentlemen's bar on the corner of NW 23rd and Savier called The Oak. Across the street from The Oak was JR Stipe Grocery, but Stipe decided to move out to the country to take up poultry farming and closed the grocery in 1903. This left a vacancy for Besaw and his old logging buddy Medric Liberty, another French-Canadian logger, and with a bit of capital provided by Henry Weinhard, they opened up the saloon Besaw & Liberty across the street from The Oak. The Oak eventually became the Tavern & Pool, currently owned by McMenamin's.

Prior to the 1905 Lewis and Clark Centennial Expo, a petition was circulated to close saloons during the fair, which was to take place just a few blocks away at Guild's Lake. Fortunately for Besaw's, which was conveniently located near the entrance of the fairgrounds, the measure was filibustered. Besaw's cheerfully provided fairgoers with all the booze they could drink before taking in the sights at the Expo. Ever the stalwart friend to Portland's drinkers, when Prohibition ended, Besaw's was the first establishment in Oregon to regain its liquor license.

During Prohibition, Medric Liberty sold his half of the interest to Besaw, who introduced a home-style menu to the saloon and renamed the business the Solo Club. The food served at Besaw's was the typical kind of saloon fare expected by foundrymen, sawyers, and other neighborhood working stiffs. The "truck driver sandwiches and longshoremen soup"— slabs of fresh bread with thick piles of sliced ham and a hearty navy bean soup—were the house specialties, sold at workingmen's prices.[52] Cheese sandwiches were also plentiful and practically given away.

Besaw's had already spent four decades as a beer hall and a home-style restaurant when George Besaw's husky, fast-talking son, Clyde, took over. With Prohibition behind them, the Solo Club was renamed back to Besaw's, and Henry Weinhard's beer once again flowed freely from the taps—a bit too freely, if Clyde got to talking with a customer. According to historian Mike Ryerson (a fourth-generation Slabtown denizen and font of neighborhood lore), Clyde had to jury-rig the tap handles with rubber bands so they would shut off automatically if he started chatting and lost track of what he was doing.[53]

In the 1960s, when *The Oregonian* threatened to give him a good review for serving the city's "biggest and juiciest sandwiches," he protested, declaring that he just wanted it to remain a regular, old neighborhood joint. He preferred serving honest fare to blue collar guys—guys with names like Yakima Jim, Scappoose Joe, and Jungle Jaimie. "God sake don't write anything about me!" he scolded journalist Ralph Friedman.[54] "I don't want publicity. . . . You put in something about me I'll have all those rich people come here. I don't want foreigners. I just want the people from Slabtown, the working stiffs who live close around here."[55]

Throughout the generations, the restaurant maintained its reputation as a place to get a stiff drink and a hearty meal. After Clyde closed the restaurant in 1979, it sat vacant for a few years until being reopened by new owners in 1987. Besaw's still looks like an old back-slapping, around-the-way type of joint, and although they still serve the ponderous portions expected by lumberjacks, the menu has grown up with the neighborhood.

DAN & LOUIS OYSTER BAR, 1907

In 1903, the twenty-six-year-old son of a German oyster farmer, Louis Wachsmuth, followed his brothers from the oyster beds in Shoalwater Bay, Washington, to the beaming metropolis of Portland, Oregon. He found a job cooking at Lemp's Oyster Parlor for a year before meeting a pretty girl named Lizzie Sauer. He married Lizzie in 1908, and they quickly produced a litter of four sons. He and his partner, L. Roland Mills, ran a seafood business, City Oyster Company, from a storefront between SW 2nd and 3rd and Ankeny, but Mills soon moved on to other things and Wachsmuth took over the business, changing the name to Oregon Oyster Company.

Wachsmuth began serving oyster cocktails from the bar, all briny pearl-liquor and tangy ketchup shot from tiny glasses, or just freshly shucked atop a ketchup-smeared cracker. It was not long before the Portland weather went all gray and sideways, and Wachsmuth had but one balm for the doldrums: a buttery, creamy stew studded with plump, silky oysters. The stew and cocktails became so sought after that Wachsmuth soon found himself without enough room to accommodate his hungry patrons, and he moved his office out to make room for two tables, seating four people each; next, the crab pot had to be moved out to make room for a few more tables. Serving only oyster cocktails and stew, Louie's Oyster Bar was now in operation, in all its kooky, nautical finery.

Wachsmuth's oyster stew was a sensation. In 1912, Wachsmuth caused a great upset when he defeated Portland Press Club chef William Souls in a spirited chowder contest. Among the losing team, there were halfhearted sour grapes, with Souls's supporters claiming that he had been "jobbed" by Wachsmuth, who had padded out his chowder by slipping "300 transplanted Eastern oysters and a bunch of small bivalve into the mixture in order to make his offering the more palatable."[56] The competition had actually been rather friendly, though, and in addition to bowls of rich chowder, the guests were treated to "crawfish, bacon and the usual 'trimmings.'"

Word of the succulent oyster stew traveled fast, and the restaurant flourished. Nonetheless, Wachsmuth always insisted that the best way to eat an oyster was alive and raw. The only proper sauce, he maintained, was ketchup. By 1927, Wachsmuth acquired his own oyster beds in Yaquina Bay, which he used to supply both the restaurant as well as Oregon Oyster Company, still operating as a seafood company. (It is somewhat surprising that he did not also acquire a cracker factory, because his restaurant served more than 3 million oyster crackers by the 1980s.) With Louis's son Dan working by his side, the restaurant took on the nickname Dan & Louie's Oyster Bar among the regulars. When Dan died suddenly of pneumonia in 1938, at only twenty-seven years old, the family was devastated. They eulogized their son by officially renaming the restaurant.

The restaurant has remained nearly unchanged for more than a century, seeing many Wachsmuths come and go over the years. Some have gone on to great culinary careers, such as James Beard Award–winning chef and cookbook author Cory Schreiber, who opened the acclaimed

Figure 6.4. Rose Festival attendees line up for a lunch at Dan & Louis Oyster Bar (also known as the Oregon Oyster Company) in 1951. Photo © Thomas Robinson

Portland restaurant Wildwood. Schreiber, a descendant of the Wachsmuths, got his start early, working at Dan & Louis Oyster Bar at age eleven.

Louis Wachsmuth was a man who truly understood oysters, and was a master of their cookery. His wizardry, however, came in his restraint, in leaving well enough alone. "Oyster soup is mighty nice," he said.[57] "So is a pepper roast and a fancy roast. A good many people prefer an oyster loaf. Others like an oyster pie. I have a book that gives 98 recipes for cooking an oyster. But as I've said before, I like them raw, and the best way of all is to eat 'em alive."[58]

OTHER OLD-TIMERS

Although Portland is a relatively young city with only a small handful of venerable restaurants of respectable age, the city has many others that have survived to their golden anniversary, turning out the same time-tested foods for more than fifty years.

Nick's Coney Island on Hawthorne and Roakes' on McLoughlin has been serving hot dogs since the 1930s, proving that old dogs do not need new tricks to stay alive. The diminutive Jim Dandy Drive-In and Skyline Restaurant have been around just as long, and their burgers and milk shakes are a testament to the utter pointlessness of reinventing the wheel. Local fast food chain Burgerville has only been around since 1969, but they are the Pacific Northwest's prodigal child, with thirty-nine locations in Oregon and Washington and using predominantly NW-sourced and sustainably raised ingredients, like seasonal Oregon berry milk shakes, Walla Walla Sweet onion rings (only available in the summer), and fresh wild smoked salmon and hazelnut salads. As of 2009, they even offer a "cycle-thru" for car-less fast-food drive-thru enthusiasts.[59]

For steaks, Ringside and Sayler's Old Country Kitchen are a study in contrasts, both borne of the 1940s. Downtown, Ringside is high-end, serving dry-aged, bone-in steaks served with ethereal onion rings that (the restaurant claims) James Beard called "the best I ever had."[60] Conversely, Sayler's started out as an East County chicken shack, built at a time when the neighborhood was still largely berry fields. They are the home of the seventy-two-ounce steak challenge: anyone who can eat the entire thing in under an hour gets it for free. Ringside is for business dinners and impressing clients; Sayler's is a casual den straight out of the *Brady Bunch*, full of families and Greatest Generation gentlemen, cozying up to giant slabs of meat in cushy vinyl booths.

Postwar, the Hollywood District was the newest suburb in town, and Sandy Boulevard was the place to go for a taste of the exotic. The "Colony" was a string of different restaurants in the district featuring international flavors: one could have "a taste of the Orient" at The Pagoda from 1940 until it closed in 2008 (nostalgic diners can see the old red-and-gold arch at chef Naomi Pomeroy's latest exploit, Expatriate). Henry Thiele's eastside restaurant served memorable German pancakes; A Taste of Sweden offered a gourmet smorgasbord; and Poncho's provided south-of-the-border flair. And after 1954, one could go to Prime Rib for juicy, pink

roast beef carved tableside from a heated steel cart, served with horseradish and rich beef *jus*.

Before restaurateur Eddie Mays opened Prime Rib, the building
housed a much more notorious restaurant that lives in Portland infamy:
Coon Chicken Inn. "Coon Chicken Inn was a routine part of the city,"
explained Portland State University professor emeritus of Black Studies,
Darrell Millner, in a statement that echoes the overarching racial relations
sentiment in the city that now prides itself as a pantheon of political
correctness.[61] The restaurant had been opened in 1930 by restaurateur
Maxim Lester Graham, after successfully opening the chain in Salt Lake
City and Seattle. The entryway to the restaurant was a giant, grotesque
blackface, requiring one to walk through the grinning mouth to access the
building.

Race relations was not at a high point in the 1930s. Although slavery
was never legal in Oregon, Portland nonetheless had a long history of
redlining and exclusion laws against people of color. In the case of the
Coon Chicken Inn, white complacency was to blame. "White people
didn't even think about [the imagery] as offensive," said Millner.[62]
"There were no thoughts given to the people who had to drive past it
every day, who had to share the city with it."[63] After the war, with
changes in popular culture and a society beginning to distance itself from
blatantly offensive imagery, the owners retired and closed the restaurant.
In 2006, Prime Rib was purchased by African American entrepreneur
Ernest Clyde Jenkins.

Most Portland restaurants offer no more controversy than the choice
between steaks and pancakes for breakfast. For those preferring the latter,
the Original Pancake House on SW 26th and Barbur has been serving
their famous Dutch baby since 1953—a gossamer pillow of farinaceous
delight, gilded with the lightest dusting of powdered sugar, served with
whipped butter and, sensibly, lemon wedges to cut through the eggy
richness. For the undecided (or those who simply prefer to eat breakfast at
3:00 a.m.), the Original Hotcake and Steak House on SE 10th and Powell
is a snapshot of classic Americana; it is a perfect greasy spoon where one
can have fluffy pancakes *and* hand-cut steaks on the same plate . . . and
French fries. And bacon and eggs. And a grilled cheese sandwich.

7

DRINK UP

Breweries, Saloons, and Bars

In the early spring of 1851, William S. Ladd arrived to an infant city with wide-open markets, and the first thing he did after stepping off the ship was to walk into a saloon. The affable twenty-five-year-old befriended saloon owner Colburn Barrell over a free drink, and the next day he opened W. S. Ladd & Company on Front, on what is now a piece of goose-speckled lawn in Tom McCall Waterfront Park. Ladd had it in mind to supply saloon owners like his new friend Mr. Barrell, and immediately put out a note to his friend Charles Tilton with one frantic plea: send more liquor, ASAP. [1]

By 1853, Ladd had already moved his liquor store from SW Ash a few blocks south to his new building on Morrison Street, the city's first brick building. Another new arrival to Portland, Simeon Reed (for whom the college would be later named), worked Ladd's front counter, while Ladd was the behind-the-scenes wholesaler. Ladd eventually expanded the business to include general goods and groceries, dubbing the new venture W. S. Ladd & Company Wholesale Grocers and Liquor Dealers. Reed was made a partner within a few years, and both Ladd and Reed went on to prosper as two of Portland's wealthiest residents. Most of the city's other early merchants made their fortunes at least in part on liquor sales. Portland was built on booze.

Between the 1840s and the Civil War, Portland was establishing itself as a destination for the East Coast's adventuresome young men to strike out on their own. After the war, Portland entered into the most dangerous, lewd, and exciting part of its history.

BREWERIES

During the Lewis and Clark Centennial Expo in 1905, one could visit Olympia Brewing Company's Swiss Chalet to drink the very same spring water used in brewing its beer, "free for the asking."[2] However, in that sultry July air, many would have preferred a nice, cold beer, and anyone reading the Expo guidebook would have known that Portland's own Henry Weinhard made "the beer that makes all others jealous."[3]

The beer that probably made no one jealous was the strange concoction that Lewis and Clark's hunter John Collins brewed from camas cakes purchased not far from the Expo site a century prior. The cakes had started to ferment on their own, and after a delicious breakfast of dog meat the Corps enjoyed "[s]ome excellent beer . . . which was verry good."[4] This was the first beer to be brewed in Portland.

The accidental camas beer of 1805 would not do much good to the people—mostly men—arriving in droves a half century later. Now that Portland was a real city, it made little sense to import beer when wheat, hops, and fresh water were aplenty in the region. Frontier towns throughout the west had begun erecting small breweries to stay abreast of the needs of thirsty men. Peter Guild (for whom the lake was named) offered his home as the first brew pub and dance hall for baby Portland in 1849, setting the stage for fur trappers to blow off some steam.[5] German immigrant Henry Saxer also arrived to Portland in the nick of time and got busy setting up a brewery on what is now First and Davis—right in the heart of the workingmen's territory. Built in 1852, Liberty Brewery was the first commercial brewery in the entire Pacific Northwest, and soon became what the papers called "a favorite place of resort for our Teutonic citizens."[6]

WEINHARD

Henry Weinhard was born in 1830 in the decidedly Oregon-like Württemberg, Germany—the region famous for its rich farmlands and the

Figure 7.1.   Built in 1852, Liberty Brewery was the first brewery in the Pacific Northwest. Early Portlanders were so grateful that they nominated Henry Saxer to the provisional government. Courtesy of Oregon Historical Society, negative ORHI 5607

Black Forest. As a young man, he apprenticed with a beer maker in the capital city, Stuttgart, and left for the United States during the deluge of emigration that brought nearly a million Germans to America. After landing in New York he made his way west, and after a couple years in Ohio he decided to keep moving. Whether he determined the Midwest already had too many breweries or had simply been bitten by the Oregon bug is perhaps moot. Oregon had plenty of thirsty, hardworking men, and Weinhard was ready to keep them slaked.

Weinhard moved westward in 1856 with copper kettle in tow, four years after Henry Saxer had set up Liberty Brewery. He took a job at a brewery owned by John Meunch in Vancouver, Washington Territory.[7] Vancouver, though, was Snoozeville compared to bustling Portland, and six months later Weinhard relocated to Stumptown's greener pastures to begin building his beer empire. He set up a brewery with George Bottler, and when that venture failed to grow sufficiently quickly, Weinhard returned to Vancouver to buy Meunch's brewery. He renamed it Vancouver Brewery and operated it for two years, then returned to Portland and bought out Henry Saxer and George Bottler. Accounts vary, but by the early 1860s, Weinhard had sold his successful Vancouver Brewery and bought out both Bottler and Saxer to focus on becoming the Pacific Northwest's foremost beer baron.

The City Brewery was set up between Burnside and Couch on NW 11th, taking up the space formerly occupied by both Saxer's Liberty Brewery and the brewery Weinhard had first opened with Bottler. He helped build the Turnverein and Arion Societies, and then supplied beer to approximately 800 people between the two societies' beer halls. He also supplied most of the major saloons in town, including Erickson's, Hof Brau, the Oro Fino, and the Gem. The saloons bought his beer on credit, and if they were late with a payment, he took a stake in the company. If they failed to pay, he would take over ownership. He acquired several saloons this way, and opened a few saloons of his own, as well, including the Germania Beer Hall.

Between the 1860s and 1870s, a slew of other breweries—mostly German-owned—began cropping up to serve Portland's booming population: Gambrinus, Jubitz & Scheland, Belinger-Weiss, and East Portland Brewing Company each had their golden moment in the rain-drenched Portland sun. Weinhard's business, too, was booming, and he soon expanded his two-block brewery into a four-block compound, eventually swallowing up a fifth block of prime Pearl District real estate.

Weinhard was a philanthropist who made great strides in helping Germans in need. He dedicated money to an elderly care home Altenheim and an orphanage, and he served on the board of the German Aid Society founded by Saxer in the 1870s. In 1888, however, Weinhard made the grand gesture that would endear him to the city more than all of his other acts of generosity. Portland lawyer C. E. S. Wood recalled with fraternal affection that Weinhard had made a special offer for the dedication ceremonies of Skidmore Fountain. "Henry Weinhard, the brewer, as fine and honest an old German as you could find" announced that he "would bear the expense of whatever hose was necessary . . . to connect his largest lager tank with the fountain, and have the fountain spout free beer!"[8] Writing in 1933—just months before the repeal of Prohibition—Wood remembered that he had thanked Weinhard for the offer ("perhaps not as gratefully as I might in these days"), but that Mayor Henry Failing "felt obliged to decline it."[9]

Prohibition began twenty years after Henry Weinhard passed away, but he would have approved of the business decision to begin manufacturing near-beer (of less than 0.5 percent alcohol), draught root beer, and "healthful thirst-quenchers with the glorious flavorings of the West's finest fruits."[10] These sodas, which were billed as "safest for the children," were sold under the Luxo, Toko, Appo, and R. Porter brand names, and came in a wide range of flavors such as strawberry, lemon, crème, pineapple, sarsaparilla, and ginger ale.[11] The R. Porter brand in particular had its own flavors that were distinguished by the "-port" suffix: graport, loganport, apport, and orangport. They even sold fruit syrups for making sodas at home. These "non-intoxicating" products were relatively successful, but the brewery nonetheless sold its malt house and merged with Blitz in 1928 so the two breweries could better divide labor of brewing, bottling, and shipping while they waited out Prohibition.

Weinhard's brewery had operated in the same location for more than 130 years when it was sold to its last owner, Miller Brewing Company. With a complete lack of regard to Portland's brewing heritage or even to financial profits (which were still healthy), Miller unceremoniously closed the brewery in 1999 and the entire five-block complex was put up for sale. An upscale gastropub that bears Weinhard's name—Henry's—is the building's last connection to its legacy. And although it no longer comes from the stately brick building in Portland, Henry's Private Reserve is still brewed more than 150 years later, from the same recipe.

SALOONS

Beer had always been more popular than hard liquor, but until the first breweries could be established, whiskey and rum was all that Portland saloons had to offer. By the time William Ladd stepped off a boat into Portland's disheveled streets in 1851, Colburn Barrell's saloon was, according to historian Kimbark MacColl, "one of the nearby Front Street saloons"; suggesting that there was more than one place to obtain a slug of whiskey.[12] Ladd likely would not have embarked on a trade in supplying saloons if there were not several potential customers in the wings, but Barrell was Ladd's first and best customer.[13] By the time of the 1855 census, Portland still had only six saloons, but within a decade the number had jumped to 105 liquor retailers (plus a dozen wholesalers). With a population of a little over 6,000, there was one liquor dealer for every fifty residents, including the children; by the 1870s, this number would be surpassed by saloons alone.

Along Portland's muddy streets, some saloons offered billiards and bowling; others were dedicated to keeping ladies happy with oysters and ice cream, serving coffee instead of liquor. In 1860, the Fashion Saloon on Washington included singing and dancing along with boxing. Sutton's Saloon on First and Morrison included both a quiet reading room to enjoy while drinking "the best liquors in the market, direct from San Francisco," and, delightfully, a shooting gallery for rifle and pistol practice. [14] Most saloons, however, were dedicated to simply getting men nice and drunk. For a modest remuneration, plenty also provided a bit of female companionship. The Bella Union Saloon on First and Stark even ensured in print that "young ladies will attend to the wishes of customers." [15]

Downtown saloons like Chambreau's, the Oro Fino, and the Gem were spectacular places to get fleeced playing cards, but for decades, Burnside Street, replete with brothels and flophouses, was affectionately known as the "Bowery of Portland." [16] Between the 1880s and Prohibition, anyone with a penchant for gambling, liquor, and a little bit of trouble was required to visit the intersection of Burnside (then still known as B Street) and Second before departing. [17] For at this hallowed intersection sat the Big Four: the Portland Club, the Blazier Bros Saloon, Fred Fritz's Saloon, and the most renowned of them all: Erickson's.

ERICKSON'S

Much has been written about the esteemed Erickson's. Founded in 1884, Erickson's "managed to create the equivalent of both New Orleans' Bourbon Street and San Francisco's Barbary Coast under a single roof," wrote cocktail historian Wayne Curtis, making it the prime destination for working men looking to part with a season's income in a single sitting. [18] Loggers, fishermen, sailors, dockworkers—each clamored for their spot at the venerable bar.

August "Gus" Erickson was a handlebar-mustachioed Scandinavian who came straight from the bracing climes of Helsinki to open what

Figure 7.2.   Columbia Saloon, on First Street, ca. 1870s. Many of Portland's early saloons accommodated hardworking men and their salacious appetites. (Note the equally hardworking women in the second-story window.) Courtesy of Oregon Historical Society, negative ORHI 11984

would become Portland's preeminent workingmen's club. Although Erickson touted his bar as "a popular resort" and ran a series of advertisements promising that "pleasant surroundings and good business management are always productive of good behavior on the part of the patrons," most people knew that this was abjectly untrue, which was entirely the point.[19] True, Erickson employed a handful of thick-necked bouncers to keep the riffraff out, but plenty of men found trouble within Erickson's doors nonetheless.

Erickson's presented so many splendid ways to part with one's cash: having a schooner of beer or three; taking in one of any variety of shows; indulging in the company of a special lady; or trying one's hand at roulette, cards (faro was a favorite), or the ponies. Eventually gambling was outlawed at the turn of the twentieth century, leading Fred Fritz and the

AUGUST ERICKSON
PROPRIETOR

Figure 7.3. Finnish immigrant August Erickson owned Portland's largest bar, a favorite haunt of sailors, loggers, and dock workers. Courtesy of City of Portland Archives, Oregon, A2004-001.232

Blazier brothers—both working for Erickson at the time—to open up their own bars across the street.

But for all the money spent on vice, not a cent would be lost on lunch. Erickson's famous (and erroneously named) "dainty lunch" was on the house, so long as one kept drinking. And plied with smoked fish and salty meats and cheeses layered atop thick trenchers of bread, keep drinking he would. A man would not even need to risk losing his seat to relieve himself, because Erickson had considerately installed a urinal trough at the foot of the stools that ran the entire length of the bar.

The bar suffered great damage during the flood of 1894, but even as the city lay submerged, Erickson, like many other heroic saloonkeepers, kept spirits up by serving drinks from a rowboat. When the waters subsided, Erickson took stock of what remained, and decided to tear down and start over. Erickson's new brick building, which opened in 1895, was astounding. Taking up a city block, the bar was touted as the world's longest: purportedly totaling 684 feet in length (comprised of five bars in the same room), hewn from old-growth Douglas fir and burnished to a gleam. There were exotic liquors, imported beers, and entertainments of every flavor. Best of all, printed *The Oregonian* in 1895, the saloon had been thoughtfully outfitted with "private rooms . . . which prove a great convenience. These rooms afford every opportunity to hear the fine music in the saloon proper, including the matchless harmonies of the $5,000 organ."[20] Of course, if a man found himself in the company of a doxy in the cribs upstairs, he might hear the harmonies of a different organ.

Although one might assume that the "husky, hardworking lot" who patronized the bar stuck to whiskey and beer, fancy cocktails were exceedingly popular at Erickson's saloon.[21] One retired sawmill worker, Charles Oluf Olsen, reminisced of drinking there in the 1890s with other loggers and sawmill workers, recalling with a bemused twinkle that although gambling in mixed company was risky, and the drinking "hectic and impulsive," that it was

> far better to go broke in one glorious, meteoric orgy of a single night than to squander your stake on a continuous drunken blow-out of three weeks' duration. Better king for an hour and then back to drudgery, with wild glory booming in your ears, than never to have tasted life's brimming cup.[22]

The wisdom of this old sawyer knew no bounds. The font of Olsen's poetry, however, came in describing Erickson's enchanting cocktails:

> I remember the delicious concoctions Erickson's accomplished bartenders could conjure from the mysterious-looking bottles on the back bar—bottles that teased my imagination with their odd shapes, suggestive labels, queer, fantastic names and attractive colors. That old-time Manhattan cocktail with its genuine marachino (*sic*) cherry on a toothpick and an ensnaring perfume![23]

The magic of Erickson's cocktails came not just from the skill of his bartenders, but from the fact that Erickson himself ensured that his bar was well-stocked with the full range of exotic liquors. One item Erickson proudly served was *Svensk punsch*, or Swedish punsch—a liqueur made with sugar, spices, citrus, and arrack (an earthy Sri Lankan liquor distilled from sugarcane juice, red rice, and coconut flowers, similar to cachaça). The cordial dates back to the eighteenth-century Swedish East India Company, and Erickson imported several different brands as soon as it became available. Traditionally served hot in a silver or tin mug as an accompaniment to Swedish pea soup, punsch started out as a sailor's grog, and considering his clientele, it is not surprising that Erickson served it in much the same way. Olsen recalled the same drink (without mentioning its name) in his typical lyricism that the hot cocktail, "the making of which one of the drink-dispensers was a wizard," was prepared with boiling water, Jamaican rum, "a silver teaspoon of powdered sugar," a shaving of lemon peel, and a light scratch of nutmeg.[24] The stimulating drink, he beamed, "would have thawed out Paul Bunyan in the memorable Winter of the Blue Snow!"[25] Tragically, Erickson's *Svensk punsch* was an innocent victim of Prohibition, lost by the wayside.

Prohibition did not kill the saloon, but one might say it killed the man. August Erickson passed away in penury on a hospital cot in 1925, nearly twenty years after selling his business to Fred Fritz. The saloon survived the dry days; the free lunches simply ceased to be free, and the beer served was non-alcoholic. Erickson's carried on for several more decades, finally closing in the early 1990s after more than a century on the same corner. The glory days of the saloon, however, died with Gus Erickson. "Erickson's belongs to the Northwest's youth, its period of wild-oats sowing," the sage sawyer Olsen concluded wistfully.[26] "It but expressed the times. It was a reckless age, a prodigal age, a mad age, if you will, but who will deny that it was an age worthwhile?"[27]

KELLY'S OLYMPIAN

Originally opened in 1902 as The Olympia Saloon, Kelly's was a fine example of a saloon opened for the express purpose of selling a single product: in this case, Olympia Brewing Company's beer. During Prohibition the bar survived selling cigars, soda pop, and sandwiches to businessmen on their lunch breaks. Making way for progress and downtown facelifts, the bar was forced to move to its current location in 1957, but the customers made the two-block crawl to the new location easily enough. The brilliant green and pink neon marquee certainly helped. A funny legend surrounds Olympia beer, according to a collection of Oregon superstitions collected in the late 1950s by western folklorist Donald M. Hines. "If you're going out on a date, take Olympia Beer along," instructed the superstition.[28] The prescription read something like tea leaves:

> By peeling off the label and looking at the dots on the back of it, you can tell how your date will turn out.
> 1 dot: you'll shake her hand.
> 2 dots: you can kiss her.
> 3 dots: you can "feel" her.
> 4 dots: you're "in."[29]

Fortunately for Portland's female dating population, this superstition was understood to be a joke.

WHITE EAGLE

The White Eagle's history is built on apocrypha of heroic proportions: shanghai tunnels that led the besotted and unwary to the waterfront's waiting ships, and ghosts of dead prostitutes plaintively roam the halls past the cribs upstairs or are more hostilely mischievous, groping the living and throwing waitresses down stairs. The basement was rumored to have been where the opium dens lulled men to long, purple-hazed slumber and where lusty ladies of color were relegated to do their lamentable work. Fondly called the "Bucket of Blood," the bar survived Prohibition by converting to an ice cream parlor for Albina kids, but if one knew how to ask, something a bit stronger could be procured downstairs.

Although ghost stories dripping with delicious vice are tempting to embrace, the true history of the White Eagle is no less significant, nor is it any less marvelous. The saloon was opened in 1905 by Polish immigrants Bronislau Sobolewski (aka Barney Soboleski) and William Hryszko (Riscoe) to serve Albina's laborers. The saloon's mascot is the white eagle of the Polish coat of arms. Similar to the disenfranchisement of Volga Germans, Russian Poles in the late nineteenth and early twentieth centuries were under increasingly demoralizing conditions because of the pressure of Czarist Russia. Poles who emigrated to Portland settled in Albina, but after acquiring enough resources they largely returned to Europe to fight the Russification of their homelands. The White Eagle served as a base camp for new Polish immigrants, and sometimes even hired them to keep them working until they got on their feet.

Records of the saloon indicate that after the building was refurbished into brick in 1914, the eleven boarding rooms upstairs were all occupied by Polish men who worked at the nearby Albina rail yards.[30] Furthermore, police records indicate that few arrests were ever made for prostitution in all of Albina between 1905 and 1921, and none were made at that address. Although it is certainly possible that the boarders had the occasional female companion, all factual evidence (perhaps disappointingly) dispels the notion a brothel was operating from the second story of the saloon.

In June of 1906, a Polish political group called Progress was accused of plotting the assassination of President Theodore Roosevelt. The government investigation led to the group's stronghold at the White Eagle Saloon, and to one *Collier's Magazine* journalist denouncing Portland as the nation's hotbed of anarchism.[31] The Secret Service and the Portland police issued a raid on the White Eagle, arresting five Polish men and threatening to revoke the saloon's liquor license.

Two Portland papers, *The Oregonian* and *The Evening Telegram*, eventually ran articles that cleared the men's names and led to their release. *The Oregonian*'s reporter was a bilingual, Polish immigrant himself, and once he talked to the arrested men it was discovered that they were "merely socialists."[32] The accusations had been falsely made after

Progress's disgruntled former president was ousted from the group. "It is the common custom in Russia and Poland to call anyone an anarchist who did not believe in the Catholic church," explained *The Oregonian*'s reporter, "and this, linked with the poor knowledge of English possessed by the accuser, was probably the basis of the sensational accusation."[33]

Decades later, the Hryszko family sold the storied saloon to thirty-year-old Brooklyn, New York, native Tony Ferrone. The White Eagle became a raucous music venue under the tutelage of the bartender/owner Ferrone, and in the 1970s, acts such as Robert Cray and the Holy Modal Rounders (of *Easy Rider* soundtrack fame) were regular fixtures, bringing working-class neighborhood guys together with hard-partying longhairs. The cribs upstairs are now budget rooms for the saloon's "Rock and Roll" hotel, lovingly restored by the McMenamin brothers. Because of the loud music and revelry of the living downstairs, the haunting cries of the wicked cannot be heard.

Although the White Eagle has borne the brunt of idle gossip and tall tales, most of Portland's deadfalls rightfully earned their bad reputations. Even glamorous places like the Oro Fino were notorious. Built in the late 1850s and named after a New Mexico gold mine, the Oro Fino on First and Stark was one of the city's first really well-known saloons. It was often described as luxurious and swanky, but it was, in all actuality, a gambling house, and its "variety theater" was a front for prostitution.

Many other saloons were the center of even better scandal. Celia Levy's Blue Light Saloon was under the microscope for being a "house of ill-fame"—an indictment for which she appeared in court in 1876. Although she was not proven to be a madam, Mrs. Levy ended up in court again later that year, after she was threatened at gunpoint for not giving the assailant a drink on credit. Considering she had already survived a gunshot wound a few years earlier, one might surmise that rough men were a hazard of the trade.

Not even the police could stay out of trouble; the Gem Saloon was owned by James Lappeus, who was also one of the Oro Fino's original owners and Portland's first chief of police. He was eventually fired for purportedly offering to accept a $1,000 bribe in exchange for the release of a convicted murderer, but not before becoming involved in the Oro Fino Ring scandal, wherein his officers intimidated voters into stuffing ballot boxes on election day. Yamhill Street was once, according to one account, lined with "poisonous dens from whence little gusts of viciousness puffed into the streets."[34] Salacious reports on the houses of disrepute and the men who frequented them filled the papers for decades, but the straw that broke the camel's back was a respectable little watering hole called the Webfoot Saloon.

"THE WAR ON THE WEBFOOT SALOON"

In the early 1870s, with new breweries and saloons opening on an increasingly regular basis, churches began holding meetings to discuss the problem of wine drinking and the Demon Rum. The Women's Christian Temperance Union had just been formed in Ohio, and local branches were forming across the country. In Portland, it was the Women's Temperance Prayer League (WPTL) who took up the cause to protect women from their drunk husbands. Drunk men were prone to violence and to indiscretions of both the financial and the corporeal. The WTPL wrote letters to saloon owners beseeching them to "desist from this ruinous traffic," which was, predictably, met with laughter from saloonkeepers.[35] "Once launched, the Great Crusade scudded forth before a gale of windy oratory," wrote historian Malcolm H. Clark Jr. in his 1957 retelling of the account titled "War on the Webfoot Saloon."[36] The women began marching, singing, and praying, and took pause at the swinging doors of the Webfoot Saloon.

Walter Moffett, the saloon's owner, was a man of fairly solid means and reputation; he was a property owner, an honest businessman, and married to a Terwilliger (for whom half of South Portland is named). However, in Moffett, the Temperance movement had a potent foe. "He had an intense dislike for female do-gooders," wrote Clark. "[H]e regarded the Temperance movement as hypocritical humbuggery, and he was possessed with an explosive temper equipped with a very short fuse."[37] When the ladies came to try and "pray him down," Moffett decided to really give them something to pray about. He shoved them out the door and told them that he could not have women in the saloon; after all, he was not running a whorehouse. The women were indignant. This meant war.

After days of vain attempts to gain entry to the saloon, the "petticoat revolution" switched tactics.[38] According to reports from *The Oregonian*, the women lined up in front of the entrance, effectively blocking the saloon's doors, and began to pray and sing. Moffett was not impressed. He made a big show of pulling out his glasses, putting them on the end of his nose, and then took out a Bible and began to loudly read verses that, when taken out of context, were exceedingly shocking and offensive.[39] The women sang louder, and Moffett volleyed back by raising his voice, as well. When one woman began sobbing and asking him why he would say such insulting things, he simply replied that "he was an educated man, and he educated his children; he generally attended to his own business and would be much obliged if they would do the same."[40] As long as the Crusaders returned, he promised, "he would always find something with which to 'stand them off.'"[41] He tossed in a few extra insults while he had the floor, though, adding that the women would be better off at home, where they belonged.

Moffett's behavior was fitfully discussed at the church that night, and although some women felt that maybe they should cut their losses and refocus on another target, most of the Crusaders took Moffett's retaliation as the sign of a guilty conscience. He could be saved yet, they thought (and perhaps a few simply did not want Moffett to win). After a few days, they regrouped in front of the Webfoot Saloon. A crowd soon gathered, and moments later it swelled to hundreds strong. "The crowd was so large that it completely jammed the sidewalks and overflowed into the streets," Clark reported.[42] Moffett did what anyone would do when faced with an angry mob: he called the cops.

Police Chief Lappeus, a saloon owner himself, had little patience for the crusaders and told them to leave. When they refused, he warned them that he had little choice but to arrest the whole lot of them. The ladies spent several loud, martyred hours in jail before being released. When the Leaguers returned to the Webfoot a week later, Moffett was waiting for them with a hand-cranked organ, whistles, and a large Chinese gong. The ladies sang and prayed, drowned out by the din but undeterred. After the "hideous clamour" of the saloon's defenders started running out of steam, one of the men turned on a fire hydrant and flooded the streets.[43] The ladies still did not budge, nor did they flinch even as the hose was turned fully on them, soaking them to the bone. The singing and praying continued. At least one of the saloon-defenders had been steadily getting drunker as the day went on, and naturally, a fight broke out. The cops came to break it up, and everyone went home for the night.

The Leaguers took another trip to jail for the riot they had caused, but their next move rattled saloonkeepers more than any direct action. They produced a handy little guide called *The Voters' Book of Remembrance*, which would intend to help voters know which candidates were in favor of temperance laws. Unfortunately, the guidebook had been written by someone who "possessed a very large vocabulary of exceedingly short words" and was filled with rather coarse accusations that those engaging in the liquor trade (which included many of the city's wealthiest and most upstanding citizens) "went hand in hand with another—older—profession."[44]

With that, the moral high ground previously enjoyed by the Women's Temperance Prayer League had been shattered. Abigail Duniway fired off a condemning shot in *The New Northwest* that blamed the male preachers for ruining everything. "After which parting blast," wrote Clark, "she climbed aboard her suffragette hobby-horse and galloped noisily off in search of new dragons."[45] Moffett did not get very long to enjoy his victory; he died a few months later of an unknown illness, and the Webfoot Saloon was razed two years later.

"A SOURCE OF ENDLESS TROUBLE"

When women were not praying for the end of all liquor, they were evidently sneaking into saloons and asking men for drinks. In the 1890s, two decades after the Temperance League simmered down, Portland's saloon owners were once more faced with female troubles. First, the Progressive morality-police wanted to keep women out of bars for their own protection. Some saloons, like Fritz's, were deemed harmless "resorts" where "respectable women might go," but one district attorney on a case involving Fritz's Saloon replied matter-of-factly that "respectable women can go anywhere, but they will not be respectable when they come away."[46] One case that grabbed headlines was when Miss Hazel Noland, the sixteen-year-old daughter of a restaurateur, was "lured into ruin" by a saloonkeeper, and ended up in the House of the Good Shepherd—a home for "wayward, delinquent and incorrigible girls."[47] The saloonkeeper was blamed not just for selling liquor to a minor, but for causing the young woman to become sullied.

Moral hygienists trotted out the same old tropes, complaining that saloons that permitted women either as employees or patrons were "practically 'combination houses,'" implying that in addition to a ground floor selling liquor, the saloon's upstairs was used for a more licentious commerce.[48] Before ordinances, some women were in the employ of saloons to act as hostesses to persuade men to buy more drinks, being paid a piece rate for every drink they convinced a man to buy. The papers noted that saloons had employed women "engaged in selling drinks on commissions ever since Portland was still a 'Wild West' town."[49] But while they were soliciting drinks, ordinance supporters intimated, women were probably making other solicitations, as well. Just in case, policemen were ordered to arrest any women found in saloons on North 3rd or North 6th in what is today's Old Town—Portland's former vice district.

In the late nineteenth century, women had already been banned from performing song or dance in saloons or working as barmaids, but the law was mostly forgotten or ignored until the new ordinance reminded everyone. In the 1900s, the mere presence of a woman enjoying a beer in a saloon was menacing, and was blamed for the problems caused by men. Women in saloons were officially deemed "a source of endless trouble," and the city passed ordinances to prevent women from entering at all, unless they were dining in a restaurant of sufficient size and reputation.[50]

Saloonkeepers were obviously not too pleased about the proposed law's effect on their bottom line. "'Cusswords' Used by Liquor Men," read the headlines, in fact, describing the "stormy session" that ensued between City Council, the Liquor Commission, temperance supporters, and the saloon owners' retail liquor representatives.[51] The "verbal thrusts administered" by two liquor reps issued forth "a generous supply of profanity, at the utterance of which the preachers cast significant glances at each other."[52] It mattered little; the ordinance was passed, barring women from saloons or restaurants serving liquor except where there were "open and public" dining rooms without obstructions such as booths or private boxes—popular in French restaurants and in heavy use in the upstairs of the Louvre.[53] Women would not get the right to drink in public without ordering a full meal until the repeal of the Eighteenth Amendment in 1933.

Although most saloonkeepers were bitterly angry about the loss in business due to the ordinance, some actually preferred to keep women out of saloons. This was not just because of some "boys' club" mentality or for altruistic reasons pertaining to what was deemed best for women, but because women's "grafting proclivities" made them a "nuisance to [the] trade."[54] According to one saloon owner, women stole anything that was not nailed down and were simply not worth the trouble:

> [T]he average woman who visits such resorts is a petty larcenist in her desire to add to her collection of souvenirs at home. It has been practically impossible for me to keep my stock of glasses and silver spoons replenished. . . . They take everything in sight that can be conveniently carried away. . . . Liquor men who want the trade of women are welcome to it. I want no more of it.[55]

Modern bar owners have had similar issues, though the complaint is no longer directed exclusively at women. One bar in Portland requires patrons to submit their drivers' licenses as collateral when ordering a Moscow mule, after the bar suffered the loss of all of its beautiful copper mugs to sticky fingers. Another bar owner, Janis Martin, has lamented the theft of the highly collectible Fu Manchu mugs used for specialty cocktails at her critically acclaimed sake bar Tanuki. "Portland is a f***ing den of thieves," she repined.[56]

PROHIBITION

Although Mark Twain called the movement justifiable, the Temperance movement has been blamed for stalling women's suffrage for decades. Very often, the same women were on both campaigns. Using her newspaper *The New Northwest*, Abigail Duniway led the march for both temperance and women's right to vote, and after years of rallying, she succeeded at the latter in 1912. She gained Oregon women the right to vote eight years before the rest of the nation—a right that they promptly exercised by voting in a complete ban on alcohol two years later, even though Duniway herself was ardently opposed to prohibition, proclaiming that "prohibition and liberty could not possibly pull together."[57] To the chagrin of liquor dealers, alcoholics, and general merrymakers across the state, Oregon's prohibition began five years before the Eighteenth Amendment was passed.

But in 1844, fifteen years before Oregon was even a state, the Oregon Territorial Government put the first prohibition laws on the books.

William Johnson's moonshine, distilled from Hudson's Bay Company molasses, was first produced in 1842—just two years before the first prohibition law—and was of an octane so potent that it may be entirely blamed for inspiring the ban. A British officer and ex-Hudson's Bay employee, Johnson had set up a still in the vicinity of what is now the corner of SW Kelly and Curry, in the Corbett-Terwilliger-Lair Hill neighborhood. The product was known by a delightfully sinister name: "blue ruin."

This cerulean spirit, claimed legislation written by the Oregon Provisional Government,

> would bring withering ruin upon the prosperity and prospects of this interesting and rising community, by involving us in idle and dissolute habits, inviting hither swarms of the dissipated inhabitants of other countries, checking emigration, destroying the industry of the country, bringing upon us the swarms of savages now in our midst, interrupting the orderly and peaceable administration of justice, and in a word producing and perpetrating increasing and untold miseries that no mind can rightly estimate.[58]

Despite such hyperbolic rhetoric (and the repeated use of "swarms" to illustrate alcohol's scourge), the law passed, effectively creating the precursor of the Oregon Liquor Control Commission (OLCC). Fortunately for the Oregon Territory's thirsty new arrivals, the law was repealed five years later by the territorial legislature. There was another early alcohol-related ordinance in 1854 intended to regulate saloons, and in 1857 the Masonic Grand Lodge of Oregon had a rule that suspended Portland's liquor-selling Freemasons "for producing drunkenness."[59] Considering that most of the town's leaders had a financial interest in alcohol, these types of rules were not enthusiastically embraced.

At around the turn of the twentieth century, a number of organizations formed in Portland concurrently with those forming around the country: the Anti-Saloon League, the Prohibition Party, and the Woman's Christian Temperance Union (comprised of the remaining membership of the defunct Women's Temperance Prayer League) all began the arduous and righteous work of drying up the state county by county, saloon by saloon. Beginning in 1904, they introduced a series of bills, resulting in several embattled years of the "wets" versus "dries" in various cities and counties across the state. A series of complicated rules and convoluted exceptions were volleyed back and forth; there were wet cities within dry counties and vice versa.

In 1908, Weinhard's brewery took out a full-page advertisement in *The Oregonian* calling prohibition "vicious" and "wrong morally," pointing out that it "betters nothing."[60] "They had prohibition agitators in Shakespeare's time," reminded the advert.[61] "But Shakespeare wrote 'Dost thou think because thou art virtuous there shall be no more cakes and ale?'"[62] Portland and Multnomah County maintained position as "wet"-friendly, but in 1910, bills proposing to affect the entire state were introduced. "Prohibition at its worst is better than any license at its best" was their slogan.[63] Within four years, Oregon passed prohibition.

During the middle of the temperance hullabaloo, one man offered a practical solution. In 1912, millionaire logging magnate and temperance advocate Simon Benson had donated $10,000 to the city for the purchase and installation of twenty four-bowl bronze drinking fountains. Some sources claim he did so to give loggers (of which he employed many) something besides liquor to drink on their lunch breaks, but others insist that he saw a crying, parched child during one Portland Fourth of July, and wanted to help. The first two fountains were installed on SW 5th and Washington and in front of Benson's home on SW 11th and Clay, to commemorate his kind and generous gift to the city. By 1917, the remaining eighteen Benson Bubblers had all been installed and turned on, quenching the thirsts of dried-out Portland during Prohibition. In the 1970s, Benson's family formally requested that the fountains only be installed within specific boundaries of downtown, so as not to squander their uniqueness; following that advice, the next fifteen were installed on the bus mall after it was constructed in 1976–1977. Today, there are more than fifty Benson Bubblers downtown, plus more than seventy of the single-bowl variants throughout the city.[64]

GETTING AROUND THE LAW

Just as it was everywhere else, Prohibition was an abject failure in Portland. People who wanted to drink did so regardless of the law, and the laws of supply and demand took care of the rest. Speakeasies popped up in the expected places; Huber's began serving booze in coffee mugs, and Scandia Restaurant sold apple cider that had gone hard. "Mysterious"

Billy Smith—the very same man who was supposedly crimping sailors at the Boss Saloon and who also happened to have been a champion welterweight boxer in the 1890s—was busted in 1906 for slipping absinthe into sarsaparilla that he was serving to a teenaged girl at his soda fountain. The blind pigger (period slang for the proprietor of illicit drinking establishments known as "blind pigs") was back at it again in the 1920s; he was busted for serving liquor at his soda stand and was charged with "maintaining a nuisance."[65]

When restaurants were busted, liquor was often unearthed in interesting places. One German restaurant owner was fined when whiskey was revealed in Heinz 57 sauerkraut barrels in his basement during a raid. "A new variety," commented the district attorney upon the discovery of the liquor; "must be the 58th."[66] Because of Portland's shipping industry and easy access to international waters, many bootlegging restaurateurs sold liquor imported directly from Canada. The cargo ship would rendezvous with a crew of lithe motor launches twelve miles off the mouth of the Columbia, in the amnesty of international waters. The trim launches could handily outrun any of the Coast Guard's sluggish boats, which provided no end of frustration for Oregon liquor law enforcement officials as they raced up the Columbia toward Portland. Being at the confluence of the Columbia and the Willamette, Sauvie Island provided a convenient waypoint for vessels running high-end whiskey from British Columbia to Portland and from there, other West Coast cities.

Thirsty Portlanders who could not afford drinking in speakeasies could always try their hand at moonshining, and many did. Early in Oregon Territory history, at least a few men found a way to craft the blue ruin from Hudson Bay Company molasses and shorts (the floor sweepings left over from grinding wheat into flour). Besides William Johnson's still in South Portland, *Oregon Native Son Magazine* reported in 1899 that another man, Richard McCrary, set up a still on Swan Island. One account of the Swan Island still reported that Dick McCrary was working with two men—James Connor and Hi Straight—and the product rendered was said to "glaze the eye, palsy the hand and confuse the feet of the intrepid drinker."[67]

In the 1840s, blue ruin was the official moonshine of Portland. It was the local alternative to bathtub gin, and some actually grew to enjoy the strong tipple: the so-called canned heat addicts. This brew, as well as a variety of other, even less-potable spirits, were favored by the hoboes who gathered around oil drum bonfires under Portland's bridges—"a tatterdemalion lot" susceptible to predation by unscrupulous liquor dealers.[68] This ended in calamity when, during Prohibition's twilight, three Portland druggists were found guilty of manslaughter for selling denatured alcohol. The victims were no strangers to rough booze; however, this denatured methyl alcohol—a wood alcohol sold as "dehorn"—was fortified with formaldehyde. Twenty-eight men died rather agonizing deaths from having their innards pickled, in a tragic case of acute methyl alcohol poisoning. One of the three druggists spent time in the state penitentiary for the offense. Much as with homeless addicts today, the truth about the deaths was at first obscured because of the victims' "renegade character, their furtive indulgence in their vice and their isolation from interested relatives and friends."[69]

Another dangerous beverage popular with Portland's desperate alcoholics was a blend of evaporated milk and gasoline. The drinker, wrote Andrew Sherbert during the Federal Writers' Project of the 1930s, "gets as 'high' on this automotive high-ball as does the wealthy nabob on Portland Heights with tall, cool horses necks [cocktails] made of Haig and Haig [Scotch whiskey]. . . . It would seem that to smoke while on a milk and gasoline bender would be fraught with . . . danger."[70]

Fortunately, most average drinkers did not reach for the embalming fluid or the gas can during Prohibition, and most moonshine was not of the ilk likely to kill two dozen men. When agents discovered a still and 446 gallons of raisin whiskey made by two Austrian brothers in the misty, mossy environs of today's Forest Park, it seems almost quaint by comparison.

HOME BREWING TAKES OFF

Oddly, Oregon's initial prohibition law, as enacted in January 1915, allowed individuals to order by mail up to two quarts of gin or twenty gallons of beer per month. One man wrote to the paper in an outcry at the ridiculousness of the fine print, because, as he put it, "it is not fair to our own breweries that can brew such excellent stuff and to our distilleries that can distil such fine old whisky. What can I do about it?"[71] An amendment for beer was proposed and supported by hop growers and industry leaders so that Oregonians could obtain their superior, homegrown product and continue to support the local economy. An "equal rights" initiative to allow local brewers to provide the rationed beer was filed in 1916, but, sadly, failed to pass.

Regardless of the law, on SW 3rd and Taylor, two doors down from the Lotus Card Room, the Malt Syrup and Supply Company kept selling and, boldly, *advertising* malt, hops, kegs, bottles, and capping machines—everything one needed to brew beer at home.[72] Before the passage of the Eighteenth Amendment to the United States Constitution in 1920 and, more importantly, the National Prohibition Act (aka the Volstead Act, which enabled the enforcement of the law), Prohibition had sparked off an explosion in home brewing in Portland and abroad. Even large, well-known companies like Budweiser offloaded gallons of malt syrup through mail order.

After 1920, many of these dealers would be fined for violating the Volstead Act, including Fred Polsky, the owner of Malt Syrup and Supply. Most dealers of brewing supplies were careful not to advertise their intended purpose, but many were nonetheless busted by undercover agents asking for supplies to give their near-beer a "kick."[73] One brewing supplier was not only brave enough to open during state Prohibition (at the cusp of the law going national), but has managed to survive for nearly one hundred years. In 1918, Frank H. Steinbart opened his eponymous Portland store, and today F. H. Steinbart's is America's oldest home brewing supply store.

Home brewing would not be legalized in Oregon for more than forty years after the end of Prohibition, but when people began to return from wars overseas, they brought a taste for European beers with them. Imported beers did not always travel well, and often went stale or became light-struck in transit. Ultraviolet light denatures the hop molecules called isohumulones, resulting in the freeing of sulfur molecules, giving an unpleasant skunky odor and flavor. This "skunked" beer did not satisfy cravings for the rich, malty beers of Europe, nor did pale, domestic lagers. A wise man once said, "I urge you, go for the dark side and forget the mellow yellow—live it up!"[74] In 1969, this wise man—beloved local beer enthusiast Fred Eckhardt—came to the rescue with his groundbreaking pamphlet *A Treatise on Lager Beer*.

Born in Olympia, Washington, in 1926, Eckhardt is a witty, congenial man with spry eyes and a neatly waxed mustache; he not only remembers the glory days of Portland brewing, but he helped build them.[75] Having lived in Portland since after the Korean War, he was a stalwart advocate of home brewing for more than a decade before it became legal in Oregon, and has called the city the "brewing capital of the world."[76] In 1997, Hair of the Dog Brewing Company in industrial SE Portland named a barley wine–style ale after the man, and beginning as a surprise party for Eckhardt's eightieth birthday in 2006, Fredfest is now a charity fundraiser held every May in his honor.

Although Portland restaurateur Greg Higgins (chef-owner of the acclaimed Higgins Restaurant) has gained renown for his exquisite beer pairings, Eckhardt takes a more irreverent approach, pairing beer with cheese, cookies, candy bars, and even breakfast cereal. His best-known pairing is stout beer and vanilla ice cream, culminating in an ice cream float, the invention of which he credits to Higgins.

THE PATH TO BEERVANA

Ten years after Eckhardt's monumental 1969 book, home brewing was legalized with a bill signed into law by President Jimmy Carter. Today, there are around a dozen home brewing supply stores in the city, and in 2011, additional legislation was passed that permits home brewers to transport and pour their own beer without a license from the OLCC. Importantly, legalized home brewing gave beer enthusiasts the opportunity to practice and experiment with minimal financial risk. Using friends and family as guinea pigs gave many amateur brewers the chance to perfect their craft before launching the small-scale breweries that have made Portland famous.

One thing that the first generation of microbrewers had in common with Eckhardt was a rebellious streak. They also shared a preference for beers besides thin, pale domestic lagers, or what Eckhardt dubbed the "pasteurized carbonated malt 'pop.'"[77] These brewers did not have delusions of grandeur; they simply wanted to drink better beer and share it with the rest of Portland.

In the late 1970s and early 1980s, several brewers began opening small craft beer operations: Brian and Mike McMenamin; the Widmer boys; Portland Brewing Company founders Art Larrance, Fred Bowman, and Jim Goodwin; and Willamette Valley winemaking power couple Richard and Nancy Ponzi opened BridgePort Brewing with the help of brewmaster Karl Ockert. But without marketing budgets or even bottling budgets to get the product into stores, these brave new beers were remaining unknown. If one was lucky, an established pub or tavern might carry the beer on tap, but this was woefully uncommon. Craft brewers needed a way to sell directly to the beer aficionado, but first they needed to change the law.

Post-prohibition laws had failed to include beer in the language that determined who could sell directly to consumers. Wine was safe, but beer was glaringly not. This stemmed from the pre-Prohibition reality, in which most saloons were owned or controlled by breweries, creating something resembling a monopoly. The law was effective at first, but had become outdated and unnecessary by the 1980s. In 1982, Washington and California had already changed their brew pub laws, so in 1984, Portland's stalwart microbreweries banded together to do the same for Oregon. The Widmer and McMenamin brothers as well as the people behind Portland Brewing Company and BridgePort lobbied tirelessly to change Oregon's brewing laws to reflect the laws governing wine making. After repeatedly failing, the bill was attached as a rider on one that would allow Coors to sell beer in Oregon, and with this backing, the law passed in 1985. Finally, breweries could serve their draught right at the source, as long as food was also served. The brew pub was born.

The magnitude of the law's benefit could not be overstated. "[T]he Brewpub Bill . . . was arguably the single most important episode in the history of Oregon brewing," wrote historian Pete Dunlop in his *Portland Beer: Crafting the Road to Beervana.*[78] Throughout the late 1980s and 1990s, new brew pubs began popping up anywhere the space was big and the rent was cheap, namely, Portland's industrial districts. Instead of having two or three large-scale producers, Portland became an intricate tapestry of the myriad beers and brewing styles perfected by men and women dedicated to the craft.

This creative freedom has allowed some brewers to concoct unconventional beers like espresso stouts and even (for better or worse) a beer flavored with maple and bacon. Mercifully, most breweries deviate little from classic techniques, instead focusing on perfecting the old styles. In 2008, during their third Fredfest, Hair of the Dog Brewing offered tastings of their Bourbon Fred beer—a barley wine aged in oak bourbon casks. Because they are conditioned with yeast in the bottle and the alcohol content of the beers is so high, brews like barley wines, sour beers, lambics, and winter ales mellow with age and develop a complexity and richness unattainable in a lager or pilsner. These are ancient European techniques that, when paired with Portland's similar climate and water, are performed to stunning effect.

When asked why Portland has become such a haven for the makers and lovers of beer, Fred Eckhardt has a few theories. "It helps to have a good law. Oregon has what may be the best brew pub law in the country. . . . A new craft brewer may choose to have a pub, or she may choose to distribute her own beer. That's very brewer-friendly."[79] Another factor dear to Eckhardt is food; Portland's brew pubs all have menus offering items besides pretzels and peanuts. Unlike in Washington, Oregon brew pubs are required by law to serve food, and many serve excellent food. Those that wish to avoid the trouble of a kitchen might opt for food carts in the parking lot.

One company took the concept of small, hand-crafted brewing a step further when it opened a small distillery called Clear Creek. Specializing in grappa, fruit liqueurs, and the "water of life" called *eau de vie*, Clear Creek has been distilling the spirits from local fruits for nearly thirty years. Like Portland's microbrewed beers, Clear Creek's eau de vies are based on the marriage of European technique with local ingredients, culminating in a range of products like the cherry schnapps *Kirschwasser*, a serene brandy distilled from Douglas-fir needles and a pear brandy with the pear grown right inside the bottle. Benevolently, Clear Creek has paved the way for the numerous other microdistilleries that have opened around Portland over the past decade.

COFFEE AND TEA

Portland has always been kind to cottage-industry drink producers. During the grunge era of the 1990s, a good many Portlanders did time working behind an espresso machine in a coffee shop—a lifestyle born in Seattle that spread southward and beyond. Analogous to microbrewed beer, specialty roasters like Stumptown Coffee Roasters, which opened in 1999, have been at the forefront of the so-called third wave of coffee. Founder Duane Sorenson began roasting coffee using a machine that dates back to 1919—the oldest in the country.[80] Bringing small-batch coffee to a range of customers, third-wave coffee follows the espresso-crazed 1990s and "gourmet" specialty coffees of the 1970s, while offering consumers the additional choices of being organically grown and fairly traded.

Other caffeinated beverages arose from the rainy city and reflect Portland's bohemian past: Stash Tea was born in a Portland Victorian house in the 1970s; new age–soaked Tazo tea (now owned by Starbucks) was named for "the whirling mating dance of the pharaohs of ancient Egypt and a cheery salutation used by Druids and 5th-century residents of Easter Island."[81] Super-sweetened Oregon Chai was inspired by a backpacking trip through the Himalayas, and America's first commercially produced kombucha came in 1994 with Portland's rose-scented Oocha Brew.

OTHER VICES

Besides serving a range of hard alcohols, many of Portland's old bars enjoyed a few other common traits: they supported gambling, the hotels upstairs were rumored to have been brothels, and the entire building is said to be haunted. The Lotus Cardroom and Café not only survived Prohibition, but had the audacity to open during Prohibition's zenith in 1924. With its high ceilings, booth seats, and cherrywood bar, one might forget that the café was once little more than a gathering place for bootleggers and cardsharps, where the liquor was covert but the gambling was out in the open. Opened in 1920, the Rialto pool room shares a similar history, with its basement betting parlor (now called the Jack London Bar—a favorite hangout of Portland's social historians).

For twenty-five years, Club Mecca (later the Desert Room, then a gay bathhouse, and now McMenamin's sanitized Zeus Café and Crystal Hotel), was once the site of a delectable variety of vice and scandal. In the 1950s, the bar boasted open gambling, dancing, canoodling, and a bawdy house upstairs, making it a natural fit for the local crime syndicate. In 1957, the raucous good times came to a head when Desert Room owner Nate Zusman found himself at the center of a racketeering scandal and was called to testify by U.S. Senate labor investigator Robert F. Kennedy. Despite claims to the contrary by an associate, brothel madam "Big Helen" Hardy, Zusman denied that he was "an expert on prostitution."[82] His wisecracking testimony famously sent the jury into a fit of giggles, but he eventually testified that the head of the Portland Police's vice squad was a tool of crime boss Jim Elkins.

Saloons, bars, and cafés provide obvious opportunities for cultural exploration, for the kindling of relationships, and even for social reform. However, staying in to drink warm mugs of coffee or to brew the family beer provides a fortuitous connection to the homebodies of Portland's past—those people who simply preferred the view from their own kitchens.

8

LIKE MOTHER USED TO MAKE

Historic Cookbooks and Home Cooking

"A good cook in the home is the surest anti-divorce influence known," wrote *The Oregonian*'s domesticity correspondent Laura Leonard in 1905. This was certainly not new advice to women, but it underscored the importance of food and cooking in the maintenance of family happiness. *The Oregonian* began printing selected "Valuable Recipes" in 1861, the same year Henry Pittock claimed ownership and began running the paper as a daily.[1] These recipes were often slightly altered versions (and sometimes carbon copies) of ones published in *Godey's* or other household magazines, but they offered Portland's new housewives instructions on American cooking with beloved dishes from around the country, as well as a vital link to the cities they had left behind. That Portland's first printed recipes came from New England, the East Coast, and the South reveals much about the city's culinary repertoire today.

Some children were fortunate enough to have grown up learning at Mother's (or Father's) knee. Raised in SE Portland, James Beard's culinary perspective—and nearly the entirety of his childhood happiness—was formed by the home cooking of his two parents and their Chinese cook Let, bolstered by the region's embarrassment of riches. In his autobiography, Beard wrote rapturously of his mother, Elizabeth's cooking; he fawned over her expertly home-canned vegetables, her "mammoth" coconut-cream birthday cakes (his favorite), her picnic lunches of cold chicken sandwiches and hard-boiled eggs wrapped in Japanese cloth napkins and packed on day trips to Oaks Amusement Park.[2] Beard's appreciation for and promotion of both domestic culinary skill and local ingredients has had a lasting impact on the way Portlanders cook at home.

Beard also developed a great knack for cooking foreign foods, thanks in large part to the family cook, Let, and the Chinese amah who cared for Beard when he was a small child. Most often, Portland cooks experimenting with foreign foods were left using domestic ingredients to poorly approximate ethnic recipes (for example, tamales made with cornmeal instead of nixtamalized masa). However, later, some recipes reflected the reverse: a growing integration of ethnic ingredients into the local culinary toolbox. Portland resident Harriet Uchiyama's recipe for "roast chicken," published in the *Portland Christian Schools Tasting Tea Cook Book* (1970), uses hoisin sauce, soy sauce, and sugar to make what is a standard teriyaki sauce (with a recommendation to source exotic ingredients at Anzen).[3] The contrast of another of Uchiyama's recipes in the fundraising cookbook, for "raisin chews," illustrates that Japanese Portlanders, like most Americans, adapted to American cooking styles while keeping at least some of their familial culinary traditions.

Culinary historian Abigail Carroll has pointed out that the current rise in American obesity can be correlated to the decline in home cooking; this has been attributed to several factors, but one of the more salient among them is that many Americans simply do not know to cook.[4] Only a generation ago, this was a rarity; people used to learn to cook at home and at school. A century ago, Portland had its own resident expert to teach "the gentle art of cookery."[5]

DOMESTIC SCIENCE

Not all women enjoyed cooking (whether they had to do it or not), but a good cook has always been a welcome addition to any home. By the turn of the twentieth century, Portland women had a place to become the masters of their kitchens. "If the Portland Y.W.C.A. have their way," wrote Laura Leonard, "the next generation of wives in the City of Roses will regard as their first and foremost wifely duty to know all about the appurtenances of a table, from selecting meats, fish and vegetables, to having them served in tempting and dainty fashions, and this, whether they have all the work to do themselves or have only the supervision of it."[6]

Domestic science, or home economics, was an emerging field for women of the late nineteenth century. Even while women were heading into higher education, there was a concern that girls would finish college only half-developed; intellectual stimulation and academic achievement meant little if she was "handless." One young Portland woman suffered from this condition; she had been the brightest girl in her class, but she had never been taught to use her hands. "It was difficult for her to lift a pan without upsetting it," lamented Lilian Tingle, the director of the Portland School of Domestic Science.[7] "She could scarcely handle a knife without cutting herself, and she was so awkward generally that she was in constant mortification."[8]

Miss Lilian Tingle's cooking classes aimed to correct that, readying the young women of Portland to take on the world. Tingle herself had been busy doing just that; born and raised in Aberdeen, Scotland, she graduated from the city's famous School of Domestic Economy (Robert Gordon's College) in 1896. She went on to higher learning at the University of London, where she studied German and Italian. After a stint in North Dakota on the faculty of State Normal Industrial School, Tingle arrived to Portland in the February of 1905, just in time to be caught in the whirlwind of the Lewis and Clark Centennial Expo celebrations. She had secured a position as the new director of the Portland School of Domestic Science run by the Young Women's Christian Association (YWCA), which had opened a year earlier.

"[H]ome-making . . . is rightly regarded as a woman's first privilege and duty," she wrote, while acknowledging that not all mothers have the time to pass on the craft to their daughters, nor have they necessarily mastered the craft in the first place.[9] Her smart solution was for parents to send their daughters to her school of domestic science for proper training. More than just a cooking school, the Portland School of Domestic Science taught nutrition, bacteriology, and "the theoretical side of gastronomic functions," as well as millinery and sewing.[10] Some of the classes catered to young women wishing to enter domestic work, with varying levels of advancement. Others were for schoolgirls or for "business girls"; another class, held on Saturday evenings, was for Japanese cooks (then as common as Chinese cooks in private homes) to learn American techniques.

Figure 8.1.   Young women in a cooking class at the Portland School of Domestic Science, ca. 1914–1915. Photo © Thomas Robinson

Lilian Tingle was a force with which to be reckoned, and she was a phenomenal role model to young women, regardless of whether or not they intended to use their new skills explicitly for landing a husband. Before her first year in Portland was over, Tingle inspired Portland women to take charge of their kitchens and everything that entered them, when she led the crusade for clean markets; her mission went national three years later when *Good Housekeeping* spotlighted her efforts to women across the country. She began writing a series of weekly columns on cooking and housekeeping for *The Oregonian* only six months after her arrival, and eventually began answering queries from the public.

She possessed an adventurous spirit that sent her traveling around the globe—unescorted by a man. The woman who called herself "merely a confirmed spinster of honorable standing" became versed in Chinese cookery after visiting China in 1907 (writing a series of travel features while abroad), and soon letters from Portland ladies came pouring in inquiring on recipes for "authentic" chop suey.[11] She explored foreign cuisines from around the world and shared her discoveries with local women in a way that was respectful to the culture and accessible to the layperson. By 1908, she had kicked off home economics programs in Portland's high schools. She spent a decade running the School of Domestic Science in Portland while writing weekly columns for *The Oregonian* before taking a position as the head of the Department of Household Arts at the University of Oregon in Eugene.

By the 1930s, Tingle had stopped writing her column, having taken once again to traveling (this time to Yugoslavia and Central Asia) and begun writing features about eating abroad and foreign foodways. Jeanette Cramer took Tingle's place at *The Oregonian* as the home ec editor, but was eventually replaced by Nancy Miller, who ran a popular "Hostess House" column starting in the 1940s. *The Portland News* had its own home ec editor, as did *The Oregon Journal*, with "Mary Cullen." Like many ladies' media personalities of the era, Mary Cullen never actually existed, but was name after Mary Goodall (*The Journal*'s domestic scientist expert in the late 1920s and 1930s) and a shortening of the word *"culinary."* By the 1940s, the woman behind Mary Cullen was Cathrine C. Hindley (née Laughton), who edited *Mary Cullen's Northwest Cook Book*.[12]

Although she was not as prolific a columnist as Lilian Tingle, Hindley was an expert of domestic science in her own right. She wrote the Household Arts Service of the *Oregon Journal* for more than thirty years and was the director of Mary Cullen's Cottage—an actual cottage owned by *The Journal* that offered "an all-embracing homemaking guide for busy homemakers."[13] Founded in 1932, Mary Cullen's Cottage provided homemakers—some of whom had never bothered learning to cook until forced to by the Depression—the opportunity to learn new skills and master the use of modern appliances as those became more available in Portland kitchens.

Hindley was a close personal friend of James Beard's; their family beach houses in Gearhart were next door to one another, and she spent four months testing and reviewing the baking recipes for his monumental *American Cookery,* a task for which she was thanked in his acknowledgments.[14] When Katie Hindley passed away in 1993, the city mourned the loss of a "kind of a Lois Lane with apron and oven gloves—a first-class journalist who had to be among the best in her field in the country."[15]

RADICAL HOMEMAKING

Today, a new culture of gastronomic do-it-yourselfers harken back to the early domestic science movement of the turn of the twentieth century, but raise the stakes: they keep backyard chickens, brew beer, grow produce for canning (or forage from neighborhood streets), ferment yogurt and pickles. Buying meat *en carcasse* is within reach for average householders, with the increased presence of large storage freezers in the average Portland home. Portlanders like knowing farmers and buying food directly from them.

Radical homemaking is not postfeminist; it is neofeminist. Unlike the homemakers from generations past, many modern householders have come to their knowledge without classical home ec training; they are fearless autodidacts who learn from trial and error and from the community's body of knowledge. Today, householding ladies are rarely society ladies, whereas a century ago, Portland's society ladies were the ones publishing the cookbooks.

FIRST COOKBOOKS

Early on, when women of Portland's upper crust came together to publish cookbooks, they brought out recipes that had traveled with them from England (Old and New) or the East Coast—recipes that they likely never actually prepared themselves, but were cooked by their domestic help.

As late as the 1870s, foreign cooking was somewhat resisted. Garlic was treated with suspicion; there was a general repugnance toward ethnicity even when meats with evident anatomy, such as cows' heels and calves' brains, were relished. Just when Oregon was on the verge of statehood, American cookbook author Eliza Leslie was rallying against French cooking, drumming that "in a country as rich as America, where good things are abundant, there is no necessity of imbibing the flatulency of weak washy soups."[16] However, when French cooking techniques began to surface in the 1880s in Portland restaurants like The Lafayette, the Arlington Club, and (later) Hotel Portland, that changed. Portland's culinary landscape became more sophisticated, more cosmopolitan. By the time *The Web-Foot Cook Book* was published in 1885, recipes for *court bouillon* and *puree de tomate* began to appear in the charity cookbooks produced by society women, suggesting that they either prepared these foods at home or at least wanted people to think they did. Provincial French cooking—with its fondness for charcuterie, artisanal ciders, and an ardor for produce at the peak of its season—still plays a significant role in Portland restaurants.

Community cookbooks first began during the Civil War as a way of empowering women to do their part, and between the war and the years following World War I, more than 3,000 church and charity cookbooks were published across the country. In the decades following the publication of *The Web-Foot Cook Book*, dozens of community cookbooks were published in Portland. One from St. David's Episcopal Parish, *Cook Book: Tried, Tested and Proved* (1899), included recipes for hot spiced rum and punch, although some owners of the book would have doubtless preferred not to see liquor.[17] The *Old Fashioned Cook Book: Containing "Mother's Favorite Recipes"* by the Ladies' Aid Society of the Forbes Presbyterian Church (1905) featured tamales, reflecting early twentieth-century Portland's craze for the hot masa pillows.[18] *Dainty Dishes* from the Grace Memorial Episcopal Church (1910s) brought a recipe for bobotee, a South African meat and egg casserole, while the church's later book, *Cooking with Grace* (1996), still included a dated tomato aspic ring with seafood salad in the center.[19] Rose City Park Community Church's cookbook, the 1922 *Choice Recipes*, would have escaped notice if not for its inclusion of a delightful booster cartoon at the end, featuring "Billy Beaver" scolding a housewife for "buying at random" instead of selecting Oregon products.[20]

Seventh Day Adventists had two vegetarian cookbooks affiliated with their sanitaria: The *Sanitarium Eclectic Cook Book* (1901), which was the first vegetarian cookbook published in Portland, reads like any of the Kellogg books, with its reliance on nut milks, granose, protose, and various other "-oses"; the other, *Vegetarian Cook Book*, had originally been published by the Mountain View, California-based Pacific Press in 1910, and was reprinted in Portland four years later. The 1920s also saw the issue of two Masonic cookbooks, produced by the local ladies' auxiliaries the Order of the Eastern Star, Mount Scott Chapter No. 110 (1924) and Amaranth's Grand Court (1928).

Besides simply sharing the recipes of a place's ordinary (if wealthy) citizens, community cookbooks offer the chance to see the broad changes in local and national cooking trends, and as they present snapshots of the many details of the home, they are invaluable to culinary historians. When examining several generations of cookbooks, one can see how recipes from the same family may be altered based on personal preferences or the rationing of ingredients. The recipes a woman saved and shared gives readers a glimpse about her relative socioeconomic status; they reveal her skill level at and interest in cooking; they reveal the most intimate detail of her home: how it smells.

WEB-FOOT COOK BOOK (1885)

Although the earliest cookbooks date back to the medieval era and were written for and by royal chefs, most average home cooks found that cookbooks were integral to achieving culinary success. Like young women across the country, Portland's brides were gifted with cookbooks and the best of wishes for keeping her husband's affections. In the nineteenth century this was typically a copy of *Boston Cooking School Cook Book*, but before the century was up, it was possible for brides to receive a locally published book: *The Web-Foot Cookbook*. Produced in 1885 by the San Grael Society of the fashionable First Presbyterian Church, the book was the first cookbook published in the Pacific Northwest. It later became one of James Beard's favorites, although it was already exceedingly difficult to find by the early 1950s.[21] Beard includes the book's layered, New England–style fish chowder recipe in his essential *American Cookery*, with the comment that most people used butter instead of salt pork, and a recommendation to pour a bit of cream over the top before serving.[22]

The majority of the book's 476 recipes were from Portland women, but a few came from elsewhere in the region, including Seattle, Salem, and Astoria. Some of the recipes came from other cookbooks, such as the Victorian bestseller *Mrs. Beeton's Book of Household Management* (1861). Mostly, though, the book serves as a culinary yearbook of the who's-who of Portland women: the daughters and wives of Failing, Hoyt, Ladd, Reed, Corbett, Dekum, Meier, and Frank, among myriad other prominent families. The recipes, nearly a quarter of which were desserts, reflect the sensibilities of wealthy women, and with numerous recipes for chowders, Shaker-style salt cod, baked beans, and biscuits, it also reflects the New England origins of the majority of Portland's more affluent residents. The cookbook also offered women an innocuous platform from which to express political perspectives like temperance, with recipes for Temperance Plum Pudding (in which the brandy is woefully missing), or woman's suffrage, represented by Mrs. Edes' Election Cake.[23]

Some of the women preferred to keep their foods, rather than their politics, coyly masked. A salad called "The Mystery" and a cake called "Mystery Pudding" both come shrouded in creamy veils, of mayonnaise dressing and vanilla whipped cream, respectively. Another mystery is the recipe for Emperor Napoleon's Salad, one that bears little resemblance to the *haricots de Soissons* (kidney beans with oil) that Napoleon was rumored to have enjoyed.[24] Composed of lettuce and chicories and topped with hard-boiled egg, olives, potatoes, beets, a cucumber pickle, and onions (and topped with a garlicky Caesar-style egg yolk, mustard, and vinegar dressing), the salad more closely resembles a *salade Niçoise*, and no explanation is given as to the salad's name.[25]

With a full chapter on camp cooking, "where the only culinary utensils carried are a frying pan and a small bucket or kettle," the *Web-Foot* reveals the recreation habits of Western families.[26] By the time the cookbook was published, most of the wealthy women of First Presbyterian had come to Oregon the easy way: by rail or steamship. These women never had to bother with baking in a Dutch oven over an open fire, or had to fry a fresh trout under the cover of starlight. In fact, the recipes in the chapter appear to have been written entirely by men. A few, like "To Roast Potatoes in Camp" and "Roast Venison," were attributed to Nessmuck, the pen name of *Field and Stream* writer and outdoorsman George W. Sears. Many recipes came from Portland poultry breeder T.N. Strong, but the most detailed of the camp recipes were written by thoroughbred horse breeder Thomas B. Merry.[27] One interesting recipe, for "Shingled Trout," offers instructions on plank cookery; Merry suggests preparing the meal by first catching a fish from the heavily timbered waters of the Wilson River at Tillamook, makes a recommendation of eating from "granite ironware with small handles, such as are used for shirred eggs," and even gives a bit of advice on how to multitask so the fish is done at the same time as one's potatoes.[28] Because the fish was to have been buttered before going over the fire, "[t]his dish requires no gravy," he promises, "and the man who proposes it should be sent to Coventry, *nem con* (a British turn of phrase meaning that anyone proposing the fish needed gravy should be ostracized, forthwith)."

The book also includes a range of very basic recipes, sometimes given names with a bit of local flair, like the one for "Trinity Church Salad" (from another of Portland's posh churches, Trinity Episcopal), which turns out to be a rather unoriginal chicken salad mixed with minced celery and mayonnaise. There is a recipe for a plain sponge cake that, according to Mrs. Wesley Jackson (whose husband sat on First Presbyterian's board of directors) is "a very old recipe, and well known among old residents of Portland." (Twenty years later, *The Portland Ideal Cook Book* referred to an identical sponge recipe as "the old fashioned 'dia bread' (diet bread) of our grandmothers; the only cake children were allowed to eat").[29] Mrs. Corbett included a recipe for "Water Ice," which sounds simple and plain enough, but is actually an early Popsicle recipe made from a simple syrup flavored with citrus peel and juice.

THE PORTLAND IDEAL COOK BOOK (1905)

The Portland Ideal Cook Book was compiled by the George Wright Relief Corps No. 2 of the Grand Army of the Republic (GAR), a veterans' fraternal organization founded at the end of the Civil War. The GAR's Women's Relief Corps was the world's largest all-women charitable organization by the late nineteenth century, and when *The Portland Ideal Cook Book* was published in 1905, the group had eighty members in the city. Unlike other charity cookbooks, *The Portland Ideal Cook Book* was not penned by society ladies. The group's president, Civil War widow Helen N. Packard, was a poet and newspaper correspondent who had moved from Massachusetts to Portland for, of all reasons, the weather.[30]

The book made the optimistic claim that "[a]ll recipes, having been tried and approved, are, therefore, warranted not to kill," while challenging anyone without a private cook (and would therefore be left to try the recipes herself) to disagree. The book's publishing was funded by selling advertising, and to keep the advertisers happy, the book warned that if satisfactory results were to be guaranteed, "supplies must be purchased from the advertisers found herein."[31]

The cookbook includes three recipes for breakfast cakes using huckleberries and recipes from popular magazines of the era like *Table Talk* (to which Charles Dickens was a frequent contributor). Oysters feature prominently. It includes a poem by Helen Packard that tends toward gallantry and unyielding loyalty to Country; however, the book's title page is graced with the work of another American poet: Eugene Field. This poem—this song of culinary patriotism—reveals the soul of a true Yankee.

Full many a sinful notion
Conceived of foreign powers,
Has come across the ocean
To harm this land of ours;
And heresies called fashions
Have modesty effaced,
And baleful morbid passions
Corrupt our native taste.
O tempora! O Moses!
What profanation these
That seek to dim the glories
Of apple pies and cheese! [32]

THE NEIGHBORHOOD COOK BOOK (1912)

The Neighborhood Cook Book was published by Portland's Council of Jewish Women in 1912. It sold out within ten months, and a second edition was issued in 1914. The book was published as a fund-raiser for Neighborhood House, a Jewish community center opened in 1905 by Jeanette Meier (widow of Meier & Frank founder Aaron Meier) and Tilly Selling (wife of legislator, businessman, and philanthropist Ben Selling). The Neighborhood House acted as a settlement for recent immigrants, opened the city's first well-baby clinic, and ran one of the first free kindergartens in Portland, educating the children of immigrants (the building is now home to Cedarwood Waldorf School). In its unwavering education and advocacy for immigrants, the Neighborhood House anchored people to their new community in South Portland.

The Neighborhood Cook Book speaks in many ways of this progressivism; it was the first cookbook in Portland to feature a recipe using the novel new California export, avocadoes (then still known as "alligator pears"), and it was only the second Jewish American cookbook written after the reform of Judaism, a fact that is revealed by the great many non-kosher recipes. It makes liberal use of the region's abundance of shellfish, for example—a testimony to the relatively high socioeconomic status of

Portland's established Jewish community.[33] However, the book also highlights a pragmatism and thrift consistent with housewives of the era, offering advice on how to select the best fish, for example, or how to put kitchen waste to best use: "the ham bone, the tough end of beefsteak, the few spoonfuls of vegetables . . . will yield up their final atoms of juiciness and flavor in the soup kettle only."[34] Although the book is not kosher, it does dissuade the reader from pork due to its indigestibility, which the book says is owing to the "large accumulation of fat between the [muscle] fibers."[35]

The cookbook features many classic Jewish recipes using local ingredients. Despite the Ashkenazic preference of freshwater fish over ocean fish is evident in the recipe for Scharfe fish, which consists of poached steelhead in a rich egg sauce, and the gefilte fish recipe uses salmon and halibut rather than carp and whitefish. Marrow ball, liver Kloesse (dumpling), and Einlauf (egg drop) soups hail straight from Germany, whence South Portland's first Jews came. The bread chapter, however, with its rusks, soda biscuit, and Sally Lunn, reflects the general American tastes of the era, rather than of Jews specifically. The recipe for "Little Breads" (*Brödchen*), made from a dough sweetened with sugar and potatoes, and enriched with butter and milk, is braided, glazed with egg, and sprinkled with poppy seeds, calling to mind challah.

In *The Neighborhood Cook Book*, one recipe stands out as an original, at least by name: "Saddle Bags a la Rothchild." This dish, a large tenderloin steak that has been slit open and stuffed with oysters and basted in a glaze of ketchup, Worcestershire sauce, and butter, is a clever nod to the luxury dish called carpetbag steak, which dates back to the 1890s. Perhaps the Council of Jewish Women supposed that saddlebags would have been more useful to a Westerner than carpetbags. The dish was named after wealthy Portland liquor distributor and banker Fred Rothchild, a man who could eat Saddle Bags anytime he pleased.[36]

THE *PORTLAND WOMEN'S EXCHANGE COOK BOOK* (1913)

The Portland Women's Exchange was comprised exclusively of society ladies, such as suffragist Sara Bard Field (who would later marry prominent lawyer C. E. S. Wood), and the wives of businessmen-cum-politicians Henry Corbett and Josiah Failing. James Beard wrote the introduction for the 1973 reprint of the *Portland Women's Exchange Cook Book*, and peppered the book with his comments and witty asides in the footnotes. Some of his notes offer that the recipe was one of his favorites, or suggest ingredient substitutions for the modern cook, while others helpfully point out that an ingredient was spelled incorrectly, or that another, such as calf's head, had become "rather difficult to come by."[37]

The Portland Women's Exchange, which began in 1891, was part of a national philanthropic movement to "help women to help themselves" by providing an honorable venue for disadvantaged women to peddle their wares and skills.[38] The movement was founded by Queen Victoria in 1880 as the "Working Ladies' Guild," and although it was meant to be self-sustaining, the only revenue for the Portland branch was generated by the club's restaurant, which was also used for private events. At first, Portland's Women's Exchange was the only one in the United States that was purportedly self-sustaining.[39] However, despite Beard's assertion in the book's foreword that the food was excellent, the costs of running the restaurant and tea room eventually exceeded its revenue. By 1912, even after years of successful charity events, *The Oregonian* reported that the Women's Exchange was nearly $2,000 in the hole—around $48K today.[40] The cookbook was a noble effort to pull the organization out of crushing debt, and it survived for a while longer, only to fold after World War II.

Despite its failure to save the organization, the cookbook had been a heroic endeavor. It drew from its restaurant's most loved menu items, such as chicken pie and creamed clams. The compilers also called on some of Portland's best-known chefs de cuisine for recipes. August Vergez of the Imperial Hotel provided his recipe for Sweetbreads Imperial: delicate slices of the hypothalamus, fried to a golden brown and served in a tureen with a sherry-cream sauce enriched with egg yolks, and "[s]ome nice brown toast on the side."[41]

One lovely little recipe in the "Custardy Things" chapter is Mabel Weidler's "Berries and Cheese," calling simply for cottage cheese to be sieved and whipped with cream until smooth, served with fresh strawberries and raspberries and a sprinkling of sugar.[42] Another, for "Tomatoes Portland," is from the chef of the Portland Hotel; it is comprised of a salad of crab and hard-boiled egg, dressed in a tarragon- and chervil-scented mayonnaise that has been piped artfully into a hollowed-out tomato half.[43] Typical of the era, there are also a dozen or so cake recipes that, aside from their creative names (such as "Bachelor Cake," "Apple Sauce Cake," or "Dumbarton Cake"), differ primarily in their respective amounts of raisins, walnuts, and nutmeg.

AN ALL-WESTERN CONSERVATION COOK BOOK (1917)

This cookbook, published in the height of World War I, offered a way for the housewife to do her part by number-crunching to victory. "Our cook books, and the recipes copied from them . . . were all published during times of plenty," wrote Inie Gage Chapel (using the *nom de plume* Aunt Prudence), head of the *Evening Telegram*'s Kitchen Department in the book's introduction. "[N]ot only are unnecessarily expensive ingredients used in them, but all things that are the least imperfect are rejected, leaving us with much of our war gardens unused."[44] Chapel's solution to this problem of waste and extravagance was to cook economically, and to stick to plain, healthy foods, perfectly cooked. To assist the housewife with this endeavor, each recipe included a breakdown of cost by ingredient (including fuel costs for cooking times!), so that one could ascertain the actual, *true* cost per serving of her meals, down to the 1/100th of a cent. "No one has tried to tell us accurately what each recipe really does cost before," she points out, while putting the onus on housewives to submit their own cost-saving recipes to do their "bit" for the war effort. Chapel noted that Portland women who had originated in "barren New England" were better suited to this task of belt-tightening than "the women who have grown up in this warm, luxuriant garden land, the fertile Willamette Valley."[45]

Thankfully, the fecund bosom of the Willamette Valley offered Portland women another way to do their patriotic duty: heavy use of the War Garden, which had been initiated in March 1917 by the newly formed U.S. National War Garden Commission. In Portland, where most lot sizes averaged 5,000 square feet, War Gardens (also known as Victory Gardens) were highly productive, miniature munitions plants.[46] In *An All-Western Conservation Cook Book*, Chapel outlines which vegetables may be harvested on a weekly basis, and provides tips for preserving them to get through the lean times. This approach paved the way for books like *Growing Vegetables West of the Cascades* in 1980, written by Oregon homesteader and Territorial Seed Company founder Steve Solomon twenty years after he began his journey into self-sufficiency, and during the economic crash of 2005, Solomon's *Gardening When It Counts: Growing Food in Hard Times*, which harkened back to the Victory Garden efforts and those of Portland's school gardens in the 1910s.

An All-Western Conservation Cook Book was ahead of its time in its presentation of several recipes for plants that may be harvested from the wild and prepared in civilized ways. Chapel asserted that *The Evening Telegram* was a newspaper for the middle class ("to which most of us belong more exclusively than any other"), and the recipes in the cookbook reflected that.[47] The treatment of wild foods and urban foraging was unashamed; elderberries, Oregon-grape (botanically unrelated to grapes), and the seedy evergreen blackberry were given their due respect with jelly recipes.

A later wartime book, *Bundles for Britain Cook Book* (1941), was produced at the onset of World War II as "a means of aiding Britain."[48] It includes restaurateur Henry Thiele's Princess Charlotte Pudding, but otherwise recycles many recipes originally printed in the *Portland Women's Exchange Cook Book* of 1913. The book contains a great many British recipes like kedgeree and cock-a-leekie, but as it was produced by Portland society ladies, it also includes many French recipes and even one for *Potage Bouillabaise* [*sic*] *Marseillaise* (French fish soup) from the prestigious Arlington Club. The recipe is no humble fisherman's stew; in addition to the usual rockfish, leeks, potatoes, and a mix of other common seafood, it contains two pounds of lobster, Rhenish wine, and French cognac, and is topped with sliced baguette browned in olive oil. "This recipe must not be used for commercial purposes," Chef Horn advises, "only for Kings, Queens, Dukes, Counts and Epicureans."[49]

MARY CULLEN'S NORTHWEST COOK BOOK (1946)

The first commercial cookbook published in Portland was *Mary Cullen's Cook Book* (1938), which included a selection of Oregon recipes in a chapter titled "Oregon Favorites—Foods with a Western Flavor" (these were mostly for wild game and fruit-based desserts).[50] Her *Northwest Cook Book* is a snapshot of Oregon life immediately following World War II, at the onset of the Baby Boom. It was written by local celebrity Mary Cullen, aka Cathrine C. Laughton, who was the *Oregon Journal*'s answer to Lilian Tingle. The book has no introduction, but instead jumps right in with a frank discussion of appetizers—"the dress-up touch to a rather commonplace meal."[51] The appetizer, Laughton suggested, bought the housewife a few minutes to finish preparing the meal for her dinner guests. Even better, it offered her the chance to trot out jazzy hors d'oeuvres like smoked salmon pinwheels and celery sticks filled with all manner of spreadable cheese.

The book is a glimpse into the meals women prepared as they were settling down in the suburbs with the handsome young men, newly returned from war. It inspired a generation of Portland housewives to produce vast crudités platters garnished with Thousand Island dressing, and to always prepare enough casserole to feed ten. In this book, ambiguous or unappetizing casserole names begin to appear: the Depression-era classic called "More" was "[a] Northwest favorite to prepare," intended to serve those fresh in from rollicking on the beach or from skiing, which are pastimes supposedly enjoyed by all Northwesterners.[52] The dish is a goulash of ground beef, tomatoes, and macaroni, with the addition of a cup each of canned black olives and peas. "Goop" was, contrary to its name, the "dressiest main dish we know of," and like More, it was intended to serve those coming in all abluster from outdoor activities.[53] The one-pot meal is comprised of an entire chicken and a whole knuckle of veal simmered with spaghetti, mushrooms, and olives, and topped with a staggering three cups of grated cheese.

True to the region, the book contains many recipes using salmon, oysters, and crab. Like *The Web-Foot Cook Book*, the *Northwest Cook Book* features a chapter on outdoor cookery for the barbecue master or chuck wagon enthusiast. Because the Weber grill was still five years away from invention, the cooking techniques were a bit more reminiscent of that of the pioneers on the wagon train, requiring a campsite or an open fire pit in one's backyard for proper execution. As such, recipes for Dutch oven beans, biscuits, and fried ham abound. There were also numerous recipes for preparing the region's wild fish and game. Laughton's recipes for Columbia River smelt, which are harvested by dip net (and "by hand, in bird cages, in shirts and in hats") from the Sandy River, are more straightforward than Lilian Tingle's, which called for placing the tail of the smelt in its mouth or through its eyes before frying, to present a dainty ring-shape.[54]

WEST COAST COOK BOOK (1952)

Helen Evans Brown despised tuna casserole. One of the earliest tuna
noodle casserole recipes published anywhere in America appears in a
community cookbook that was written to help Portland families embrace
their immigrant neighbors. Although there is nothing German about the
"German Noodles and Tuna Fish" recipe from the 1932 *Cook Book of
Many Lands*, it does bear a striking resemblance to a recipe that appeared
in *Sunset* magazine two years prior from a reader in Kennewick, Washington, made from the same Holy Trinity of noodles, tuna, and white
sauce, with a pretty pimento garnish. The recipe by the mysterious "Mrs.
W. F. S." adds the mushrooms and the cheese topping familiar today; in
fact, the addition of mushrooms may have inspired the widespread switch
to canned cream of mushroom soup in lieu of labor-intensive white
sauce.[55] Helen Evans Brown may not have realized that this dish—this
invaluable tool in the midcentury housewife's culinary arsenal—originated in the Pacific Northwest when she wrote about why she intentionally
omitted recipes for which she did not much care, regardless of their favor
among others. "If, for instance, a dish composed of tuna fish, canned
mushroom soup, and corn flakes is in any danger of becoming a dish of
the region, I prefer to ignore it. If by doing so I can give it ever so gentle a
nudge toward oblivion, that is good."[56] Ms. Brown may have shoved with
all her might toward oblivion's abyss in 1952, but more than six decades
later, tuna casserole appears to be staying safely put.

West Coast Cook Book, while not specifically from or about Portland,
is a masterpiece of regional gastronomy and is written with a deftness and
wit rivaled only by M. F. K. Fisher. Helen Evans Brown was a prolific
cookbook author and a very close friend of James Beard's—their correspondence was more than enough to fill a book, which culminated in
Love and Kisses and a Halo of Truffles. She wrote in *West Coast Cook
Book* that the three types of recipes included in her book were steadfast
historic recipes (that she *liked*, mind), dishes that were well known in the
West (and known elsewhere as being of the West), and recipes from the
region's famous eateries. Although several of Portland's earliest cookbooks featured recipes from the Portland Hotel, the Multnomah Hotel, or
the Arlington Club, these had been treated as the carrot that made the
book worth the price. Brown, however, took a different approach, prefer-

ring the stories about the establishments (and customers) themselves rather than dwelling on the fame of the chef.

Brown proclaimed that denizens of the West excelled at barbecue; although those are fighting words to Southerners and Midwesterners, she had done her homework. "The pioneers … roasted much of their meat and game in the open, over campfires," she sagely pointed out, and "[t]hey also learned pit-roasting from the Indians, who used that cookery technique for their camas roots."[57] These same pioneers, she wrote, satisfied their sweet tooth with pies baked from wild berries. She included many Chinese and Mexican recipes, recognizing the contributions these immigrants made to the West's culinary landscape. Although many of her recipes were made "Oregonian" by simply tacking "Oregon" on the name (or in one instance, "Clackamas Pheasant Casserole," without explanation as to what made it "Clackamas"), she does offer much insight as to how early Oregonians and Portlanders ate. Her recipe for "Pheasant with Cream Gravy" is spot-on in its claim that, to the pioneers, pheasant was simply what one ate instead of chicken.

"The entire history of the West Coast is flavored with oysters," Brown aptly wrote.[58] If the rest of her seafood chapter is any indication, it is also flavored with the crab legs served by Dan & Louis downtown, "where you can dine like a king without paying his ransom."[59] It is flavored with Columbia River smelt, "so rich that the aborigines dried and burned them like candles, and gave a lovely light."[60] She includes a recipe for steelhead cooked *en papillote*, and unlike earlier Portland cookbooks, which relied on canned fish, Brown's salmon recipes call for fresh fillets of "the red red gold."[61]

HISTORIC PORTLAND RECIPES

Although modern Portland seems to have largely forgotten its historic love of seafood, cookbooks of the past reveal a town that was enrapt with fish and shellfish. Oddly, despite the magnificent abundance of salmon practically leaping into boats, most historic recipes called for canned salmon, a fact that did not escape Helen Evans Brown. Even a century ago, fresh salmon was more expensive than meat, for reasons less obvious than they are now. (Fifty years prior, salmon was the penny-pincher's protein of choice.)

Portlanders were similarly enamored of cakes and other baked goods, and still are; Portland bakeries consistently top Best Of lists in *Saveur*, *Food and Wine*, and *Bon Appetit*. Portland's historic cookbooks often relied heavily on baked goods, and not just because sliced bread had yet to be invented.

Presented here is a small selection of recipes that stand out as being either evocative of or unique to the historic City of Roses, or that showcased the best the city had to offer. They are arranged by the era in which they were most heartily relished by Portlanders.

Portland Oyster Rabbit

Keith's Oyster House was "where the gay blades of the '50s ate oysters, drank wine and made whoopee and goodness knows what all, until 3 o'clock [a.m.] and after," wrote Helen Evans Brown. At Keith's, which was at its height in the mid-nineteenth century, one might order oyster stew or the Olympia fry with a side of the famous cabbage slaw and buttered bread. This rarebit (aka "rabbit"), Brown supposed, may have been enjoyed by some of those wild late night/early morning revelers:

> Cook a cup of small oysters in their own liquor until their edges curl. In a pan over hot water, melt a tablespoon of butter, add ½ pound of Oregon Cheddar, and a little salt and pepper. Stir and cook *slowly* while the cheese melts. Then add the oyster liquor also slowly, and 2 beaten eggs. When smooth, stir in the oysters and serve at once on toast, and don't forget some ice-cold beer! Serves 4. [62]

Duck Salmi

This recipe, submitted by a "Portland Amateur Sportsman," was one of the few in *The Web-Foot Cook Book* furnished by a man (outside of the camping chapter). Portland's first citizens were largely men, and more than one took to duck hunting in Portland's vast wetlands, such as Guild's Lake.

> Take two nice mallards, draw them and place the giblets in a stew-pan, with a little mace, bay leaf, cayenne pepper and salt, and a little water, and let simmer slowly until tender. Then take out giblets and chop fine with a small onion. Return them with the liquor in the stew-pan, and

add a glass of good sherry; stew slowly for ten minutes, then add bread crumbs, a little sage and pounded celery seed, and stuff the ducks with this compound. Place the ducks in a large stew-pan, a half pound of good butter, and when it is quite hot place the ducks in it, stirring them around until they get nicely browned, then add boiling water just to cover the ducks. Chop one-quarter pound of bacon into dice and add two onions stuck with cloves, one carrot, with pepper and salt to suit taste. Let simmer very slowly until ducks are tender, then add one bottle of claret and skim off the fat rising to the surface. After adding the wine, let the ducks simmer eight or ten minutes in it and add two cans of mushrooms sliced. Cook slowly ten minutes and serve hot—ducks in the center, dry toast around edges, mashed potatoes on side. If you have two ducks and have only one friend to assist you, and it kills him when done, he will die contented and happy.[63]

Lumber Camp Doughnuts

"The slogan of the camp foreman is pretty apt to be, 'Feed the men, so I can get logs,'" read a 1919 issue of *The Four L Lumber News*.[64] The doughnut recipe included in the magazine called for three cups of sugar, 1½ pints of egg yolks, 2½ quarts milk, eight ounces of baking soda, and ten pounds of flour, and was flavored with vanilla and lemon. This recipe from the *West Coast Cook Book* differs in that it is a raised (rather than cake-style) doughnut, and it makes a bit fewer than 150 doughnuts. Helen Evans Brown pointed out that bear lard would have been used in the early days, but as that ingredient is difficult to come by (and just imagine the flavor), regular pig lard is recommended here—preferably the lard from Tails and Trotters' pigs, which are fattened in hazelnut orchards.[65] The lumberjack's suggested addition of lemon zest and vanilla is a nice touch, or they could be tossed with cinnamon sugar when hot.

A cup of evaporated milk is mixed with a cup of hot water, 1 cup of dark brown sugar, a cake of yeast dissolved in ¼ cup of water, 2/3 cup of lard (bear lard was used in the early days), 2 teaspoons of salt, and enough flour to make a soft dough, about 4 cups. This is allowed to rise, then rolled and cut with a doughnut cutter. It is then allowed to rise again (on a floured board), before frying in deep fat (370°). Camp cooks often pinched off big hunks of the soft dough instead of rolling and cutting it, an idea which should be used more often. These dough-nuts are light as a feather, as anyone who has eaten them can testify.[66]

Pink Gefilte Fish

Portland's Jewish mothers and grandmothers brought traditional recipes to the Northwest in the 1860s, but made adjustments based on local ingredients. Plentiful and affordable, salmon made its way into even gefilte fish, yielding a lovely pink version of the classic dish. This recipe for "Gefullte Fish," from *The Neighborhood Cook Book*, is similar to the handwritten recipe by Edith Zusman—the grandmother of Portland judge and *Artisan Jewish Deli at Home* co-author Michael Zusman.

> In making this dish, some people use the skin of the fish, and serve the balls in it, fastening the skin together with toothpicks. Others serve the balls plain. Pass two pounds of halibut and two pounds of salmon through a meat grinder. Add salt and pepper to taste, finely sliced onion, which has been smothered in butter, from one to three whole eggs, three or four slices of bread, which have been soaked in water and most of the moisture pressed out, and some parsley. Form the above mixture into balls. Into a deep stew pan place the fish bones (for flavoring), some sliced carrots, celery, onion and parsley, and add the fish balls, covering all with water. After boiling steadily for twenty minutes, remove the balls carefully, strain the gravy, and add a cube of sugar. Beat the yolks of three eggs well, add the hot gravy slowly, stirring constantly while doing so, and serve with the fish. [67]

Huckleberry Breakfast Cake

Although *The Portland Ideal Cook Book* could be fairly heavy-handed with the product placement, this specific recipe did not mention brands by name. Suffice it to say, it would have been best made with Portland Flouring Mills' Olympic Cake and Pastry Flour ("especially prepared to make flaky pie crust and delicate cake"), Northwest-grown beet sugar, and wild-harvested berries. [68]

> One pint of flour before sifting, ½ cup of sugar, 1 cup of milk, 1 egg, 2 tablespoonfuls of melted butter, 2 teaspoonfuls of baking powder, 1½ cups of huckleberries. Bake in a long pan, pour in about 1 inch deep. Eat hot with butter for breakfast or lunch. [69]

Lewis and Clark Fair Cake

The Lewis and Clark Centennial, celebrated in 1905, brought out revelers from around the country. And as with any celebration, there was cake. This one comes from the Ladies Aid Society of the Piedmont Presbyterian Church, who produced the charity cookbook *Choice Recipes*—a common name for cookbooks at the time; there were four books with this title produced in Portland alone by the 1920s. Since Portland Flouring Mills was one of this cookbook's sponsors in addition to the *Portland Ideal Cook Book*, the brand Olympic flour is specified here, as well. Unfortunately, the recipe's author, Mrs. Swinton, seems to have forgotten to include the baking instructions.

> One cup white sugar, one-half cup of butter, one-half cup of milk, one and one-half cups of sifted Olympic flour (before), three eggs, beaten separately, three teaspoons baking powder. ICING FOR CAKE. Six tablespoons grated chocolate, one-half cup of sugar, four tablespoons of milk; put this on the stove until it dissolves, cool, pour on the cake, flavor with Woodlark's vanilla; use boiled frosting.[70]

Rose Petal Conserve

For the opening of the 1909 Rose Festival, Lilian Tingle thoughtfully offered several recipes using roses, found within her personal collection of old cookbooks, some of which she claimed were more than 150 years old. "Rose petal conserve put up in tiny glasses, with a decorated label in water color makes a dainty present. The conserve may be spread on wafers, used as sweet sandwiches for afternoon tea or passed with cream cheese, like Bar-le-duc preserves [a French currant jelly]."[71] Her recipe comes from an unnamed source, but would be a delightful addition to any Portland cook's repertoire.

> Take the opening buds of the true scarlet roses. Clip off all the red part. To each pound of roses, beat and sift two pounds of fine sugar; pound the roses very well in a marble mortar, then stir in the sugar by degrees, and continue pounding until all the sugar is thoroughly incorporated with the roses. If you think it too thin, add more sugar until they will receive no more. So put into small pots for use.[72]

Schacht Cocktail

This simple seafood appetizer appeared on the menu at the Portland Hotel in the 1910s, but was missing by 1921. Despite the fact that half of its ingredients are not kosher, the recipe was published in *The Neighborhood Cook Book*. The use of expensive seafood reveals the hotel's high status, and the inclusion of the recipe in the book reveals a Jewish community that was well-integrated economically and socially. [73]

> One oyster, one clam (hard shell), two crab claws on lettuce, caviar on lettuce, one piece of lobster, two anchovies, a teaspoon of minced onion, one-half lemon. Serve on ice. [74]

Crab Louis

As noted by James Beard, this dish arose in San Francisco and Portland at approximately the same time, so its origin is uncertain. A recipe appears on the menu of the Old Poodle Dog in San Francisco in 1908, and another appears in *The Neighborhood Cook Book* just four years later. [75] The book's recipe for "Crab a la San Francisco," notes historian Richard Engeman, is much closer to modern Crab Louis recipes.

> Crab Louis—Three tablespoons oil, one of vinegar, one-half of catsup, two teaspoons Worcestershire sauce, paprika, salt, little English mustard, two hard boiled eggs, one shredded crab and shredded lettuce; mix together. Serve on lettuce leaves. [76]

> Crab a la San Francisco—Take out the meat of a large cooked crab in as large pieces as possible, put in cocktail glasses and, just before serving, pour over it the following sauce: One cup cream, half cup tomato catsup, one tablespoon Worcestershire sauce, salt and paprika. Let stand on ice for at least two hours. This will serve six people. [77]

Eben Gläce

These strawberry dumplings (also spelled *Eben Kloese*) were standard fare among the Volga Germans who settled the Albina neighborhood between the 1890s and 1910s. This recipe, from Portland resident Marcia Staunton, was one of her grandfather's favorites. "[Aunt] Abeth cooked for the whole family every so often and she would do the special dishes, gläce (a dumpling that was a bit heavy), chili, cabbage rolls, etc. If Grandpa wasn't feeling good she would have to make gläce for him. Always said it made his stomach feel better."[78] *Eben Gläce* would be sublime with local Hood strawberries.

> 4 c. flour 2 eggs 1 c. hot water. Make dough. Let rest. Divide dough [into four] and roll one 1/4 at a time. Roll as for pie dough. Cut into 4" squares. Top with sweetened fresh strawberries (use only fresh berries) and 1/2 teas. dried bread crumbs. Bring corners up and pinch well. Drop into boiling water—cook 5-7 minutes. Drain. Cover with cream and melted butter. This is a meal not a dessert. My grandparents came from Norka [village near present-day Saratov, Russia]. This what they ate and what I grew up eating.[79]

Indian Cocktail

Served by the Portland Hotel and the Multnomah Hotel, much mystery surrounds the Indian cocktail, the recipe for which has never been published. Its death knell appears to have been Prohibition, as the cocktail was invented in 1912, only two years prior to Oregon's enactment of the law. The Multnomah took matters to absurd heights by putting out a want ad in the *East Oregonian* in Pendleton in 1914, seeking "an Indian maid to serve Indian cocktails."[80] The hotel manager beseeched the mayor of Pendleton "to supply him with a redskin lassie. . . . She must be young, pretty, and able to speak good English," in addition to being willing to wear a costume.[81]

The Neighborhood Cook Book features several cocktail recipes of the same period, including the Portland Hotel's "Wild Irish Rose" (different from the bottom-shelf fortified wine preferred by hoboes) and another called "Indian Milk Punch." It is quite possible that the latter is the Indian Cocktail in disguise; the recipe makes an amount typically only needed by a professional bartender.

> Indian Milk Punch—Remove the thin yellow part from the rinds of six lemons, steep in one-half bottle of rum for twenty-four hours. Take five bottles rum, two pounds sugar, the juice of the lemons already used with that of six more. Mix in a large vessel, add two quart bottles of water, one-fourth ounce each of ground nutmeg, cloves, cinnamon

and one-half ounce ginger. Mix well, pouring over all two quarts boiling milk. Let stand a moment, then stir well, cover closely until next day, then strain through a four-folded flannel bag. Fill in clear bottles. The longer it is kept the better it is. If the spices are not perfectly fresh and strong, use a slightly larger quantity. [82]

Crab or Lobster in Casserole

This fantastic gratin recipe, from the *Bundles for Britain Cook Book,* is unattributed, but is a glorious example of a purely Oregon dish made from local ingredients. It is not only the first recipe for a crab casserole to appear in a Portland cookbook, but it is the earliest recipe calling for Tillamook cheese in any Portland cookbook—particularly notable at a time when American cheese was the first choice for Mornay sauce. In the 1940s, the only cheese Tillamook made was cheddar, so that is what this recipe would presumably use. This dish would be sublime with Dungeness crab and freshly foraged lobster mushrooms or chanterelles.

1 ½ cups crab or lobster
4 hard-boiled eggs
½ lb. sauted (sic) mushrooms
3 tablespoons butter
3 tablespoons flour
1 ½ cups milk
½ cup grated Tillamook cheese
3 tablespoons sherry
¾ cup walnut meats, whole
Salt and pepper

Mix butter and flour over low fire and then add milk, stirring until thick. Add grated cheese, sherry, salt and pepper. Simmer awhile. Butter baking dish, place alternate layers of crab, eggs, mushrooms with walnuts, sprinkled throughout. Cover with sauce and on top a thin coating of bread crumbs. Place in oven at 350 degrees for about an hour. [N.B. about half this cooking time would suffice.] [83]

Dutch Babies

Helen Evans Brown says that German pancakes, also known as "Dutch" (Deutsch) babies are "immensely popular in Seattle," but they are popular with a similar intensity in Portland, where they have been served at the Original House of Pancakes since 1953.[84] German pancakes are a long-time Portland favorite; they were a top-selling item at Henry Thiele Restaurant in the 1930s, and a recipe for Dutch babies (by name) is published in *Mary Cullen's Cook Book*.[85] They resemble a Yorkshire pudding, which Lilian Tingle has claimed was her second-favorite recipe (when asked for her favorite recipe by a reader of her column, she coyly replied that most of her favorite recipes would be unsuitable to share). Tingle wrote that "there are a very large number of recipes for German pancakes" and shared one for her readers in 1920. Although it is far less rich than Brown's Dutch baby recipe, it is a bit simpler to prepare.

> 2 eggs, 1 cup milk, three-quarters to 1 cup flour, one-half teaspoon salt, two or three tablespoons fat. Mix the eggs, flour and milk to a smooth, very thin batter about the consistency of thin cream. Place the fat in a large oven spider [or cast-iron frying pan] and heat it in the oven. When both fat and pan are hissing hot, pour in the batter and bake in a hot oven for 20 to 30 minutes. The heat may be slightly reduced after it is well puffed and brown, but the pancake should not be taken from the oven until it is firm and crisp or it may fall. Serve very hot with [powdered] sugar and lemon, or with syrup and butter, or with syrup and lemon as preferred.[86]

Oregon Centennial Birthday Cake

In 1951, Portland celebrated its centennial birthday with modest fanfare. Disappointingly, no mentions of the birthday cake remain, other than to say who blew out the candles (Mayor Dorothy McCullough; she only extinguished ninety-eight with one breath) and who cut it (the city health bureau, who unceremoniously distributed the slices to other city employees). In 1959, the Oregon Centennial cake received marginally more press, mostly because it was a sensational five-ton behemoth in the shape of Mount Hood, festooned with candy-covered wagons and tiny candy trees, designed to feed 40,000 people.[87] The mastermind behind the cake was Mardi Jacob, an unassuming woman who ran a party-planning business that designed dresses to coordinate with her cakes. A frosting recipe was developed specifically for the centennial by White Satin Sugar (made from local sugar beets), and was printed in *The Oregonian* as part of the company's promotion:

Oregon Birthday Frosting
1 cup White Satin Granulated sugar
1 egg white
¼ teaspoon cream of tartar
1 teaspoon vanilla
¼ teaspoon other flavoring*
½ cup boiling water
1 cup tiny marshmallows

(*The recipe makes several suggestions for pairing frosting with cake, such as mint with chocolate cake, orange with yellow cake, etc.)

Place marshmallows over hot water to soften. Place sugar, egg white, cream of tartar and flavorings in deep mixing bowl. Bring water to boil and pour immediately over bowl ingredients. Turn mixer to high; beat 8 minutes. Add softened marshmallows to mixture and continue beating on high speed for two more minutes. Makes enough frosting for two cake layers. [88]

Hosted at what is today the site of the Oregon Expo Center in Portland's Kenton neighborhood, the official centennial birthday party was a very big deal. There were months of revelry and merrymaking; a thirty-one-foot-tall statue of Paul Bunyan was dedicated to the event and still stands at N. Interstate and Denver; Harry Belafonte, Lawrence Welk, and Roy Rogers played the event; the cake was cut by Secretary of State Francis Wilcox with help from Mardi Jacob, who wore a fabulous chiffon frock of her own making. But despite all of this attention to throwing the biggest bash the state had ever seen, no one bothered to report on how the birthday cake tasted.

EPILOGUE

A Gustatory Wonderland

Some say that Portland's signature dish is the Voodoo Doughnut.

No, no, others counter; it is Stumptown coffee. It is bacon-everything. It is microbrewed beer.

The truth is, all of these are correct. They are also completely wrong. Portland does not have baked beans or cheesecake or deep dish pizza to define it. Portland is a *meibutsu*-less city, adrift in a sea of regional specialties.

But how? How can a town so steeped in cuisine—so famous for its culinary prowess—lack a signature dish?

The foods that many people associate with Portland are derived from and defined by its history: Portland is the First People's deference to deities Salmon and Huckleberry; the pioneers' reliance on salt pork and fruits foraged along the way; the lumberjack's utter dependence on biscuits and gravy, strong coffee, and pie.

It is its farmers' handiness with tools and the fruits of their labor.

It is its immigrants and their traditions; it is the Chinese industriousness and yes, the German propensity for beer.

But Portland is more than its ingredients. It is greater than the sum of its parts. Portland is an eater's paradise and a cook's playground. Portland is a gustatory wonderland.

NOTES

I. THE MATERIAL RESOURCES

1. Harvey Whitefield Scott, *History of Portland, Oregon, with Illustrations and Biographical Sketches* (Syracuse, NY: D. Mason & Company, 1890), 147.

2. There are only three other volcanoes located within American city limits: Pilot Butte in Bend, Oregon; Jackson Volcano in Jackson, Mississippi; and Diamond Head in Honolulu, Hawaii.

3. John Eliot Allen, "Volcanoes of the Portland Area, Oregon," *The Ore Bin Vol. 37, No. 9* (Portland, OR: State of Oregon Department of Geology and Mineral Industries, 1975), 145.

4. Cain Allen, "The Columbia River Trade Network," Oregon Historical Society, Oregon History Project. Available: http://www.ohs.org/the-oregon-history-project/historical-records/the-columbia-river-trade-network.cfm Accessed: February 9, 2013.

5. Meriwether Lewis, William Clark, Elliott Coues, and Thomas Jefferson, *History of the expedition under the command of Lewis and Clark: to the sources of the Missouri river, thence across the Rocky mountains and down the Columbia river to the Pacific ocean, performed during the years 1804-5-6, by order of the government of the United States, Volume 2* (New York: F. P. Harper, 1893), 641.

6. Ibid.

7. Oregon Bureau of Labor, *50 Years of Progress, Volume 10* (Salem, OR: State Printing Dept., 1922), 95.

8. United States Fish Commission, *Report of the Commissioner for the Year Ending June 30, 1893* (Washington, DC: Government Printing Office, 1895), 254

9. Advertisement for Thlinket Packing Corporation placed in *Western Canner and Packer, Volume 14* (Miller Freeman Publications of California, 1922), 87.

10. Ibid.

11. United States Bureau of Fish and Fisheries, *Part IV, Report of the Commissioner for 1875-76* (Washington DC: U.S. Government Printing Office, 1878), 815.

12. United Kingdom House of Commons, "American Tariffs; Hudson Bay Company's Posts in Oregon; Willamette Valley," *Accounts and Papers: Twenty-Eight Volumes, Commercial Tariffs, Vol. XXIV* (1846), 170.

13. Ibid.

14. Alexander Innes Shand, "Salmon Cookery," *The Salmon* (London: Longmans, Green, 1898), 196.

15. Shand, Salmon Cookery, 211.

16. James Henry Worman and Ben James Worman, "Salmon Fishing with the Indians," *Outing, Volume 33* (New York: Outing Publishing Company, 1899), 126.

17. W.A. Jones, "Salmon Fisheries of the Columbia River," *Congressional Edition, Volume 7* (Washington DC: U.S. Government Printing Office, 1888), 15.

18. Marshall McDonald, "Salmon Fisheries of the Columbia River Basin," *Bulletin of the Bureau of Fisheries, Volume 14* (Washington DC: United States Government Printing Office, 1895), 155.

19. City of Portland, Bureau of Planning, "Guild's Lake Industrial Sanctuary Plan" (PDF), 15–16. Available: http://www.portlandonline.com/shared/cfm/image.cfm?id=58694. Accessed: February 14, 2013.

20. Katrine Barber, Portland State University, "Celilo Falls," *The Oregon Encyclopedia*. Available: http://www.oregonencyclopedia.org/entry/view/celilo_falls/. Accessed: February 15, 2013.

21. Joseph E. Taylor III, Oregon Historical Society, "Saving Salmon," *The Oregon History Project*. Available: http://www.ohs.org/the-oregon-history-project/narratives/canneries-on-the-columbia/nature-of-salmon-canneries/saving-salmon.cfm. Accessed: February 14, 2013.

22. Ian C. Campbell, "Lamprey harvest is under way at Willamette Falls by tribes of the Columbia River basin," *The Oregonian, OregonLive* (published July 13, 2012). Available: http://www.oregonlive.com/environment/index.ssf/2012/07/lamprey_harvest_at_willamette.html. Accessed: February 18, 2013.

23. Ibid.

24. Meriwether Lewis, William Clark, *The Journals of the Lewis and Clark Expedition*, University of Nebraska Lincoln. Available: http://lewisandclarkjour-

nals.unl.edu/read/?_xmlsrc=1805-11-03.xml&_xslsrc=LCstyles.xsl#n25110305. Accessed: May 22, 2013.

25. Charles Hallock, *Forest and Stream, Volume 36* (New York: Forest and Stream Publishing Company, 1891), 348.

26. Hallock, 348.

27. Audubon Society of Portland, "Important Bird Areas." Available: http:// audubonportland.org/local-birding/iba/summary. Accessed: February 8, 2013.

28. Julian Hawthorne, *The Story of Oregon: A History, With Portraits and Biographies, Volume 2* (New York: American Historical Publishing Co., 1892), 436–437; Multnomah Anglers and Hunters Club, "Some of Our History," Available: http://mah1883.org/web%20pages/History.html. Accessed: February 22, 2013.

29. Anonymous letter to *Forest and Stream, Volume 36* (New York: Forest and Stream Publishing Company, 1891), 4.

30. Anonymous, 4.

31. Anonymous, 4.

32. George Herman Ellwanger, *The Pleasures of the Table: An Account of Gastronomy from Ancient Days to Present Times* (New York: Doubleday, Page, 1902), 333.

33. Martin Biddle, *Henry VIII's Coastal Artillery Fort at Camber Castle, Rye, East Sussex: An Archaeological, Structural and Historical Investigation* (London: Oxford Archaeological Unit for English Heritage, 200), 310.

34. W. Mackay Laffan, "Canvas-Back and Terrapin," *Sport with Gun and Rod in American Woods and Waters, Volume 2* (Edinborough: D. Douglas, 1884), 744.

35. John Shertzer Hittell, *Pacific Coast Guide Book* (San Francisco: A.L. Bancroft & Company, 1882), 207.

36. William Thomas Shaw, *The China or Denny Pheasant in Oregon, with Notes on the Native Grouse of the Pacific Northwest* (Philadelphia: J. B. Lippincott Co., 1908), 16.

37. Shaw, *China or Denny Pheasant in Oregon*, 17.

38. Shaw, *China or Denny Pheasant in Oregon*, 17.

39. William L. Finley, "N.O.A. (Northwestern Ornithological Association) Work," *The Oregon Naturalist, Volume III No. 7* (Oregon City, OR: Naturalist Publishing Company, 1896), 102.

40. Herbert Bashford, *Nature Stories of the Northwest* (San Francisco: The Whitaker & Ray Company, 1900), 42.

41. Oregon State Board of Agriculture, *The Resources of the State of Oregon: A Book of Statistical Information Treating Upon Oregon as a Whole, and by Counties* (Salem, OR: W. H. Leeds, 1898), 85.

42. Jean Anthelme Brillat-Savarin (translated by M. F. K. Fisher), *The Physiology of Taste: Or, Meditations on Transcendental Gastronomy* (New York: Counterpoint Press, 2000), 374.

43. Léon Brisse (baron.); (translated by Mrs. Matthew Clark), *366 menus and 1200 recipes of the Baron Brisse in French and English* (London: Sampson Lowe, Marston, Searle, and Livingston, 1882), 251.

44. James Beard, *James Beard's American Cookery* (New York: Little, Brown, and Company; Reprint edition, 2010), 243–44.

45. Oregon Department of Fish and Wildlife, "Oregon's Large Mammals." Available:http://www.dfw.state.or.us/resources/viewing/docs/largemammals.pdf. Accessed: April 15, 2013.

46. W. H. Greenfell, *The Pall Mall Magazine, Volume 11* (London: George Routledge & Sons, Limited, 1897), 333.

47. The Portland Woman's Exchange, *The Portland Woman's Exchange Cook Book* (Portland: The Exchange, 1913), 95.

48. Sara Bosse and Onoto Watanna, *Chinese-Japanese Cook Book* (Chicago: Rand McNally, 1914), 90.

49. B. J. Noles, "Lloyd Center deer draws crowd," *The Oregonian*, June 17, 1978, 34, NewsBank/Readex, Database: The Historical Oregonian, 1861–1972, SQN: 131F4CC16E3C0970. [Note: archives date up to 1987, not 1972.]

50. Annie Laura Miller, "Mushrooms Are Thick on Edges of Portland," *Sunday Oregonian,* November 30, 1913, 4. NewsBank/Readex, Database: The Historical Oregonian, 1861–1972, SQN: 11C1B056126CDBA0.

51. "Promoting the Culture of Mushrooms," *Morning Oregonian*; February 9, 1897, 5; NewsBank/Readex, Database: The Historical Oregonian, 1861–1972, SQN: 1238A98D5D3C96B0.

52. Harry Lane, "Edible Mushrooms—Here Is Information of Value to the Oregon Epicure," *Sunday Oregonian*, November 8, 1896, 6, NewsBank/Readex, Database: The Historical Oregonian, 1861–1972, SQN: 1238A89982D386A8.

53. Harry Lane, "Edible Mushrooms—Here Is Information of Value to the Oregon Epicure," *Sunday Oregonian*, November 8, 1896, 6, NewsBank/Readex, Database: The Historical Oregonian, 1861–1972, SQN: 1238A89982D386A8; Harry Lane, "Poisonous Russulas—Dr. Lane Writes Another Article on Mushrooms," *Morning Oregonian*, November 13, 1896, 7. NewsBank/Readex, Database: The Historical Oregonian, 1861–1972, SQN: 1238A8AA2C8ABD90.

54. Harry Lane, "Edible Mushrooms—Here Is Information of Value to the Oregon Epicure," *Sunday Oregonian*, November 8, 1896, 6, NewsBank/Readex, Database: The Historical Oregonian, 1861–1972, SQN: 1238A89982D386A8.

55. Harry Lane, "Edible Mushrooms—Here Is Information of Value to the Oregon Epicure," *Sunday Oregonian*, November 8, 1896, 6, NewsBank/Readex, Database: The Historical Oregonian, 1861–1972, SQN: 1238A89982D386A8.

56. Harry Lane, "Edible Mushrooms—Here Is Information of Value to the Oregon Epicure," *Sunday Oregonian*, November 8, 1896, 6, NewsBank/Readex, Database: The Historical Oregonian, 1861–1972, SQN: 1238A89982D386A8.

57. Peter Gillins, "Violence Clouds Wild Mushroom Harvest in U.S. as Demand Takes Off: Oregon: U.S. Forest Service says prices are high because of demand in Eastern Europe, where the 1986 Chernobyl nuclear accident contaminated traditional growing areas," *Los Angeles Times*, August 1, 1993. Available: http://articles.latimes.com/1993-08-01/local/me-19088_1_forest-service.

58. Burkhard Bilger, "Letter from Oregon: The Mushroom Hunter," *The New Yorker*, August 20, 2007, 62–69.

59. Bilger, "Letter from Oregon," 62–69.

60. Gregory Bonito, James Trappe, Pat Rawlinson, and Rytas Vilgalys, "Improved resolution of major clades within *Tuber* and taxonomy of species within the *Tuber gibbosum* complex," *Mycologia*, September/October 2010, 1042–57.

61. Meriwether Lewis, William Clark, Elliott Coues, and Thomas Jefferson, *History of the expedition under the command of Lewis and Clark: to the sources of the Missouri river, thence across the Rocky mountains and down the Columbia river to the Pacific ocean, performed during the years 1804-5-6, by Order of the Government of the United States, Volume 3* (New York: Francis P. Harper, 1893), 821.

62. Oregon State University, *Station Bulletin—Agricultural Experiment Station, Oregon State College, Issues 1–48* (Corvallis, OR: Agricultural Experiment Station, 1888), 360.

63. Laura Schenone, *A Thousand Years over a Hot Stove: A History of American Women Told Through Food, Recipes, and Remembrances* (New York: W. W. Norton & Company, 2004), 150.

64. Euell Gibbons, *Stalking the Wild Asparagus* (New York: David McKay Company, Inc., 1962), 55.

65. Lewis, Clark, Coues, and Jefferson, *History of the Expedition*, 929.

66. Lewis, Clark, Coues, and Jefferson, *History of the Expedition*, 929.

67. Merriwether Lewis, William Clark, Gary E. Moulton, and Thomas W. Dunlay, *The Journals of the Lewis & Clark Expedition: March 23–June 9, 1806. Vol. 7* (Lincoln: University of Nebraska Press, 1991), 266.

68. John. C. Fremont, *Narrative of the Exploring Expedition to the Rocky Mountains: in the Year 1842, and to Oregon and North California in the Years 1843–44* (New York: Hall & Dickson, 1847), 154.

69. Fremont, *Narrative of the Exploring Expedition*, 199–200.

70. Herbert O. Lang, *History of the Willamette Valley, Being a Description of the Valley and its Resources, With an Account of its Discovery and Settlement by White Men, and its Subsequent History: Together with Personal Reminiscences of its Early Pioneers* (Portland: Himes & Lang, 1885), 570.

71. Lang, *History of the Willamette Valley,* 570.

72. Lang, *History of the Willamette Valley,* 570.

73. Lewis Ankeny McArthur, and Lewis L. McArthur. *Oregon Geographic Names*, 7th ed. (Portland, OR: Oregon Historical Society Press, 2003), 170.

74. Lang, *History of the Willamette Valley,* 570.

75. Rebecca T. Richards and Susan J. Alexander, *A Social History of Wild Huckleberry Harvesting in the Pacific Northwest*. Gen. Tech. Rep. PNWGTR-657, (Portland, OR: U.S. Department of Agriculture, Forest Service, Pacific Northwest Research Station, 2006), 8.

76. Don Minore, *The Wild Huckleberries of Oregon and Washington—A Dwindling Resource* (Portland: USDA Government Printing Office, 1972).

77. Fanny Lemira Gillette, *White House Cook Book: A Selection of Choice Recipes Original and Selected, During a Period of Forty Years' Practical Housekeeping* (Chicago: R. S. Peale & Co., 1887), 414.

78. Reuben Gold Thwaites, *Original Journals of the Lewis and Clark Expedition, 1804–1806, Volume 4, Parts 1–2* (Scituate, MA: Digital Scanning, Inc., 2001), 21.

2. THE CHINOOK AND KALAPUYA PEOPLE

1. Harvey Whitefield Scott, *History of Portland, Oregon, with Illustrations and Biographical Sketches of Prominent Citizens and Pioneers* (Portland: D. Mason & Company, 1890), 15.

2. National Parks Service, *National Historic Landmarks Program Database*, "Sunken Village Archaeological Site," Available:http://tps.cr.nps.gov/nhl/detail.cfm?ResourceId=2081&ResourceType=Site. Accessed: June 18, 2013. Once published, research by Tracy J. Prince and Linda Coons will contradict the theory of population density on Sauvie Island (pers. comm. Tracy J. Prince, May 5, 2014).

3. Contrary to their name, the Flathead Indians of Montana did not practice head flattening.

4. Ralph Friedman, *The Other Side of Oregon*, (Caldwell, ID: Caxton Press, 1993), 200.

5. Ibid.

6. Meriwether Lewis, William Clark, et al., March 29, 1806 entry in *The Journals of the Lewis and Clark Expedition*, ed. Gary Moulton (Lincoln, NE: University of Nebraska Press / University of Nebraska-Lincoln Libraries-Electronic Text Center, 2005). Available:http://lewisandclarkjournals.unl.edu/read/?_xmlsrc=1806-03-29.xml&_xslsrc=LCstyles.xsl. Accessed: April 7, 2014.

7. Meriwether Lewis, William Clark, et al., November 4, 1805 entry in *The Journals of the Lewis and Clark Expedition*, ed. Gary Moulton (Lincoln, NE: University of Nebraska Press / University of Nebraska-Lincoln Libraries-Electronic Text Center, 2005). Available:http://lewisandclarkjournals.unl.edu/read/?_xmlsrc=1805-11-04.xml&_xslsrc=LCstyles.xsl. Accessed: April 7, 2014.

8. John Kaye Gill, *Gill's Dictionary of the Chinook Jargon: With Examples of Use in Conversation and Notes Upon Tribes and Tongues* (Portland: J. K. Gill Company, 1909), 7.

9. Kenneth M. Ames and Herbert Maschner, *Peoples of the Northwest Coast: Their Archaeology and Prehistory* (London: Thames and Hudson, 1999), 25.

10. Bruce Smith, "Low-Level Food Production and the Northwest Coast," *Keeping It Living: Traditions of Plant Use and Cultivation on the Northwest Coast of North America* (Seattle: University of Washington Press, 2005), 38.

11. Gill, *Dictionary of Chinook Jargon*, 9.

12. Meriwether Lewis, William Clark, et al., April 7, 1806 entry in *The Journals of the Lewis and Clark Expedition*, ed. Gary Moulton (Lincoln, NE: University of Nebraska Press / University of Nebraska-Lincoln Libraries-Electronic Text Center, 2005), Available: http://lewisandclarkjournals.unl.edu/journals.php?id=1806-04-07.

13. Melville Jacobs, "World View of the Clackamas Chinook Indian," *The Journal of American Folklore*, Vol. 68, No. 269 (July–September, 1955), 285.

14. Jacobs, "World View of the Clackamas Chinook Indian," 286.

15. Jacobs, "World View of the Clackamas Chinook Indian," 286.

16. Jacobs, "World View of the Clackamas Chinook Indian," 286.

17. Gill, *Dictionary of Chinook Jargon*, 8.

18. Tracy J. Prince, "Why Tillicum is the right name for TriMet's new bridge: Guest opinion," *The Oregonian OregonLive*, February 27, 2014. Available:http://www.oregonlive.com/opinion/index.ssf/2014/02/why_tillicum_is_the_right_name.html. Accessed: March 11, 2014.

19. Linda Coons, via pers comm with Tracy J. Prince, email March 25, 2014.

20. Ames and Maschner, *Peoples of the Northwest Coast*, 175.

21. Also known as Pacific serviceberry (*Amelanchier alnifolia*).

22. Robert Ruby and John Brown, *The Chinook Indians: Traders of the Lower Columbia River* (Norman: University of Oklahoma Press, 1976), 55.

23. Alexis Steinberg, "Review of *The Flanagan site 6,000 years of occupation in the upper Willamette Valley, Oregon*," Available:https://scholarsbank.uoregon.edu/xmlui/bitstream/handle/1794/2130/Steinberg1.pdf?sequence=1. Accessed: June 19, 2013.

24. Megan K. Walsh, Cathy Whitlock, and Patrick J. Bartlein, "1200 years of fire and vegetation history in the Willamette Valley, Oregon and Washington,

reconstructed using high-resolution macroscopic charcoal and pollen analysis,"
Palaeogeography, Palaeoclimatology, Palaeoecology (297: 2, 2010), 286.

25. Walsh, Whitlock, and Bartlein, "1200 years of fire and vegetation history," 286.

26. Franz Boas, *Chinook Texts* (Washington, DC: U.S. Government Printing Office, 1894), 265.

27. Franz Boas, *Chinook Texts* (Washington, DC: U.S. Government Printing Office, 1894), 265.

28. Franz Boas, *Chinook Texts* (Washington, DC: U.S. Government Printing Office, 1894), 265.

29. Gill, *Dictionary of Chinook Jargon,* 10.

30. Gill, *Dictionary of Chinook Jargon,* 10.

31. Although Coyote was a benevolent deity, he was also a trickster who tried to sneak his way into heaven. For this, he was punished by being cast down from the sky. Coyote was condemned to forever wander and cry for his sins, and this is why coyotes howl at night, hungry and friendless wherever they go.

32. Erna Gunther, "An Analysis of the First Salmon Ceremony," *American Anthropologist* (28:4, 1926), 615.

33. Boas, *Chinook Texts*, 104.

34. Boas, *Chinook Texts*, 105.

35. Before the Columbia River was dammed, the ocean's tidal influence was observed upstream as far as Cascade Locks. Today, the Columbia is considered to be tidally influenced up to Bonneville Dam.

36. Boas, *Chinook Texts*, 106.

37. Boas, *Chinook Texts*, 106.

38. Warm Springs and Grand Ronde Indians also use Willamette Falls for lamprey fishing.

39. Helen H. Norton, "Evidence for Bracken Fern as a Food for Aboriginal Peoples of Western Washington," *Economic Botany* 33, no. 4 (October–December, 1979), 386.

40. Meriwether Lewis, William Clark, et al., January 23, 1806 entry in *The Journals of the Lewis and Clark Expedition*, ed. Gary Moulton (Lincoln: University of Nebraska Press / University of Nebraska-Lincoln Libraries-Electronic Text Center, 2005), Available:http://lewisandclarkjournals.unl.edu/journals.php?id=1806-01-23.

41. Henry Wetherbee Henshaw, *Perforated Stones from California* (Washington, DC: U.S. Government Printing Office, 1887), 11.

42. In Jacobs's transcription of Mrs. Howard's story, Cat Ear is named as a type of camas, but is probably the mariposa lily known as Tolmie's star-tulip, or *Calochortus tolmiei*. Because of its hairy, triangular petals, cat's ear is another colloquial name for *Calochortus*.

43. Harold Mackey, *The Kalapuyans* (Salem: Mission Hill Museum Association, 2004), 43.

44. William Jackson Hooker, *The London Journal of Botany: Containing Figures and Descriptions of . . . Plants . . . Together with Botanical Notices and Information and . . . Memoirs of Eminent Botanists, Volume 5* (London: Hippolyte Baillière, 1846), 295.

45. Hooker, *The London Journal of Botany*, 295.

46. Missouri Historical Society, Lewis and Clark National Bicentennial Exhibition, "Nez Perce: Collecting and Preserving Plants," Available:http://www.lewisandclarkexhibit.org/4_0_0/page_4_1_3_2_3_3.html. Accessed: July 1, 2013.

47. Gill, *Dictionary of Chinook Jargon,* 10.

48. Although the island maintains a largely agricultural presence, much of the island is managed by the Oregon Department of Fish and Wildlife as the Sauvie Island Wildlife Area.

49. William R. Swagerty, *The Indianization of Lewis and Clark* (Norman, OK: The Arthur H. Clark Company, 2012), 410.

50. Linda Coon, via Tracy J. Prince, personal communication., e-mail March 25, 2014.

51. Meriwether Lewis, William Clark, et al., March 29, 1806 entry in *The Journals of the Lewis and Clark Expedition*, ed. Gary Moulton (Lincoln: University of Nebraska Press / University of Nebraska-Lincoln Libraries-Electronic Text Center, 2005), Availabe: http://lewisandclarkjournals.unl.edu/journals.php?id=1806-03-29.

52. Jacobs, "World View of Clackamas Chinook Indians," 285.

53. Rebecca T. Richards and Susan J. Alexander, "Social History of Wild Huckleberry Harvesting in the Pacific Northwest," Gen. Tech. Rep. PNW-GTR-657 (Portland, OR: U.S. Department of Agriculture, Forest Service, Pacific Northwest Research Station), 7

54. Richard I. Ford (ed.), *An Ethnobiology Source Book: The Uses of Plants and Animals by American Indians* (New York: Garland Publishing, Inc., 1986), 76.

55. Paul Kane, *Wanderings of an Artist Among the Indians of North America: From Canada to Vancouver's Island and Oregon, Through the Hudson's Bay Company's Territory and Back Again* (London: Longman, Brown, Green, Longmans, and Roberts, 1859), 185.

56. Kane, *Wanderings of an Artist*, 185.

57. Hugh Murray, *Historical Account of Discoveries and Travels in North America* (London: Longman, Rees, Orme, Brown, & Green, 1829), 107.

58. Murray, *Discoveries and Travels in North America*, 107.

59. John Doerper and Alf Collins, "Pacific Northwest Indian Cooking Vessels," Oxford Symposium on Food and Cookery, 1988, *The Cooking Pot: Proceedings* (London: Prospect Books, Ltd., 1989), 28.

60. Doerper and Collins, "Pacific Northwest Indian Cooking Vessels," 29.

61. Gill, *Dictionary of Chinook Jargon,* 10.

62. Lewis, Clark, et al., *The Journals of the Lewis and Clark Expedition,* March 4, 1806 entry.

63. Meriwether Lewis, William Clark, et al., February 24, 1806 entry in *The Journals of the Lewis and Clark Expedition,* ed. Gary Moulton (Lincoln: University of Nebraska Press / University of Nebraska–Lincoln Libraries-Electronic Text Center, 2005). Available: http://lewisandclarkjournals.unl.edu/journals.php?id=1806-02-24.

64. Lewis, Clark, et al., *The Journals of the Lewis and Clark Expedition,* February 24, 1806 entry.

65. Robert T. Boyd, *People of the Dalles: The Indians of Wascopam Mission* (Lincoln: University of Nebraska Press, 2004), 232.

66. Lillian Ackerman, *A Necessary Balance: Gender and Power Among Indians of the Columbia Plateau* (Norman: University of Oklahoma Press, 2003), 18.

67. Meriwether Lewis, Elliott Coues, William Clark, and Thomas Jefferson, *History of the expedition under the command of Lewis and Clark: to the sources of the Missouri River, thence across the Rocky Mountains and down the Columbia River to the Pacific Ocean, performed during the years 1804-5-6, by order of the government of the United States, Volume 2* (New York: F.P. Harper, 1893), 641.

68. Coues, *History of the Expedition,* 641.

69. Meriwether Lewis, William Clark, et al., March 4, 1806 entry in *The Journals of the Lewis and Clark Expedition,* ed. Gary Moulton (Lincoln, NE: University of Nebraska Press / University of Nebraska–Lincoln Libraries-Electronic Text Center, 2005), Available: http://lewisandclarkjournals.unl.edu/journals.php?id=1806-03-04.

70. Charles A. Geyer, "Notes on the Vegetation and general character of the Missouri and Oregon Territories, made during a Botanical Journey in the State of Missouri, and across the South Pass of the Rocky Mountains, to the Pacific, during the years 1843 and 1844," *The London Journal of Botany: Containing Figures and Descriptions of . . . Plants . . . Together with Botanical Notices and Information and . . . Memoirs of Eminent Botanists, Volume 5* (London: H. Baillière, 1846), 300.

71. Erna Gunther, *Ethnobotany of Western Washington* (Seattle: University of Washington Press, 1973), 43.

72. Yeffe Kimball and Jean Anon, *The Art of American Indian Cooking* (New York: Lyons and Burford, 1965), 20.

73. Gunther, *Ethnobotany of Western Washington*, 22.

74. Walter Shelley Phillips, *The Chinook Book: A Descriptive Analysis of the Chinook Jargon in Plain Words, Giving Instructions for Pronunciation, Construction, Expression and Proper Speaking of Chinook with All the Various Shaded Meanings of the Words* (Seattle: R. L. Davis Printing Company, 1913), 79.

75. Ruby and Brown, *Chinook Indians*, 73.

76. Boas, *Chinook Texts*, 268.

77. Jill E. Martin, "'The Greatest Evil' Interpretations of Indian Prohibition Laws, 1832–1953" (2003). Great Plains Quarterly.Paper 2432, 36. Available: http://digitalcommons.unl.edu/greatplainsquarterly/2432. Accessed: August 6, 2013.

3. THE OLD WORLD MEETS THE WILD WEST, OR: "CONGRATULATIONS! YOU HAVE MADE IT TO OREGON"

1. Lansford W. Hastings, *The Emigrant's Guide to Oregon and California* (reprint of original 1845 edition) (Bedford, MA: Applewood Books, 1994), 6.

2. Cathy Luchetti, *Home on the Range: A Culinary History of the American West* (New York: Villard Books, 1993), 39.

3. Hastings, *Emigrant's Guide to Oregon and California*, 144.

4. Hastings, *The Emigrant's Guide to Oregon and California*, 144.

5. Hastings, *The Emigrant's Guide to Oregon and California*, 144.

6. Sylvester Graham, *A Treatise on Bread: and Bread-Making* (Boston: Light & Stearns, 1837), 96.

7. Fred Lockley, *Conversations with Pioneer Women* (Eugene, OR: Rainy Day Press, 1983), 96.

8. Tracy J. Prince, "Why Tillicum is the right name for TriMet's new bridge: Guest opinion," *The Oregonian OregonLive*, February 27, 2014. Available:http://www.oregonlive.com/opinion/index.ssf/2014/02/why_tillicum_is_the_right_name.html. Accessed: March 11, 2014.

9. Richard Byron Johnson, *Very Far West Indeed: A Few Rough Experiences on the North-west Pacific Coast* (London: S. Low, Marston, Low, & Searle, 1872), D2.

10. Eugene Snyder, *Early Portland: Stump-Town Triumphant* (Portland: Binford & Mort, 1970), 11.

11. Thomas Jefferson Farnham, *Farnham's Travels* (Reprint of original 1843 edition) (Bedford, MA: Applewood Books, 2007), 66.

12. Snyder, *Stump-Town Triumphant*, 126.

13. Tracy J. Prince, *Portland's Goose Hollow* (Charleston, SC: Arcadia Publishing, 2011), 31

14. Lockley, *Conversations with Pioneer Women*, 15–16.

15. John G. Abbott, "To Oregon by Ox Team 59 Years Ago," *Lane County Historian* 27, no. 2 (Summer 1982): 44.

16. Cathy Luchetti, *Home on the Range* (New York: Villard Books, 1993), 28.

17. Harvey Whitefield Scott, *History of Portland, Oregon, with Illustrations and Biographical Sketches of Prominent Citizens and Pioneers* (Portland: D & Mason Company, 1890), 144.

18. Joseph R. Conlin, "Old Boy, Did You Get Enough of Pie? A Social History of Food in Logging Camps," *Journal of Forest History* 23, no. 4 (October 1979): 164–85.

19. Allan Hendricks, "Summer Logging," *Lippincott's Monthly Magazine, Vol. 62* (Philadelphia: J. B. Lippincott Company, 1898), 274.

20. Conlin, "Old Boy, Did You Get Enough of Pie?" 169.

21. Conlin, "Old Boy, Did You Get Enough of Pie?" 169.

22. Robert L. Tyler, *Rebels of the Woods: The IWW in the Pacific Northwest* (Eugene: University of Oregon Books, 1967), 104.

23. Anna M. Lind, "Women in Early Logging Camps, A Personal Reminiscence," *Journal of Forest History* 19, no. 3 (1975): 128–35.

24. Lind, "Women in Early Logging Camps," 131.

25. Oregon-California Trails Association, "Archer and Whitlock Correspondence in 1879 from Oregon City to U.K." *Paper Trail Website*. Available: http://www.oregonpioneers.com/archer.htm. Accessed: September 10, 2013.

26. Scott, *History of Portland, Oregon*, 247.

27. Scott, *History of Portland, Oregon*, 247.

28. Scott, *History of Portland, Oregon*, 247.

29. Portland Bureau of Planning and Sustainability, *East Portland Historical Overview & Historic Preservation Study*, Revised: March 2009. Available:http://www.portlandoregon.gov/bps/article/214638. Accessed: September 18, 2013.

30. Sara Wrenn, "Early Days and Ways In and Around Milwaukie," *Oregon Folklore Studies from the Federal Writers' Project, 1939*. Available: http://lcweb2.loc.gov/wpa/30010924.html. Accessed: September 19, 2013.

31. Wrenn, "Early Days and Ways In and Around Milwaukie."

32. Finn J.D. John, "Bing Cherry Has Roots on Oregon Trail," *Offbeat Oregon History,* January 11, 2010. Available: http://www.offbeatoregon.com/H1001b_Lewellings.htm. Accessed: September 19, 2013.

33. John, "Bing Cherry Has Roots on Oregon Trail."

34. E. R. Lake, "The Apple in Oregon," *Oregon Agricultural Experiment Station Bulletin* (Corvallis, OR: Agricultural College Printing Office, July 1904), 6.

35. Michael Pollan, *The Botany of Desire: A Plant's-eye View of the World* (New York: Random House, 2001), 9.

36. Robert J. Cromwell, Ph.D, "A Short History of the 'Old Apple Tree,' Located in the Old Apple Tree Park, Vancouver National Historic Reserve, Vancouver, Washington, Compiled from Various Historical Sources," *Northwest Cultural Resources Institute Short Report No. 34* (Prepared for the Fort Vancouver National Historic Site, September 2010), 9.

37. Cromwell, "A Short History of the 'Old Apple Tree,'" 11.

38. Seth Lewelling, "Pioneers of Fruits Early Horticulture in Oregon: Interesting Reminiscences of the First Cultivated Trees and Plants Grown in the State," *The Sunday Oregonian,* October 16, 1892. Provider: NewsBank/Readex, Database: The Historical Oregonian, 1861–1987, SQN: 12349BCE853D8998.

39. Based on an inflation calculator from Oregon State University's Department of Political Science, $1 in 1858 would be worth $28.54 in 2013. Calculator available here: http://oregonstate.edu/cla/polisci/individual-year-conversion-factor-tables. Accessed: September 24, 2013.

40. Thomas C. McClintock, "Henderson Luelling, Seth Lewelling and the Birth of the Pacific Coast Fruit Industry," *Oregon Historical Quarterly* 68, no. 2 (June 1967): 167.

41. Ben F. Dorris, "Filbert Culture: High Spots in the Commercial Production of Filberts in Oregon," *The Oregon Grower, Volumes 3–5* (Corvallis, OR: Oregon Growers Co-operative Association, 1921), 167.

42. *Oregon Native Son and Historical Magazine, Volume 1* (Portland: Native Son Publishing Company, 1899).

43. Howard and Grace Horner, eds., *History and Folklore of the David Douglas Community* (Portland: David Douglas Historical Society, 1989), 131.

44. "Bulletin Board," *The New Majority*, August 5, 1922, 7.

45. United States Department of Agriculture, *Farm Work for City Youth* (Washington, DC: U.S. Department of Agriculture, 1947), 7.

46. Greg Hall, "The Fruits of Her Labor: Women, Children, and Progressive Era Reformers in the Pacific Northwest Canning Industry," *Oregon Historical Quarterly* 109, no. 2 (Summer 2008): 239.

47. I. D. Ransley, Henry Schoen, and Tom Burns, "On the Job in Oregon," *The International Socialist Review*, Volume 14, 163.

48. Hall, "Fruits of Her Labor," 226.

49. "Court Warning Out: Judge Stevenson Says 'Broken Head Your Punishment,'" *The Oregonian*, July 19, 1913, 8.

50. E. Mowbray Tate, *Transpacific Steam: The Story of Steam Navigation from the Pacific Coast of North America to the Far East and the Antipodes, 1867–1941* (Cranbury, NJ: Associated University Presses, 1986), 111.

51. Daniel J. Meissner, "Theodore B. Wilcox: Captain of Industry and Magnate of the China Flour Trade, 1884–1918," *Oregon Historical Quarterly* 104, no. 4 (Winter 2003): 518.

52. *The Weekly Northwestern Miller*, Volume 48 (Minneapolis: Miller Publishing Company, 1899), 786.

53. Meissner, "Theodore B. Wilcox," 528.

54. Lucile Saunders McDonald, "Letter to the Editor," *Oregon Historical Quarterly* 61, no. 1 (March 1960): 66.

55. "Industries of Portland," *The West Shore*, Volume 14, No. 8 (Portland: L. Samuel, 1888), 407.

56. A. D. Bowen, *Oregon and the Orient: A Work Designed to Show the Great Natural and Industrial Advantages of Oregon and Its Unequaled Position Relative to Trade with the Orient* (Portland, OR: C. H. Crocker Co., 1901).

57. Advertisement, *The Oregonian*, June 6, 1916, 12

58. Advertisement, *The Oregonian*, June 6, 1916, 12

59. John Harvey Kellogg, *Modern Medicine*, Volume 15, Issue 1 (Battle Creek, MI: Modern Medicine Publishing Company, 1906), 27.

60. "Prospects Were Slim. Little Encouragement for Promoter of Vegetarian Restaurant," *The Oregonian*, January 17, 1898, 8.

61. "Prospects Were Slim," 8.

62. "Vegetarian Restaurant: Portland Eating-House Which Sells No Meat," *The Oregonian*, March 23, 1900, 10.

63. Robert D. Johnston, "The Myth of the Harmonious City: Will Daly, Lora Little, and the Hidden Face of Progressive-Era Portland," *Oregon Historical Quarterly*, Vol. 99, No. 3, "Aspects of Portland History" (Fall 1998), 275.

64. Regan Lee, "Moveable Feasts, Mobile Slaughter," *Oregon L.O.W.F.I.: Oregon's Oddities Reviewed in a New Light*, Available: http://forteanswest.com/wordpress-mu/oregonlowfi/tag/william-h-galvani/. Accessed: October 23, 2013. For more information about the Scottish Rite, read Charles Thompson McClenachan's *The Book of the Ancient and Accepted Scottish Rite of Freemasonry* (New York: Masonic Pub. & Manufacturing, 1868).

65. William H. Galvani, "Vegetarian Philosophy Bills of Fare for That Plantigrade Frugivorous Mammal Known as Man," *The Sunday Oregonian*, December 20, 1896, 15.

66. Alexander Patterson, "Terrasquirma and the Engines of Social Change in 1970s Portland," *Oregon Historical Quarterly* 101, no. 2 (Summer 2000): 168.

67. Mike Francis, "Firm Takes a Wild Ride on Food Chain," *The Oregonian*, September 3, 1991. Available via NewsBank: http://0-docs.newsbank.com. cata-

log.multcolib.org/openurl?ctx_ver=z39.88-2004&rft_id=info:sid/
iw.newsbank.com:NewsBank:ORGB&rft_val_format=info:ofi/
fmt:kev:mtx:ctx&rft_dat=0EB086A7A27B0C5F&
svc_dat=InfoWeb:aggregated5&req_dat=0D10F2CADB4B24C0. Accessed: October 23, 2013.

68. Vegetarian Research Group, *Vegetarian Times*, Harris Interactive Service Bureau, data taken June 18, 2013. A 2009 poll by People for the Ethical Treatment of Animals placed Portland as second best, but other polls in subsequent years rank Portland as the world's most vegan-friendly city.

69. Fred Lockley, *Conversations with Pioneer Women* (Eugene, OR: Rainy Day Press, 1993), 47.

70. F. G. Young and Joaquin Young, "Ewing Young and His Estate: A Chapter in the Economic and Community Development of Oregon," *The Quarterly of the Oregon Historical Society* 21, no. 3 (September 1920): 175.

71. Young and Young, "Ewing Young and His Estate," 179.

72. Wrenn, "Early Days and Ways In and Around Milwaukie."

73. "How and What to Cook: The Secret of Success in Preparing First-Class Meals," *The Oregonian*, May 14, 1892, 8. Accessed: October 28, 2013.

74. "New Meat Company Is Not a Monopoly," *The Sunday Oregonian*, October 22, 1893, 12. Provider: NewsBank/Readex, Database: The Historical Oregonian, 1861–1987. Accessed: October 28, 2013.

75. "New Meat Company Is Not a Monopoly," *The Sunday Oregonian*, October 22, 1893, 12. Provider: NewsBank/Readex, Database: The Historical Oregonian, 1861–1987. Accessed: October 28, 2013.

76. United States Department of the Interior, National Park Service, National Register of Historic Places, "Multiple Property Documentation Form for Historic and Architectural Properties in the Early Kenton Neighborhood of Portland, Oregon." Prepared by City of Portland Bureau of Planning, August 2001. Available: http://pdfhost.focus.nps.gov/docs/NRHP/Text/64500509.pdf. Accessed: October 23, 2013.

77. Erin deJesus, "Watch Portland Meat Collective's Camas Davis Talk Whole-Animal Butchery, Ethical Meat-Eating," *Eater PDX*, September 5, 2013. Available: http://pdx.eater.com/archives/2013/09/05/watch-camas-davis-talk-portland-meat-collective.php. Accessed: October 28, 2013.

78. "Portland Upholds Pure Milk Record: Quiet Investigation Convinces Federal Officials of Correctness of Rating," *Morning Oregonian*, June 13, 1916, 8. Provider: NewsBank/Readex, Database: The Historical Oregonian, 1861–1987. Accessed: October 30, 2013.

79. "Milk Inspectors to Try Surprises. Dairies Will Not Know of Calls in Future," *The Morning Oregonian*, April 18, 1929. NewsBank/Readex, Database: The Historical Oregonian, 1861–1987. Accessed: October 31, 2013.

80. Kimberly Jensen, *Oregon's Doctor to the World: Esther Pohl Lovejoy and a Life in Activism* (Seattle: University of Washington Press, 2012), 116.

81. Dana, Marshall N. *Newspaper Story: Fifty Years of the Oregon Journal, 1902–1952* (Portland: Binfords, 1951), 100.

82. Finn John, "Before newspaper 'crusade,' tainted milk was killing babies," *Offbeat Oregon History*. Available: http://offbeatoregon.com/1208b-bad-milk-was-killing-babies-in-portland.html. Accessed: October 31, 2013.

83. Dana, *Newspaper Story,* 99.

84. "Bailey Clinches with News Getter. Journal Report Roughly Handled by State Dairy and Food Commissioner," *The Oregonian*, August 29, 1909, 14. NewsBank/Readex, Database: The Historical Oregonian, 1861–1987. Accessed: November 4, 2013.

85. Dana, *Newspaper Story*, 100.

86. Dana, *Newspaper Story*, 100.

87. John, "Before Newspaper Crusade."

88. Jensen, *Oregon's Doctor*, 117.

89. Jensen, *Oregon's Doctor*, 117.

90. "What Oregon Will Show the World," *The Oregonian*, January 2, 1905, 12. NewsBank/Readex, Database: The Historical Oregonian, 1861–1987. Accessed: November 5, 2013.

91. Census data from http://www.censusrecords.com/.

92. Dale Skovgaard, "Oregon Voices: Memories of the 1948 Vanport Flood," *Oregon Historical Quarterly* 108, no. 1 (Spring 2007): 93.

93. Skovgaard, "Memories of the 1948 Vanport Flood," 93.

94. Manly Maben, *Vanport* (Portland: Oregon Historical Society Press, 1987), 106.

95. "Vanport Deemed Ghetto," *Oregon Journal*, March 10, 1952.

96. Tom Nash and Twilo Scofield, *The Well-Traveled Casket. Oregon Folklore* (Eugene, OR: Meadowlark Press, 1999), 59–60.

4. IMMIGRANTS

1. Paul G. Merriam, "The 'Other Portland': A Statistical Note on Foreign-Born, 1860–1910," *Oregon Historical Quarterly* 80, no. 3 (Fall 1979): 260. Portland had a foreign-born population of 37.4 percent of the whole population; San Francisco was 42.4 percent foreign per capita.

2. City News section of *The Oregonian*, August 17, 1875, 3, Provider: NewsBank/Readex, Database: The Historical Oregonian, 1861–1987, SQN: 12329E2200F84A80. Accessed: April 7, 204.

3. Tracy J. Prince, *Portland's Goose Hollow* (Charleston, SC: Arcadia Publishing, 2011), 18.

4. Tracy J. Prince, *Portland's Goose Hollow* (Charleston, SC: Arcadia Publishing, 2011), 18.

5. Leora Sidwell, *Cook Book of Many Lands . . . Foreign Recipes* (Portland: Americanization Department, District of Parents and Teachers of Portland, Oregon, 1932), i.

6. Advertisement in *Morning Oregonian*, January 1, 1880, 4. Provider: NewsBank/Readex, Database: The Historical Oregonian, 1861–1987, SQN: 1233F80382277BB0. Accessed: April 7, 2014.

7. Advertisement in *Morning Oregonian*, throughout October and November 1867, alerting customers of move to new location on SW First. NewsBank/Readex, Database: The Historical Oregonian, 1861–1987, Accessed: November 22, 2013.

8. Harvey Whitefield Scott, *History of Portland, Oregon, with Illustrations and Biographical Sketches of Prominent Citizens and Pioneers* (Portland: D. Mason & Company, 1890), 561.

9. Advertisement in *Morning Oregonian*, July 02, 1868, 2. Provider: NewsBank/Readex, Database: The Historical Oregonian, 1861–1987, SQN: 1233F83E5F861D38. Accessed: December 17, 2013.

10. Eugene Snyder, *Portland Names and Neighborhoods: Their Historic Origins* (Portland: Binford & Mort, 1979), 65.

11. "Where Aged Live in Comfort: 'Altenheim' Erected by German Aid Society, Is Model of Kind," *Morning Oregonian*, March 30, 1912, 10. NewsBank/Readex, Database: The Historical Oregonian, 1861–1987, Accessed: November 22, 2013.

12. Aukjen T. Ingraham, "Henry Weinhard & Portland's City Brewery," (*Oregon Historical Quarterly* 102, no. 2 (Summer 2001): 187.

13. Polina Olsen, *Stories from Jewish Portland* (Charleston, SC: History Press, 2011), 70.

14. Polina Olsen, *Stories from Jewish Portland* (Charleston, SC: History Press, 2011), 70.

15. *Volga Germans in Portland*, "Arrival in Portland," compiled by Steve Schrieber. Available:http://www.volgagermans.net/portland/arrival_portland.html. Accessed: December 1, 2013.

16. Lucile Saunders McDonald, "Letter to the Editor," *Oregon Historical Quarterly*, Vol. 61, No. 1 (March 1960), 66.

17. McDonald, "Letter to the Editor," 66.

18. Vickie Willman Burns, "Wire Down: Memories of the Hop Harvest," an oral history of Mollie Schneider Willman. Available:http://www.volgagermans.net/portland/docs/Wire_Down-Hop_Harvest.pdf. Accessed: December 17, 2013.

19. James Beard, *Delights and Prejudices* (Philadelphia: Running Press, 2001), 8.

20. Marie Rose Wong, *Sweet Cakes, Long Journey: The Chinatowns of Portland, Oregon* (Seattle: University of Washington Press, 2004), 267.

21. Wong, *Sweet Cakes, Long Journey*, 268.

22. Rose Hum Lee, "The Decline of Chinatowns in the United States," *American Journal of Sociology* 54, no. 5 (March 1949): 425–26.

23. Mike Ryerson, Norm Gholston, and Tracy J. Prince. *Portland's Slabtown* (Charleston, SC: Arcadia Publishing, 2013), 15, 19

24. Marie Rose Wong, *Sweet Cakes, Long Journey*, 215; "Our Mongolian Gardens," *The West Shore*, September 21, 1889, 41. Available:http://oregonnews.uoregon.edu/lccn/2012260361/1889-09-21/ed-1/seq-9/. Accessed: January 7, 2013.

25. "Our Mongolian Gardens," 41–42.

26. Portland State University in collaboration with the Chinese Consolidated Benevolent Association, *Dreams of the West: A History of the Chinese in Oregon, 1850–1950* (Portland: Ooligan Press, 2007), 50.

27. Lilian Tingle, "Answers to Correspondents," *Sunday Oregonian*, June 27, 1915, 8. Available:http://oregonnews.uoregon.edu/lccn/sn83045782/1915-06-27/ed-1/seq-64/. Accessed: January 6, 2014.

28. Tingle, "Answers to Correspondents."

29. "Vegetable Vendors Fight But Chinese Beat Italians in First Round at Municipal Court," *Morning Oregonian*, August 28, 1901, 12. Available:http://oregonnews.uoregon.edu/lccn/sn83025138/1901-08-28/ed-1/seq-12/. Accessed: December 31, 2013.

30. Ryerson, Gholston, and Prince, *Slabtown*, 22

31. Robert Clark, *James Beard: A Biography* (New York: Harper Collins, 1993), 23.

32. James Beard, *Delights and Prejudices* (Philadelphia: Running Press, 2001), 14.

33. "Society," *The Sunday Oregonian,* March 8, 1903, 18. Available:http://oregonnews.uoregon.edu/lccn/sn83045782/1903-03-08/ed-1/seq-18/. Accessed: January 6, 2014.

34. "Society," March 8, 1903, 18.

35. Wong, *Sweet Cakes, Long Journey*, 157.

36. Marie Rose Wong, personal communication e-mail, January 7, 2014.

37. Eiichiro Azuma, "A History of Oregon's Issei, 1880–1952," *Oregon Historical Quarterly* 94, no. 4, "The Japanese in Oregon" (Winter 1993/1994): 319.

38. Dave Conklin, personal communication e-mail, January 17, 2014; Azuma, "Oregon's Issei," 318.

39. William Shurtleff and Akiko Aoyagi, *History of Tofu and Tofu Products (965 CE to 2013)* (Lafayette, CA: SoyInfo Center, 2011), 2808.

40. Shurtleff and Aoyagi, *History of Tofu*, 6.

41. Eric Eto, "Some eats in Okayama, Japan," *CHOW,* December 4, 2003. Accessed: January 22, 2014. Available:http://chowhound.chow.com/topics/ 263642. Accessed: January 22, 2014.

42. Dave Conklin, cited by William Shurtleff and Akiko Aoyagi, *How Japanese and Japanese-Americans Brought Soyfoods to the United States and the Hawaiian Islands—A History (1851–2011): Extensively Annotated Bibliography and Sourcebook* (Lafayette, CA: SoyInfo Center, 2011), 295; Food and Agriculture Organization of the United Nations, Fisheries and Aquaculture Department. Cultured Aquatic Species Information Programme *Crassostrea gigas (Thunberg, 1793)*. Available:http://www.fao.org/fishery/culturedspecies/Crassostrea_gigas/ en. Accessed: January 22, 2014.

43. Azuma, "Oregon's Issei," 328.

44. Jim Iwasaki, personal communication, telephone conversation, January 29, 2014.

45. Azuma, "Oregon's Issei," 340.

46. Shurtleff and Aoyagi, *How Japanese and Japanese-Americans Brought Soyfoods to the United States*, 295.

47. Norimitsu Onishi, "Spaghetti Stir-Fry and Hambagoo: Japan Looks West," *The New York Times*. Available:http://www.nytimes.com/2008/03/26/ dining/26japan.html?pagewanted=all&_r=1&. Accessed: January 22, 2014.

48. Leora Sidwell, *Cook Book of Many Lands . . . Foreign Recipes* (Portland: George E. Sandy Printing Company, 1932), 24.

49. Shurtleff and Aoyagi, *How Japanese and Japanese-Americans Brought Soyfoods to the United States*, 295.

50. Shizue Iwatsuki and Lawson Fusao Inada, *Legends from Camp: Poems* (Minneapolis: Coffee House Press, 1992), 151. Inada's family was interned in Amache Camp in Colorado during the war, but Iwatsuki and her family were at Minidoka. Iwatsuki and Inada collaborated on this poem, which is inscribed on a granite boulder in Portland's Japanese American Historical Plaza that commemorates the unlawful internment of Japanese Americans during World War II.

51. Dana Beck, "Century Porco," *The Bee*, March 2013, 6.

52. Charles F. Gould, "Portland Italians, 1880-1920," *Oregon Historical Quarterly* 77, no. 3 (September 1976): 246.

53. Evan Jones, *Epicurean Delight: Life and Times of James Beard* (New York: Simon and Schuster, 1992), 35.

54. Jones, *Epicurean Delight*, 34.

55. Gould, "Portland Italians," 249.

56. Gould, "Portland Italians," 249.

57. United States Department of the Interior, National Park Service, National Register of Historic Places Registration Form, August 15, 1988 (approved March, 1989). Prepared by the Hawthorne Blvd. Business Association, 5. Available:http://pdfhost.focus.nps.gov/docs/NRHP/Text/89000087.pdf. Accessed: January 29, 2014.

58. NPS, National Register of Historic Places Registration Form, 1.

59. Alessio Baking Company, "Our Story." Available:http://www.alessiobakingcompany.com/alessio-story.php. Accessed: January 30, 2014.

60. John Guernsey, "No Cakewalk: Retiring Eludes Veteran Baker," *The Oregonian*, January 5, 1978, 35. Provided by NewsBank/Readex, Database: The Historical Oregonian, 1861–1987, SQN: 12C2B30CE2E4ACBC. Accessed: January 31, 2014.

61. Guernsey, "No Cakewalk: Retiring Eludes Veteran Baker."

62. Advertisement seen in *The New Age* for The Mobile Restaurant, March 24, 1900, 6. Other ads seen in *Oregon Daily Journal* and *The Oregonian* as early as 1895.

63. "Town Topics," *Oregon Daily Journal*, August 12, 1905, 5. Available: http://oregonnews.uoregon.edu/lccn/sn85042444/1905-08-12/ed-1/seq-5/.

64. "Help Wanted," *Morning Oregonian*, June 02, 1904. Available:http://oregonnews.uoregon.edu/lccn/sn83025138/1904-06-02/ed-1/seq-10/. Accessed: February 1, 2014.

65. Lilian Tingle, "Answers to Correspondents," *Sunday Oregonian,* November 12, 1912, 7, and December 11, 1910, 6. Available:http://oregonnews.uoregon.edu/lccn/sn83045782/1912-11-17/ed-1/seq-67/andhttp://oregonnews.uoregon.edu/lccn/sn83045782/1910-12-11/ed-1/seq-66/. Accessed: February 1, 2014.

66. Lilian Tingle, "Answers to Correspondents," *Sunday Oregonian*, September 01, 1912. Available:http://oregonnews.uoregon.edu/lccn/sn83045782/1912-09-01/ed-1/seq-58/. Accessed: February 1, 2014.

67. Inie Gage Chapel, *All-Western Conservation Cookbook* (Portland: Modern Printing & Publishing Co., 1917), 87. The author also claims that chop suey was invented by a Mexican.

68. Nancy Nusz and Gabriella Ricciardi, "Oregon Voices: Our Ways: History and Culture of Mexicans in Oregon," *Oregon Historical Quarterly* 104, no. 1 (Spring 2003): 123.

69. Nusz and Ricciardi, "History and Culture of Mexicans in Oregon," 116–17.

70. Nancy Morris, "Meals in Minutes," August 20, 1951, 17. Provided by: NewsBank/Readex, Database: The Historical Oregonian, 1861–1987, SQN: 12B72CB5E3ED84B3. Accessed: February 1, 2014.

71. Morris, "Meals in Minutes," 17.

72. Robert F. Allen, "The Gourmet Touch," *The Oregonian*, July 24, 1950, 13. Provided by NewsBank/Readex, Database: The Historical Oregonian, 1861–1987, SQN: 12B62903FA957CE9. Accessed: February 1, 2014.

73. William Moyes, "Behind the Mike," *The Oregonian,* September 22, 1950, 20. Provided by NewsBank/Readex, Database: The Historical Oregonian, 1861–1987, SQN: 12B629CBA3EDF33E. Accessed: February 1, 2014.

74. Moyes, "Behind the Mike," 20.

75. Moyes, "Behind the Mike," 20.

76. Debra L. DeLaet, *U.S. Immigration Policy in an Age of Rights* (Westport, CT: Greenwood Publishing Group, 2000), 79.

77. David Card and Ethan G. Lewis, "The Diffusion of Mexican Immigrants during the 1990s: Explanation and Impacts," *Mexican Immigration to the United States* (Chicago: University of Chicago Press, 2007), 206.

78. US Department of Commerce, Bureau of the Census, Neighborhood Statistics Program, Oregon, *Special Report: 1980 Census of Population and Housing,* 140 pp. Available:http://www.portlandoregon.gov/oni/article/328525. Accessed: February 2, 2014.

79. Samuel Howe, "'We Help Together': Refugees building new businesses," *The Oregonian*, July 19 and 20, 1981, 7. Provided by NewsBank/Readex, Database: The Historical Oregonian, 1861–1987, SQN: 13244DC7F14BBCF4. Accessed: February 2, 2014.

5. TO MARKET, TO MARKET

1. Jean-Nicolas Perlot, *Gold Seeker: Adventures of a Belgian Argonaut During the Gold Rush Years* (translated in 1967 by Helen Harding Bretnor) (New Haven, CT: Yale University Press, 1998), 318.

2. E. Kimbark MacColl, *Merchants, Money and Power: The Portland Establishment 1843–1913* (Athens, GA: The Georgian Press, 1988), 20. Inflation calculator provided by http://www.davemanuel.com/inflation-calculator.php.

3. MacColl, *Merchants*, 36.

4. MacColl, *Merchants*, 36.

5. George Eigo and Richard Engeman, *A Market for the City: The History of Portland's Public Markets* (Portland: Oregon Historical Society, 2002), 2.

6. Eigo Engeman, *Market for the City*, 2.

7. "Central Market Opened. The First Grand Opening Night," *Morning Oregonian*, October 6, 1872, 3. Provided by: NewsBank/Readex, Database: The Historical *Oregonian*, 1861–1987, SQN: 1236553881830238.

8. Eigo and Engeman, *A Market for the City*, 4.

9. "War on Bad Meats," *Sunday Oregonian*, July 27, 1902, 24. Available: http://oregonnews.uoregon.edu/lccn/sn83045782/1902-07-27/ed-1/seq-24/. Accessed: February 24, 2014.

10. "Keep Meat Pure. Officials Say City Inspection Is Needed. Some Butchers Admit It," *Morning Oregonian*, June 04, 1903, 16. Available: http://oregonnews.uoregon.edu/lccn/sn83025138/1903-06-04/ed-1/seq-16/. Accessed: February 24, 2014; "Of Wood and Steel," *Morning Oregonian,* February 18, 1904, 10. Available: http://oregonnews.uoregon.edu/lccn/sn83025138/1904-02-18/ed-1/seq-10/. Accessed: February 24, 2014; "Gets Monopoly on Billboards," *Morning Oregonian*, May 18, 1905, 8. Available: http://oregonnews.uoregon.edu/lccn/sn83025138/1905-05-18/ed-1/seq-8/. Accessed: February 24, 2014.

11. "Keep Meat Pure," 16.

12. "Keep Meat Pure," 16.

13. Lilian Tingle, "Clean Markets," *Good Housekeeping* 45 (October 1907): 425.

14. Tingle, "Clean Markets," 425.

15. "He Eats No Flesh," *Morning Oregonian*, April 13, 1905, 8. Available:http://oregonnews.uoregon.edu/lccn/sn83025138/1905-04-13/ed-1/seq-8/. Accessed: February 24, 2014.

16. "He Eats No Flesh," 8.

17. "Reform Demanded in City Markets," *Sunday Oregonian*, February 27, 1903, 25. Available:http://oregonnews.uoregon.edu/lccn/sn83045782/1903-01-25/ed-1/seq-25/. Accessed: February 25, 2014.

18. Tingle, "Clean Markets," 427.

19. "Clean Market Day, November 13. A National Visiting Day Proclaimed, for Market Inspection, and a Cash Award," *Good Housekeeping* 45 (1907): 569.

20. "Reform Demanded in City Markets," 25.

21. "A Move Toward Monopoly," *Morning Oregonian,* February 14, 1908, 8. Available:http://oregonnews.uoregon.edu/lccn/sn83025138/1908-02-14/ed-1/seq-8/. Accessed: February 24, 2014.

22. "Move Toward Monopoly," 8.

23. "Move Toward Monopoly," 8.

24. "Move Toward Monopoly," 8.

25. "Need of a Public Market," *The Evening Telegram*, April 8, 1913, 6.

26. "Public Markets Urged," *Sunday Oregonian,* April 6, 1913, 12. Available:http://oregonnews.uoregon.edu/lccn/sn83045782/1913-04-06/ed-1/seq-12/. Accessed: February 23, 2014.

27. Eigo and Engeman*, A Market for the City*, 12.

28. "Farm Products to Arrive. Albina Market Promises Many New Features for Today," *Morning Oregonian,* May 9, 1914, 9. Available: http://oregonnews.

uoregon.edu/lccn/sn83025138/1914-05-09/ed-1/seq-9/. Accessed: February 24, 2014.

29. "Market Change Asked," *Morning Oregonian,* June 27, 1914, 12. Available:http://oregonnews.uoregon.edu/lccn/sn83025138/1914-06-27/ed-1/seq-12/. Accessed: February 25, 2014.

30. "Tomorrow Portland's Marvelous New Million Dollar Market Opens!" *Morning Oregonian*, December 14, 1933, 8–9.

31. "New Million Dollar Market," 8.

32. Max Mandell Zimmerman, *Super Market, Spectacular Exponent of Mass Distribution* (New York: Super Market Publishing Co., 1937), 87.

33. Zimmerman, *Super Market*, 93.

34. "New Million Dollar Market," 9.

35. "New Million Dollar Market," 9.

36. Zimmerman, *Super Market,* 87.

37. Zimmerman, *Super Market*, 87.

38. David A. Horowitz, "The Crusade against Chain Stores: Portland's Independent Merchants, 1928–1935," *Oregon Historical Quarterly* 89, no. 4 (Winter 1988): 341.

39. "City Gets Chain Stores," *Sunday Oregonian*, July 17, 1921, 46. Available:http://oregonnews.uoregon.edu/lccn/sn83045782/1921-07-17/ed-1/seq-46/. Accessed: March 1, 2014.

40. "Huge Chain Store System Born Here," *Morning Oregonian,* February 16, 1929, 5. Provided by NewsBank/Readex, Database: The Historical Oregonian, 1861–1987, SQN: 12A0672BF9196230. Accessed: March 1, 2014.

41. Horowitz, "The Crusade against Chain Stores," 343.

42. Montaville Flowers, *America Chained; A Discussion of "What's Wrong With the Chain Store"* (Pasadena: Montaville Flowers Publicists, Limited, 1931), 81.

43. Flowers, *America Chained*, 83.

44. Horowitz, "The Crusade against Chain Stores," 344.

45. Horowitz, "The Crusade against Chain Stores," 355.

46. "Quarter Block Leased: Failing Property at Fifth and Yamhill Taken," *Sunday Oregonian*, June 19, 1921, 62. Available:http://oregonnews.uoregon.edu/lccn/sn83045782/1921-06-19/ed-1/seq-62/. Accessed: March 2, 2014.

47. "Quarter Block Leased," 62.

48. Harvard Business School, Baker Library Collections, "Fred Meyer, Inc." *Lehman Brothers Collection—Contemporary Business Archives.* Available:http://www.library.hbs.edu/hc/lehman/industry.html?company=fred_meyer_inc. Accessed: March 2, 2014.

49. "The Birth of One-Stop Shopping," Fred Meyer website archive from July 11, 1998. Access provided by Internet Archive Wayback Machine. Avail-

able:http://web.archive.org/web/19980611072322/http://www.fredmeyer.com/
fmshbirth.htm. Accessed: March 2, 2014.

50. "New Market Attracts," *Morning Oregonian*, June 27, 1931, 5.

51. "Fred-Speak," Fred Meyer website archive from July 11, 1998. Access provided by Internet Archive Wayback Machine. Available:http://web.archive.org/web/19980611072425/http://www.fredmeyer.com/fmshspeak.htm. Accessed: March 2, 2014.

52. E. Kimbark MacColl, *The Growth of a City: Power and Politics in Portland, Oregon, 1915–1950* (Portland: The Georgian Press, 1979), 630.

53. John Harvey Kellogg, *The Stomach* (Battle Creek, MI: Modern Medicine Publishing Company, 1896), 372.

54. Advertisement in *Sunday Oregonian,* April 27, 1930, 38. Provided by: NewsBank/Readex, Database: The Historical Oregonian, 1861–1987, SQN: 12A11D30961E98F5. Accessed: March 3, 2014.

55. *Sunday Oregonian,* April 27, 1930, 38.

56. Gerry Pratt, "Organic Food Store Taps New Market," *The Oregonian*, November 14, 1970, 27. Provided by NewsBank/Readex, Database: The Historical Oregonian, 1861–1987, SQN: 1303A4BD7927DB55. Accessed: March 3, 2014.

57. *The Oregonian*, November 14, 1970, 27.

58. *The Oregonian*, November 14, 1970, 27.

59. "Daily Grind Closing Its Doors," *Willamette Week*, October 27, 2007. Available:http://www.wweek.com/portland/blog-9833-daily_grind_closing_its_doors.html. Accessed: March 3, 2014.

60. Julie Tripp, "Natural Food Industry Sheds 'Hippie' Image," *The Oregonian,* November 26, 1982, 44. Provided by: NewsBank/Readex, Database: The Historical Oregonian, 1861–1987, SQN: 132685A7AF600795. Accessed: March 3, 2014.

61. Marc D. Brown, "Building an Alternative: People's Food Cooperative in Southeast Portland," *Oregon Historical Quarterly* 112, no. 3 (Fall 2011): 301.

62. Brown, "Building an Alternative" (*Portland Scribe*, November 17–23, 1972).

63. Rod Patterson, "NW Portland has local neighborhood atmosphere all its own," *Sunday Oregonian*, August 8, 1976, 43. Provided by: NewsBank/Readex, Database: The Historical Oregonian, 1861–1987, SQN: 131D589EDE5FB6E0. Accessed: March 5, 2014.

6. PERUSING THE MENU

1. Edward Gardner Jones, *The Oregonian's Handbook of the Pacific Northwest* (Portland: Oregonian Publishing Company, 1894), 151.

2. Steward Holbrook, *Wildmen, Wobblies and Whistle Punks* (edited and introduced by Brian Booth) (Corvallis: Oregon State University Press, 1994), 219.

3. Lawrence Barber, "Last Stop for Ferry No. 2," *Sunday Oregonian*, August 22, 1954, 100. Provider: NewsBank/Readex, Database: The Historical Oregonian, 1861–1987, SQN: 12BA815CC3AAC735. Accessed: March 17, 2014.

4. Joseph Gaston, *Portland, Oregon, Its History and Builders: In Connection with the Antecedent Explorations, Discoveries, and Movements of the Pioneers that Selected the Site for the Great City of the Pacific, Volume 2* (Portland: S. J. Clarke Publishing Company, 1911), 666.

5. "Alisky's," *Morning Oregonian*, February 9, 1886, 3. Provider: NewsBank/Readex, Database: The Historical Oregonian, 1861–1987, SQN: 12340913F3152600. Accessed: March 10, 2014.

6. "Alisky's," *Oregonian*, 3.

7. "Alisky's," *Oregonian*, 3.

8. Harvey Whitefield Scott, *History of Portland, Oregon: With Illustrations and Biographical Sketches of Prominent Citizens and Pioneers* (Portland: D. Mason & Company, 1890), 561.

9. "Hof Brau Grille Opens Today," *Morning Oregonian*, July 18, 1908, 5. Provider: NewsBank/Readex, Database: The Historical Oregonian, 1861–1987, SQN: 11BE4B7D0BE07F30. Accessed: March 11, 2014.

10. "Hof Brau Grille Opens Today," 5.

11. "Theodore Kruse Home. Missing Hotel Man Returns After Long Absence. Mysterious Disappearance and Trip Abroad," *Morning Oregonian*, March 27, 1912, 4. Available: http://oregonnews.uoregon.edu/lccn/sn83025138/1912-03-27/ed-1/seq-4/.

12. George Painter, "The Louvre Restaurant," *Gay and Lesbian Archives of the Pacific Northwest* website. Available:http://www.glapn.org/6080louvre.html. Accessed: March 12, 2014.

13. "A Bestial Story from Portland," *The Daily Capital Journal,* November 18, 1912, 4. Available: http://oregonnews.uoregon.edu/lccn/sn99063957/1912-11-18/ed-1/seq-4/. Accessed: March 12, 2014.

14. "Rainbow Grill Outdoes Nature in Its Decorative Beauties," *Morning Oregonian*, October 5, 1913, 74. Available:http://oregonnews.uoregon.edu/lccn/sn83045782/1913-10-05/ed-1/seq-74/. Accessed: March 12, 2014.

15. "Rainbow Grill Outdoes Nature in Its Decorative Beauties," 74.

16. "Rainbow Grill Is Open," *Morning Oregonian*, October 3, 1913, 2. Available:http://oregonnews.uoregon.edu/lccn/sn83025138/1913-10-03/ed-1/seq-2/. Accessed: March 12, 2014.

17. "Rainbow to Re-Open," *Sunday Oregonian*, March 12, 1916, 17. Available:http://oregonnews.uoregon.edu/lccn/sn83045782/1916-03-12/ed-1/seq-17/. Accessed: March 12, 2014.

18. "Council Modifies Mooted Measure. Rushlight Amendment to the 'Women-in-Saloons' Ordinance Adopted," *Morning Oregonian*, October 29, 1908. Provider: NewsBank/Readex, Database: The Historical Oregonian, 1861–1987, SQN: 11B976911358F508. Accessed: March 11, 2014.

19. "Big Fight Certain. Council Will Tackle Problem of Women in Saloons," *Morning Oregonian*, July 19, 1908, 10. Provider: NewsBank/Readex, Database: The Historical Oregonian, 1861–1987, SQN: 11BE4B7F86630280. Accessed: March 11, 2014.

20. "Big Fight Certain," 10.

21. "Big Fight Certain," 10.

22. "Big Fight Certain," 10.

23. Frederick B. Warde, *Fifty Years of Make-Believe* (New York: International Press Syndicate, 1920), 257.

24. There was also a Georgian Room at the Heathman Hotel in the 1920s.

25. Jan Whitaker, *Tea at the Blue Lantern Inn: A Social History of the Tea Room Craze in America* (New York: St. Martin's Press, 2002), 167.

26. William R. Leach, *Land of Desire: Merchants, Power, and the Rise of a New American Culture* (New York: Random House, 2011), 25.

27. Christine Curran, "Oregon Places: The Georgian Room at Meier & Frank," *Oregon Historical Quarterly*, Vol. 107, No. 3 (Fall 2006), 442.

28. James Beard, *James Beard's Delights and Prejudices* (Philadelphia: Running Press, 2001), 122.

29. Beard, *Delights and Prejudices*, 122.

30. "Get in Line," *Sunday Oregonian*, September 29, 1907, 2. Available:http://oregonnews.uoregon.edu/lccn/sn83045782/1907-09-29/ed-1/seq-2/. Accessed: March 17, 2014.

31. "The Cafeteria," *The Oregon Daily Journal*, September 20, 1907, 9. Available:http://oregonnews.uoregon.edu/lccn/sn85042444/1907-09-20/ed-1/seq-9/. Accessed: March 17, 2014.

32. "Announcing a New Kind of Cafeteria" (advertorial), *Morning Oregonian*, August 18, 1921, 7. Available:http://oregonnews.uoregon.edu/lccn/sn83025138/1921-08-18/ed-1/seq-7/. Accessed: March 17, 2014.

33. E. Kimbark MacColl, *Merchants, Money & Power: The Portland Establishment 1843–1913* (Athens, GA: The Georgian Press, 1988), 19.

34. Reser's Fine Foods Product Sheet. Available:www.insideresers.com/docs/nutrition/product%20guide.xls. Accessed: March 18, 2014.

35. David Sarasohn, "The meals with Ross," *The Oregonian*, June 6, 1985, 37. Provider: NewsBank/Readex, Database: The Historical Oregonian, 1861–1987, SQN: 13282DEBF7FD9296. Accessed: March 19, 2014.

36. Sarasohn, "The meals with Ross."

37. "Café Retains 1910 Locale," *The Oregonian*, October 9, 1956, 63. Provider: NewsBank/Readex, Database: The Historical Oregonian, 1861–1987, SQN: 12C9E90AE8FFF403. Accessed: March 20, 2014.

38. "Café Retains 1910 Locale."

39. Stewart Holbrook, "Round About the Town," *Morning Oregonian*, February 8, 1935, 6. Provider: NewsBank/Readex, Database: The Historical Oregonian, 1861–1987, SQN: 12A4A76A5F57A247. Accessed: March 19, 2014.

40. The Huber's website says that Frank Huber died in 1912, but the announcement of his death and funeral appear in *The Oregonian* on May 1 and May 2, 1911, respectively.

41. Holbrook, "Round About the Town."

42. "Louie family continues Huber's 105-year tradition," *The Oregonian*, April 11, 1984, 48. Provider: NewsBank/Readex, Database: The Historical Oregonian, 1861–1987, SQN: 13269BC927793C89.

43. Mueller & Meier has been also spelled "Mueller & Meyer" and "Miller & Meier."

44. "Louis Feurer Has Opened The Quelle as a First Class Beer Hall," advertisement in *The Oregonian* beginning January 19, 1880. Provider: NewsBank/Readex, Database: The Historical Oregonian, 1861–1987, SQN: 1233F83C1E9EE5D0. Accessed: March 21, 2014.

45. "Opening of the Quelle. Formal Opening Will Take Place Tonight. Excellent Taste Has Been Shown," *Morning Oregonian*, March 15, 1902, 7. Available:http://oregonnews.uoregon.edu/lccn/sn83025138/1902-03-15/ed-1/seq-7/. Accessed: March 21, 2014.

46. "Opening of the Quelle."

47. "Quelle Is to Be No More. Owner of Crawfish Headquarters to Buy Hof Brau Café," *Morning Oregonian*, February 2, 1912, 9. Provider: NewsBank/Readex, Database: The Historical Oregonian, 1861-1987, SQN: 11C1A447E7423778. Accessed: March 24, 2014.

48. "Jake's 90th Anniversary—Our History," *Sunday Oregonian,* November 7, 1982, 6. Provider: NewsBank/Readex, Database: The Historical Oregonian, 1861–1987, SQN: 1325F2134BA85655. Accessed: March 24, 2014.

49. "Jake's 90th Anniversary."

50. Historic Places Inventory for Jake's, 13–14.

51. United States Department of the Interior Heritage Conservation and Recreation Service, National Park Service, National Register of Historic Places Inventory, Nomination Form for Whitney and Gray Building and Jake's Famous Crawfish Restaurant. 1983, 9. Available:http://pdfhost.focus.nps.gov/docs/NRHP/Text/83002177.pdf. Accessed: March 21, 2014.

52. Ralph Friedman, "Northwest 23rd," *Sunday Oregonian, Northwest Magazine,* November 6, 1966, 150 (page 25 of magazine insert). Provider: NewsBank/Readex, Database: The Historical Oregonian, 1861–1987, SQN: 12F41D4212E0981F. Accessed: March 25, 2014.

53. Mike Ryerson, personal communication, e-mail, March 25, 2014.

54. Friedman, "Northwest 23rd," 5.

55. Friedman, "Northwest 23rd," 5.

56. "'Padded' Chowder Wins. Press Club Chef Loses in Contest with Louis Wachsmuth," *Morning Oregonian*, September 15, 1912, 37. Provider: NewsBank/Readex, Database: The Historical Oregonian, 1861–1987, SQN: 11C1ACA9CCBA54D0. Accessed: March 27, 2014.

57. Edward M. Miller, "Eat 'Em Alive, Says Louis Wachsmuth," *Sunday Oregonian,* March 23, 1930, 65. Provider: NewsBank/Readex, Database: The Historical Oregonian, 1861–1987, SQN: 12A15C12C26C659F. Accessed: March 27, 2014.

58. Miller, "Eat 'Em Alive."

59. Margeret Haberman, "Burgerville says sorry to bicyclist for drive-through ban," *The Oregonian, Oregon Live.* Available:http://www.oregonlive.com/news/index.ssf/2009/08/burgerville_apologizes_to_bicy.html. Accessed: March 27, 2014.

60. Ringside Steakhouse website. Available:http://www.ringsidesteakhouse.com/. Accessed: March 27, 2014.

61. Darrell Millner, personal communication (telephone) March 14, 2014.

62. Darrell Millner, personal communication (telephone) March 14, 2014.

63. Darrell Millner, personal communication (telephone) March 14, 2014.

7. DRINK UP

1. E. Kimbark MacColl, *Merchants, Money & Power: The Portland Establishment 1843–1913* (Athens, GA: The Georgian Press, 1988), 18.

2. Lawson G. Bradley, *Official Guide to the Lewis and Clark Centennial Exposition* (Portland: Lewis and Clark Centennial and American Pacific Exposition, 1905), 56.

3. Bradley, *Official Guide to Lewis and Clark Expo*, 47.

4. Meriwether Lewis, William Clark, et al., October 21, 1805 entry in *The Journals of the Lewis and Clark Expedition*, ed. Gary Moulton (Lincoln, NE: University of Nebraska Press/University of Nebraska-Lincoln Libraries-Electronic Text Center, 2005). Available:http://lewisandclarkjournals.unl.edu/read/?_xmlsrc=1805-10-21&_xslsrc=LCstyles.xsl. Accessed: April 7, 2014.

5. Mike Ryerson, Norm Gholston, and Tracy J. Prince, *Portland's Slabtown* (Charleston, SC: Arcadia Publishing, 2013), 8.

6. News, *Morning Oregonian,* July 18, 1864, 3. Provider: NewsBank/Readex, Database: The Historical Oregonian, 1861–1987, SQN: 1233AC68221EF088. Accessed: April 7, 2014.

7. Aukjen T. Ingraham, "Henry Weinhard & Portland's City Brewery," *Oregon Historical Quarterly* 102, no. 2 (Summer 2001): 184. Various sources spell Meunch's name as Meunich, Meney, or Meany.

8. Charles Erskine Scott Wood, "The Skidmore Fountain," *Oregon Historical Quarterly* 34, no. 2 (June 1933): 100.

9. Wood, "Skidmore Fountain," 100.

10. Advertisement, *Morning Oregonian,* June 5, 1919, 9. Available:http://oregonnews.uoregon.edu/lccn/sn83025138/1919-06-05/ed-1/seq-9/. Accessed: April 7, 2014.

11. Advertisement, *Morning Oregonian,* June 5, 1919, 9.

12. MacColl, *Merchants, Money & Power*, 18.

13. MacColl, *Merchants, Money & Power*, 18.

14. Advertisement, *Morning Oregonian*, March 11, 1863, 2. Provider: NewsBank/Readex, Database: The Historical Oregonian, 1861–1987, SQN: 1233A68378E6C5C0. Accessed: April 2, 2014.

15. Advertisement, *Morning Oregonian*, May 5, 1865, 4. Provider: NewsBank/Readex, Database: The Historical Oregonian, 1861–1987, SQN: 1233F0B760DA9178. Accessed: April 2, 2014.

16. Eugene Snyder, *Portland Names and Neighborhoods* (Portland: Binford & Mort, 1979), 103.

17. David Hazen, "Romantic Portland Streets," *Morning Oregonian*, April 5, 1934, 4. Provider: NewsBank/Readex, Database: The Historical Oregonian, 1861–1987, SQN: 12A355412FE2A6A2. Accessed: April 2, 2014.

18. Wayne Curtis, "Boomtown Imbibing. The storied history of Erickson's saloon in Portland, Oregon," *Imbibe Magazine*, March/April 2014. Available:https://imbibemagazine.com/History-of-Portland-s-Erickson-s-Saloon. Accessed: April 2, 2014.

19. "A Popular Resort. The Refitting of Erickson's on Second and Burnside," *Morning Oregonian,* November 23, 1895, 10. Provider: NewsBank/Readex, Database: The Historical Oregonian, 1861–1987, SQN: 1238E9B12418E010. Accessed: April 2, 2014.

20. "Erickson's New Place," *Morning Oregonian,* June 29, 1895, 5. Provider: NewsBank/Readex, Database: The Historical Oregonian, 1861–1987, SQN: 1236E4CB860C1880. Accessed: April 1, 2014.

21. Ralph W. Andrews, *This Was Sawmilling* (Seattle: Superior Publishing Company, 1957), 172.

22. Andrews, *This Was Sawmilling,* 172.

23. Andrews, *This Was Sawmilling,* 172.

24. Andrews, *This Was Sawmilling,* 172.

25. Andrews, *This Was Sawmilling,* 172.

26. Andrews, *This Was Sawmilling,* 172.

27. Andrews, *This Was Sawmilling,* 172.

28. Donald M. Hines, "Superstitions from Oregon," *Western Folklore* 24, no. 1 (January 1965): 16.

29. Hines, "Superstitions from Oregon."

30. Hills, "White Eagle Saloon," 525. Federal census records show 93 male Polish boarders living in Portland in 1920.

31. "Polish Society Not Anarchistic," *Morning Oregonian*, June 25, 1906, 9. Available:http://oregonnews.uoregon.edu/lccn/sn83025138/1906-06-25/ed-1/seq-9/. Accessed: April 5, 2014. See also Hills, "White Eagle," 528.

32. "Polish Society Not Anarchistic," 9.

33. "Polish Society Not Anarchistic," 9.

34. Malcom H. Clark Jr., "War on the Webfoot Saloon," *War on the Webfoot Saloon and Other Tales of Feminine Adventures* (Portland: Oregon Historical Society, 1969), 5–7.

35. Letter from the Women's Temperance Prayer League, printed in Clark, *War on the Webfoot Saloon*, 3.

36. Clark, "War on the Webfoot Saloon," 7–8.

37. Clark, "War on the Webfoot Saloon," 10.

38. Clark, "War on the Webfoot Saloon," 10–11.

39. "Visiting the Saloons," *Morning Oregonian*, April 1, 1874, 3. Provider: NewsBank/Readex, Database: The Historical Oregonian, 1861–1987, SQN: 12326487AAB1BFA0. Accessed: April 7, 2014.

40. "Visiting the Saloons," 3.

41. "Visiting the Saloons," *Morning Oregonian*, April 1, 1874, 3. Provider: NewsBank/Readex, Database: The Historical Oregonian, 1861–1987, SQN: 12326487AAB1BFA0. Accessed: April 7, 2014.

42. Clark, "War on the Webfoot Saloon," 13.

43. Clark, "War on the Webfoot Saloon," 15.

44. Clark, "War on the Webfoot Saloon," 22.

45. Clark, "War on the Webfoot Saloon," 23t

46. "Girl Bares Life of Ex-Policeman. Convicted Woman Tells of Relations with Former Portland Officer," *Morning Oregonian*, May 24, 1910, 9. Provider: NewsBank/Readex, Database: The Historical Oregonian, 1861–1987, SQN: 11B9BFB1775E83C8. Accessed: April 2, 2014.

47. "Keep Women Out of All Saloons. Council Will Consider Drastic Ordinance," *Morning Oregonian*, January 21, 1908, 1. Provider: NewsBank/Readex, Database: The Historical Oregonian, 1861–1987, SQN: 11B2CFB872757330. Accessed: April 8, 2014.

48. "Women in Saloons—Councilman Flegel Makes an Investigation," *Morning Oregonian*, April 30, 1905, 24. Provider: NewsBank/Readex, Database: The Historical Oregonian, 1861–1987, SQN: 12383A2AEDD4D190. Accessed: April 8, 2014.

49. "Barmaids Are to Go. Chief of Police Issues Order to Saloonkeepers. Ordinance to Be Enforced," *Morning Oregonian,* January 24, 1905, 14. Provider: NewsBank/Readex, Database: The Historical Oregonian, 1861–1987, SQN: 1235F1E1A4C96B60. Accessed: April 8, 2014.

50. "Keep Women Out of All Saloons," 1.

51. "'Cusswords' Used by Liquor Men," *Morning Oregonian*, October 27, 1908, 10. Available:http://oregonnews.uoregon.edu/lccn/sn83025138/1908-10-27/ed-1/seq-10/. Accessed: March 31, 2014.

52. "'Cusswords' Used by Liquor Men."

53. "'Cusswords' Used by Liquor Men."

54. "Liquor Dealer Favors Law. Saloonkeeper Says Women Are Nuisance to His Trade," *Morning Oregonian*, November 11, 1908, 11. Available:http://oregonnews.uoregon.edu/lccn/sn83025138/1908-11-11/ed-1/seq-11/. Accessed: March 31, 2014.

55. "Liquor Dealer Favors Law."

56. Janis Martin, pers comm., March 20, 2014.

57. Abigail Duniway, *Path Breaking: An Autobiographical History of the Equal Suffrage Movement in Pacific Coast States* (Portland: James, Kerns & Abbott Company, 1914), 231.

58. Oregon State Archives, "Liquor Control, Temperance and the Call for Prohibition." Available:http://arcweb.sos.state.or.us/pages/exhibits/50th/prohibition1/ardentpg1.jpg. Accessed: March 31, 2014.

59. MacColl, *Merchants, Money & Power*, 72.

60. Advertisement in *Sunday Oregonian,* May 31, 1908, 11. Available:http://oregonnews.uoregon.edu/lccn/sn83045782/1908-05-31/ed-1/seq-35.pdf. Accessed: April 14, 2014.

61. *Sunday Oregonian,* May 31, 1908, 11.

62. *Sunday Oregonian,* May 31, 1908, 11.

63. John E. Caswell, "The Prohibition Movement in Oregon II. 1904–1915," *Oregon Historical Quarterly* 40, no. 1 (March 1939): 76.

64. Lindsay Wochnick, "Benson Bubblers Celebrate Centennial Birthday," City of Portland, Portland Water Bureau website. Available: http://www.portlandoregon.gov/water/article/410923?archive=yes. Accessed: April 9, 2014.

65. News in Brief, *Morning Oregonian*, March 21, 1924, 5. Provider: News-Bank/Readex, Database: The Historical Oregonian, 1861–1987, SQN: 129E114DF8EACF21. Accessed: April 29, 2014.

66. "Jury Soon Finds Café Sold Liquor—Joe Mazzini Convicted in 3 Minutes and Third Case of Day Is Started," *Morning Oregonian*, February 10, 1916, 15. Provider: NewsBank/Readex, Database: The Historical Oregonian, 1861–1987, SQN: 11C7F1654EAF8D50. Accessed: April 12, 2014.

67. Andrew Sherbert, "Oregon Blue Ruin," published in *The Food of a Younger Land*, ed. Mark Kurlansky (New York: Penguin, 2009), 360.

68. Sherbert, "Oregon Blue Ruin."

69. Frank R. Menne, "Acute Methyl Alcohol Poisoning: A Report of Twenty-Two Instances with Postmortem Examinations," *Archives of Pathology* 26 (1939): 77–92.

70. Sherbert, "Oregon Blue Ruin," 362.

71. "Home Brewery Rights," *Morning Oregonian*, February 2, 1915, 6. Provider: NewsBank/Readex, Database: The Historical Oregonian, 1861–1987, SQN: 11BE4E5B7903E6C8. Accessed: April 8, 2014.

72. Advertisements appear in *The Oregonian* beginning in September 1919 and continue in the daily paper for several months.

73. "Home Breweries Are Hit. Dry Enforcement Officers Are Making Many Arrests," *Morning Oregonian,* November 23, 1920, 20. Provider: NewsBank/Readex, Database: The Historical Oregonian, 1861–1987, SQN: 11D63BE20F897E48. Accessed: April 9, 2014.

74. Fred Eckhardt, "Making the Case for Beervana," *All About Beer Magazine,* July 2013. Available:http://allaboutbeer.com/article/making-the-case-for-beervana/. Accessed: April 9, 2014.

75. Alan Sprints, owner of Hair of the Dog Brewing, pers comm about Fred Eckhardt's birthplace. April 10, 2014.

76. Eckhardt, "Making the Case for Beervana."

77. Fred Eckhardt, *A Treatise on Lager Beers* (Portland: Hobby Winemaker, 1977), 1.

78. Pete Dunlop, *Portland Beer: Crafting the Road to Beervana* (Charleston, SC: The History Press, 2013), 87.

79. Eckhardt, "Making the Case for Beervana."

80. E. Saelens, "Stumptown ogresses on with attitude," *Portland Business Journal,* July 6, 2003. Available:http://www.bizjournals.com/portland/stories/2003/07/07/story3.html?page=2. Accessed: April 15, 2014.

81. Jonathan Nicholas, "This Hot New Trend—Being Really Cool —Fits Portland to a Tea," *The Oregonian,* September 1, 1994, D01. NewsBank on-line database (America's Nws). Accessed: April 15, 2014.

82. Wallace Turner, "Hint Given to Charge of Perjury," *The Oregonian,* March 7, 1957, 1. Provider: NewsBank/Readex, Database: The Historical Oregonian, 1861–1987, SQN: 12BF12FD98858FB2. Accessed: April 14, 2014.

8. LIKE MOTHER USED TO MAKE

1. "Valuable Recipes," *Morning Oregonian*, February 28, 1861, 2. Provider: NewsBank/Readex, Database: The Historical Oregonian, 1861–1987, SQN: 12349C728D3EF208. Accessed: April 18, 2014.

2. James Beard, *James Beard's Delights and Prejudices* (Philadelphia: Running Press, 2001), 138.

3. Harriet Uchiyama, "Roast Chicken," *Portland Christian Schools Tasting Tea Cook Book*, 1970 (unpublished community cookbook). Author's personal collection.

4. Abigail Carroll, "Reinventing Home Economics," December 3, 2013, *UVM Food Feed, Sustainable Food Systems at the University of Vermont*, Available:http://learn.uvm.edu/foodsystemsblog/2013/12/03/reinventing-home-economics/. Accessed: April 25, 2014.

5. "Teaching the Gentle Art of Cookery: What Miss Tingle, the New Director, is Doing at the Portland School of Domestic Science," *Morning Oregonian*, April 2, 1905, section 4, 39. Available:http://oregonnews.uoregon.edu/lccn/sn83045782/1905-04-02/ed-1/seq-39/. Accessed: April 17, 2014.

6. "Teaching the Gentle Art of Cookery."

7. "Teaching the Gentle Art of Cookery."

8. "Teaching the Gentle Art of Cookery."

9. "Teaching the Gentle Art of Cookery."

10. "Teaching the Gentle Art of Cookery."

11. Lilian Tingle, "Hints on Training Husbands; by One Who Never Had One," *Morning Oregonian,* February 21, 1909, 8. Provider: NewsBank/Readex, Database: The Historical Oregonian, 1861–1987, SQN: 11B9BDE66FAC21D0. Accessed: April 18, 2014.

12. Harvard University, *The Harvard University Catalogue* (Cambridge, MA: Harvard University, 1922), 375.

13. International Newsmedia Marketing Association, "1940s: Public Relations, Women and War," May 2003. Available:http://web.archive.org/web/20030503075318/www.inma.org/about_40shistory.cfm. Accessed: April 18, 2014.

14. James Beard, *James Beard's American Cookery* (New York: Little, Brown & Co., 2010), 845.

15. "Ex-Director of Oregon Journal's Mary Cullen's Cottage Dies at 91," *The Oregonian*, February 26, 1993, E04. Provided by NewsBank on-line database (America's News). Accessed: April 25, 2014.

16. Eliza Leslie, *Miss Leslie's New Cookery Book* (Philadelphia, T. B. Peterson, 1857), 35.

17. Southern Methodist University, DeGoyer Library Acquisitions Checklist, 2001–2002, 19. Available:https://smu.edu/cul/degoyer/pdfs/acq01-02.pdf. Accessed: April 22, 2014. It appears that this is the only copy of this book in existence in any American library; fortunately, the library has included a brief description of the cookbook in this checklist.

18. Richard Engeman, "Hot Tamales in the Gay Nineties," *Oregon Rediviva*, March 23, 2014. Available:http://oregonrediviva.blogspot.com/2014/03/hot-tamales-in-gay-nineties.html. Accessed: April 22, 2014. Website includes a photo of the cookbook and a recipe for Chicken tamales.

19. Mrs. A.S. of Grace Memorial Episcopal Church, *Dainty Dishes* (Portland: Schwab Bros. P. & L. Company, 1910), 17. Jane Hewitt, "Tomato Aspic Seafood Salad," *Cooking with Grace Cookbook*, posted to Grace Memorial Episcopal Church website on January 23, 2014. Available:http://www.grace-memorial.org/recipe/tomato-aspic-seafood-salad/. Accessed: April 22, 2014.

20. Rose City Park Community Church, *Choice Recipes* (Portland: Rose City Park Community Church, 1922), 62.

21. James Beard, *Love and Kisses and a Halo of Truffles: Letters to Helen Evans Brown* (New York: Arcade Publishing, 1995), 7–8. Letter to Helen Evans Brown asking her to pick up a copy of *Web-Foot Cook Book*, to which she replies that she had been trying years to find a copy. Beard also mentions on page 173 of his *American Cookery* (1972) that the book is a "scarce book on the market."

22. Beard, *American Cookery,* 180.

23. San Grael Society, *The Web-Foot Cook Book* (Portland: W.B. Ayer & Company, 1885), 124, 135.

24. Andrew Kirwan, *Host and Guest* (London: Bell & Daldy, 1864), 212.

25. San Grael Society, *The Web-Foot Cook Book*, 177–178.

26. San Grael Society, *The Web-Foot Cook Book*, 201.

27. San Grael Society, *The Web-Foot Cook Book*, 203.

28. T.B. Merry, "Shingled Trout," *The Web-Foot Cook Book*, 207.

29. Mrs. Wesley Jackson, "Sponge," *The Web-Foot Cook Book* (Portland: W. B. Ayer & Company, 1885), 138, and M.B. Caukins, "Sponge Cake," *The Portland Ideal Cook Book* (Portland: George Wright Woman's Relief Corps, No. 2, 1905), 77.

30. Julia Ward Howe and Mary Hannah Graves, *Representative Women of New England* (Boston: New England Historical Publishing Company, 1904), 185.

31. Helen N. Packard, *The Portland Ideal Cook Book* (Portland: George Wright Woman's Relief Corps, No. 2, 1905), 9.

32. Helen N. Packard, *The Portland Ideal Cook Book* (Portland: George Wright Woman's Relief Corps, No. 2, 1905), 3.

33. Michigan State University Libraries, "Aunt Babette's Cook Book," *Feeding America—The Historic American Cookbook Project.* Available:http://digital.lib.msu.edu/projects/cookbooks/html/books/book_41.cfm. Accessed: April 22, 2014.

34. Council of Jewish Women, *The Neighborhood Cook Book* (Portland: Bushong & Company, 1914), 43.

35. Council of Jewish Women, *The Neighborhood Cook Book*, 116.

36. "Portland. Bankers and Lumbermen's Bank." *The Bankers Magazine, Volume 73* (New York: Bradford-Rhodes & Company, 1906), 981.

37. James Beard, note on recipe for "Calf's Head Rolled," *Portland Women's Exchange Cook Book* (Portland: Oregon Historical Society, 1973), 77.

38. Portland Women's Exchange, *Portland Women's Exchange Cook Book*, 7.

39. "Women's Exchange First Year Was a Prosperous One," *Morning Oregonian*, June 18, 1892, 3. Provider: NewsBank/Readex, Database: The Historical Oregonian, 1861–1987, SQN: 12345CC50D246910. Accessed: April 23, 2014.

40. "Exchange Loses $1970. Portland Women Forced to Sell $2000 City Bonds," *The Oregonian*, May 14, 1912, 5. Available:http://oregonnews.uoregon.edu/lccn/sn83025138/1912-05-14/ed-1/seq-5/. Accessed: April 23, 2014. Inflation calculator for $2000 in 1912 to $47,559 in 2013: http://www.westegg.com/inflation/infl.cgi.

41. August Vergez, "Sweetbreads Imperial," *Portland Women's Exchange Cook Book,* 62.

42. Mabel Weidler, "Berries and Cheese," *Portland Women's Exchange Cook Book*, 153.

43. Chef of Portland Hotel, "Tomatoes Portland," *Portland Women's Exchange Cook Book*, 122.

44. Inie Gage Chapel, *An All-Western Conservation Cook Book* (Portland: Modern Printing and Publishing Co., 1917), 1.

45. Chapel, *All-Western Conservation Cook Book*, 1.

46. Charles Lathrop Pack, Commissioner of the National War Garden Commission, *The War Garden Victorious* (Philadelphia: J. B. Lippincott & Co., 1919), iv.

47. Chapel, *All-Western Conservation Cook Book*, 2.

48. Harriet Cumming Corbett, *Bundles for Britain Cook Book* (Portland: F.W. Baltes & Company, 1941), Acknowledgement page.

49. Fred Horn, "Potage Bouillabaise (sic) Marseillaise," *Bundles for Britain Cook Book*, 9.

50. Mary Cullen's Department of The Journal, *Mary Cullen's Cook Book* (Binford & Mort, 1938), 412–33.

51. Cathrine C. Laughton, *Mary Cullen's Northwest Cook Book* (Portland: Journal Publishing Company, 1946), 1.

52. Laughton, *Northwest Cook Book*, 34.

53. Laughton, *Northwest Cook Book*, 44.

54. Laughton, *Northwest Cook Book*, 52.

55. Mrs. W. F. S. "Noodles and Tuna Fish en Casserole," *Sunset Magazine*, May 1930, 57.

56. Helen Evans Brown, *West Coast Cook Book* (New York: Little, Brown and Co., 1960), iii.

57. Brown, *West Coast Cook Book*, 26.

58. Brown, *West Coast Cook Book*, 143.

59. Brown, *West Coast Cook Book*, 136.

60. Brown, *West Coast Cook Book*, 168.

61. Brown, *West Coast Cook Book*, 156.

62. Brown, *West Coast Cook Book*, 147.

63. San Grael Society, *The Web-Foot Cook Book,* 46.

64. Charles Sharkey, "Department of Camp Cooking," *The Four L Lumber News* (Portland: The Loyal Legion of Loggers and Lumbermen, March, 1919), 18.

65. Brown, *West Coast Cook Book*, 33.

66. Brown, *West Coast Cook Book*, 33.

67. Council of Jewish Women, *Neighborhood Cook Book*, 100–101.

68. Packard, *The Portland Ideal Cook Book,* 1.

69. Packard, *The Portland Ideal Cook Book,* 13.

70. Ladies Aid Society of the Piedmont Presbyterian Church, *Choice Recipes* (Portland: 1905), from Richard Engeman's blog *Oregon Rediviva*. Available:http://oregonrediviva.blogspot.com/2012/04/choice-recipes-lewis-clark-fair-cake.html. Accessed: April 25, 2014.

71. Lilian Tingle, "How Dainty Rose Leaves May Be Used with Fancy Dishes," *Sunday Oregonian*, June 06, 1909, 12. Provider: NewsBank/Readex,

Database: The Historical Oregonian, 1861–1987, SQN: 11B97C9A476F9468. Accessed: April 25, 2014.

72. Tingle, "Dainty Rose Leaves."

73. Michigan State University Libraries, "The Neighborhood Cook Book," *Feeding America—The Historic American Cookbook Project.* Available:http://digital.lib.msu.edu/projects/cookbooks/html/books/book_68.cfm. Accessed: April 19, 2014.

74. Council of Jewish Women, *Neighborhood Cook Book*, 16.

75. Erica J. Peters, *San Francisco: A Food Biography* (Lanham, MD: Rowman & Littlefield Studies in Food and Gastronomy, 2013), 182, and Council of Jewish Women, *The Neighborhood Cookbook* (Portland: Bushong & Co., 1912), 175.

76. Council of Jewish Women, *Neighborhood Cook Book*, 175.

77. Council of Jewish Women, *Neighborhood Cook Book*, 78.

78. Marcia Staunton, "My Remembrances of Grandpa Pfenning," *The Volga Germans in Portland,* November, 2000. Available:http://www.volgagermans.net/portland/grandpa_pfenning.html. Accessed: April 19, 2014.

79. Staunton, "Remembrances."

80. "Here's a new job," *East Oregonian*, June 2, 1914, 8. Available:http://oregonnews.uoregon.edu/lccn/sn88086023/1914-06-02/ed-1/seq-8/. Accessed: April 19, 2014.

81. "Here's a new job."

82. Council of Jewish Women, *Neighborhood Cook Book*, 309.

83. "Crab or Lobster in Casserole," unattributed recipe in *Bundles for Britain,* 23.

84. Brown, *West Coast Cook Book*, 34.

85. The Journal, *Mary Cullen's Cook Book*, 138.

86. Lilian Tingle, "Answers to Correspondents," *Morning Oregonian*, March 28, 1920, 5. Provider: NewsBank/Readex, Database: The Historical Oregonian, 1861-1987, SQN: 11D636AA412A0110. Accessed April 27, 2014.

87. "There's 40,000 Slices of Good Eating in This Cake," *The Oregonian,* June 25, 1959, 9. Provider: NewsBank/Readex, Database: The Historical Oregonian, 1861–1987, SQN: 12C36643334C74CA. Accessed: April 24, 2014.

88. White Satin Sugar, Advertisement with recipe, *The Oregonian*, February 6, 1959, 30. Provider: NewsBank/Readex, Database: The Historical Oregonian, 1861–1987, SQN: 12C2AB74E2CFCC20. Accessed: April 25, 2014. *The Oregonian* printed the same recipe two days earlier without crediting White Satin Sugar.

SELECTED BIBLIOGRAPHY

Ackerman, Lillian. *A Necessary Balance: Gender and Power Among Indians of the Columbia Plateau*. Norman: University of Oklahoma Press, 2003.

Armitage, Susan and Elizabeth Jameson, eds. *The Women's West*. Norman: University of Oklahoma Press, 1987.

Beard, James. *James Beard's Delights and Prejudices*. Philadelphia: Running Press, 2001.

Boyd, Robert T., Kenneth M. Ames, and Tony A. Johnson. *Chinookan Peoples of the Lower Columbia River*. Seattle: University of Washington Press, 2013.

Brooks, Karen. *The Mighty Gastropolis: Portland: A Journey Through the Center of America's New Food Revolution*, San Francisco: Chronicle Books, 2012.

Brown, Helen Evans. *West Coast Cook Book*. New York: Little, Brown, 1952.

Chandler, J. D. *Hidden History of Portland, Oregon*. Charleston, SC: The History Press, 2013.

Dunlop, Pete. *Portland Beer: Crafting the Road to Beervana*. Charleston, SC: The History Press, 2013.

Engeman, Richard. *Eating It Up in Eden*. Portland: White House Grocery Press, 2009.

Gaston, Joseph. *Portland, Oregon, Its History and Builders*. Portland: S. J. Clarke Pub. Co., 1911.

Holbrook, Stewart. *Wildmen, Wobblies and Whistle Punks: Stewart Holbrook's Lowbrow Northwest*. Corvallis: Oregon State University Press, 1994.

John, Finn J. D. *Wicked Portland: The Wild and Lusty Underworld of a Frontier Seaport Town*. Charleston, SC: The History Press, 2012.

Johnson, David Allan. *Founding the Far West: California, Oregon, and Nevada, 1840–1890*. Berkeley: University of California Press, 1992.

Jones, Edward Gardner. *The Oregonian's Handbook of the Pacific Northwest*. Portland: The Oregonian Publishing Company, 1894.

Laughton, Cathrine C. *Mary Cullen's Northwest Cook Book*. Portland: Binfords & Mort, 1946.

Luchetti, Cathy. *Home on the Range: A Culinary History of the American West*. New York: Villard, 1993.

MacColl, Kimbark E. *The Growth of a City: Power and Politics in Portland, Oregon, 1915–1950*. Athens, GA: Georgian Press, 1979.

———. *The Shaping of a City: Business and Politics in Portland, Oregon, 1885–1915*. Athens, GA: Georgian Press, 1976.

MacColl, Kimbark E. and Harry Stein. *Merchants, Money and Power: The Portland Establishment, 1843–1913*. Athens, GA: Georgian Press, 1988.

Olsen, Polina. *Stories from Jewish Portland*. Charleston, SC: The History Press, 2011.

Oregon Black Pioneers and Kimberly Stowers Moreland. *African Americans of Portland*. Charleston, SC: Arcadia Publishing, 2003.

Parr, Tami. *Pacific Northwest Cheese: A History*. Corvallis: Oregon State University Press, 2013.

Pintarich, Paul. *History by the Glass: Portland's Past and Present Saloons, Bars & Taverns*. Portland: Bianco Publishing, 1996.

Prince, Tracy J. *Portland's Goose Hollow*. Charleston, SC: Arcadia Publishing, 2011.

Rubin, Rick. *Naked Against the Rain: The People of the Lower Columbia River 1770–1830*. Portland: Far Shore Press, 1999.

Ryerson, Mike, Norm Gholston, and Tracy J. Prince. *Portland's Slabtown*. Charleston, SC: Arcadia Publishing, 2013.

Scott, Harvey Whitefield. *History of Portland, Oregon, with Illustrations and Biographical Sketches of Prominent Citizens and Pioneers*. Syracuse, NY: D. Mason & Company, 1890.

Snyder, Eugene Edmund. *Early Portland: Stump-Town Triumphant*. Portland: Binford & Mort, 1970.

———. *Portland Names and Neighborhoods: Their Historic Origins*. Portland: Binford & Mort, 1979.

Swagerty, William. *The Indianization of Lewis and Clark*. Norman, OK: Arthur C. Clark Company, 2012.

Wingo, Karen. *Hotels and Restaurants*. Portland: K. Wingo, 1980.

Wong, Rose Marie. *Sweet Cakes, Long Journey: The Chinatowns of Portland, Oregon*. Seattle: University of Washington Press, 2004.

Williams, Jacqueline B. *The Way We Ate: Pacific Northwest Cooking, 1843–1900*. Seattle: Washington State University Press, 1996.

———. *Wagon Wheel Kitchens: Food on the Oregon Trail*. Lawrence: University Press of Kansas, 1993.

INDEX

ABOUT THE AUTHOR

Heather Arndt Anderson, a Portland native, is a freelance journalist and food writer. She is the author of *Breakfast: A History* (2013). She is presently writing *Chilies: A Global History*. In a previous life, she was a plant ecologist and blogger. She plays hobby-homesteader in Portland with her husband, son, cats, and chickens.